BUSINESS POLICY: A FRAMEWORK FOR ANALYSIS

BUSINESS POLICY: A FRAMEWORK FOR ANALYSIS

Fourth Edition

Robert G. Murdick
R. Carl Moor
Richard H. Eckhouse
Florida Atlantic University
Thomas W. Zimmerer
Clemson University

JOHN WILEY & SONS

New York • Chichester • Brisbane • Toronto • Singapore

Copyright © 1980, 1984, by John Wiley & Sons, Inc.

Library of Congress Cataloging in Publication Data:
Main entry under title:

  Business policy.

  Bibliography: p.
  Includes index.
  1. Industrial management.   I. Murdick, Robert G.
HD31.B8543   1984   658   82-24266
ISBN 0-471-84132-3

Printed in the United States of America

10   9   8   7   6   5   4   3

CONTENTS

PREFACE

This book is intended for use in undergraduate courses in Business Policy, in management seminars, and as a desk reference for practicing managers. It emphasizes a down-to-earth approach to business policy and strategy and includes treatment of frequently encountered problems in the functional areas of business.

Changes from the third edition, published in 1980, are substantial. Three new chapters have been added, providing improved coverage of strategic management, the environment of business, the systems concept in business, and management information systems. All chapters have been brought up to date and include many new contemporary examples and revised charts and tables.

The authors wish to express special thanks to Diane Krause and Amy Anderson for their excellent research support.

Robert G. Murdick
R. Carl Moor
Richard H. Eckhouse
Thomas W. Zimmerer

THE STUDY OF BUSINESS STRATEGY, POLICIES, AND PROBLEMS

TO WHOM THIS BOOK IS ADDRESSED

This book is addressed to "students of business" in the broadest sense. This includes practicing managers, college business administration students, and professors of business administration.

Practicing managers usually suffer from tunnel vision caused by starting in a functional field and progressing up through this one functional field. They finally reach a point where lack of breadth of knowledge and lack of experience in dealing with complex total-business problems become a barrier to advancement. These managers need an overall review of typical problems in all functional areas. They often recognize their need to develop their skills for systematic analysis and solution of complex interrelated problems.

The other major audience for this book consists of college students in business programs. Such students have been so busy regurgitating facts and theories that they have no idea how to attack real-world business problems. Business problems are complex; vital information is often lacking, unreliable, or conflicting; the problems themselves are neither clearly defined nor easily definable; and usually there are multiple feasible solutions in the face of multiple conflicting business goals. When such students ultimately are exposed to a case method course such as Business Policy, they are totally unprepared. This book is designed to show them how to do the job expected of them.

Many professors, both experienced and inexperienced, will find this book helpful in touching base with real business problems and in broadening their perspectives.

WHY MANAGERS FAIL

Businesses fail because managers fail. The history of American business shows that many businesses, large and small, have a *relatively short successful life span*. In Exhibit 1.1 we have listed just a sample of the many firms that rose high and fell far. Obviously, few, if any, executives *want* their businesses to *fail*. They want to perpetuate the lives and increase the profits of the firms that they manage. Why, then, the poor track record? There is only one answer—management *does not know how to determine the specific actions necessary to maintain the ongoing health and vigor of their organizations.*

But, you say, why shouldn't management know what to do? Haven't they had experience with the past? Haven't they read books or taken courses on the concepts, practices, procedures, and thinking in every area of business? Of course, they have. The problem is that such fragmented knowledge in minute detail has obscured the real skill which management needs. Management needs most the skill to *formulate complex decision-problems in understandable action terms.* This means management must be able to identify a situation where action is required. Management must identify the constraints upon courses of action. Management must be able to specify at least several good courses of action. Management must be able to evaluate these alternatives relative to each other. Management must then have the courage to *decide on the best action and take that action.*

Both managers and students have trouble differentiating between symptoms and problems. R. H. Eckhouse, a consultant to many small business firms, illustrates this point in the following anecdote.

Recently, I asked the owner of a small business what his problems were. He immediately went into a long harangue about the difficulties of getting good people who were interested in doing a creditable piece of work. "In fact, all they are interested in," he said, "is to get their paychecks and go home before it is quitting time." Then he gave me a lecture on the problems of the younger generation, finally ending up with a "So you see, to be concise, our problems are first, getting good help, second, getting our sales up more and third improving our earnings." It was only after several hours of discussion that he began to realize that the *end result* he was seeking was a healthy business (he would eventually turn over to one or both of his sons) which could be described by a specific set of objectives instead of just in general terms. His real problem was that he had no competitive edge with which to entice customers to buy more.

Once the *competitive edge* was agreed upon as *the* problem, we discussed the possible alternatives. On a subsequent visit we agreed on the competitive edge that seemed to be most suitable and most practical for him to achieve. At this point he became really excited because now for the first time he knew specifically what he was going to do—his course of action was clear. Eliminate the low quality, low price items, stress *quality* and *custom design* making use of the real talent of his younger son; keep an accurate record of design and testing *time costs* charging his

EXHIBIT 1.1

Examples of Business Failures

Company	High Flight	Nose Dive	Possible Causes
Curtiss-Wright	1940-44 - Second place in sales in defense and prime contractor list	1967 - 66th on the list for defense sales	Failure to make transition from reciprocating engine technology to jets and rockets
General Dynamics	1957 - Earnings of $56 million on sales of $1.7 billion	1960-1962 - Lost $425 million on its Modal 880 and 990 airplanes. Went over $70 million in the hole for 1960-62	Lack of central control. Strong personalities making unilateral decisions in distant divisions
Litton	1967 - Stock sold at $101/share	1973 - Stock sold at $9/share.	Lack of centralized management and operating skills
Memorex	1969 - Stock sold at $173/share	1973 - Stock sold at $3.60/share Funded debt of $206 million with $50 million due in 1973. Net income of $1.2 million in 1972	Entry into a systems (main frame computer) market dominated by strong competitors. Lack of strong marketing organization and financial difficulties
W. T. Grant	Stock price $70 in 1971 1238 stores in 1973	In bankruptcy in 1975 1082 stores in 1975 $663 million debt	Poor store locations. Too rapid expansion. Lack of data on sales and inventory by department
Braniff Airlines	1978 - Earnings per share $2.26	1979 - Loss per share $2.21. Declared bankruptcy 1982, $1 billion debt	Too rapid expansion. High level of borrowing, high interest rates. Deregulation of airlines

usual overhead rate (to be updated quarterly), plus a percentage for expenses and profit (10%), redirect his sales force to customers interested in quality and unique design, etc.

As he said when he paid me, "You know you really didn't give me a single new idea, but what you did was worth even more than I'm paying you and I'll be eternally grateful—you made me focus on my real problem instead of thinking about 100 different things. Once you had organized my thinking, the answers were automatically clear as they should have been all along but weren't."

Both practicing business executives and students in Business Policy courses have a variety of *backgrounds, skills,* and *natural abilities.* It is well known that students are ill-prepared for their capstone course of business problem solving. It is less well known that *many business executives are unprepared for their present jobs or unprepared to advance into general management.* This is reflected in Exhibit 1.2, which shows types and total number of business failures in the U.S. in 1980.

GENERAL OBJECTIVES OF THE BUSINESS POLICY COURSE

The following are commonly established general objectives:

1. Business Policy courses are designed to make the student aware of the nature of policies, their impact on the firm, and the differences in management that account for the rise and fall, success or failure, of business firms. As has been already pointed out, business firms come and go. Some grow and prosper rapidly and equally rapidly fade into obscurity, eventually going bankrupt. Others seem to be able to remain in business over long periods of years but never or only rarely gain *both* large sales and profits. Still other firms seem to do well, both sales- and profit-wise, despite the vagaries of the economic climate, general business conditions, peace and war. *What is it that makes the huge difference in the success or failures of business firms?* This is a major question which the Business Policy course seeks to answer.

2. The Business Policy course makes the student aware of the field of action in which executives must operate and make decisions. It is an uncertain, highly competitive world, requiring the manager to fathom and figure the risks and odds. The manager's decisions are sometimes on long shots and at the other times on the favorites, but always on the prospects of gains versus losses in the long run. In summary, the student learns the facts of life in the field of business.

3. The Business Policy course serves the student further by:

a. Integrating his or her knowledge of all previous courses. In particular, the student learns to relate the separate disciplines to a given problem. He or she learns the "systems approach" to business problem solving, which favors the total business over special internal interests.

EXHIBIT 1.2

Causes of Business Failures in 1981

Percentage of Business Failures	Underlying Causes	Apparent Causes		
.7	Neglect	Due to	Bad Habits	.2
			Poor Health	.2
			Marital Difficulties	.1
			Other	.2
.3	Fraud	On the part of the principals, reflected by	Misleading Name	.0
			False Financial Statement	.1
			Premediated Overbuy	.0
			Irregular Disposal of Assets	.1
			Other	.0
11.1	Lack of Experience in the Line	Evidenced by inability to avoid conditions which resulted in	Inadequate Sales	59.4
12.5	Lack of Managerial Experience		Heavy Operating Expenses	24.7
19.2	Unbalanced Experience*		Receivables Difficulties	6.4
45.6	Incompetence		Inventory Difficulties	6.9
			Excessive Fixed Assets	3.1
			Poor Location	2.2
			Competitive Weakness	16.3
			Other	3.5

EXHIBIT 1.2 (Continued)

Percentage of Business Failures	Underlying Causes	Apparent Causes	
			Fire .2
			Flood .0
			Burglary .0
.5	Disaster	Some of these occurrences could have been provided against through insurance	Employees Fraud .0
			Strike .1
			Other .1
10.1	Reason Unknown		
100.0	Total		
16,794	Number of Failures		
$414,147	Average Liabilities Per Failure		

Source: The 1981 Dun & Bradstreet Business Failure Record, New York: The Dun & Bradstreet Corporation, pp. 12-13.

b. Making the student realize that a decision made by a manager is likely to affect every other department because they are so closely interrelated. For example, a marketing decision is likely to affect production, finance, engineering, personnel, etc. The whole business is a single entity comparable to an orchestra in which various groups must blend together.

SPECIFIC OBJECTIVES OF THE BUSINESS POLICY COURSE

More specifically, the objectives of the Business Policy course are:
1. To help the student *improve his or her analytical ability.* Unfortunately, under our present educational system, too often the student comes to believe *without realizing it* that (a) what is written is true and (b) that most teachers give good grades for regurgitation of the so-called facts.

In the Business Policy course, students improve their analytical abilities by *not* accepting all that is written as true and by not feeding back so-called *facts.* In fact, quite the opposite is true. Students must learn to question what seem to be facts. If they are to analyze a business situation, perhaps their efforts should be to sort out their thinking by dividing the descriptive written material into three groups.

a. "Facts" that seem to be true.
b. "Facts" that may or may not be true and hence require additional investigation. A rereading of the case or outside information may permit these "facts" to be reclassified as probably true or probably false.
c. "Facts" which are not facts at all but merely "thinks," or opinions and beliefs of the characters in the case. Often in cases given to students, one individual or more will be quoted as to how they view the problems of the firm being studied or the problems of one department of the firm. Frequently, what a person merely "thinks" is taken by students as true. Recently, when studying a case which required the students to choose a new president, a number of students picked an individual merely because one of the firm's vice-presidents said he "thought" the individual chosen had been a graduate of Harvard Business School. Nowhere in the case was this stated as true, and even if it had been, this alone is a mighty slim reason for picking a new president!

Sorting out the "thinks" from the true situational elements is the first part of the analytical process. The second step is to guess at the *probable facts.* This not only takes intuitive reasoning but also "listening with the third ear" by seeking things *not* stated which may be as important as what is said. The third step requires an application of an *organized system for reaching conclusions* based upon probable facts as well as intuitive reasoning (see Chapter 14). In other words, the objective is to train students to bring order out of murky complexity.

Here, too, the importance of searching for imaginative and creative *alternative solutions,* can be learned by the students as they listen to the ideas of their peers during the case discussion. The controversial analyses and evaluations of the merits of each alternative course of action, provoked by class discussion, shows how the final decision of the firm should be forged.

Once a final decision is made, students need to learn the necessity for proper controls to insure the implementation of the decision as intended and to have a *test* for the *validity* of the decision through good feedback.

2. *To develop the student's awareness of the need to make decisions lacking complete information.* A parallel objective is to develop the student's skill in making decisions, as he or she must do in the real world, with lack of facts and under conditions of uncertainty. *Specified action* is the required answer to a business problem situation. An executive once said when talking about the managers in his company, "It is far easier to find people who make sins of omission rather than sins of commission." That is, more executives go wrong by failing to act on problems than by taking really wrong actions. In the vernacular, the unwritten rule of a good executive is "the buck stops here." (Passing the decision on to the next higher position in the chain of command is the last resort.)

A manager's effectiveness should be measured by the number of decisions made as opposed to the number ducked, as well as the percentage of good decisions made versus the bad. Many decisions cannot be measured because the results often cannot be evaluated for many years, if at all. Therefore, usually a person's superior will act upon, when it comes time for promotion or pay increases, some intuitive feeling about the decisiveness of the individual and the value of his or her decisions. One company kept a record of the number and results of each executive's hirings over a period of years. It was found that the most skilled interviewers had a record of 68% to 73% of what could be called above average hirings whereas less skilled interviewers dropped below 55%. This low success rate occurred despite the elaborate testing and interviewing techniques that had been set up. This example is cited to indicate to the student that no one can possibly be right in every decision. Further, just as in choosing prospective employees, the good manager *must make decisions* if the business is to remain viable.

The case method forces students to make decisions in the classroom, often on incomplete information (which the student, like the executive, must *never* learn to like but only accept to the extent that time and economics dictate). It thus sharpens students' decision-making abilities in a wide variety of situations which might well take them far longer to experience in business life.

3. To teach the student how to *improvise and compromise from previously learned concepts and theories.* In other words, the student learns how to *put previous learning into practice* in a simulated business situation. The student needs to be shown vividly that there

is room for unorthodoxy, imagination, and personality in business. Such things as "reversing the field" or swimming against the tide of majority opinion will undoubtedly be brought out in class discussion. Likewise, personality of the actors (managers) will be shown as having an important bearing upon management consensus.

Reversing the Field

Malcolm McLean is an extremely successful but little known entrepreneur who is turning back to the shipping business. McLean was a pioneer in containerized shipping who built Sea-Land Service, Inc., into the largest U.S. shipping company before selling out in 1969.

In 1978, McLean bought U.S. Lines, Inc., a company with less than half of Sea-Land's container capacity and running a poor third in the industry. McLean plans to extend U.S. Lines to match Sea-Land in size by 1985. He has ordered 12 giant container ships each with a capacity of over 50% greater than Sea-Land's largest. He believes that he will obtain greater efficiency by means of around-the-world routes which eliminates the problem of half-empty back-hauls on back-and-forth routes.

His strategy is just the opposite of the rest of the industry, which is building smaller ships because of fear of partially empty hauls and higher fuel costs.

The give-and-take of classroom discussion and the act of defining one's own viewpoint and trying to optimize decisions will hopefully sharpen the student's judgment in much the same fashion as the business manager's judgment is sharpened through repeated decision making in the real world. Even the discovery by the student that there is no way of knowing "the answer" or "the one best solution," when coupled with the sharpening of his or her own judgment, will build confidence in the student's decision-making ability.

4. To develop the student's ability *to recognize the need for additional factual material* which is readily available, can be found through research, or can be bought from technical experts such as accountants, attorneys, or industrial engineers. The first questions to be asked are (a) What are the *time* constraints? and (b) What are the *money* constraints? If the constraints are such as to prevent getting additional information, then the decision must be made without them. Often, however, this is not the case, either additional light can be shed upon the matter quickly and cheaply by further conversation with executives of the firm or by consultation with the experts. Other long-range important decisions will require that patient, costly research, or consultation with broad-gauge consulting firms be undertaken.

Consulting Helps

> A heavy equipment manufacturer located a new plant in a remote rural area with the expectation of obtaining skilled labor by training farmers. Highly skilled workers were essential for the product to meet rigid quality standards. The training proved to be very difficult and staffing objectives were not met. As a result the company suffered severe financial losses and damage to its reputation due to poor quality and delayed deliveries.
>
> A plant location expert or a training expert should have been consulted on this, the most critical factor in the move.

No hard and fast rules can be laid down as to how to recognize the need for additional factual material, but the Business Policy student should improve decision-making ability in this area by class discussion in a variety of situations.

5. *To develop the student's communication skills* by case writing and oral presentations to the class and definition of position on decisions. The prerequisites to good communications—outlining, organizing, selecting important points to emphasize, deleting unimportant matters, and choosing the right words—can only be mastered by practice. Such practice is demanded by the Business Policy courses.

It is fine to have great ideas backed up by relevant, competent research, but these ideas are of no value unless others can be convinced of their merit. This requires communication skills.

INTRODUCTION TO THE CASE METHOD OF LEARNING

Who would have thought that the once mighty Penn Central Railroad with nearly three billion dollars in assets in 1968 and a net income of over $90 million would be bankrupt two years later with a loss in 1970 of $241 million? Why of the 100 largest businesses in the United States in 1900 were only 40 of them alive after 40 years? And only two left in 1968?

A study by R. G. Murdick and Scott P. Gygli showed that of 169 of the top 200 industrial firms in 1970, by 1978 only 58% had improved their profit/sales ratio. Although 76% improved their return on investment (ROI), only 56% improved *both* profit/sales and ROI.

If the performance and failure rates in our strongest and largest firms are that bad, just imagine how poor the record must be for weaker, smaller companies. In the "normal" year before the energy squeeze, 1972, over 70% of businesses that failed were small businesses (liabilities under $100,000). The past poor performance record of business makes it obvious that our time-honored methods of training business managers leave a great deal to be desired. Our performance record is not good. Hundreds of management seminars which are given each year are failing to develop managerial problem solvers. Management's time-honored and time-consuming method of on-the-job learning is only inbreeding inadequate thinking. The usual seminar and lecture methods simply do not teach people how to think. All the theory, wise advice, or stories of how successful managers operate do not transmit analytical skills into the repertoire of the listener.

The only way to learn analytical skills for application to unstructured problems is to exercise the mind on dozens of such problems subject to critique and coaching. Colleges of Business have therefore turned to the *case method*. The case method puts the student in the place of the decision maker in an actual situation. He or she actually "experiences" in the classroom a variety of situations which might take years to experience in real business life.

Relevance of course content to the real world must be the dominant criterion for professional business schools. This is because professional schools are concerned with their students for specific careers. Case courses provide the most relevant experience next to fieldwork that the business school can offer.

The case "tells it like it is" in describing a situation, much as some in-company reports do. Direct quotes from managers or workers often give important personal insights that enter into the situation. The true problems of the firm are usually obscured by the symptoms, just as in real life.

The case method in business policy provides the means for students to integrate all the rules, principles, and theory they have learned in all previous courses. It does more than this, however. It calls upon them to improvise, compromise, and optimize in realistic situations where neatly developed principles only provide guidelines. In short, it requires them to utilize that most complex quality of the mind—judgment. The case method improves a student's ability to make decisions founded upon rational analysis sufficiently sound to stand up against the arguments of peers. The student learns that there is no way of knowing "*the* answer" or "the one best solution" either before a decision has been made or even after it has been implemented. This frustrating fact, however, eventually helps to build students' confidence in their own solutions which they learn to think through.

The business policy case methods, in most instances, introduce the student to a variety of industries. Whereas an individual's work experience tends to be narrowly limited by the characteristics of the company for which he or she works, wide "experience" is achieved by the study of many companies.

In real life, the pressure of the need to solve a particular problem immediately, or often just to get rid of the symptom, builds shallow problem-solving habits. In case courses, even apparently simple problems are often found to be, under the rigorous scrutiny given to the case, like the tip of an iceberg. You may see how this works in the following case of a shoe company:

Management of a shoe manufacturing company noted that there was a high turnover among its salespeople in the field. The first assumption made was that its compensation plan was out of line with its competitors. Investigation showed that, indeed, the salespeople had low incomes. The commission rates, however, were checked with competitors' and turned out to be as high or higher. A parallel check of average sales showed that the average per salesperson had been declining steadily over the past years.

Top management brought a number of salespeople in for lengthy discussions on the problem. They learned that late deliveries, incomplete deliveries, wrong sizes to fill orders, and shoddy workmanship were causing a loss of shoe accounts. This was traced back to the factory where the production control system had degenerated over the years. Manufacturing management had continued to shrug off complaints from salespeople with myopic perversity.

In most case methods, a student's analysis is subject to the sharp and open peer criticism. He or she learns to prepare the analysis better and to anticipate objections. In business, such free and open criticism is often not made. Instead, covert or unexpressed criticism undermines the executive's position without his being able to benefit by spoken criticism.

The business policy case method gives students the perspective of the company as a whole. They see the interrelationships of the operations and the many problems. They will carry this perspective with them even though their first assignment with a company is usually small and narrow.

The students must put themselves in the place of the company's decision makers so that they actually "experience" in the classroom a variety of situations. They can make serious mistakes in their decisions without fear of being fired or suffering monetary loss. In one course they can make as many major decisions as they would in years of business life.

An added advantage of the case method of learning over an individual's work experience is the emphasis on finding a *number* of alternative, feasible solutions before making one proposed decision. Sometimes in business, due to the urgent need for a decision *now,* the emphasis in some firms is wrongly placed on finding the first workable solution and getting on with the job. Weighing the merits of as many alternatives as possible would likely produce a far better decision.

Business policy cases are abstracts of highly complicated business situations. Just as the business executive is limited in the amount of information available because of time and money, the case analyst is similarly limited, although to a greater degree.

While business decisions often rest upon incomplete facts, under *no* circumstances should either the businessperson or the student learn to like sloppy, rushed, forced decision making. Both should learn to push to the utmost within the time and money constraints for every relevant fact. Often it is found that a better decision can be reached through the use of easily available sources for facts that had too carelessly been overlooked. The similarity is that both the executive and the case student must find the best workable solution they can *with the information available*. There is no passing the buck: *action must be decided upon*.

In the case approach to business study and decision making, the student must:

1. Identify present problems and issues by a careful study of the case material.
2. Analyze the case material to determine the causes or sources of these problems and issues.
3. Anticipate future problems and issues based upon present policies and activities of the company as well as upon personalities and the central figures.
4. Synthesize the above findings and focus upon the most significant and/or the central problem or issue.
5. Develop and recommend the policies, strategies, plans, operations and controls for the business situation, radiating from the focal problem. *He or she must propose action.*

On the basis of the above, a number of methods have been used to conduct business policy case courses. The most common method is to assign cases to students for written and/or oral reports. Each individual in the entire class may be required to turn in a written case analysis, or the class may be divided into groups, with each group turning in a written report. An individual or panel may present the case in class where the presentation is subject to the criticism of the class members.

With large classes, the oral student presentation of the case may be omitted. The instructor asks key probing questions of class members and conducts a tightly time-controlled session by calling upon class members at random to answer specific questions or give rebuttals to arguments presented.

The content of the course may consist of a variety of cases from different industries. Some instructors prefer to use only cases from a single industry because the basic background for each case becomes better known. For the "live" case method, the instructor provides background material on a company at one class session. At the next class session, an executive from the company presents the current picture of the company and its problems and also answers questions after the presentation. This session is followed up by a written analysis by each student. Other instructors use a combination of readings, lectures, cases, and incidents to present the course.

WHAT WE SHOW IN THIS BOOK

We show in this book how to diagnose a firm that is obviously in trouble or potentially in trouble and how to arrive at a specific program of action. The skill required to carry out such action is learned by repetitive application of case-method problem-solving techniques. In this book, therefore,

1. We present the field of action in which the manager operates. This will highlight the constraints and processes of the business system.
2. We emphasize and describe throughout *common major problems* which, if not *identified* and *solved,* will prevent a business from prospering. These major problems, which must be overcome, are called Critical Success Factors (CSF).
3. We provide a framework for developing a *unified sense of direction,* for integrating functional activities and business portfolios, and for relating the company to its environment. This framework is the strategic management concept.
4. We give a synopsis of key policies and problems in the functional and behavioral areas of business.
5. Following the above basic topics, we present the main topic, an operational approach to systematic methods for *identifying complex business problems, organizing and structuring the pertinent information, analyzing the information, formulating and evaluating alternative action programs,* and *prescribing a specific action program.* This includes a guide to clear expression of such a program.

2

THE FIELD OF ACTION: ENVIRONMENT OF THE BUSINESS SYSTEM

LEGITIMACY—THE ROLE AND RESPONSIBILITIES OF BUSINESS IN SOCIETY

Too many business managers have too restricted a perspective of their businesses. They see the business firm as an institution endowed from on high with innate rights and obligations only to itself. The educated manager realizes that businesses, as they exist in our society, do so only because society believes that it is best served by such institutions. There are many other types of societies in the world which believe that private enterprise is not the best way to have goods produced and distributed. This *rightness* of an institution is called its *legitimacy*.

Legitimacy of a business is secured by its satisfying to a sufficient degree its *stakeholders,* such as:

1. Customers,
2. General public,
3. Suppliers,
4. Industry to which the company belongs,
5. Government,
6. Special interest groups,

and by acting in a morally responsible manner towards them. This does not mean that a business must satisfy all stakeholders completely to stay in business. One or two powerful stakeholder groups may be sufficient to provide legitimacy *or* to force the company out of business. Management must, therefore, establish policies for each stakeholder group, which clarify the degree of "social responsibility"

15

it will bear. Exhibit 2.1 indicates how a company might be profiled for analysis.

Management may make the corporation act as a morally responsible person by (a) holding individuals accountable for specific actions, (b) following rules established by externally imposed social norms,

EXHIBIT 2.1
Example of a Profile Chart for Policy Analysis

Policies	Customers	General Public	Suppliers	Industry	Government	Special Interest Groups
Fight for greater social responsibilities for all business in society						
Lead your industry in social responsibility						
Be as socially progressive as your industry as a whole	◯					
Do only what is required to avoid conflict		◯	◯	◯		◯
Resist pressures in the system for social responsibilities that will reduce profits					◯	
Do whatever you can get away with to maximize short-term profits						

Stakeholders

and (c) allowing individuals to make decisions that produce in others a feeling of trust, belief in reliability, respect, and rationality (Kenneth E. Goodpaster and John B. Matthews, Jr.). The decision-making aspect of responsibility is considered the most important by some. It may be measured in terms of answers to such questions as:

1. Has the problem been defined without the bias of loyalties?
2. How would the problem be defined by others with opposing interests and views?
3. How did past action lead to this situation?
4. What loyalties do you have to others in the corporation and to the corporation itself?
5. Who are the stakeholders in the decisions arising from this problem?
6. Who would be benefited and who would be injured by your decision?
7. Will your decision appear as right in the future as it does now?
8. Could you make your decision public in a newspaper without embarrassment or guilt?
9. What is the implication of decision as a precedent for the future and in terms of broader scope?
10. Is your decision consistent with your past decisions?

MONITORING AND FORECASTING THE ENVIRONMENT

The strategies, plans, operations, and decisions of a company represent the company's attempt to survive and prosper in an environment which seems all too hostile. Any study, analysis, or evaluation of a company must include *in parallel* a study of the environment and a study of the anatomy of the company.

The two basic questions that the analyst must ask are "How well is top management anticipating environmental opportunities and constraints?" and "How well is management developing and matching company capabilities (resources) to opportunities?"

Environmental areas which must be described (current) and forecast are:

1. Economic health of the world, country, and region of operation of the firm,
2. Industry structure and nature of the competition,
3. Markets, market segments, and needs and preferences of customers,
4. Political-legal constraints,
5. Social and demographic features and trends,
6. Technology.

> Longtime photographic equipment market leader, Eastman Kodak Co., became aware of changes in its competition, markets, and technology and, by 1982, had implemented a strategy to respond to these changes.
>
> Strong Japanese competition, decreased demand for amateur photography products, and radical technological breakthroughs were monitored and recognized by Eastman Kodak as environmental opportunities. The company began its response to the environment while still in a position of financial and productive strength.
>
> Kodak's team of strategic planners cultivated new markets in nonphotographic fields such as medical, office, and industrial products, for which Kodak already possessed the necessary technological expertise. The company also introduced the position "chief of market intelligence" to oversee worldwide market research and to monitor demographic trends in the environment.

7. Detailed files on the environment, as maintained by one of the largest firms in the U.S., are listed in Exhibit 2.2.

Whether top management is trying to diagnose its company's problems and plan for the future, or whether a business student is presenting a solution to a case study, there is no escape from explicitly describing the anticipated environment. It is all too common for businesspeople in smaller companies to say, "We can't predict the future, and anyway, our problems are in the present." *Many of the present problems are there because the businessperson did not attempt to look ahead and take action at an earlier point in time!* Anticipations will change as time passes and operations should be adjusted accordingly. The student who prepares a case report should state as the *premise* for solution his or her anticipation of the environment. The complaint of inadequate data is not a valid excuse for failure to do this.

Some major methods of forecasting the environment are:

1. Cross impact analysis—Select about 25 events, estimate probabilities of occurrence and time of occurrence, assess relationships, and interpret the impact on the future.
2. Trend impact analysis—Forecast some event in the environment in terms of a trend. Identify unprecedented events. Combine the events' probabilities and judgment of the impacts of the events on the trend to be forecast.
3. Delphi process—A group of experts individually estimate future events and their probabilities. The results of the individual estimates are combined and returned to the experts for a second round of estimating.

One of General Electric's former approaches to forecasting the environment is outlined in Exhibit 2.3. General Electric first used a Delphi process. Both trend impacts on the future and cross-impacts of possible events on the future were considered to develop a picture, or scenario, of the future.

While a rigorous treatment of environmental forecasting is beyond the scope of this text, we have provided references at the end of Chapter 2. We also discuss in later sections the development of the most immediate and urgent factors, namely industry and market environ-

EXHIBIT 2.2

Environmental Data Files

International

Balance of trade	Investment
World energy	Political situations
World mineral resources	Taxes
Food production	World Bank activities
Technology	Productivity

United States

Economic

GNP
Expenditures by GNP segments
Construction, commercial and
    residential
Disposable Personal Income
Personal savings
Corporate profits and
    cash flow
Federal government expenditures
Local and state
    expenditures
Employment rate
Money supply
Inflation rate
Economic indicators
Interest rate
Productivity
Wage levels
Hourly work week
Personal debt
Corporate debt
Pension funds
Taxes
Physical distribution
Land use
Farm subsidies
Social and Cultural
Categories of spending
Dwelling types
Leisure interests
Life-styles
Mobility
Purchase of services
Shopping habits
Work week

Government

Antitrust activities
Law enforcement
Consumer interests
Credit
Employment
    Equal opportunity
    Discrimination
Ethical practices
FCC
ICC
IRS
OSHA
Postal service
Privacy
Resource restrictions
Taxes
Education
Research in science
Monetary policy
Fiscal policy
Defense expenditures
Foreign aid
Ecology
Inner-city development
Medical and Health

EXHIBIT 2.2 (*Continued*)

Demographic
Age distribution
Age of workers
Education
Unions
Education of workers
Income distribution
Income levels
Labor force size
Occupations
Parttime workers
Population concentrations
Population size
Urban/surburban proportions
Women workers
Technology
Scientific research policy
   and funding
Alternate energy sources
Mass transportation
Weather modification
Medicine and health care
Communications
Food
Home construction
Defense

Resources
Coal
Electricity
Fabrics
Fertilizer
Food
Gas
Metals
Oil
Outdated sources
Scarce material restrictions
Transportation systems (people)

Public Attitudes
Work
   Benefits
   Trade and professional
   Working conditions
   Hours
   Retirement
   Women/minority managers
Business
   Profits
   Ethics
   Products
   Disclosure
Consumerism
      Advertising
   Pricing
   Privacy
   Packaging (labeling)
   Product quality
   Product safety
   Product type
   Service quality
Economic conditions
   Income
   Taxes
   Economy in general
   Inflation
Education
   Cost
   Effectiveness of system
   Benefits
Environment
   Air, water, noise
   Energy, resources
   Land use
   Material resources
   Solid waste
Equal opportunity
Government
         Regulation of business
         Regulation of individuals
         Effectiveness
         Honesty of leaders
      Competence of leaders
         Belief in institutions
         Law enforcement
   Inner cities
   Quality of life

ments. Finally, we point out that many of the business periodicals as well as trade association data will help keep management aware of estimates of coming events which have an impact on business in general.

EXHIBIT 2.3
How Scenarios Have Been Constructed at General Electric Company with
Trend Impact Analysis (TIA)

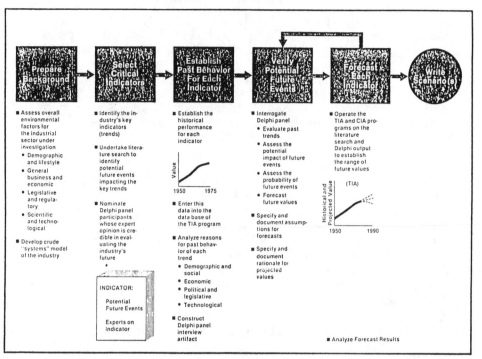

Source: General Electric Company. The Business Environmental Analysis Component
Corporate Strategic Operation annually constructs and updates scenarios focusing on
issues of concern to G.E.'s Business Sectors. From these scenarios, guidelines for planning are issued to the Strategic Business Units.
TIA-Trend Impact Analysis   CIA-Cross Impact Analysis

OPPORTUNITIES AND THREATS

OPPORTUNITIES

The environment poses both opportunities and threats to firms. Opportunities should be divided into immediate and long-term for purposes of search and identification. Immediate opportunities usually
require special insights and creative focusing of attention. They are
there but not visible to other companies who could exploit them. A few
examples of immediate opportunities are:

1. Previously unrecognized needs of individuals, companies, or government;
2. New applications of products and services;
3. Sudden growth of demand (designer jeans, for example);
4. Synergy achieved through merging;

5. New method of distribution;
6. New manufacturing process or substitution of materials;
7. New and better method for customer service.

Immediate opportunities are those for which the company is presently prepared; that is, the company must have a special competence or a competitive edge that allows it to pursue a program leading to achievement of greater sales and profits.

Long-term opportunities must be identified in terms of both the environment and the capability of the firm to reshape itself, if necessary. The preparation of the firm to take advantage of some opportunity in the future is the concern of strategic management. (See Chapter 4.)

THREATS

By the time environmental threats to the firm are immediately present, the firm may be in mortal danger. Major immediate threats are evidence of past strategic errors and management incompetence. As the environment has grown more complex and rapidly changing, the pages of history are being cluttered with records of great firms falling by the wayside. Management incompetence has been hidden by high rewards for short-term performance rather than long-time survival. A few sources of environmental threats are:

1. Competitors,
2. Changes in customer wants,
3. Dwindling resources and rising prices,
4. Legislation,
5. Inflation,
6. Recession,
7. International political and monetary relationships,
8. Technological breakthroughs.

> DuPont Co. was slow to identify environmental threats to the market it created (synthetic fibers) and failed to take preventive actions. Its fibers earnings fell from $126 million to $6 million in just one year.
>
> Even after demand for synthetic fibers had begun to decline, DuPont was building four new fibers plants. DuPont, as well as Monsanto and Celanese Corp., failed to heed economists' warnings of increasing Middle East political instability and subsequent rise in oil prices. These companies' earnings were hit hard as a result of failure to track environmental threats of declining demand and precarious source of major raw materials.

D. A. Hurd and E. R. Monfort, in their article "Vulnerability Analysis," describe a formal approach to analyzing environmental threats to a company. This approach is based on identifying "underpinnings," i.e., factors essential to the continued existence of the firm. The steps in the approach are:

1. Identify specific underpinnings in each of the 12 categories given in Exhibit 2.4,

EXHIBIT 2.4

Classes of Underpinnings

1. Needs and Wants:	Has traditionally been applied almost exclusively to customers but necessarily must be extended to other stakeholder groups.
2. Resources:	Refers to all people, physical assets, materials, and services employed in running a business.
3. Relative Costs:	The relationship of a company's key cost elements with those of competitors.
4. Customer Base:	This refers to the number and composition of the customer base.
5. Technology:	This refers to product and process technology.
6. Special Abilities:	The ability of one company to significantly outperform its competition in certain ways.
7. Identifying Symbols:	Logos and other means whereby the company's product or services are identified by the customer.
8. Artificial Barriers to Competition:	Various laws and regulations which help keep potential competitors out of a market.
9. Social Values:	Those clusters of social values which create demand for specific products and services.
10. Sanctions and Supports:	The enabling permission or public endorsement given to business by governments and other groups.
11. Integrity:	The basic trust a customer places in a product or service.
12. Complementary Products:	Products and services which are essential to the performance of other products or services.

2. List events—no matter how far-fetched—that could seriously damage an underpinning,
3. Evaluate these potential threats in terms of probability of occurrence and impact on the business,
4. Plot the results of the evaluation on the diagram in Exhibit 2.5.

CONSTRAINTS

Constraints imposed by the environment require careful attention to uncover. Legal constraints may be obvious, but political constraints

EXHIBIT 2.5
Vulnerability Analysis Threat Assessment Diagram

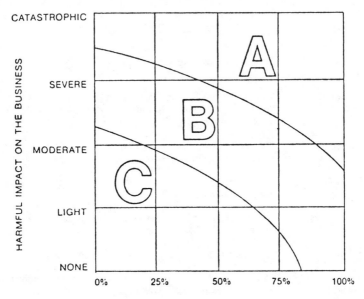

Source: Douglas A. Hurd and E. Riggs Monfort III, "Vulnerability Anaylsis: A New Way to Assure Future Trends," *Planning Review,* A Bimonthly Publication of the North American Society for Corporate Planning, Nov. 1979, pp. 32, 33.

may be more subtle. In the latter case, politicians or government agencies may be aroused to mobilize public opinion or introduce legislation if a company exceeds certain bounds in raising prices, closing down plants, polluting the environment, or compensating foreign officials in international trade.

Constraints to growth may be present due to lack of natural resources, well-established competitors, declining productivity, declining GNP, or a deteriorating transportation system. Cost of capital, cost of equipment, or costs of union labor may also be constraints. Political instability in countries where the company does business is another constraint in the world today.

SUMMARY

The environment with which the company interacts has grown increasingly complex because of many more factors that are changing at rapid rates. A few well-known companies that have suffered a severe impact in recent years are Chrysler (foreign competition, recession, high interest rates), Mobil Oil (loss of overseas sources of oil), U.S. Steel (foreign competition), AT&T (government anti-trust settlement), and many large savings and loans associations (government constraints on interest rates, high-interest borrowing rates, competition from money funds of innovative institutions such as Merrill Lynch).

As a result, entrepreneurship and survival plans for companies require monitoring and forecasting selected key variables in the environment. In addition, the general environment must be monitored for early warning signals of other factors that may affect the future of the firm. Opportunities, threats, and constraints must be identified through such forecasting. Formal methods, such as vulnerability analysis, can help in assessments.

SELECTED BIBLIOGRAPHY ON THE ENVIRONMENT OF THE BUSINESS SYSTEM

Berger, Peter L. New Attack on the Legitimacy of Business. *Harvard Business Review,* September-October, 1981.

Coates, Joseph F. Technological Change and Future Growth. *Technological and Social Forecasting,* Vol. 11, No. 1, 1977.

Edmunds, Stahrl. Which Way America? Six Scenarios for the Future of the United States. *The Futurist,* February, 1979.

Epstein, Edwin M., and Votaw, Dow (eds.). *Rationality, Legitimacy, Responsibility.* Santa Monica, Calif.: Goodyear Publishing Co., 1978.

Fahey, Liam; King, William R.; and Narayanan, Vadake K. Environmental Scanning and Forecasting in Strategic Planning—The State of the Art. *Long Range Planning,* February, 1981.

Gatewood, Elizabeth, and Carroll, Archie B. The Anatomy of Corporate Social Response: The Rely, Firestone 500, and Pinto Cases. *Business Horizons,* September/October, 1981.

Goodpaster, Kenneth E., and Matthews, John B., Jr. Can a Corporation Have a Conscience? *Harvard Business Review,* January-February, 1982.

Hurd, Douglas A., and Monfort III, E. Riggs. Vulnerability Analysis: A New Way to Assure Future Trends. *Planning Review,* November, 1979.

Kahn, Herman; Brown, William; and Martel, Leon. *The Next 200 Years: A Scenario for America and the World.* New York: William Morrow & Company, 1976.

Keegan, Warren J. Multinational Scanning. *Administrative Science Quarterly,* September, 1974.

Nash, Laura L. Ethics Without the Sermon. *Harvard Business Review,* November-December, 1981.

Neubauer, F. Fredrich; Soloman, Norman B. A Managerial Approach to Environmental Assessment. *Long Range Planning,* April, 1977.

O'Connor, Rochelle. *Multiple Scenarios and Contingency Planning,* Report 741. New York: The Conference Board, 1978.

Segey, Eli. How to Use Environmental Analysis in Strategy Making. *Management Review,* March, 1977.

Sethi, S. Prakash. A Conceptual Framework for Environmental Analysis of Social Issues and Evaluation of Business Response Patterns. *Management Review,* January, 1979.

Starling, Grover. *The Changing Environment of Business.* Boston: Kent Publishing Company, 1980.

Terry, P. T. Mechanisms for Environmental Scanning. *Long Range Planning,* June, 1977.

Tullock, Gordon, and Wagner, Richard E. (eds.). *Policy Analysis and Deductive Reasoning.* Lexington, Mass.: Lexington Books, 1978.

3

THE FIELD OF ACTION: THE BUSINESS SYSTEM

THE SYSTEMS CONCEPT

For many years and in many companies, the analysis of business problems focused on each functional area separately. As companies grew larger, the need to deal with problems in terms of interrelationships between departments became apparent. The search for solutions to problems and for new opportunities for the company by focusing on the company as a whole is called the "systems approach." Optimization of total company performance takes precedence over optimization of any single part.

The systems approach starts with definition of a system. A system is, simply, a set of elements and/or subsystems related and working together to achieve common (system) objectives. A business system, for example, consists of people, equipment, and facilities, which process input from the environment to produce such output as goods, services, information, scrap, and waste. A business system may be divided into subsystems in various ways as shown in Exhibit 3.1.

In planning, operating, or controlling a business, total business objectives should be established. For each of the sets of systems shown in Exhibit 3.1, the subsystems of the set should be managed to optimize total business results. Thus, allocation of resources to the subsystems will not likely optimize performance of any single subsystem. Specifically, resources allocated among marketing, manufacturing, and engineering will not allow any of these activities to reach their highest level, but any other allocation will reduce total business performance. Similar reasoning holds for the subsystems of products. Thus, in analyzing cases, recommendations for solutions must consider tradeoffs among subsystems of both resources and achievement of subsystem objectives.

EXHIBIT 3.1

Dividing the Business into Subsystems in Five Ways

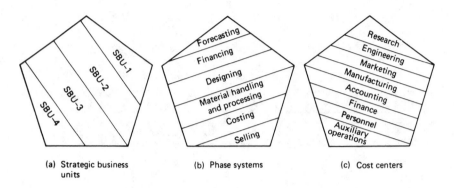

(a) Strategic business units

(b) Phase systems

(c) Cost centers

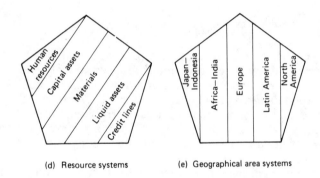

(d) Resource systems

(e) Geographical area systems

THE GENERAL MANAGEMENT PERSPECTIVE

The general manager in business is an individual responsible for a business system. Titles for general management positions are:

Chairman and CEO (Chief Executive Officer)
Vice-Chairman and CEO
President and CEO
President
VP (Vice-President)
Group VP or Division VP
General Manager
Director (foreign or international).

The general manager (GM) is responsible for the profit and loss of the business system and for the long-term survival. The GM must think and act as a generalist rather than as a specialist; he or she must take a systems view and systems approach to the management of the organization.

Judgment and wisdom must be guiding perspectives in seeking balance among (1) conflicting objectives of subsystems, (2) differing value systems of internal and external influences, (3) opposing views of priorities and emphasis, and (4) conflicting proposals for criteria in all areas. Changing market outlooks, shifting societal wants, and changing world conditions require that the GM maintain both fundamental ethical attitudes but flexibility in understanding and applying these in the rapidly changing environment.

> Edwin H. Land, founder and CEO of Polaroid Corp. for 43 years, was an inventor first and a manager second. Ninety percent of his time was spent in a laboratory. Land's research and technological orientation and his total devotion to photography dictated the objectives, values, and policies of the company. He never deviated the company's course from developing and refining the instant camera.
>
> Land's successor wanted to diversify Polaroid's base into commercial and industrial products, in light of a declining amateur photography market. However, Land felt that amateur photography was in a growth, not a maturity stage. As Polaroid's single largest stockholder, he attempted to wield his influence and preserve the company's one-product strategy.

The GM for the total enterprise must (a) develop the concept of the enterprise, (b) guide the development of a set of visions, goals, values, and policies, and (c) conduct the strategic management tasks of entrepreneurial renewal and growth.

ORGANIZATION—THE STRUCTURE OF THE SYSTEM

ORGANIZING FOR ACTION

What makes one business an aggressive innovative leader and another a ponderous obsolescing fumble-bum? Why are large companies seeking desperately to introduce entrepreneurship into their work climate—and failing? The answers to these questions lie in *organization* of the firms. By this we mean organization in its broadest sense. Organization consists of interpersonal relationships, communication processes, and a climate of open cooperation which are held together in the formal organizational framework for overall control.

Good organization facilitates rapid responses by all members to the day-to-day operating demands. Good organization minimizes useless paperwork and formal ties yet assures control through key reports. Organization is tied directly to the strategy of a company. *A major change in strategy usually requires a major change in the organization of a company.* This is most evident when a small single-product company explodes into a large volume company. The degree to which the organization is redirected by restructuring determines whether its required changes in strategy will work.

When General Foods Corp. changed its strategy from growth due to stringent cost controls to growth through diversification, it introduced organizational changes to facilitate the change in strategy.

To encourage the necessary change from a conservative to a more entrepreneurial perspective, authority for new-product and most capital spending decisions was shifted from a central committee to middle management. Compensation was tied to increased sales volume.

General Foods' strategic business units were granted more control and authority, to expedite quicker entry into the marketplace and ultimately to develop the desired volume and product-line growth.

When Schlumberger Ltd., premier oil services company, acquired Fairchild Camera & Instrument Corp., it moved quickly to introduce its organizational style and corporate culture into the chip maker. To facilitate decentralization and to instill operating people with more responsibility and decision-making power, Schlumberger reduced Fairchild's headquarters staff by two-thirds. It also reorganized Fairchild's operations into business units by market instead of by manufacturing process.

Schlumberger further encouraged its own long-run orientation by eliminating Fairchild's bonus program, which was based on short-run performance.

ORGANIZATIONAL FORMS PRESCRIBED BY LAW

From a legal viewpoint, the basic organizational forms are

1. Individual proprietorships,
2. Partnerships,
3. Limited partnerships,
4. Corporations,
5. Joint-venture companies for international ventures.

The decision as to the legal form of organization or *change* to a different legal form is extremely critical to the owners of the company. In analyzing a particular company, the following questions should be answered:

1. Is the form the most effective from the viewpoint of both strategy and prompt response to competition? For example, an individual proprietor may set his own objectives and take big entrepreneurial

risks, whereas in the corporate form, the board of directors may provide restraints.

2. Is the risk appropriate to the desires and resources of the owners? For example, individual proprietorships, partnerships, and general partners of limited partnerships risk not only their investments but their personal resources as well. Partnerships are subject to conflicts among partners and imprudent actions by any of the partners.

The risk for the limited partners in a limited partnership is that they may be forced to stand by helplessly while the general partner flounders and dissipates the assets of the company.

In corporations, joint ventures, and holding companies, the capital risk is limited to the investments of the owners.

3. What is the intended life of the company? Proprietorships and partnerships may be forced to dissolve upon the death of one of the owners, whereas corporations continue "forever." Joint-venture companies are usually designed for a limited life for a special project and may be dissolved upon completion. U.S. government policy and law have been erratic with regard to permitting companies to join together for joint foreign ventures.

4. What are the capital requirements? Individual proprietorships and partnerships do not have access to the great capital markets which corporations listed on the stock exchange have.

5. What are the tax advantages? This is often the dominant consideration.

Since 1983, corporation income has been taxed at a rate of 15% on the first $25,000; 18% on the next $25,000; 30% on the next $25,000; 40% on the next $25,000; and 46% on income over $100,000. This contrasts with proprietorships or partnerships in which earnings are taxed only once at the individual's income tax rate.

However, a corporation owned by 10 or fewer people (and fulfilling some other conditions) may be considered a "small business corporation" under subchapter S of the Internal Revenue Code. Undistributed taxable income is then taxed to the shareholders rather than the corporation.

If the owners are in high income tax brackets, partnerships and joint-ventures often offer tax shelters. Large depreciation expenses which do not affect cash flow out are subtracted from cash incomes of shareholders before they are taxed.

We have presented only the major managerial decision or policy questions which should be asked. Obviously, considerable legal assistance may be required to answer some of these questions in actual cases.

ORGANIZATIONAL GUIDES FOR SMALL FIRMS

The small unincorporated company, which heaven must like because there are so many in our economy, is often guided and led by a single individual or two partners. In one of the most workable forms, there may be no "president," "chief executive officer," or other fancy leadership title. The organization may appear as shown in Exhibit 3.2.

EXHIBIT 3.2

An Effective Organization
for a Small Manufacturing Firm

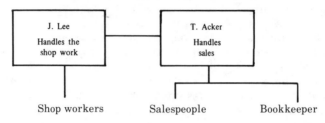

Although specification of assets, equity, sales, earnings, or number of employees have been used to differentiate the "small" firm from the "medium-size" firm, these are of dubious value. What is important are the limitations of strategy imposed on a firm by its limited capabilities. Thus, in small firms, the managers are usually the owners, capital is supplied by a single owner or small group (10 or fewer), and the area of operations (although not necessarily its markets) are local. It would be a mistake to classify a firm which is smallest in its industry as "small" when it employs thousands of people, has tremendous assets, and has access to the major money markets.

The biggest mistake which the consultant, new president, or student can make in trying to doctor a sick small firm is to impose the formidable hierarchy and staff of the giant firm upon it. A tight formal structure imposed upon a small or medium-size firm can easily choke it to death.

In the highly successful medium-size Buffalo Forge Company in western New York state no formal organization chart and policy manual have been prepared. The management of the firm works together in close personal relationship, and the chief executive supplies more than average personal direction to the key people, both individually and in numerous meetings and conferences.

As the small firm grows in sales and production, the owner-manager often finds that some specialized skills are required which he or she does not possess. The solution is *not* to bring one or several $50,000/year vice-presidents into the firm. The owner-manager should first attempt to hire outside assistance on a part-time basis to aid, say, the bookkeeper or the sales manager who may lack advertising expertise or the plant manager who may lack industrial engineering training. He or she may arrange to attend a concentrated one-week seminar or workshop to gain some particular skill.

The owner-manager may possibly decide that it is not possible to run the daily operations any longer because the size of the work force and variety of activities have increased too much. He finds that he should be devoting some of his time to forward thinking or longer-range investment decisions. In such a case he would look for people in the company to designate as managers. The purpose is to *delegate some of the responsibilities* so that the owner-manager may work where he is most effective. Exhibit 3.3 shows an example of such an organization.

EXHIBIT 3.3

**Small Wholesaling Firm
Growth and Delegation**

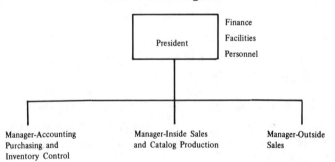

Many small firms incorporate in order to limit liability. They often fail to exploit the potential to be obtained from the board of directors. The owner-manager continues to dominate all decisions. It is surprising but true that many local professional and businesspeople welcome the opportunity of serving as directors, but small entrepreneurs are reluctant to use their services. Exhibit 3.4 suggests how a president might augment his or her own skills in the corporate form of business at no or nominal cost.

How do we get an organization designed for effective action in the small company? We attempt to get a *working team* based on the actions and objectives specified. Generally, the more informal the organization, the better the firm will perform. Specialized knowledge in a number of fields is required for every business organization. The small firms cannot usually afford to buy all that they need; so the alert ones will make full use of a diversified board of directors as a source.

EXHIBIT 3.4

**The Board of Directors in the
Fiberglassy Boat Company**

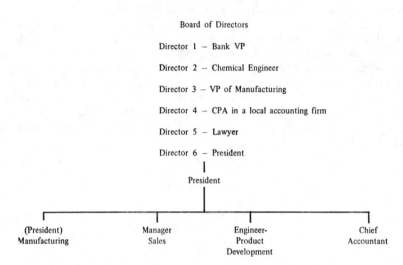

In analyzing the case of your own company or another company, the data in Exhibit 3.5 will be helpful.

ORGANIZATIONAL GUIDES FOR MEDIUM-SIZE FIRMS

There are no clear-cut generally accepted boundaries between medium and large firms. Common measures are assets, sales, equity, and number of employees.

Since strategy and operations are so dependent upon management skills and financial resources, we find that organizational problems depend upon company size. The discrete step up from a small firm to a medium-size firm occurs when the number of employees, the sales, and the other operations have grown to the point where a functional manager is required for each functional area. In a medium-size firm we no longer have a president who is also a manager of some function such as sales or production. In addition, full-time key specialists such as legal counselor and treasurer are required.

The other important characteristic of a medium-size firm is that it has access to the great financial markets if it wants such access. We mean that the firm is large enough that a strategy of "going public" will permit it to be listed on the American Stock Exchange (Amex). Four of the requirements for listing on Amex are

1. Minimum net tangible assets of $4,000,000,
2. Minimum net after-tax earnings of $400,000 and minimum net income before taxes and extraordinary items of $750,000,

EXHIBIT 3.5

Small Business Organizational Problems

Symptoms	Possible Problems	Needed Action
1. Confusion on customers' orders such as duplication, failure to fill, incorrect size or model.	Owner-manager has assigned the sales function to one of his employees but keeps getting into the act and dealing sporadically with customers.	Owner-manager should either take over the sales or clearly delegate the responsibility and funnel all information to his sales manager.
2. Administrative costs have grown more rapidly than sales.	Big-company organization is being put onto a small company.	Reduce number of managers by broadening area of responsibility for the remaining. Don't hire specialists; train current workers in needed specialties.
3. One activity such as sales, production, or purchasing just cannot keep abreast of the work.	Is there a relative on the payroll? Is the manager up to his job? Is the manager being choked by too tight a budget? Are personality problems pitting the workers against the manager?	An objective and immediate study is needed. If the owner-manager doesn't know the cause of the problem by now, he should hire a local business consultant to take a look.
4. The company seems to be drifting aimlessly or trying to go in all different directions.	The organization lacks someone skilled in planning. The owner-manager is a volatile unsystematic entrepreneur.	If there is a board of directors, the symptoms should be called to their attention. The board should be able to provide a steadying influence by formulating some simple 1- to 3-year plans.
5. When the owner-manager is not around, things seem to rest on dead center; the organization is paralyzed.	The owner-manager is dictatorial and believes no one else can do any job or make any decision without him on the spot.	Eventually, the company will start running down hill. A committee of the more capable employees may suggest to the owner-manager that they be given more freedom and responsibility in decision making. A memo of agreement is desirable so that the owner-manager doesn't forget such delegation of responsibility by the next week.
6. Supervisors make decisions which frequently are reversed by the owner-manager.	The owner-manager has not taken time to develop a consistent set of policies.	Some policies, guidelines, and procedures should be put into writing to cover the major areas of repetitive action and decision-making.
7. Conflicts among managers and key personnel. Confusion about current objectives and operations. One manager is dominating his co-workers.	The owner-manager is not working closely and personally with his people to develop a team approach and unified objectives.	Daily conferences between the owner-manager and his staff to build a working organization, not just a paper organization.

- 3. Minimum public distribution of 400,000, shares (exclusive of certain officers' and family holdings),
- 4. Minimum market value of shares of $3,000,000.[1]

The medium-size firms generally retain centralized corporate control of functions although there is usually geographical dispersion of sales units or manufacturing plants. The organization tends to be fairly "flat"; that is, there are relatively few levels in the formal hierarchy. Exhibit 3.6 illustrates this type of functional organization.

It may often be beneficial to combine these functions or further segregate them. For example, engineering and manufacturing are sometimes combined when manufacturing processes pose difficult problems or represent the competitive edge of the firm and the engineering of new products is insignificant. Employee, public, and stockholder relations are often combined into one group. At times, production appears as two separate organizations, (1) planning and control and (2) manufacturing.

EXHIBIT 3.6

General Organization for a Medium-Size Firm

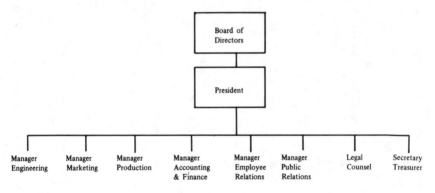

In medium-size firms which produce clearly differentiated product lines, a characteristic of large firm organization structure may be advisable. This is organization by product division with some duplication of functional activities for the divisions.

Several very undesirable organization forms should be avoided. One is the many-layered hierarchy. An example of multiple layers in manufacturing is shown in Exhibit 3.7.

Good management dictates a broad span (number of people reporting to a single manager) and *decentralized* decision making. Thus a span of one, plant superintendent over the manager of production in Exhibit 3.7 is pointless. One of the positions should be abolished. The manager of production has only two people reporting to him. Generally, a span of management of at least six people is desirable.

EXHIBIT 3.7

Too Many Layers in the Medium-Size Firm

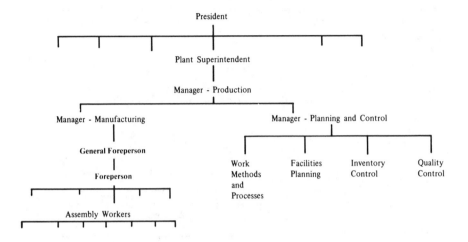

Organizations are said to be "centralized" or "decentralized" according to where most decisions are made. In a centralized organization, the top person is making most decisions. On a continuing basis, this results in weak lower and middle management. People who never make key decisions never develop their executive skills. However, in a period of crisis, centralized decision making may be desirable to provide prompt, decisive, and consistent company-wide action.

The big advantages of decentralized organization are: (1) making daily operating decisions develops the executives, (2) the executives who are on the spot know the situation best and can make prompt decisions, (3) a climate for creativity is established, and (4) the minimization of control tends to motivate the managers.

While we have dwelt on the basic functional organization structure, new dynamic forms of organization have been developed to suit the characteristics of individual manufacturing, wholesaling, retailing, or service firms. The choice of one of these depends upon that characteristic—function, product, process, project, or system—which deserves the most attention and control. Exhibit 3.8 summarizes and compares these structures.

Let us explain Exhibit 3.8 in more detail. Exhibit 3.8a through 3.8e shows legal counsel and manager-finance reporting to the president. Because a high degree of specialization is required in each of the functional areas of engineering, marketing, production, and personnel, the firm is organized on the basis of these functions. Each function is then responsible for applying *its own special skills* to each product line, to each process (such as engineering, manufacturing, or marketing) within its proper purview, to all special projects undertaken, and to all *systems* which may be developed. The principal advantage of this form of organization is the grouping together of people with the same specialty to encourage exchange of ideas. The principal disadvantage is that functional areas such as marketing and manufacturing have conflicting goals *at their level of operation*. This is developed in detail later on in this text.

EXHIBIT 3.8

Basic Organizational Forms for Medium-Size Firms

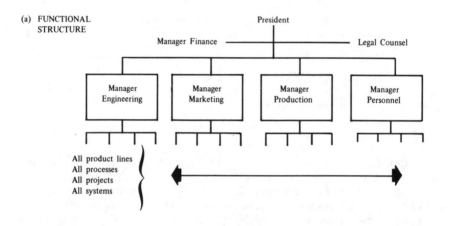

(a) FUNCTIONAL STRUCTURE

Exhibits 3.8b focuses on the product. Every stage of development, production, and distribution of a product is the responsibility of one manager, the product manager. This is not the case for the functional organization where managers are more concerned with high priority for pet jobs.

Exhibit 3.8c represents a departmentalization by process. *Like equipment* is grouped together. It is typical of the job shop in manufacturing where a variety of products is made. This form of organization generally has the advantage of optimum use of equipment in each department. Maintenance is also made easier by having like machines together.

Exhibit 3.8d is typical of a company which is engaged primarily in large research projects, large construction projects, or large venture projects. All the resources required to carry out a project are placed under the line control of the project managers. In practice, some common activities such as an engineering test laboratory or a drawing, drafting, and processing unit are separated out. The project managers then deal with these organizations by "buying" their services on a planned basis. This form of organization is very important for the development of complex, ill-defined projects which require considerable control to keep costs down and quality high. It has been used

EXHIBIT 3.8 (*Continued*)

(b) PRODUCT-
ORIENTED
STRUCTURE

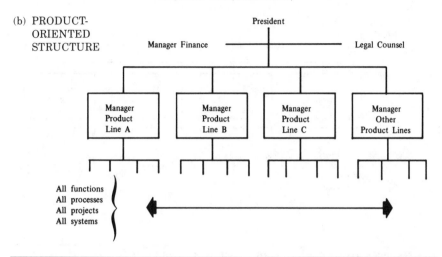

(c) PROCESS-
ORIENTED
STRUCTURE

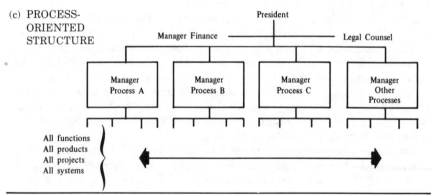

(d) PROJECT
ORGANIZATION

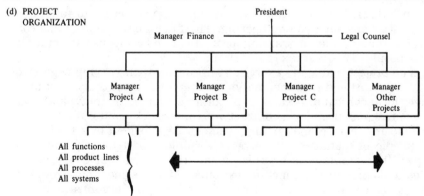

EXHIBIT 3.8 (*Continued*)

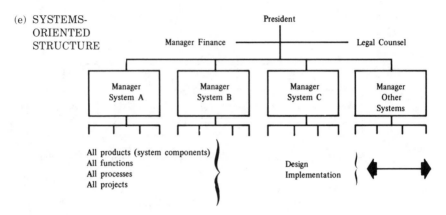

(e) SYSTEMS-
   ORIENTED
   STRUCTURE

most successfully in defense-project work because the reporting system ties in so closely to the organization.

Exhibit 3.8e shows an organization form for the design of large systems. Electronic control systems, electro-mechanical operating systems, management information systems, or urban transportation systems would be examples. Systems design is considerably different from component design, so that this is the reason for this form.

Another completely different interpretation may be placed on this form. These systems may refer to the operational systems of the company itself. Thus, processing systems, logistical systems, control systems, and marketing systems are examples.

Finally, all the organizations of Exhibit 3.8 may be converted to the matrix type. For our purposes, let us illustrate the matrix form by converting the functional organization to this form. The matrix form is shown in Exhibit 3.9.

In Exhibit 3.9 individuals are assigned permanently to functional organizations such as engineering. The functional manager has control over assignments, training, promotion, and compensation of his or her people. This is *line* organization.

The project managers exercise staff control with varying degrees of authority. At one extreme, individuals report daily to the project manager for technical direction. At the other extreme, the individuals perform tasks as if under a contract with few check points.

One drawback of matrix management is spelled out by a traditional principle of management—a person should report to only one manager. Its advantage is organizational stability in that every person has a "home" in the functional groups. At the same time, the planning, motivation, and control of project-type organizations are present.

Some common symptoms and problems for medium-size organizations are listed in Exhibit 3.10.

EXHIBIT 3.9

Matrix Organizational Form

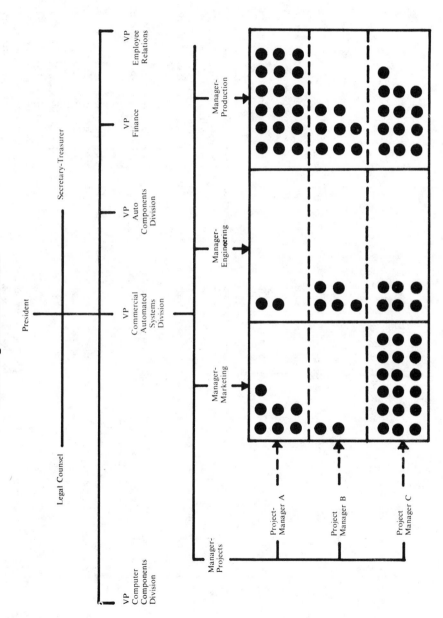

EXHIBIT 3.10

Medium-Size Business Organizational Problems

Symptoms	Possible Problems	Needed Action
1. One functional area is failing to perform well.	Organizational responsibilities not well defined. Manager not adequate for the job. Manager from another function dominating his comanagers.	Clarification of responsibilities and measurements. Further training of the manager. Review manpower requirements.
2. Communication is very slow.	Too many layers of management. Only formal lines of communication are followed.	The CEO should minimize number of organizational levels. Establish cross-functional committees and liaison positions.
3. Matrix-type organization is not working.	Jealousy between line manager and product manager.	The CEO should classify responsibilities of managers. Put line managers in product review teams.
4. The president is too busy to work on 1- to 3- year plans.	President is failing to delegate. Managers lack confidence and refer too many decisions to the president.	President must coach his managers and then refuse to make their decisions for them. He must allow them to make some mistakes so that they can learn.
5. One aggressive manager appears to be taking on broader and more diversified duties at the expense of the other managers.	We have an "empire-builder."	The CEO should clarify the scope of each manager's work in a position description or policy guide.
6. Managers appear to be going in all different directions and enjoying it.	The president has "overdelegated," in fact he has relinquished control which is necessary to hold the organization together.	The president must work closely with all managers to set a unified set of objectives. He must work with the personnel to develop a system of measurement by objectives. Further, he must work with the financial manager to control activities by means of cost/performance/time standards.
7. General and administrative costs are rising rapidly.	Staff people are being added too rapidly as the organization expands.	Keep the organization lean by cutting back on reports and delegating more responsibility to line managers.

ORGANIZATIONAL GUIDES FOR LARGE FIRMS

Organization of large firms varies from the relatively traditional divisional (product) type of firm to complex mixtures of types of organizations. Large firms are generally *re*organized to slim down operations, to reflect a change of emphasis from say, products to market segments, to provide greater control over wide-flung diversified operations, or to handle acquisitions and expansions in the changing environment.

New Organization Structure in a Large Company

In many ways the most significant internal change has been Genesco's new management organization structure ... Reporting to the chief operating officers are the group presidents, each of whom is responsible for a number of related operating companies. Reporting to the group presidents are the presidents of the operating companies. (See Exhibit 3.11.)

In this chain of command, each executive knows his responsibilites, has the authority to take the action necessary to produce results, and knows that he is accountable for those results. This organization permits the rapid, decentralized decision-making necessary in the apparel industry.

Source: Genesco Inc., *Annual Report,* 1973, p. 3.

FEATURES OF LARGE COMPANIES

In very large firms, the organization is usually very complex. It is probably true that hundreds of organizational forms could be established successfully for any single firm. A well-designed organization structure facilitates effective performance of the company, although it certainly does not guarantee it. An inappropriate organization structure will very likely impede effective performance, but it is possible for good personal relationships to overcome this handicap.

The most noticeable characteristic of the organization of large companies is the addition of many "staff" people to "line" personnel. The line personnel are those who have been delegated responsibility for the production and distribution of the product or service. Staff people provide solely advisory and/or supporting general or technical services. In Exhibit 3.12 showing the top management of Exxon Company, we see two distinct staff groups: the Coordination and Planning group and the Advisory and Service group. The *line* management and line personnel fall in the Operations Management organizational components.

The second most noticeable feature of the large company is the greatly increased number of layers of management. The General Electric Company has made a determined effort to hold down the number of layers from the lowest rung on the organizational ladder to the president to only six or seven.

EXHIBIT 3.11

Genesco Organization

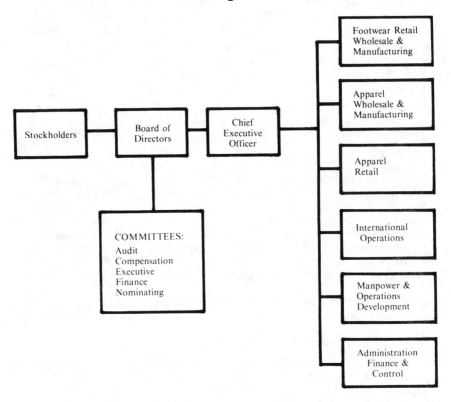

Another outstanding feature of large companies is the subdivision of the parent company into nearly autonomous divisions or companies. Exhibit 3.13 shows how Rapid-American is subdivided. This permits great flexibility of organization for each subcompany.

Other common characteristics of large companies are standardization, rigidity, and tight control systems. Large companies which have tried to maintain a free-wheeling, free-form organization eventually find themselves in trouble.

An offbeat type of organization was that of Boise Cascade. Headed by a three-member office of the president, R. V. Hansberger, W. D. Eberle, and R. Halliday. Boise Cascade experienced a fantastic growth in the 1960s. After a decade of growth, sales fell 1% in 1970 but profits dropped 55%. High turnover of executive personnel and ecological problems have forced the company to rethink its organizational approach.

Some common symptoms and problems in organization for large companies are listed in Exhibit 3.14.

EXHIBIT 3.12

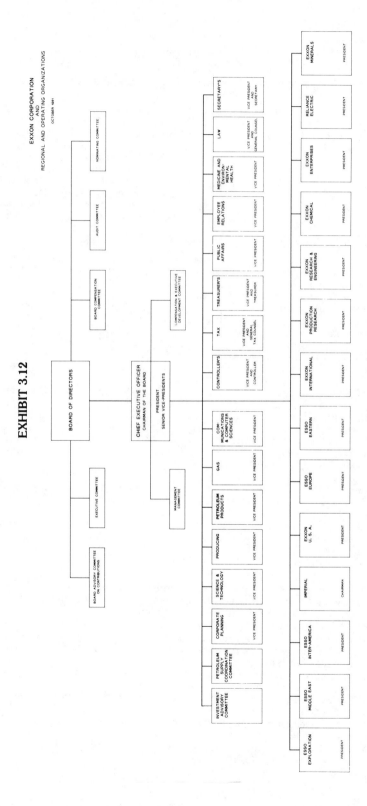

EXXON CORPORATION
AND
REGIONAL AND OPERATING ORGANIZATIONS

OCTOBER 1981

EXHIBIT 3.13

Table of Rapid-American Corporation and Subsidiaries

The following table sets forth certain information, as of April 15, 1981, with respect to the subsidiaries of Rapid, other than certain subsidiaries which, if considered in the aggregate as a single subsidiary, would not constitute a significant subsidiary.

	Percentage of voting securities owned by its immediate parent (%)	State or other jurisdiction in which incorporated
Parent[1]		
Subsidiaries of Rapid:		
McCrory Corporation	100[2]	Delaware
Schenley Industries, Inc.	100[3]	Delaware
McGregor-Doniger, Inc.	100[3]	New York
Melville Knitwear Co., Inc.	100[4]	New York
Shenandoah Corporation	100	Delaware
Plastic Toy and Novelty Corp.	100	Delaware
Donagain Corp.	100	New York
Anvil Brand, Inc.	100[3]	Delaware
Rapid-American Menswear, Inc.	100[3]	Delaware
Rapid Distribution Service, Inc.	100	Delaware
RAAM Information Services Corporation	100	Delaware
View Top Corporation	100	Delaware
ILC Industries	74	Delaware
Leeds (Israel) Ltd.	100	Israel
Theatre Venture, Inc.	100	Delaware
Triple Eight Corporation	100	Delaware
Subsidiaries of McCrory Corporation:		
Lerner Stores Corporation	100[5]	Maryland
Otasco, Inc.	100	Nevada
J. J. Newberry Co.	100[6]	Delaware
Whimsy, Incorporated	100	California
S. Klein Department Stores, Inc.	100	New York
Subsidiaries of Lerner Stores Corporation:		

[1]For information concerning Riklis Family Corporation and AFC, see "Introductory Note," Item 4 – "Security Ownership of Certain Beneficial Owners and Management" and Note 2 to Financial Statements.

[2]Rapid has approximately 100% of the voting power except for the election of directors where it has approximately 81% of such voting power. These shares are pledged to secure Rapid's guarantee of McCrory's bank indebtedness. See Note 6 to Financial Statements.

[3]All voting securities are pledged to secure Rapid's guarantee of McCrory's bank indebtedness. See Note 6 to Financial Statements.

[4]All voting securities are pledged to secure certain Rapid bank indebtedness. See Note 6 to Financial Statements.

[5]All voting securities are pledged to secure borrowings of McCrory. See Note 6 to Financial Statements.

[6]Arrearages in preferred dividends entitle the holders of such stock to elect two directors to the Board of Directors of J. J. Newberry Co.

EXHIBIT 3.13 (*Continued*)

	Percentage of voting securities owned by its immediate parent (%)	State or other jurisdiction in which incorporated

Lerner owns 100% of the voting securities of its 14 subsidiaries, five of which are real estate companies, and nine operate retail stores.

Subsidiary of Otasco, Inc.:

Otasco Credit Corporation	100	Nevada

Subsidiary of J. J. Newberry Co.:

J. J. Newberry Canadian Ltd.[7]	100	Canada

Subsidiaries of Schenley Industries, Inc.:

AGE Bodegas Unidas, S.A.	49.3	Spain
D.W.S. Corporation	100	Quebec
Distributors of New England, Inc.	100	Mass.
Dreyfus-Ashby & Co., Limited	100	United Kingdom
Dubonnet Wine Corporation	100	New York
L.E. Jung & Wulff Co., Inc.	100	New York
Knickerbocker Market Research Corp.	100	New York
Schenley Affiliated Brands Corp.	100	New York
Schenley Charge Plan, Inc.	100	New York
Schenley Distillers, Inc.	100	Delaware
Schenley Enterprises, Inc.	100	Delaware
Schenley Export Corporation	100	New York
Schenley Far East, Ltd.	100	Japan
Schenley International Co., Inc.	100	Delaware
Trans-American Distributing Corp.	100	Delaware
Virgin Islands Rum Industries, Ltd.	100	Virgin Islands

Subsidiary of D.W.S. Corporation:

Schenley Canada, Inc.	100	Quebec

Subsidiaries of Schenley Canada, Inc.:

Canadian Gibson Distillery Ltd.	100	Canada
Park & Tilford Canada, Inc.	100	British Columbia
Quebec Distillers, Ltd.	100	Quebec
John MacNaughton Co., Ltd.	100	Quebec
Schenley Wines and Spirits, Ltd.	100	Canada

Subsidiaries of Knickerbocker Market Research Corp.:

Merit House, Inc.	100	Delaware
World Network, Inc.	100	Illinois

Subsidiary of Schenley Affiliated Brands Corp.:

Wine & Spirits Merchandisers, Inc.	100	Illinois

Subsidiary of Schenley Distillers, Inc.:

Tennessee Dickel Distilling Co.	100	Tennessee

Subsidiaries of Anvil Brand, Incorporated:

[7]Includes 37.4% owned by non-significant Canadian subsidiaries of J. J. Newberry Co.

EXHIBIT 3.13 (*Continued*)

	Percentage of voting securities owned by its immediate parent (%)	State or other jurisdiction in which incorporated
Almar Manufacturing Corp.	100	Delaware
The Botany Shirt Company, Inc.	100	Delaware
Beau Brummell Ties, Inc.	100	New York
Friedman Marks, Inc.	100	Delaware
Gilead Manufacturing Corporation	100	Rhode Island
Wonderknit Corporation	100	New York
Subsidiary of ILC Industries, Inc.:		
ILC Data Device Corporation	100	Delaware
Subsidiaries of ILC Data Device Corporation:		
ILC Data Device Export Corporation	98.8	Delaware
Beta Transformer Technology Corporation	100	New York
DDC United Kingdom, Ltd.	100	Delaware
DDC Electronique, S.A.	100	France

BASIC ORGANIZATIONAL FORMS

The organization of companies usually follows either one of the "pure" forms below or, in the case of large companies, a complex mixture of these. The basic patterns are:

1. By people. Talented people are given work assignments according to their particular talents. The organization structure changes whenever a manager is replaced in order to obtain the best assignment of tasks among the managers. This basis of formal organization is extremely rare but often emerges in the actual functioning of small firms.

2. By product. The use of product divisions is quite common because it permits easy establishment of profit centers. (See Exhibit 3.15, Archer-Daniels-Midland Company.)

3. By geographic area. Companies requiring strong local marketing effort find this method appropriate.

4. By process. Small companies often base their organization upon manufacturing departments or processes.

5. By function. Practically all organizations are structured at the lowest level on the basis of function. That is, "like" skills are grouped together to form an organizational component. Large as well as small companies are also organized near the top level on the basis of functions (or disciplines) such as finance, marketing, engineering, production, and personnel. At the top level, these functions appear as staff components.

EXHIBIT 3.14

Large-Business Organization Problems

Symptoms	Possible Problems	Needed Action
The firm is always late in getting new products on the market.	Management is too conservative. Too much inertia and red tape. R & D organization is too small. Organization is not structured to achieve a clear-cut strategy. Organization changes have not been made as the company has expanded.	Organize to fix responsibilities for product lines on specific individuals. Utilize "Product Manager" organizational concepts to get products developed and on the market. Break the company up into smaller divisions or businesses with wide freedom to act in developing new products and seeking new markets.
The firm's former strength (marketing, finance, low operating costs, rapid innovation, etc.) appears to have become its weakness.	Strong single-minded president who has been in office many years. Functional executive has been promoted to president and follows past strategy. Company has grown too fast for president of limited ability.	Board of directors must broaden either the office of president or the CEO himself, or move the president out. "Office of the President" may be established. A task force to restructure the organization to give greater power to executives in areas of problems may be established.
Company is drifting. The "bottom line" earnings, are decreasing each year. Glowing projections in the annual report accompanied by excuses for last year's poor results.	Incompetent CEO. High level executive conflict preventing unified direction of strategy and operations. Family ownership of a large block of stock and family interference with company strategy.	Immediate action is needed to get a new management team. The board of directors must get a new president or clear the way for the current president to act. Family with large stock block may be encouraged to put stock in trust or sell out.
Poor performance of a company at each level for a company engaged in extraction, manufacturing, wholesaling, and retailing (oil, lumber, or minerals).	A vertically integrated company is organized by vertical divisions, each division having responsibility for all steps from extraction to retailing.	Reorganize company into divisions based upon processing levels, extraction, refining or manufacturing, wholesaling, retailing.
Sales are increasing but profits sinking despite energetic top management.	Unprofitable acquisitions or retention of losers. Retention of companies which are unrelated to the central corporate scope of products and markets. Lack of financial control over largely autonomous companies.	Organize like-companies into divisions, and make division VP's responsible for achieving standard profit goals. Making operating company controllers accountable to the chief accounting officer of the corporation.

EXHIBIT 3.14 (Continued)

Symptoms	Possible Problems	Needed Action
Sales are increasing but profits sinking despite energetic top management.	Unprofitable acquisitions or retention of losers. Retention of companies which are unrelated to the central corporate scope of products and markets. Lack of financial control over largely autonomous companies.	Organize like-companies into divisions, and make division VP's responsible for achieving standard profit goals. Making operating company controllers accountable to the chief accounting officer of the corporation.
The company performs large development and production projects and constantly has cost and time over-runs.	A functional organization and lack of a project control system.	Organize along line projects or give more authority to matrix-project managers.
Line and staff conflicts at the top corporate level.	Growth of a large aggressive staff organization.	Reduce the staff organization and issue position descriptions which delegate full responsibility for division performance with division VP's. Issue a policy which permits line managers to either use company staff services or purchase services outside. Make the staff organization pay its way by "selling" staffhours to line management.

EXHIBIT 3.15

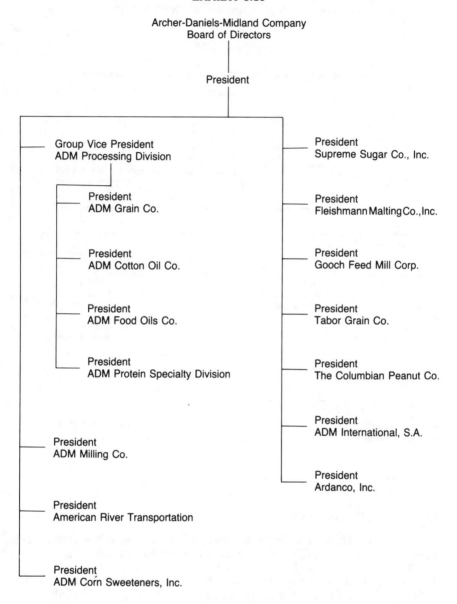

Archer-Daniels-Midland Company
Board of Directors

President

Group Vice President
ADM Processing Division

President
ADM Grain Co.

President
ADM Cotton Oil Co.

President
ADM Food Oils Co.

President
ADM Protein Specialty Division

President
ADM Milling Co.

President
American River Transportation

President
ADM Corn Sweeteners, Inc.

President
Supreme Sugar Co., Inc.

President
Fleischmann Malting Co., Inc.

President
Gooch Feed Mill Corp.

President
Tabor Grain Co.

President
The Columbian Peanut Co.

President
ADM International, S.A.

President
Ardanco, Inc.

6. By phase of activity. A petroleum company's operations, for example, may be organized into organizational components of exploration, extraction, refining, and marketing.

Large firms are often organized according to complex mixes of these basic forms. Dravo, which is listed on the New York Stock Exchange,

52

provides us with an example of mixed functional, product, process, and geographic organization as shown in Exhibit 3.16.

EXHIBIT 3.16

Dravo Corporate Organization Chart, Courtesy of Dravo Corporation

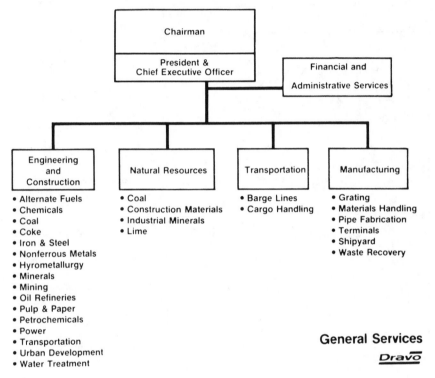

February 1983

ORGANIZATIONAL POLICIES

Policies which deal with organizational structure, other than personnel and staffing policies, may spell out such information as:

1. Principles to be followed in structuring organizational components.
2. Relationships to be maintained among major organizational components.
3. Restrictions or guidance for the establishment of position titles.
4. Associated functional descriptions of components, position guides, and organization charts which are to be maintained and distributed.
5. Maximum and minimum spans of management or, stated in a different way, the maximum number of levels of management permitted.

In addition, organizational policies may be developed for each major functional component or profit center of the company.

KEY QUESTIONS FOR EVALUATING THE COMPANY ORGANIZATION

In analyzing a company some important organizational problem areas may be identified by asking such questions as:

1. Is the company over-organized for its size? For example, if it is a small company are there five or six layers of management, rigid procedures, lack of channels for communicating horizontally, and large staff groups?
2. Is the structure appropriate for the major source, operational, and customer emphasis of the company? For example, is the focal point for company strength found in its utilization of natural resources or of specialized manpower? Is the company's competitive strength based upon certain phased operations, such as oil exploration, drilling, refining, storing, and distributing? Or is the basis for the existence of the company dependent upon matching company services and facilities to clearly defined customers or customer groups?
3. Are the organizational units combined or separated in a way which makes sense? For example, we would not expect sales forecasting to be located in manufacturing. Neither would we expect to find product control in the accounting department.
4. Has the company as few layers of management as possible to expedite communications and response by top management to serious operating problems? Does the structure *facilitate* rapid communication among people working on the same projects or in the same disciplines?
5. Is the vertical integration or the horizontal integration appropriate to the industry, the size of the company, and efficiency of marketing?
6. Is responsibility for product lines and businesses clearly placed on individuals? Joint responsibility and committees should be viewed with suspicion.
7. Is the responsibility for decision making clearly identified with a single individual for each class of decisions? Is each individual given clear responsibility for his work so that he may be held accountable for all work performed by himself and those people who report to him?
8. Is there an effective control *structure* if the company is a large conglomerate?

HOW TO EVALUATE THE BOARD OF DIRECTORS

"In the years that I've spent on various boards, I've never heard a single suggestion from a director (made by a director at a board meeting) that produced any result at all."

Robert C. Townsend, former President of Avis

◆ ◆ ◆

Arthur Goldberg stalked off the board of Trans World Airlines in October 1972. He stated that management wouldn't provide significant information for him to fulfill his "ultimate legal responsibility for the management of a corporate enterprise" as a director.

ARE THE DIRECTORS CARRYING OUT THEIR BASIC RESPONSIBILITIES?

The directors of a company, as a group and individually, may have considerable impact upon the policies, direction, and success or failure of a company. This impact may be caused by what the directors actually do or *because of what they fail to do*.

The board has certain legal functions and responsibilities outlined in the charter and bylaws of the particular firm. These include:

1. Approval of the long-range direction of the firm's products,
2. Determination of company objectives and philosophy,
3. Trusteeship—a fiduciary responsibility for conserving the corporate assets for the stockholders,
4. Selection of executives, including confirmation of certain high level executive candidates,
5. Review of pay scales, stock option plans, and other awards to executives,
6. Review of executive promotions,
7. Labor relations approach,
8. Insuring that there is a structure or information system which provides planning and control of product lines, functional systems (engineering, manufacturing, marketing, etc.), geographical areas, resources (human, capital, materials, etc.), profit and cost centers, and phases,
9. Participation in public affairs by the corporation, including contributions to education, etc.,
10. Distribution of earnings,
11. Exposing problems and malfeasance of officers,
12. Approval of public reports.

General Tire & Rubber Co.'s outside directors are pressuring management to do strategic planning and to develop a logical organizational structure.

Run by the three O'Neil brothers, Thomas, Jerry, and John, who have had an aversion to long-range planning, General Tire may be worth more broken up than remaining as a conglomerate.

The directors have worked on possible divestitures since 1976 but have been blocked by several legal problems. Meanwhile, the O'Neil brothers have been motivated by sibling rivalry in some management decisions, ensuring that one brother does not have more power than does another brother.

In the late 1970s, the outside directors required Jerry O,Neil to repay $257,400 of personal political contributions to the company.

The above list certainly does not draw attention to the three most important responsibilities of the modern board of directors. _The most important responsibility of the board of directors is to obtain the best management possible for the company._ While boards often go to considerable expense and spend much time on searching for a new president, they fail miserably with respect to auditing executive performance and firing chief executives who fail to measure up. We need only look at many companies listed on stock exchanges which have shown losses or nominal profits over the past five years and yet have not changed leadership. Exceptions make the news.

A second prime responsibility of the board of directors is to guard the company against illegal activities of the president and officers, particularly those which may seriously damage the company's financial strength or its reputation. This requires that directors do not accept management's reports as facts, but develop some means for independent and unexpected sampling of operations.

> Lamar Hill, former director and president of the First National Bank of Cartersville, Georgia, says stealing is easy. The bank says he embezzled $4,611,473.35 from it. Lamar was caught in February 1973 after 21 years of removing bank funds. "I could have hid it again but I got tired," he is quoted as saying.
>
> There are controls to keep things like that from happening, Mr. Hill said. The reason that many banks don't have such controls is that they have incompetent directors who don't understand banking.
>
> Source: Wall Street Journal, 26 January 1973.
>
> Robert Loeffler, trustee in bankruptcy of Equity Funding Corp. filed a civil suit on behalf of the company for $1 million against Stanley Goldblum, former chairman and president.
>
> The suit was filed in May 1973 after disclosure of a massive fraud. Mr. Goldblum's reports to directors were alleged to include fictitious sales of life insurance with a face amount of at least $1 billion.

A third important responsibility of directors is to act as an early warning system for management. Management is usually too absorbed in the specific running of the company to develop the breadth of knowledge to detect incipient and subtle changes in the environment. Directors with diversified backgrounds provide a means for scanning new trends in the environment.

SELECTION AND EVALUATION QUESTIONS

The evaluation of a company's future should include an evaluation of its directors as well as its management. Below is a checklist of questions to be explored for each director.

1. Is he or she an "inside" director or "outside" director? "Inside" directors, i.e., employees of the company such as vice-presidents, tend to rubberstamp. Since the president of the company is on the board and often Chairman of the Board, new ideas critical of manage-

ment are not usually welcomed by "inside" boards. On the other hand, the "outside" director doesn't usually have the time to verify information supplied by management because he or she is busy with his or her own concerns.

> Edgar H. Griffiths, chairman and chief executive of RCA Corp., resigned after several years of dissidence between himself and some RCA outside directors. Griffiths' inflexible and undiplomatic management style won him few friends on the board, and outside directors asserted that he did not confer with them enough and followed no one's recommendations but his own.
>
> On his part, Griffiths felt that his time was too valuable to spend it instructing board members how to run the business.

2. What is a person's reason for serving as director? There are many reasons for a person serving as director. He or she may have connections with other top business people and like to keep abreast of the business world. There is the ornamental director whose contribution is his name and whose reward is the status of directorship. Friends of the president may serve to help the president control board meetings.

   The investor, a representative of the company's investment banker, or a banker may serve to protect their interests. They tend to restrict the opportunities for the company.

   Lawyers, insurance executives, real estate executives, suppliers, and bankers may serve in order to throw business to their own firms.

   Women, foreign nationals, or minority members may be called upon as directors because of their expertise or because of public relations. They may elect to serve because they are dedicated or simply because of status.

3. Does the director have long experience as a chief operating executive? This may be a strong, favorable point. Professional directors with such backgrounds or with consulting experience have been very effective. Lawyers who conduct themselves as businesspeople first and lawyers second may work out well.

4. What is the person's age and length of service? A wide range of ages for the board is helpful. Generally young individuals are greatly concerned with their own business and can give only limited time as director.

   Length of service should be examined along with productivity. A director may just be coasting or may become very valuable because of a long association with the company.

5. Is the person a good listener, frank in voicing opinions, compatible with the other directors, and of comparable status?

6. Does the person have a unique contribution to make? A scientist, inventor, ex-admiral, economist, management consultant, medical

doctor, or professor of sociology may provide special technical estimates of the present and future environment for particular companies.

7. Is there a possible conflict of interest? The FTC is looking more closely at interlocking directorates. The ethics of businesspeople are receiving closer scrutiny by the public and legislative bodies.

8. Will the person be able to give time and interest and be motivated by the compensation paid him or her as director? If the director has multiple outside business interests, he or she is likely to be spread too thin to undertake the three basic responsibilities discussed above.

NEW LIABILITIES OF DIRECTORS

The lack of interest by stockholders and the greedy and elitist viewpoint of a few individuals have led to some spectacular abuses of position in recent years. A reaction in terms of new morality standards, government investigations, and court decisions has now placed the most dedicated director in a position of jeopardy. A body of law which has been described as "federal corporation law" has developed to counteract historical state trends of reducing protection for the stockholder.

Directors must now show "due diligence" in approving the registration of securities; they must make a reasonable inquiry of their own and not simply take the word of management. Directors who serve on several boards are subject to suits for conflict of interest. Mergers increase conflict-of-interest situations. In a number of cases, partners of investment firms have accepted finders' fees in cases where they served as directors of companies and have also been paid large commissions for underwriting stock issues of the companies.

Directors are not only liable collectively in the recent surge of stockholder suits based on "inside" activities, but they are liable individually for the entire amount. Their entire estates may be tied up for years. As a result of attacks from all sides, the most angelic candidate for a director's position would think twice before accepting. Corporations are indeed finding it more difficult to interest capable people despite greatly increased compensation.

HOW POLICIES DEFINE AND BOUND THE FIELD OF ACTION

Generally, a business policy is a verbal, written, or implied guide to decision making for repetitive situations which an organization faces in its attempt to attain its objectives. Objectives are both reflected by policies and interpreted by them. Therefore, most policies underlie the firm's planning. Major policies are broken down into derived policies at each lower level of the organization structure. Thus, a policy may be as broad as stating product areas to be served and as minor as requiring two signatures on expense vouchers. Policies supply general limits and boundaries within which a manager may use his discretion.

Policies serve to keep managers from going off half-cocked on some wild inspiration. At the same time, they reflect the values and biases of the company leadership. They often serve as an excuse for doing nothing. Some are very simple in nature as indicated by the note below.

Dear Professor Murdick:

In reference to your letter of May 10, we regret to advise that company policy will not permit material such as organization charts, etc. to be distributed outside the company.

Thank you for your interest in Milgo.

CHARACTERISTICS OF BUSINESS POLICIES

Policies may originate with the so-called purpose clause of the company charter and hence be very broad in scope. Such "originated" policies reflect the basic objectives of the company. Policies also are developed from decisions which are made in particular instances and withstand appeal at higher levels in the firm. These are called "appealed" policies. Finally, there are "imposed" policies which are produced by groups outside the firm. Trade associations, government regulations, or industry standards lead to the development of such policies.

Policies may be *formal, written* statements or *informal, implied* restrictions. A formal policy is a carefully worded statement which is usually published and distributed to all managers and staff personnel who have been issued a loose-leaf binder. Exhibit 3.17 shows a formal policy of E-Systems Inc., one of many for the company. Another example of a policy is shown in Exhibit 3.18.

In some companies, an unwritten policy may take precedence over a written policy with which it is in direct conflict. That is, the written policy is for public or legal consumption, while the unwritten policy represents the true feelings of the management.

Caterpillar Tractor Co. remains successful and competitive in a mature and cyclical industry by consistently following its broad policy of developing long-term relationships with its customers. Caterpillar implements this general policy by meeting customer needs through its high-quality proudcts and its preeminent service and parts system.

Caterpillar subscribes to long-range planning, spending today for future growth, and operates comfortably with its 10-year lead times for new product development. Potential managers begin on the production line and work their way up. This long-run orientation, reflecting company values, is seen in its managerial and operating functions.

EXHIBIT 3.17

E-SYSTEMS	Number: 154.1D
CORPORATE POLICY DIRECTIVE	Date of Issue: 22 May 79

SUBJECT: Inventions and Patents

PURPOSE

To assure ideas submitted by employees and nonemployees or obtained under government research projects are properly processed.

POLICY

The corporation is always receptive to new ideas and inventions to be used as a basis for new products and to otherwise support the business endeavors of the company. Thus, inventions available to the company which are consistent with corporate objectives and standards are developed by the company in this regard. Such inventions come primarily from company employees; however, some ideas and inventions of this nature are received from nonemployees. In either case, it is company policy to treat the individuals involved fairly, while simultaneously assuring adequate legal protection to the company.

Ideas and inventions submitted by nonemployees must be carefully processed to protect both E-Systems and the inventor against potential liability and/or loss of the invention. E-Systems personnel or organizational segments will decline to discuss oral or proposed invention submittals and should advise any nonemployee submitter to contact the E-Systems Corporate Patent Office. The Patent Office will then conduct negotiations with the inventor to obtain the disclosure, if desired, while providing the company with the maximum protection possible. Circumstances, however, may make it advantageous for a division to receive invention disclosures and to conduct negotiations directly with an inventor. In this instance, adequate safeguards by internal procedures and prior permission from the Corporate Patent Office must be established before receiving disclosures or conducting negotiations.

Each employee, temporary hire (i.e., job-shop, etc.) and certain consultants and representatives shall be subject to the E-Systems Employee Invention Agreement or similar agreements, whereby they agree to disclose their inventions. Each new employee shall read, sign and have witnessed the E-Systems Employee Invention Agreement while being processed by Industrial Relations as a new hire. The agreement shall also be signed by an appointed company agent.

EXHIBIT 3.17 (*Continued*)

E-SYSTEMS	Number: 154.1D
CORPORATE POLICY DIRECTIVE	Date of Issue: 22 May 79

Any invention disclosure by an employee, temporary employee, consultant or representative shall be processed in accordance with this procedure. Division management shall first review the invention to determine whether or not the invention is of interest to the division. If not, the disclosure and supporting documentation shall be forwarded to Corporate Patents for further processing with respect to interest of other sections of the company. If there is no interest in any section of the company with respect to the invention, the disclosure will be made a matter of record only. Any division interested in the invention may request assistance from Corporate Patents to determine whether patent coverage is available and in the best interest of the company.

The Corporate Patents Office will file all patent applications and perform all other patent related work requested or approved by any division of the company or by appropriate corporate personnel. Outside patent counsel will be used, as required, and fees for outside patent counsel will be monitored and approved by Corporate Patents and paid by the division for whom the work was accomplished.

All invention disclosures shall utilize the E-Systems Record of Invention form and will be routed through a Patent Liaison Representative of the respective division for forwarding and coordinating with the Corporate Patent Counsel. Corporate Patent Counsel shall acknowledge receipt of each invention disclosure.

Payment of $100 may be made to each inventor upon the filing of an original U.S. patent application and the completion of the assignment of same to the company. An additional payment of $250 (or $500 divided equally in the event there are two or more inventors) may be made when such an application issues as a U.S. patent. Neither payment will be made, however, if the inventor is no longer employed by the company at the time the payment would otherwise have been made.

Ideas and inventions conceived, developed, or reduced to practice in the performance of a government contract must be reported to the government by the operating division. This requirement also includes the reporting of such matters by vendors or subcontractors of E-Systems when appropriate. A copy of the required reports shall be sent to the Corporate Patent Counsel.

EXHIBIT 3.17 (*Continued*)

E-SYSTEMS	Number: `154.1D
CORPORATE POLICY DIRECTIVE	Date of Issue: 22 May 79

RESPONSIBILITY

The general manager of each division and subsidiary is responsible
for the processing and coordination of those inventions generated
or accepted by his division. The Corporate Patent Office shall
be responsible for coordinating inventions between facilities,
as required, and serve as the cognizant corporate function.

John W. Dixon
Chairman of the Board
President

→   ·Indicates revision

EXHIBIT 3.18

	Number: 511.1B
	Date of Issue: 1 Sep 81

SUBJECT: Advertising

PURPOSE

To provide an advertising and promotion program which reflects the appropriate image of the corporation and advances the objectives of all operating units with minimum expenditures and the greatest possible return on investment.

POLICY

The company's advertising program shall use the most effective advertising techniques and promotional programs in a manner that creates a strong, positive and consistent corporate image.

All materials designed to favorably impress the company's various publics, to promote sales and to recruit employees are considered a part of the corporate advertising program under the overall policy direction of Corporate Public Relations.

Each division and subsidiary shall submit budget requests for the following year plus current and estimated year-end expenditures for each item listed below to Corporate Public Relations by October 1 of the preceding year.   Requests shall include the following:

Item	Required Information
Product Advertising	Products to be promoted
	Recommended Publications
	Suggested Advertising Schedule
Recruiting Advertising	Recommended publications/media
Recruiting Brochures, Pamphlets, etc.	New material required and use
Product Literature	New literature required by product
Presentations	Proposed audio/visual presentations, motion pictures, etc.
Speciality Advertising	Items and quantity being considered

Upon receipt of the above information, Corporate Public Relations shall prepare and submit a corporate-wide plan to the Chief Executive Officer for review and approval. After final review, all divisions and subsidiaries will be notified of approved activities and appropriate budgets.

EXHIBIT 3.18 (*Continued*)

	Number: 511.1B
	Date of Issue: 1 Sep 81

GUIDELINES

Corporate Public Relations is responsible for the direction and centralized coordination of all product advertising, recruiting advertising and sales promotion material produced by individual divisions and subsidiaries and all corporate promotion activities. Proposed division and subsidiary advertising and literature shall .be submitted on a timely basis to Corporate Public Relations for review and approval by the Chief Executive Officer (as appropriate) in accordance with the following:

A.   Product and Recruitment Advertisements - Advertisements (with the exception of recruitment advertising for daily newspapers) shall be submitted in layout format, with copy for corporate approvals after clearance at appropriate levels in the operating unit.

B.   Capabilities Brochures - Defined as multiple-page, black and white or color brochures designed to promote the overall capabilities of an operating unit to customers and prospective customers. In general, these brochures are designed to continue in use for three years and an adequate supply should be ordered at first printing. Layout and final copy stage shall be submitted for review and final approval before printing.

C.   Product Brochures and Folders - Defined as multiple-page, black and white or color brochures designed to describe an individual product of an operating unit. Layout and final copy stage shall be submitted for review and final approval before printing.

D.   Product Sheets - Defined as single sheets, printed both sides, usually in one or two colors only, and designed to describe an individual product of an operating unit. These items do not require advance corporate approval, but, fifty (50) copies of each product sheet shall be provided to Corporate Public Relations.

E.   Recruiting Brochures, Pamphlets, etc. - Material used for recruiting shall be submitted in layout format with copy for corporate approval. This material includes brochures, booklets, pamphlets, audio-visual materials, billboards, posters and displays used for recruiting purposes.

F.   Presentations - Audio/visual or film materials intended to project the division and/or company image to our publics shall be reviewed

EXHIBIT 3.18 (*Continued*)

	Number: 511.1B
	Date of Issue: 1 Sep 81

with Corporate Public Relations prior to preparation.
The proposed presentation shall be submitted in outline
and copy form as stated in Corporate Policy 511.3,
Audio/Visual Presentations.

Preparation of material listed above must be in accordance with E-Systems
Graphics Styleguide.

RESPONSIBILITY

The general manager of each division and subsidiary is responsible for
issuing internal instructions necessary to ensure compliance with
this policy.

The cognizant corporate function is Corporate Public Relations.

John W. Dixon
Chairman of the Board
President

Revised Completely

EVALUATING COMPANIES WITH WRITTEN POLICIES

If a company does not put its policies in writing it may be attributed to ignorance or to strategy. Its strategy would be to prevent competitors from anticipating major lines of action. Thus, the company may act inconsistently and opportunistically. It pursues this strategy at the risk of confusing its own personnel.

Generally, the gains of establishing unified rules of action known to the entire organization outweigh such devious strategies. The advantages of putting policies in writing are:

1. Managers are required to think through the policy's meaning, content, and intended use.
2. The policy is explicit, and misunderstandings are reduced.
3. Equitable and consistent treatment of problems is most likely to be obtained.
4. Unalterable transmission of policies is insured.
5. Authorization of policy, helpful in many cases, is provided.
6. A convenient and authoritative reference of policies can be supplied to all concerned with their use.

The analyst should check to see if the written policies are mutually consistent and consistent with the actions and beliefs of management in each case.

DO POLICIES EXIST FOR ALL APPROPRIATE ACTIVITIES?

Policies may be established for two types of activities:

1. Those that concern the managerial functions
   a. Planning
   b. Organizing
   c. Staffing
   d. Directing
   e. Controlling
2. Those that concern the operating functions
   a. Sales
   b. Production
   c. Finance
   d. Public and personnel relations
   e. Production selection and development

DECISION MAKING AND EXECUTIVE ACTION

In business we are concerned with *decision-problems*. A decision-problem is a problem whose solution requires *action* based upon executive decision to pursue a particular course of action. This is in contrast to, say, a mathematical problem whose solution requires no action to be taken.

Since decisions are so closely interwoven with problems in the business arena, we will provide a brief introduction to the nature of problems. In the simplest sense, a problem exists when there is a state of ambiguity and two or more methods for resolving it are available. In other words, if something "bugs" you, you've got a problem. You still may have a problem, however, and not be aware of it because you have not searched for it. Such problems appear eventually as crises, or "flaps" or "fires" as they are called by executives who never seem to anticipate them.

The symptoms that a business problem exists and requires a solution are:

1. Performance is *presently* not meeting *currently established objectives.*
2. It is *anticipated* that at some future time performance will not continue to meet *present objectives.*
3. It is *anticipated* that *future objectives* will not be met by *present* policies and methods of operation.

Problems may lie along a continuum from well-structured problems to ill-structured problems. Well-structured problems are those that are closely defined with regard to objective, data required, method of solution, and desired variables in the solution. Ill-structured problems are those which are so complex that they are not even defined. The problem solver must structure the problem (usually a cluster of problems with a focal problem), construct alternative solutions in a combination of qualitative and quantitative terms, and analyze the alternatives to reach a decision.

To arrive at a major decision, many sub-decisions must be made. The manner in which a set of problems is to be structured represents such a decision. Once the problem and the related goals are defined, the constraints of the situation must be identified and decided upon. In general, a way of arriving at decisions for complex problems is to find answers to the following questions:

1. *What are all the apparent problems?*
   Don't jump to conclusions that there is one large ambiguous problem.
2. What *major problem* appears to underlie lesser problems? What are the *problem clusters?*
   Usually a central problem produces related problems. For example, sales representatives are resigning because their commissions do not support them. This is due to customers not renewing orders because deliveries are late. The late deliveries are caused by a poor production planning and control system. A poor personnel selection

and hiring system and incompetent present manufacturing management exist.

3. *What are the objectives of the organization?*

Decisions must be made which will best achieve organizational objectives. It is usually impossible to find a course of action which fully achieves every objective. Rather, tradeoffs must be made among objectives to obtain the best balance. High priority on a particular objective may dominate in some instances, such as a problem of financial liquidity.

4. *What are the data?*

Many students erroneously accept the given data as "facts." All data should be evaluated and cross-checked with other data or accepted only tentatively. Inferences from data may often be made and checked against information given in the case problem.

A structure should be established for organizing the search for data. The following decision factors may be used to provide such a structure:

a. The *situation* factor—What has happened, is happening, and probably will happen?

b. The *time* factor—The environmental factors change with time so that the calendar time of the problem and the environmental situation at that time must be considered.

c. The *people* factor—Who are the principals in the case? What are their values, views, influences, capabilities?

d. The *place* factor—What is the geographical location of the company? Where did the problems occur within the company?

e. The *causation* factor—How did the problem arise?

f. The *goal* factor—What are the goals of the organizational components, the company, and the executives?

g. The *constraint* factor—There are usually constraints on decisions due to limited resources of the company, company policies of long standing, governmental regulations, or even the personalities of the owners or top executives.

h. The *uniqueness* factor—Is the situation unique in that it will never occur again? Unique events are rare, and if the same class of problem may arise again, a generic solution should be sought. Generic solutions have more generality and are, therefore, often expressed as policies.

5. *What is the best solution?*

Analyze the pros and cons of each alternative, and then make a choice based on the evaluation of these. The evaluation and selection process is the heart of the decision process.

6. *How are the decisions expressed?*

The decisions should be clearly expressed as recommendations for

a. Objectives
b. Policies
c. Resolution of issues
d. Short- and long-range plans

e. Procedures
f. Schedules
g. Budgets

ENDNOTE

1. *American Stock Exchange Guide,* Vol. 2. Commerce Clearing House, Inc., Chicago, Ill. (Updated).

SELECTED BIBLIOGRAPHY ON
MANAGEMENT AND ORGANIZATIONAL STRUCTURE

Benton, Lewis (ed.). *Management for the Future.* New York: McGraw-Hill, 1978.

Dale, Ernest. *The Great Organizers.* New York: McGraw-Hill, 1960.

Drucker, Peter F. *Management: Tasks, Responsibilities, Practices.* New York: Harper & Row, 1974.

_____. New Templates for Today's Organizations. *Harvard Business Review,* January–February, 1974.

Galbraith, Jay R. *Organization Design.* Reading, Mass.: Addison-Wesley, 1977.

Goggin, William C. How the Multidimensional Structure Works at Dow Corning. *Harvard Business Review,* January–February, 1974.

Janger, Allen R. *Corporate Organization Structures: Service Companies.* New York: The Conference Board, 1977.

Kast, Fremont E., and Rosenzweig, James. *Organization and Management: A Systems Approach.* New York: McGraw-Hill, 1970.

Kilman, Ralph; Pondy, Louis R.; and Slevin, Dennis P. (eds.). *The Management of Organization Design: Strategies and Implementation.* New York: Elsevier North-Holland, 1976.

Mintzberg, Henry. *The Structuring of Organizations.* Englewood Cliffs, N.J.: Prentice-Hall, Inc., 1979.

Murdick, Robert G. *MIS: Concepts and Design.* Englewood Cliffs, N.J.: Prentice-Hall, 1980.

_____. MIS for MBO. *Journal of Systems Management,* March, 1977.

Perrow, Charles. The Short and Glorious History of Organizational Theory. *Organizational Dynamics,* Summer, 1973.

Sargent, Howard. *Fishbowl Management: A Participative Approach to Systematic Management.* New York: John Wiley & Sons, 1978.

SELECTED BIBLIOGRAPHY ON
CORPORATION DIRECTORS

Bacon, Jeremy. *Corporate Directorship Practices.* New York: The Conference Board, 1977.

Bacon, Jeremy, and Brown, James K. *The Board of Directors: Perspectives and Practices in Nine Countries.* New York: The Conference Board, 1977.

Burger, Chester. *The Chief Executive: Realities of Corporate Leadership.* Boston: CBI Publishing, 1978.

Furlong, James C. *Labor in the Boardroom: The Peaceful Revolution.* Princeton, N.J.: Dow Jones Books, 1977.

Mace, Myles L. *Directors: Myth and Reality.* Boston: Harvard Business School, 1971.

————. Should the Retiring CEO Stay on the Board? *Harvard Business Review,* May–June, 1978.

Mueller, Robert Kirk. *New Directions for Directors: Behind the Bylaws.* Lexington, Mass.: Lexington, Books, 1978.

Vance, Stanley C. *Corporate Leadership: Boards, Directors, and Strategy.* New York: McGraw-Hill, 1983.

4

STRATEGIC MANAGEMENT

WHAT IS STRATEGIC MANAGEMENT?

Strategic management provides the framework for the "business policy" field. Whereas previously, policy problem solving was learned by experience, the discipline of strategic management has developed systems, concepts, and tools that guide the general manager in setting the direction of his business. Strategic management is the systems approach that leads to a *unified sense of direction* and integrates all subsystems of the firm.

Strategic management is the responsibility of general managers. It is a process for conducting the entrepreneurial activities of organizational renewal, growth, and transformation in a dynamic and risky environment. Seven major tasks comprise the strategic management process:

1. Formulation of the philosophy of management, corporate purpose, and goals,
2. Environmental analysis and forecast,
3. Internal analysis of strengths and weaknesses,
4. Formulation of strategy,
5. Evaluation of strategy,
6. Implementation of strategy,
7. Strategic control.

The first task deals with the purpose and legitimacy of the corporation in society and long-term general aims. It describes what the corporation is *reaching* for rather than specific *objectives* to be *grasped* or attained.

Tasks 2 and 3 we have discussed at length previously because they provide the setting for management.

The formulation of strategy is the most complex task, except perhaps for implementation. It requires a clear definition of strategy. We define strategy as (1) a statement of strategic objectives of the organization, (2) courses of action to be taken in moving the organization from its present position to a position defined by its principal strategic objectives, and (3) policies and standards of conduct pursued for one long-range cycle of the organization. Strategy applies to four possible levels: corporate, portfolio, business, and functional. Exhibit 4.1 provides a simplified framework to guide the case analyst in solving case problems.

This part deals with the left branch of Exhibit 4.1, the development of strategy for integration of parts of the business and solutions to strategic problems. Chapters 6–12 provide background for the development of solutions to operating problems. The remainder of the text demonstrates the case-analysis method.

To continue with the major tasks of strategic management, we note that most analytical tools used to formulate strategy may be used to evaluate strategy. In addition, Seymour Tilles proposed six criteria that are useful to the case analyst:[1]

1. Internal consistency of objectives and policies,
2. Consistency with the environment,
3. Appropriateness in terms of available resources,
4. Acceptable risk,
5. Appropriate time horizon,
6. Adequacy of results achieved.

Implementation of strategy is carried out by means of preparation of strategic and operating plans, administrative action, and operating activities. A strategic control system may then be established to measure total business system performance against strategic plans and to take corrective action.

INDICATIONS THAT A COMPANY DOES NOT UNDERSTAND STRATEGIC MANAGEMENT

If we are analyzing and evaluating a company, we may quickly detect whether that company truly understands strategic planning, whether or not the company goes through the motions of planning. Look for such signs as:

1. Shifting back and forth on a tactical basis with no clear strategy. (Chrysler Corp. cannot seem to find a basis for full-line competition with Ford and GM. It misses trends completely. The shift to subcompacts occurred while Chrysler was spending $200 million to redesign its big cars.)
2. Much talk about long-range plans but no serious effort to develop formal procedures for developing strategy and plans.
3. The company maintains a stable of "losers," either product lines or subsidiary companies. (Dart Industries carried many low-profit Rexall Drug Stores for years. Genesco carried S. H. Kress stores

EXHIBIT 4.1

Framework for Case Analysis

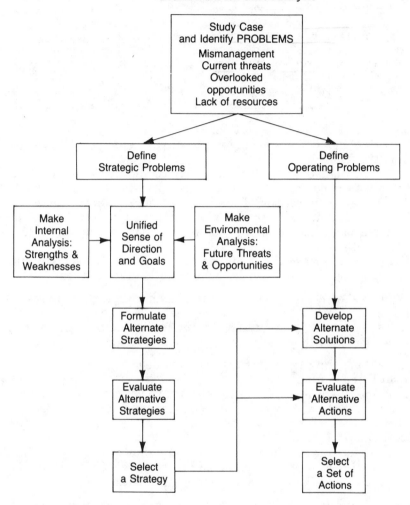

and others for years before finally writing them off in 1973 in one big $60 million financial "bath.")

- 4. Slowly deteriorating market position.
- 5. Suddenly deteriorating market position. (This is caused by failure to develop strategy by following changes in the outside world. Producers of electrical-mechanical rotary desk calculators who failed to move quickly to digital electronic calculators suffered. The Swiss watch industry suffered a shock by ignoring the development of electronic watches with no gear trains and other mechanical parts.)

In the 1970s, the switch to long-wearing radial tires, combined with the trend toward smaller cars and the elimination of the conventional spare tire caused severe overcapacity in the tire industry. While some firms were slow to react, B.F. Goodrich Company developed a strategy appropriate to the new conditions. Goodrich designated its tire business as a "cash cow" to be milked to provide funds for investment in other fields where growth prospects were brighter. Goodrich closed two plants and streamlined its dealer network. As a result, Goodrich was operating at full capacity, while the industry average was only 85% of capacity.

  6. Deteriorating capital position.
  7. Lack of agreement among top executives as to the basic direction of the firm.
  8. Acquisition sprees without a clearly established policy for selection of companies.
  9. Unbalanced allocation of resources among the functional organization so that, for example, manufacturing receives a big capital allocation when it is the marketing effort which needs to be strengthened.
10. Lack of a written five-year master plan with major milestones, time schedules, and cost for achieving these milestones.

When asked if his or her company conducts strategic planning, almost every president will answer yes. If we look at what companies are actually doing, we find that they perform some mish-mash of the following, which they designate as long-range planning:

Capital budgeting for two or three years ahead
Product line planning
Pro-forma financial schedules for one or two years ahead
Descriptions of great expansions and hopes in the annual report
Policies which are equated to plans
Budgets for the coming year
Informal plans which do not establish corporate strategic goals for at least three years, nor define specific programs of "who," "what," "when," and "how" to implement such programs.

In examining the success or lack of success of a company, we may almost always relate its position to planning or lack of planning. Careful analysis and correction of operating problems will not compensate for lack of strategic planning. Exhibit 4.2 shows the difference that formal planning makes in a company's success.

STRATEGY FORMULATION

In order to determine whether management, in a particular case, is guiding the company by means of strategic planning, we must have a

EXHIBIT 4.2

Performances of Formal and Informal Planners During Planning Period

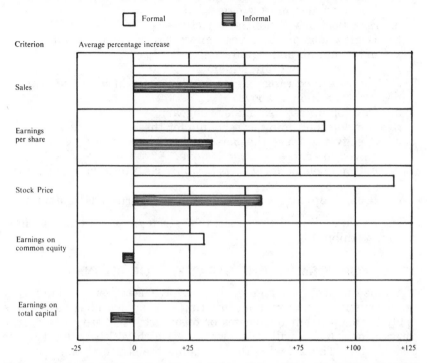

☐ Formal   ▥ Informal

Source: Stanley S. Thune and Robert J. House, "Where Long Range Planning Pays Off," *Business Horizons,* August 1970.

very specific understanding of the process and structure of strategic planning.

Strategic planning consists of two basic phases: (1) developing the strategy and (2) developing the plans. We will first describe the process in simple terms and then amplify. The steps in the *process* are:

1. Settle on the values, character, or personality of the company by open discussion among top executives.
2. Take a look *outside the company* to see what is going on, what the future will be like, and what opportunities exist for a firm of the general nature yours can be.
3. Take a look *inside the company* to determine what your resources and *capabilities for change* are.
4. Creatively match your internal capabilities to external opportunities to define the kind of company which you want to *be* in five or ten years. This definition of the "shape" of the company is in the form of a set of strategic components:
   a. Scope—products, markets, channels, price/quality categories

    b. Dynamics—timing for achievement of objectives

    c. Competitive edge—discussed previously

    d. Risk—probability of gain as related to probability and size of loss for major substrategies

    e. Specifications—financial objectives

    f. Deployment of resources—allocation of resources among human, capital, and liquid categories

    g. Acquisitions and divestments.

5. Develop the long-range strategic plan for achieving the strategy derived from item 4, above.

    a. Develop milestones (major subgoals).

    b. Develop the timing or schedule for these milestones.

    c. Specify the task, the personnel, and the other resources required to achieve each milestone.

    d. Estimate elements of costs for all tasks, milestones, and strategic goals.

    e. Prepare pro-forma statements, work descriptions, and budgets.

The above outline of the process for strategic planning is summarized in Exhibit 4.3.

TOOLS FOR FORMULATING STRATEGY FOR BUSINESS

A wide range of tools and techniques have been developed in recent years to assist managers in formulating strategy for a business. These apply to independent businesses or businesses that are part of large corporations. A few will be shown here which will be helpful to the case analyst. These deal with developing the strategic objectives (or components of strategy).

Product/Market Scope

Definition of the product/market scope essentially defines the business. D.F. Abell concluded that the business should be defined in terms of three components: customer functions, customer groups, and alternate technologies. Exhibit 4.4 illustrates this concept for Docutel. Such a diagram shows what markets Docutel competes in and what directions it may take for growth or contraction.

Some believe that the single most important variable for analyzing the product/market scope is the stage of the product life cycle (PLC). Guides for strategy for the various stages of the PLC are given in Exhibit 4.5.

Competitive Edge

We have discussed competitive edge throughout this book in terms of price, product service, product design, financial service, brand loyalty, credit terms, and delivery. Once again, a visual tool may be very helpful to management in evaluating a company's competitive edge. One such tool, developed by William K. Hall, is based on his research into strategies of successful and unsuccessful companies. He found

EXHIBIT 4.3

Development of Corporate Long-Range and Master Plans

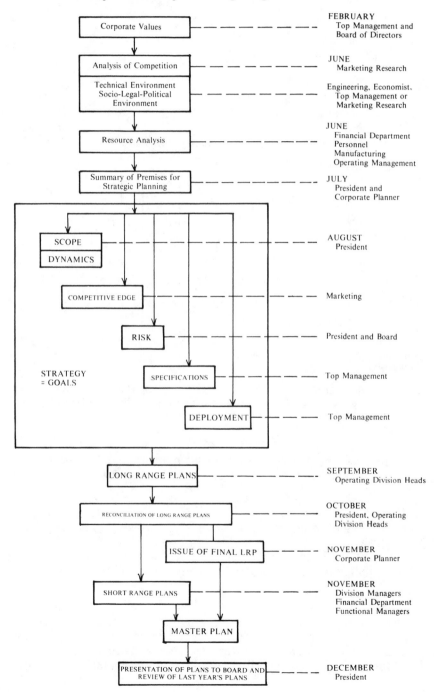

EXHIBIT 4.4

Docutel's Definition of the Financial Transactions Systems Business

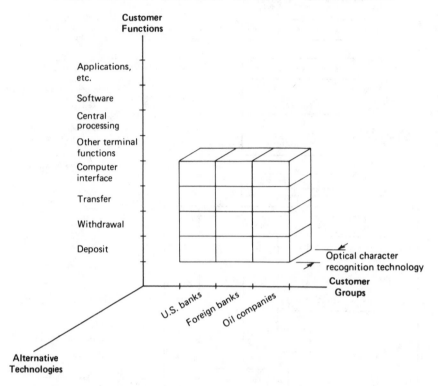

Source: Derek F. Abell, *Defining the Business,* Englewood Cliffs, N.J.: Prentice Hall, Inc., 1980, p. 80. Copyright © 1978 by the President and Fellows of Harvard College. Reproduced by permission of the Harvard Business School.

that successful companies pursued continuously and with determination one or both of the following competitive positions within their industries:

1. Lowest delivered cost position plus an acceptable quality/price policy to gain profitable volume and market share growth.
2. Highest product/service/quality differential position relative to competition, coupled with both an acceptable delivered cost and price policy to fund additional product/service differentiation.

Risk

Risk may be defined from the viewpoint of the outsider as the expected return on investment in the company less the risk-free rate of return from such investments as government securities. An index, beta, for an individual security is used to measure volatility of return.

EXHIBIT 4.5

Strategy Guides for Stages of the Product Life Cycle

Stage and Characteristics	Guides
1. *Introductory Stage* Virtual monopoly, low buyer awareness, high production and marketing costs, low profits, selective distribution	Exploit own strengths, select narrowest product/market slope, remedy defects early, quickly gain trial by early adopters to gain early high market share. If rate of change of product is rapid, focus R & D efforts on the product; if slow, focus on process.
2. *Growth Stage* Rapid increase in industry demand, entry of competitors, increased customer awareness and acceptance, repeat sales, increasing productive efficiency	For dominant firms, emphasize innovation and intense marketing; avoid persecution of and confrontation with smaller firms. Small firms should concentrate on their initial customers and consolidate their hold by means of special services. Seek to increase market share by establishing brand preference. Modify and improve products. Tailor prices to decreased production costs. Distribution channels should be intensively developed.
3. *Maturity Stage* Rate of sales growth declines. Shakeout of weak competitors. Fewer new customers and more reorders. Profit margins decline. Longest stage of the PLC.	In early part, continue to build preference; in later part, try to hold market share against aggressive competition. Shift from product design to product promotion. Tailor promotion to maintenance of market segments. Concentrate on distribution outlets and direct communication with the consumer to maintain brand loyalty. Don't increase market share through internal expansion.
4. *Decline Stage* Sales drop. The number of competing products declines. New (replacement) type of products appears. A small loyal group of customers may continue to buy the product.	Reduce R & D expenditures. Seek production efficiencies. Reduce product inventory but stock spare parts. Harvest by minimizing investment and costs. Divest when capital can generate a greater ROI elsewhere or until net present value of earnings is less than liquidation value.

For example, if the value of the security increases 1.5% when the stock market goes up 1%, beta is 1.5. The greater is beta, the greater is the risk.

EXHIBIT 4.6

Company	Beta
Campbell Soup	0.65
Eastern Air Lines	1.40
Ford Motor Co.	0.80
Gerber Scientific	1.70
Honda Motor Co.	0.60
E.F. Hutton	1.80
National Utilities	0.50
Olympia Brewing	0.65
Revlon, Inc.	1.00

Source: Value Line Investment Survey, August 27, 1982.

From management's perspective, risk may be defined in terms of the average size of investments in new capital projects, the probability of success, and the equity of the company. If a small company with equity of $3,000,000 were to make average investments of $2,000,000 with a probability of success of 0.70, it would represent a high-risk attitude on the part of management. That is, two consecutive failures would be disastrous. A large company, on the other hand, could play for the long run if the returns were high.

Eric von Bauer has proposed the chart in Exhibit 4.7 for looking at risk in strategy formulation. Suppose that a company, Vogue Creations, Inc., decides that it wishes to be an aggressive company, i.e., high risk and return. It has in the past considered as undesirable variations of cash flow from planned cash flow if they exceed 8%. Cost of capital for Vogue is currently 18%, and the risk-free rate for investments is 13.5%. From this data, we may sketch the chart in Exhibit 4.7.

Allocation of Resources

The allocation of resources is often considered to be reflected in only the capital budget. This is a very limited view. Earlier in Chapter 3, we discussed various ways that the firm could be broken down into various sets of subsystems of which capital resources was only one subsystem. Allocation of resources to each set of systems is required to define the business strategy.

TOOLS FOR FORMULATION OF STRATEGY FOR PORTFOLIOS OF BUSINESS OR STRATEGIC BUSINESS UNITS

Large companies are usually organized into product divisions that consist of "autonomous" businesses. Smaller, but still large companies

EXHIBIT 4.7

Positioning Vogue for ROI and Risk

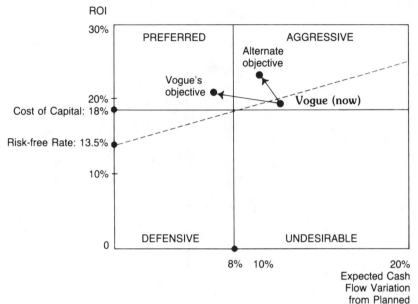

may be organized into simply a collection of businesses. In either case, the problem of managing the strategy of such sets, or *portfolios,* of business arises. In the early 1970s, General Electric found that strategic planning for the product/market matches of sets of businesses left some weaknesses. General Electric, therefore, combined some businesses or operations, regardless of level of organization, into Strategic Business Units (SBUs), solely for the purpose of strategic planning. The criteria for a component to be an SBU are:

1. It must have a unique business mission,
2. It must have a clearly identified set of competitors,
3. It must be a full-fledged competitor,
4. It must have the ability to accomplish strategic planning and implementation relatively independent of other SBUs,
5. The SBU strategic manager must be able to make decisions crucial to the success of the SBU, including, at a minimum, technology, manufacturing, marketing, and cash management.

The companies, or SBUs, in a portfolio are considered to be related to the PLC. In the early stages of a life cycle, companies are considered to be "cash users." In the maturity and decline stage, they are "cash generators." Therefore, it appears desirable to have companies at various stages of the life cycle to have a balanced portfolio.

A matrix developed by General Electric permits the top management of a corporation to see the positioning of SBUs within a portfolio so that appropriate strategic decisions may be made. Exhibit 4.8 shows a version of this matrix.

EXHIBIT 4.8

Positioning Matrix for Portfolio Strategy

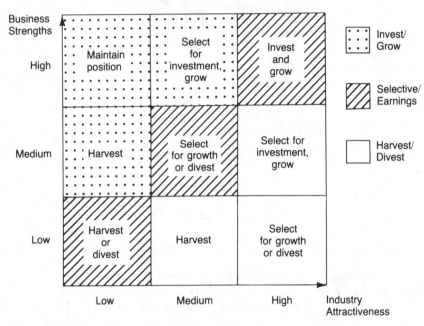

Criterion Factors

Business Strengths

Size
Growth
Share
Position
Profitability
Margins
Technology position
Strengths/Weaknesses
Image
Pollution
People

Industry Attractiveness

Size
Market growth, pricing
Market diversity
Competitive structure
Industry profitability
Technical role
Social
Environment
Legal
Human

SEGMENT SPECIALIZATION VS. MAJOR-FACTOR EXPERIENCE IN SETTING STRATEGY

The Boston Consulting Group has been proposing the concept of the Experience Curve as a planning tool for the past 10 years.[2] The essence of the idea is that unit costs decrease as accumulated volume increases (see Exhibit 4.9).

EXHIBIT 4.9

Representation of Experience Relationships

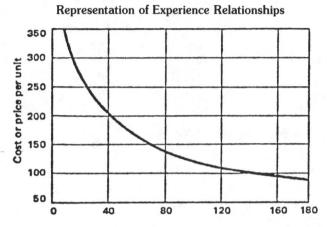

Therefore, if a company has a market share of, say, 60%, it will always be further down the curve in terms of price than its competitors. As a result, it will be able to price lower and maintain or increase its market share. The implication for the companies holding small shares of the market is to drop dead.

There are, however, two arguments in favor of hanging in there if you're a small market-share holder. First, an examination of the learning curve shows that the unit cost differential between the large and small market-share holders continually decreases.

Second, it is possible through efficient operations and selection of the strategy components to carve out a very profitable niche in the industry.[3] This form of strategy has been documented for several industries as illustrated in Exhibit 4.10.

MAJOR THRUSTS OF STRATEGY

We have pointed out that the six components of a strategy are scope, dynamics, competitive edge, risk, specifications, and deployment of resources. The actual thrust or direction of the company to which these components are related may be one of the following:

1. Forward vertical integration as when a manufacturer of clothing opens up retail outlets.
2. Backward vertical integration such as when a retailer, Sears, buys a manufacturing company which produces its clothes washers.
3. Horizontal integration which occurs when a retail chain buys another retail chain or a manufacturer of shoes buys out a competitor.
4. Product, service, or market extension.

EXHIBIT 4.10

Comparative Performance Through 1981

Company	1981 Sales ($ Millions)	5-Yr. Average Sales Growth (%)	Return on Equity 5-Yr. Average (%)
IBM	29,070.0[2]	12.7[2]	22.7[2]
Burroughs	3,540.4	12.5	10.0
Sperry	5,544.1	10.4	14.0
NCR	3,432.7	8.7	19.0
Honeywell	5,351.2	10.9	15.1
Control Data	3,101.3	14.3	9.8
Crown Cork & Seal	1,373.9[3]	13.0[4]	15.4[4]
Continental Group	5,194.4	9.2	13.9
National Can	1,534.0	12.7	12.9
American Can	4,836.4	10.9	10.9

[1]*Business Week,* March 15, 1982, p. 92.
[2]*Forbes,* January 4, 1982, p. 144.
[3]*Business Week,* p. 80.
[4]*Forbes,* p. 221.

5. Conglomerate formation—the purchase of unrelated businesses by a company.
6. Holding on with no attempt to expand.
7. Contracting to adjust to changing market or strong competition. A&P and J.M. Fields are examples of retail chain stores which have been obliged to follow this thrust.
8. Applying a tourniquet. When a firm has gotten in serious trouble, such as the Chrysler Corporation losing $1.7 billion in 1980, the strategy must be to change direction to stop the company from bleeding to death.

STRATEGIC PLANNING AND IMPLEMENTATION

PLANNING

Strategic planning is the beginning of implementation. Actual operations, corporate transactions, and control complete the implementation. The implementation of strategy and the strategic plan requires the participation and the acceptance of managers and key personnel; it cannot be imposed by the CEO upon the organization and be a success. A corporate planning director may coordinate the effort by issuing requests for all division managers to submit strategies and plans for their divisions.

The formulation of the plan usually involves putting down on paper what is to be done, when it is to be done, how it will be done, and who will do it. Formulation of complex plans is somewhat similar to literary writing. Several drafts may be required in a cut-and-try approach to achieve a satisfactory plan. A typical cycle might be as follows:

1. Prepare a list of goals which must be achieved to fulfill the strategy of the plan as stated. Alternative sets of goals or courses of action are likely to be listed.
2. By selecting from among alternative goals and courses of action, the planner may prepare one or several possible programs.
3. A schedule for achieving each goal is established and the total time required to achieve the objective can then be determined.
4. The plans are examined in terms of resources and manpower which are available and the plans are then modified accordingly. At this point, goals or lines of action may be revised.
5. Each entire plan is refined and detailed further.
6. The *scheduled* end date is reviewed in terms of a *desired* end date. There may be a tradeoff of time against money and manpower if the scheduled date is to be moved forward or back. This will involve modification of the details of plans.
7. The several plans will be reviewed and evaluated in terms of utilization of resources, probability of success, and potential costs and profits in particular.
8. Assignments of responsibility for various parts of the selected plan are made. The plan in tentative form is circulated for comment and review by the operating managers who will carry out the plan. These comments are then evaluated for incorporation in the plan before the plan is prepared in final form.

The planning cycle given above could equally be one followed by line executives or one in which a staff group at a high level within the organization prepares the plan. If a staff group proposes the plan, the staff people would obtain basic objectives from top management. They would then circulate among operating line managers and key technical personnel to determine what needs to be done to accomplish the objectives. The plans which the staff group prepares represent a synthesis of their own ideas, top management's ideas, and the line organization's thoughts.

It may be that the staff group which prepares the plans is the financial group. Often, financial analysts within an organization, knowing the objectives of the organization and the nature of the operating functions, essentially formulate the master plans. They request that operating managers propose projects or work to be accomplished during the next one to five years. From this raw material and discussions with line managers regarding costs, the financial analysts put together operating plans based upon budget plans.

A different type of planning cycle runs as follows. Top management says, in effect: "Here are some of the short-range and long-range objectives which we think are important. Prepare plans to show us how to accomplish these." Top management passes this information and request on to the next lower level of management where each manager cuts out the area he or she will be responsible for in terms of basic job function. Each manager then passes these *objectives* plus some restrictions or comments down the line. At the first line management level, each manager then elicits *plans* from the individual workers. These plans are reviewed by the first line manager, integrated and modified. He or she then passes the plans in written form up the line where the process is completed. At any point in this process, an individual may propose new projects or new approaches which would extend the list of basic objectives originally put forth. In short, general objectives are analyzed and transmitted *down* the line; individual detailed plans are started at the lowest organizational level and evaluated and synthesized at progressively higher levels of management.

Finally, the chief executive receives a set of plans from each of the top managers which represent comprehensive detailed plans. A meeting of top line executives, top staff executives, and the chief executive is then held to review the plans. The plans are subjected to severe criticism and analysis at the meeting. The end result is likely to be some recommendations for specific changes, or even further study and reformulation. Each manager coming to such a review meeting will normally have prepared a thorough defense of the recommendations.

The final formulation of a plan is likely to be fairly detailed, yet leave some opportunity for flexibility. Plans are designed with the idea that achievement of goals takes precedence over details of method of implementation. On the other hand, failures to adhere to the plan and then subsequent failure to achieve the goals as well is likely to be questioned. The formulation of large-scale plans may be expressed in a report varying from a few dozen pages to several volumes. The plans may be expressed in decimal or outline hierarchical systems so that every step may be traced back to the main objective. Another way of looking at this presentation is that every major goal is achieved by a major course of action. Every major course of action consists of a number of lesser actions. Every lesser action is in turn expanded into a number of more detailed actions.

King C. Gillette first opened his business in 1901 in a small walk-up factory in Boston. Two years later he placed his first safety razor on the market and sold 51 razors and 168 blades.

By 1905, blade sales passed the one million mark and razor sales reached 277,000. From a one-product company in 1901, Gillette, through careful planning, expanded its products in the men's shaving field and expanded its markets, both domestic and foreign, through 1946.

In the years following World War II, the carefully developed and implemented plans to strengthen its traditional men's toiletry product fields and enter the women's hair care and toiletry fields continued. The steady upward trend of profits, equity, sales, and dividends paid is a tribute to the thorough planning employed by The Gillette Company.

ACQUISITIONS, MERGERS, AND DIVESTMENTS
FOR IMPLEMENTATION OF STRATEGY

The development of the strategy for a company may lead to the alternatives of buying or merging with another firm or selling out. Reasons for buying a company may be:

1. To obtain skilled management, broader markets, new products, additional production capacity, raw materials or components, or other assets.
2. To satisfy a strategy of rapid growth or desire for greater power.
3. To get a good buy from a tax viewpoint.
4. To put idle cash to work at a better return.
5. To acquire a company that has huge unrecognized sales and profit growth which the buyer can exploit with expertise, raw materials, or access to capital.

Reasons for selling, after careful analysis, may be:

1. Problems of lack of competent top management, lack of management depth, lack of management succession in a family-owned firm.
2. A gradually disintegrating market and inadequate resources to shift to new markets or new products. For example, a brass pipe and fittings producer may see profit margins eroded by price-competition and plastic substitutes reducing the market for brass hardware.
3. Your company fills the need of another company because of complementary lines, production capacity, or marketing skills. You are offered a price which seems very attractive.
4. Your company has no valuable assets but a big loss for tax carryover benefits to a profitable company.

Some Pitfalls in Acquiring a Company

Obviously, the search for, selection of, and evaluation of a prospective acquisition is very complex. A company may be acquired by an offer of cash, stock, notes, exchange of stock, or some combination of these. There are many pitfalls which arise because the bride or groom does not look closely enough at the new spouse to see what is being taken on. Just a very few pitfalls are suggested below:

1. A food distributor, Groom, Inc., buys a rack merchandising company at 125% of book value. After the purchase, the distributor finds that most of the inventory consists of stale potato chips in store racks.
2. A technical company, Bride, Inc., purchases another technical company, Groom, Inc., on the basis of two large government contracts. After the acquisition, Bride finds that Groom had bid below cost and faced extensive losses on these R & D contracts.

3. Groom Company purchased Bride Land Development Co. in order to develop its mineral rights. Several years after the purchase, Groom discovered that the title to the land was not a clear one and lawsuits were lodged by a third party.
4. Bride, Inc., bought the Groom Manufacturing Company without a thorough appraisal of Groom's equipment. It discovered that the average age of machines in an outlying plant was 10 years and they were practically worthless.
5. Groom Company purchased Bride Company because of its lucrative large foreign construction contracts. Too late Groom learned that Bride was behind schedule on these contracts and heavy penalties for each week late were written into the contracts.
6. Bride Co. purchased Groom Co. only to discover that most accounts receivable were really bad debts.

Thus, pitfalls in purchases occur because the buyer did not investigate thoroughly such items as inventory, contingent liabilities, impending fraud charges, tax audits, or especially today, falsified computer data. Do not be rushed into a purchase.

→ Some pitfalls may be avoided by buying only part of the balance sheet. For example, if we were to buy a motel, we might purchase only the physical assets. We let the seller worry about accounts payable and accounts receivable, short-term and long-term debt, etc. Similarly, if we were to purchase a store, we do not purchase the inventory but we let the seller dispose of it before closing.

Making Ball-Park Estimates of Valuation

It never hurts to apply common sense to obtain upper and lower bounds for the value of a company which you are considering purchasing. Profile analysis, detailed financial analysis, and management science models are all valuable, but if these valuations lie outside simple rule-of-thumb estimates, pause before leaping. Here are some crude ways of estimating the value of a company.

1. Book value × 125%. Book value should be tempered by judgment as to worth of assets.
2. Average earnings over the past three years capitalized at 10% to 20%. For example, suppose average earnings have been $1.2 million. To capitalize at 10% means that a sum of X dollars invested at 10% will yield $1.2 million annually. X = $1.2 million ÷ .10 = $12 million as the value of the company.
3. Five-year payback. The buyer forecasts earnings for each of the next five years for the potential acquisition and adds these together to estimate a purchase price.
4. Present value of estimated earnings over the next 10 years. The well-known formula is:

$$\text{Present Value} = \frac{E_1}{(1 + r)} + \frac{E_2}{(1 + r)^2} + \ldots \frac{E_{10}}{(1 + r)^{10}}$$

Where E is earnings for a particular year and r is the cost of capital or desired rate of return.

5. Market value of the stock × 2.
6. Price/earnings ratio multiplied by average earnings over the past three years.
7. Upper limit = 8 × earnings *before* interest and depreciation; lower limit = 3 × earnings *before* interest and depreciation.

The above methods of valuation are for the simple case of purchase of a company with cash. Stock exchanges plus other considerations are quite involved. In addition, "pooling of interest" type of mergers are differentiated from purchases. There are many very important tax ramifications in acquisitions or mergers so that management needs highly specialized accounting assistance before a final decision is made.

Exhibit 4.11 shows how one company, E-Systems, has issued guidelines for acquisition in the form of a corporate policy statement.

GOING PUBLIC

The entrepreneur who has built his or her business into a fairly large company may face at some time one of several possible situations.

1. He or she would like to sell out and retire.
2. He or she would like to provide for his or her spouse and neither the spouse nor other members of the family are capable of managing the company.
3. The company is expanding rapidly, but lack of capital is a severe restriction on further expansion.
4. The company has been very successful over the years, but the owner can no longer keep up with changing times, and earnings are declining.

The student of business policy who observes one of these situations in a case, glibly proposes that the owner "sell out." Sell out to whom? That is the question which must be answered. Occasionally the owner may find a private buyer, but the larger the company, the more likely it will have to sell out to a listed company (listed on one of the stock exchanges regulated by the S.E.C.) or have to "go public." Going public means issuance of a fairly large number of shares of stock which must be sold in a public offering. Unfortunately, just as banks make loans only when you don't need them, people are willing to buy a company only when the owner doesn't need to sell.

The owner of a private company must therefore prepare long-range plans which will eventually include sale of the company at some future specified date. The owner must probably, although not necessarily, resign himself or herself to loss of control over the "baby." Going public and being listed on a stock exchange also means that the owner must divulge many financial facts which were previously kept secret.

Finally, and importantly, going public is not free, and may be very

EXHIBIT 4.11

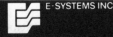 E-SYSTEMS INC.

CORPORATE POLICY DIRECTIVE

Number:	101.1
Date of Issue:	1 Jan 73

SUBJECT: Corporate Acquisition

PURPOSE

To provide the standards and responsibilities for the reasonable, safe and continued growth of our company through acquisition activity.

POLICY

The company will devote the necessary resources and management time to acquire companies or product lines that will be compatible with our overall growth objectives.

Diversification into commercial or industrial markets is a necessity to preclude preponderant dependence upon military and other government customers. This does not imply a lack of interest in continuing to expand sales to the U. S. Government. The acquisition of Memcor and Melpar has produced sound government business. Both of these divisions have contributed to corporate profits and have high promise for the future. While we are committed to expanding our commercial business, we also will be equally interested in acquiring companies or product lines for sales to the U. S. Government. E-Systems, however, must start now to substantially increase our business in commercial markets. This expansion can be achieved by acquisitions serving the industrial and/or consumer markets.

To diversify into commercial business, we will need new products, new product development capabilities, commercial marketing capabilities, and separate facilities. All of these can be satisfied by acquiring the right company.

Desirable attributes for acquisition are those companies whose -

Products or services are now selling to the commercial markets.

Name is recognizable nationally.

Gross sales between 30 and 60 million dollars a year.

Most product lines are profitable.

Growth capability possible.

Technology can relate to E-Systems Inc., if only in a broad sense.

EXHIBIT 4.11 (*Continued*)

E-SYSTEMS INC.	Number:	101.1
CORPORATE POLICY DIRECTIVE	Date of Issue:	1 Jan 73

Improvement in profitability and future growth can be enhanced by being related to E-Systems Inc.

Conversely, companies may have undesirable characteristics which by their very nature become so costly to correct, or present such a high risk in terms of cost to correct that they do not therefore fit within our first screening. E-Systems would not want to acquire a company with -

Outdated product lines or services.

New product lines only, as yet untested in the marketplace.

A history of continual labor difficulties.

Repeated profit losses due to competitive pricing problems.

A poor reputation in reliability and services.

There are some allowable deficiencies in candidate corporations for acquisition that E-Systems must be prepared to make improvement or changes in the candidate company where needed. These could be in one or more of the following categories:

Changes in management.

Improvement in products.

Changes and/or increased marketing efforts.

Modification of plant facilities by capital expenditure.

Changes in accounting and/or budget practices.

Expansion of product lines and plant facilities.

Retraction of product lines and/or markets served.

The foregoing changes or improvements must be in consonance with the ultimate profit and growth potential of the candidate company.

EXHIBIT 4.11 (*Continued*)

	Number: 101.1
E·SYSTEMS INC. **CORPORATE POLICY DIRECTIVE**	**Date of Issue:** 1 Jan 73

Where E-Systems may require outside services in the investigating phase or where the expertise does not exist within the company, finders fees or consultant services will be paid.

Under no circumstances will fee or consultant arrangements be made on a verbal basis, but only under a formal agreement and by the direction of the corporate President or Executive Vice President. Further, no one within E-Systems Inc., is authorized to make direct contact with the principals of another company for acquisition purposes except under the explicit direction of the President or the Executive Vice President. This policy exists because of legal ramifications, the artificial ballooning of the price of the acquisition, and improper stock manipulations, which must be avoided at all costs.

In the payment for acquisitions, E-Systems Inc., is in an excellent position to acquire capital and may propose to acquire another corporation with cash or stock exchange or combinations of both. This will depend upon the current selling price of our stock, debt structure of our company and the candidate company, and our own cash requirements.

Final acquisition action will not be consummated without a series of careful screenings of the candidate corporation's records, products, facilities, markets, contracts, obligations, inventories, total assets, legal liabilities, customer contact for reputation, reliability of products, and overall position in the marketplace with reference to competition.

When acquisition has been agreed to by both parties, a plan of integration shall be developed. The integration plan shall cover legal requirements, management functions, organization, accounting and controls, marketing operations, purchasing, economics in production, budgeting control of expenses, capital outlays, etc. The integration plan shall be implemented by a task force of key personnel headed by the Executive Vice President.

<u>RESPONSIBILITY</u>

The corporate Executive Vice President shall have overall responsibility for development of the acquisition program. Other company personnel shall assist as required.

J. W. Dixon
J. W. Dixon
President

3 of 3

costly. Selling to friends, as a way of going public, simply does not pan out, as a rule. The larger the company, the greater the need for utilizing an underwriter. Commonly, the underwriters buy the stock from the owner at a negotiated discount and then sell to the public.

CONTROLLING THE TOTAL COMPANY

It is not enough to observe that a company plans well; the plans may never be implemented. It is not enough to observe that a company operates efficiently and at low cost; it may not be adhering to its strategic plans. The analysis of any company requires an investigation of management control over the total company.

In order to obtain proper control, the long-range plans must be written so that Key Performance Areas (KPAs) are identified. Then a monitoring system must be in force which calls to the attention of management deviations of performance from plans and KPA objectives. KPA goals are specific goals in such areas as:

1. A set of indicators of financial condition,
2. Market position,
3. Organization and human resource development,
4. Productivity—aggregate, by division and by broad classes of employees, by balance of capital and labor costs,
5. Technological leadership (engineering and/or manufacturing),
6. Customer relations,
7. Government relations,
8. Social responsibility,
9. Balance between short-range and long-range goals.

Such KPA goals must be selected and tailored to the particular company. A sample of a few such goals for an electric utility company is shown in Exhibit 4.12.

EXHIBIT 4.12

Total Control System for an Electric Utility

This report form indicates the proposed areas for reporting and their key indicators as well as the types of reports to be made. Reports with an asterisk (*) are kept on large five-year graphs.

Key Performance Areas and Indicators	Jan.	Feb.	Mar.	Apr.	May	June	July	Aug.	Sept.	Oct.	Nov.	Dec.
1. Power Supply												
Key Indicators												
*a. Cost per KWH purchased.	X	X	X	X	X	X	X	X	X	X	X	X
b. Cost per KWH delivered.	X				X		X			X		
*c. Hrs. outage per customer per year.	X	X	X	X	X	X	X	X	X	X	X	X
d. Average voltage/standard voltage.			X			X			X			X
e. Percent voltage regulation at supply												
point or points.			X				X		X			X
*f. Ratio power cost to revenue.	X	X	X	X	X	X	X	X	X	X	X	X
2. Financial Condition												
Key Indicators												
*a. Percent operating expense to total revenue.	X	X	X	X	X	X	X	X	X	X	X	X
*b. Percent margin of revenue dollar.	X	X	X	X	X	X	X	X	X	X	X	X
*c. Percent return on plant investment.	X	X	X	X	X	X	X	X	X	X	X	X

EXHIBIT 4.12 (*Continued*)

Key Performance Areas & Indicators	Jan.	Feb.	Mar.	Apr.	May	June	July	Aug.	Sept.	Oct.	Nov.	Dec.
*c. Percent return on plant investment.	X	X	X	X	X	X	X	X	X	X	X	X
d. Reserve funds to requirements.						X						X
e. Percent of depreciation expenses to gross plant.					X						X	
*f. Percent cash available to requirements (1½ times accounts payable).	X	X	X	X	X	X	X	X	X	X	X	X
g. Ratio plant to annual revenue.				X						X		
3. Market Position **Key Indicators**												
*a. Percent revenue spent on power use.	X	X	X	X	X	X	X	X	X	X	X	X
*b. Percent KWH used to saturation (saturation being that amount for all energy requirements, except heat, for which electric power can be used).	X	X	X	X	X	X	X	X	X	X	X	X
c. Percent saturation electric ranges.		X				X			X			X
d. Percent saturation water heaters.	X		X			X			X			X
e. Percent increase in power use cost to percent increase in revenue.		X			X			X			X	
f. Percent customers attending power use meetings each year.	X			X			X			X		

Key Performance Areas & Indicators	Jan.	Feb.	Mar.	Apr.	May	June	July	Aug.	Sept.	Oct.	Nov.	Dec.
4. Service Leadership **Key Indicators**												
a. Average voltage/standard voltage.		X						X				
b. Percent regulation of voltage at customer's premises.		X						X				
*c. Outage time per customer per month.	X	X	X	X	X	X	X	X	X	X	X	X
d. Average time after new customer ready for service until he gets service (1) temporary, (2) permanent.					X				X			
*e. KWH used per res. consumer per month.												
f. Substation capacity to peak load (by substations).	X	X	X	X	X	X	X	X	X	X	X	X
g. Ratio distribution transformer capacity to peak load.					X						X	
					X						X	
5. Productivity **Key Indicators**												
a. Average rate of return on reserve funds invested.			X							X		
*b. Operating man-hours per M-KWH sold.	X	X	X	X	X	X	X	X	X	X	X	X
c. Distribution line operating cost per customer.		X			X			X			X	
d. Billing and collecting cost per customer.		X			X			X			X	
e. Maintenance cost per customer.		X			X			X			X	

EXHIBIT 4.12 (*continued*)

Key Performance Areas & Indicators	Jan.	Feb.	Mar.	Apr.	May	June	July	Aug.	Sept.	Oct.	Nov.	Dec.
f. Administration cost per customer.		X			X			X			X	
g. Power use per customer.		X			X			X			X	
h. Percent line loss.			X			X			X			X
*i. Labor cost per plant unit to standard.	X	X	X	X	X	X	X	X	X	X	X	X
j. Percent peak load to capacity on lightest loaded 3-phase feeder.				X						X		
k. Percent peak load to capacity on heaviest loaded 3-phase feeder.				X						X		
l. Operating cost per KWH sold.		X			X			X			X	
m. Cost per truck mile (1 ton or less).		X			X			X			X	
n. Cost per truck mile (above 1 ton).		X			X			X			X	
o. Average time delay after pole is condemned until replaced.	X						X					
6. Customer Relations												
Key Indicators												
a. Percent of customers attending annual corporation meetings.									X			
b. Percent of complaints justified to those received: (1) amount of bill, (2) voltage, (3) outage time, (4) radio and TV interference, (5) employee actions, (6)other.	X			X			X			X		
c. Percent customers reading newsletter.			X					X				
d. Percent return on customer understanding & appreciation surveys (analysis).											X	
e. Rate of response of customers to corporation support.			X					X				
f. Percent of hours of power use employees spent on customer relations (including preparation of newsletter).		X						X				

Key Performance Areas & Indicators	Jan.	Feb.	Mar.	Apr.	May	June	July	Aug.	Sept.	Oct.	Nov.	Dec.
7. Employee Development												
Key Indicators												
*a. Percent of total available man-hours lost due to accidents.	X	X	X	X	X	X	X	X	X	X	X	X
b. Hours safety instruction to each outside employee per month.				X				X				
c. Annual percent decrease or increase workmen's compensation cost.					X						X	
d. No. days institute, workshop, or conference training per employee per year.					X						X	
e. Percent employees appraised as having satisfactory performance.									X			
f. Percent of promotable employees advanced in grade per year.									X			
g. Percent of employees advanced from one grade to next each year.									X			
8. Public & Government Relations												
Key Indicators												
a. No. of man-hours spent in public relations activities to total man-hours (manager, assistant manager, department heads, power use people).			X					X				
b. Percent of public response favorable.			X					X				
c. Percent of appliance dealers cooperating fully with corporation.			X					X				

Source: Reprinted by permission of the publisher from *A Total Systems Approach to Management Control,* by Paul M. Stokes, © 1968, by the American Management Association, Inc.

ENDNOTES

1. Tilles, Seymour. How to Evaluate Corporate Strategy. *Harvard Business Review*, July–August, 1963.
2. *Perspectives on Experience* (Boston: Boston Consulting Group, 1968, 1970, 1972), and "Experience Curves as a Planning Tool," reprinted from *IEEE Spectrum*, June, 1970.
3. R. G. Hamermesh; M. J. Anderson, Jr.; and J. E. Harris. Strategies for Low Market Share Businesses. *Harvard Business Review*, May–June, 1978.

SELECTED BIBLIOGRAPHY ON STRATEGIC MANAGEMENT

Bing, Gordon. *Corporate Acquisitions*. Houston: Gulf Publishing Co., 1980.

Cozzolino, John M. A New Method for Risk Analysis. *Sloan Management Review*, Winter, 1979.

Hall, William K. SBU's: Hot, New Topic in the Management of Diversification. *Business Horizons*, February, 1978.

———. Survival Strategies in a Hostile Environment. *Harvard Business Review*, September–October, 1980.

Hapselagh, Philippe. Portfolio Planning: Uses and Limits. *Harvard Business Review*, January–February, 1982.

Herzog, John P. Operational Audit. *Journal of Systems Management*, October, 1977.

Hofer, Charles W., and Schendel, Dan. *Strategy Formulation: Analytic Concepts*. St. Paul: West Publishing, 1978.

Lindberg, Roy A., and Cohn, Theodore. *Operations Auditing*. New York: AMACOM, 1972.

Mooso, Sandra O., and Zakon, Alan J. Frontier Curve Analysis: As a Resource Allocation Guide. *Journal of Business Policy*, Spring, 1972.

Mueller, Robert Kirk. *New Direction for Directors: Behind the Bylaws*. Lexington, Mass.: Lexington Books, 1978.

O'Connor, Rochelle. *Planning Under Uncertainty: Multiple Scenarios and Contingency Planning*. New York: The Conference Board, 1978.

———. *Corporate Guides to Long-Range Planning*. New York: The Conference Board, 1976.

Ohmae, Kenichi. *The Mind of the Strategist*. New York: McGraw-Hill, 1982.

Schendel, Dan E., and Hofer, Charles W. (eds.). *Strategic Management*. Boston: Little Brown and Co., 1979.

Schoeffler, Sidney. Cross-Sectional Study of Strategy, Structure and Performance: Aspects of the PIMS Program. In: *Strategy plus Structure equals Performance*, edited by Hans B. Thorelli, Bloomington, Ind.: Indiana University Press, 1977.

von Bauer, Eric E. Meaningful Risk and Return Criteria for Strategic Management Decisions. *Mergers and Acquisitions*, Winter, 1981.

Wind, Yoram, and Mahajan, Vijay. Designing Product and Business Portfolios. *Harvard Business Review*, January–February, 1981.

5

THE STRUGGLE FOR SURVIVAL AND PROSPERITY

Who today remembers, or has even heard of, these once great firms of yesteryear?

Baldwin Locomotive
U.S. Cordage Co.
Pacific Mail
American Cotton Oil Co.
Central Leather
Auburn Motors
American & Foreign Power
Hudson Motors

In Chapter 1 we pointed out that of the 100 *largest* businesses in the United States in 1900, only two of them were left as independent enterprises in 1968. An even more astounding situation exists for *small* businesses. Of the 4.3 million firms (mainly small) in operation in a particular year, only one-third were in operation under the same management four years later! A death toll of 67 percent in four years![1] It appears from Exhibit 5.1 that the first five years of a firm are extremely critical. Exhibit 5.1 shows that about 55 percent have failed in the first five years in a recent period of seven years. From six to ten years in business the chances for survival are better—only 25 percent fail within this range. Failure rates decrease even further for businesses that have been in operation for more than 10 years: a 19 percent failure rate.

What causes this shockingly high turnover rate in business? Why do one firm's profits and sales zoom up like a skyrocket while others fizzle and fall to the ground dead? Numerous studies and many writ-

EXHIBIT 5.1

Age of Business Failures, 1974–1980

Year	% In Business 5 Years or Less	% In Business 6 to 10 Years	% In Business Over 10 Years
1974	59.9	20.8	19.3
1975	57.4	22.7	19.9
1976	54.8	26.0	19.2
1977	53.1	27.5	19.4
1978	53.2	27.4	19.4
1979	54.5	27.0	18.5
1980	53.6	28.1	18.3

Sources: *The Business Failure Record* 1980, New York: Dun & Bradstreet, 1980, p. 11.

ers have examined this mortality enigma, including the Office of Business Economics of the U.S. Department of Commerce which collects and publishes statistics on business turnover.[2]

After analyzing the reasons for the failure of a large number of small businesses, we found that rarely can the cause be pinpointed with accuracy to only one factor. To the contrary, generally several major management errors can be found. It is interesting and instructive to note that the same problems (to be described in this chapter) occur so frequently and are of such major causal significance that they become pitfalls to be forewarned about.

The student of business policy and the practicing manager both will benefit by studying the basic causes of business failures. For the student, such knowledge provides a base point for analysis of cases. For the new businessperson, this chapter will serve as a checklist of pitfalls. For the seasoned, highly successful business executive who is thinking of acquiring a new business, this review may stimulate reconsideration of the problems involved.

Questions to be answered in the highly competitive business inevitably include the following:

— Why is our ROI stagnant, declining, or growing at a slower rate than our competitors'?
— Why is our share of the market slipping?
— What causes our excessive management turnover?
— Why do we always seem to be short of capital?
— Why do environmental changes such as resource shortages, antitrust campaigns, consumerism, sudden changes in our customers' desires, pollution, and geopolitical events keep catching us by surprise and producing crises in our business?

Let us examine typical failings in firms from small to large.

PROBLEMS IN SMALL FIRMS

We could say that almost all problems in small firms stem from lack of managerial competence. It is also true that many problems are inherent in small businesses because of their characteristics. We will identify firms as "small" when:

— 1. Management is independent because the managers are the owners.
— 2. There are three or fewer top managers so that several functional areas must be managed by a single manager. That is, there is not a complete roster of separate managers to cover marketing, engineering, production, finance and accounting, personnel, etc.
—3. The area of operations is localized.
— 4. The market area is localized unless direct mail type of sales is used.

Small businesses are usually started by risk takers (entrepreneurs) without formal training in professional management. Such companies often start with insufficient funds and lack access to further capital. Once an owner has invested his or her life savings, however, the basic problem is how to avoid pitfalls and survive.

Both in doing consulting work for small business and in analyzing a case problem, we have found it helpful to answer a series of penetrating questions in basic areas in which companies fail.

How Big Is Small?

A small business firm is defined as one having assets not greater than $9,000,000; a net worth not greater than $4,000,000; and an average net income after taxes for the preceding two years of not more than $400,000.

Source: Small Business Administration

LACK OF A COMPETITIVE EDGE

For success, meaning anything but marginal survival, every business needs some reason for being, something that the firm does that is desirable from its customer's viewpoint that sets it apart from, and gives it an edge over its competition. The things the firm can do better than competitors can be the providing of unique services or products and not necessarily lower prices. Price cutting admittedly is a powerful, but an overworked, competitive edge.

Because so many small businesses are started with little or no attention paid to competitive-edge strategy—the means for survival—we put this first on our list. To work well over a period of years, the competitive edge must be *realistic*. We suggest the following questions be asked:

1. *Is the Competitive Edge Based on Facts?*

Hunches, generalities, and "thinks" are not good enough. Does the entrepreneur know *specifically* what customers are looking for? What is an important enough competitive edge to wean the customer away from a present source of supply? Has market research proven this beyond the shadow of a doubt? Students and businesspeople alike seem to equate the words *market research* with high cost. This simply is not true—market research can often be done at little or no cost, except the time and effort involved in a "do-it-yourself" project, including finding out what is already available.

2. *Is the Competitive Edge Based on Accurate Cost Data?*

If the competitive edge costs the firm so much that product prices will soar sky high, then the edge disappears. Often it is a matter of judgment. The question that must be answered is "Can the cost of the competitive edge be included in the selling price without driving customers away?" To answer the question the businessperson must first find out exactly what the extra cost will be and how much must be added to the sales price. This requires an accurate pro-forma statement reflecting complete costing. (Look up *pro-forma* if you do not understand the meaning. See Definitions and Calculations, chapter 7.) For example, if added quality is to be the "edge," exactly how much will it cost? Will the quality added entail more frequent inspections for quality control (added labor costs), more expensive materials, greater supervisory costs, slower production, or what?

3. *Is the Competitive Edge Compatible with the Firm's Capabilities and Constraints?*

A small firm with *limited* financial means and management capabilities must wisely choose its competitive edge within the constraints of the available resources. This truism is all too often forgotten by statements such as, "We will cross the bridge (more capital) when we come to it," or "If we don't have the technological capability we can learn, can't we?" or, "If Jones Brothers can do it so can we." (The old college spirit is fine until it comes time to pay the bills.)

Other ways of phrasing this question might be, "Can we afford the competitive edge?" "Do we know enough to give us the competitive edge?" "Do we have the staff to accomplish it?" "Is it really feasible for us?"

4. *Is the Competitive Edge Based on Conditions That Are Likely to Change Rapidly?*

Because a small firm cannot afford many mistakes without going under, a competitive edge based on conditions that will change rapidly can be a sure course to disaster. Small apparel firms dependent upon the whim of fashion, for example, usually have very short lives. Some changes in the political, economic, social, or technological conditions are to be expected and anticipated. Small firms should stay out of rapidly changing industries where the change will severely reduce the competitive edge. Suppose the competitive

edge is a new improved "hula hoop"—with a short life expectancy—
or a unique part for one type of airplane, the risk odds for longevity
will be reduced to say the least. Examples of competitive edges are
plentiful.

Firm A, wholesaler of boat supplies, based its success on complete stocks
and immediate delivery. Despite six other wholesalers in the immediate
vicinity, Firm A, by maintaining meticulous sales and inventory
records, lived up to its promise and prospered despite a slower inventory
turn and hence a lower ROI. (See Definitions and Calculations in chapter 7 of this book.)

◆ ◆ ◆

Firm B, a dry cleaning establishment with eighteen competitors in its
small town location, decided that its competitive edge would be "exqui-
sitely fine service" meaning such extras as spotting before cleaning or
washing, tailoring service (shortening hems, cuffs for trousers), bache-
lor service on laundry, inspection before delivery, etc. Within five years
they had the outstanding business in the community and seven competitors had closed their doors.

◆ ◆ ◆

Firm C, an independent supermarket owned by three brothers in a Chicago suburb, was enlarged four times in nine years. It then opened two
additional stores despite intense chain competition. Its competitive edge
was the extra traffic generated by having the outstanding meat and
delicatessen departments in the entire Chicago area. The departments
were run by all three brothers, one of which was always "on the floor"
personally helping customers to select the right cut and type of cheese to
satisfy the family tastes. Because it was discovered that patrons had a
tendency to shop at more or less the same time, although perhaps on
different days, each brother was on the floor the identical four hours per
day every day. This helped each to get to know personally a large number of customers and to cater to their needs.

◆ ◆ ◆

Firm D, a producer of specialty stainless steel machined parts that were
sold to other manufacturers, concentrated on small volume parts that
its competitors did not want to bother with. Despite numerous requests
to bid on large volume runs, the firm steadfastly refused for fear its
competitive edge would vanish. Instead, in order to grow, Firm D enlarged the numbers of parts it made and even expanded into small as-
semblies but always with an eye to avoiding the areas where they would
run headlong into much larger competitive firms.

RELYING ON "THINKS" INSTEAD OF FACTS

We have already referred to small business managers' penchant for
following hunches, guesses, and intuition which we group together
and refer to as "thinks." This is such an important and oft-repeated

error that we feel it deserves special mention. We would be remiss if we did not also say that "thinks" instead of facts are the basis for many decisions of all humans. Managers of large businesses as well as small (and even students) have been known to rely on "thinks." Although intuition and imagination are tools for all of us, to run a small business based completely or mainly upon "thinks" is a common error often causing small businesses to fail.

Despite the large amount of data (facts) published by trade associations, U.S. Government agencies, and the many good trade magazines and papers, it is a rarity to find a small-business manager who makes full use of these *low cost* readily available resources. To give some idea of the breadth of subjects covered would be to list every imaginable subject from site location for a new business to financial ratios and optimum expense costs to be used during the life of the firm.

Just for fun, we have asked owners of small businesses why they don't use the facts so abundantly available. Usually the answers are extremely weak ones such as, "I didn't know they were available," or "I can't afford them" (meaning, "I didn't bother to look at them"), or "I have to run my business; I don't have time."

A different kind of "thinks" substituted for facts is hearsay evidence. Perhaps the reader has not heard of the parlor game where those playing sit around in a large circle. A detailed set of facts is whispered to the first player who then whispers it to the next, who passes it on to the next and so on around the room. At the end, the last person tells aloud what he or she heard. Any resemblance to the original set of facts is purely accidental. In business the same thing happens. R passes it to S who tells it to T's spouse who tells it to U at a dinner party who tells V in the strictest confidence. It is then on the flimsiest of evidence that V relies on the information and makes a business decision.

To prevent such poor decision-making "thinks" from being used, we suggest firmly ingraining a habit of asking oneself the following questions regarding every set of facts that might be used as the basis for making a decision:

1. How can I check to find out if the so-called facts are really true? (Often a small amount of research will negate or substantiate the facts.)
2. Is there any contradictory evidence?
3. What other interpretation of the "thinks" would fit the situation but result in a different decision?
4. What additional solid facts are needed to make a good decision, and how can I get them?

CRISES RESULTING FROM FAULTY OR NO PLANNING

Faulty or *no planning* is evident time after time to consultants to small firms. It is of such crucial and extreme importance we might well have put it first on our list of the errors small business firms most often make. We did not do this for two reasons: first, because it is so broad in implication that it cuts across practically every other small business pitfall. For example, choosing a competitive edge is part of planning. Making decisions on facts instead of "thinks" is a vital part of *good planning*. Second, telling someone to use good planning in running their business is like telling a twelve-year-old to use good management in running his grass cutting business. Both are meaningless—there is *no* communication.

If the reader would mentally substitute the well-known Boy Scout motto "Be Prepared" when thinking about planning, perhaps it would make the meaning clearer. Timid souls and the most experienced guide alike would never think of going on a safari in deepest Africa without long, thoughtful preparation. Yet, look at the number of individuals who recently bought fast food franchises (to their ultimate dismay) with only the barest of thought regarding the future. Optimism, an American characteristic, coupled with a penchant for gambling—a chance to strike it rich—blinds many small business entrepreneurs to the necessity of planning. Even the dyed-in-the-wool horse bettor spends hours poring over the racing forms to increase his odds, but the usual small businessperson rushes in with blind hope.

Robert B. Buchele says, "Planned action is efficient action. . . . Planning can discover flaws in a proposed new product or a proposed new system of distribution or a proposed new production process more economically than can trial and error methods. Plans based on solid facts about the market will win nine times out of ten over hunches, guesses and prejudices."[3]

Consider the thousands of individuals opening new retail shops every month who are doomed to failure even before they open their doors for business because *they don't plan*. What kind of planning should prospective retailers do *before* they open? At the very least they should:

a. Decide upon the type of merchandise or service to be offered based upon *research*. (Including a market survey to determine profit potential, sales that can reasonably be expected, pitfalls to be avoided, helpful suggestions, etc.)
b. Determine the "competitive edge" of the store.
c. Analyze the physical requirements based upon space-productivity ratios (usually readily available from the S.B.A. or trade sources) and normal rent range (costs) as a percentage of estimated sales.
d. Evaluate the store location—including community and area and specific site evaluation, all in terms of a, b, and c above.
e. Assess the competition—what is their competitive edge? How does it compare?
f. Segment the market target group.
g. Decide upon *all* of the merchandising policies (price, markup, fashion, customer services, hours, promotion, resources, merchandise classifications, etc.).
h. Plan the financial management of the store—capital requirements, budgets, systems and controls, projected P & L statement, etc.).

Similar lists need to be drawn up for planning a manufacturing business or a service business, and once the business is operating, *planning* lists must be prepared for the venture's continued success. Here are the ABCs of planning.

The first step is to OUTLINE EVERY FACTOR YOU ARE GOING TO PLAN. Be certain in drawing up your list to include emphasis on your competitive edge, the reasons why the selected target customers are going to prefer buying from you, and the benefits you offer that are different from and better than those of your competition. You need to constantly sharpen and deepen your competitive edge, relentlessly striving to improve every facet of your operation, product, service, and research.

A small business might make a list of the factors it wishes to plan, such as the following:

a. The competitive edge,
b. Marketing research (how much to spend, sources of data, growth rate, market targets, market segmentation, new markets, channel information, etc.),
c. Product information (new and present),
d. Marketing plans (salesmen, promotion, investment),
e. Action timetable,
f. Numbers plan (based on facts from *a* through *e* and including projected sales by product and market, profits return on investment, etc.),
g. Controls, so that necessary evaluation and changes can be made based on *facts* accumulated.

The second step is to DETERMINE POSSIBLE SOURCES OF INFORMATION.

The amount of information available to the small business planner is so enormous as to be incredible and much of it at little or no cost. The Small Business Administration has field offices in major cities and has personnel that are most anxious to help find the desired information (which they have in abundance).[4] If they do not have exactly what is needed, they are helpful in directing you to other sources, particularly within the U.S. Department of Commerce. Trade publications, both magazines and newspapers, can often be extremely helpful. For example, *Women's Wear Daily,* a Fairchild publication headquartered in New York City, through its research department has mimeographed research material for each of the various types of women's apparel. Other excellent sources are the many trade associations which collect data, research departments of daily newspapers, university, business, and public libraries, *Sales Management's* "Annual Survey of Buying Power" (the "Bible" of marketing personnel), U.S. Bureau of the Census publications, etc.[5, 6]

Many small business managers do not even *attempt* to plan their major moves nor ferret out sources of information. There simply is no excuse for such an omission. It is exactly like the traveller who wanted to buy a halfway airplane ticket from New York to London—it is a sure ticket to disaster.

3   Finding sources of information is relatively easy but the third step in planning, GATHERING THE FACTS AND ORGANIZING THEM, seems to present difficulties. The lazy person keeps delaying the writing of letters asking for information, simple as that chore seems to be. It takes time and effort to stir oneself sufficiently to read, digest, and ORGANIZE the facts under the appropriate individual subjects so as to have an *informed* opinion on which to base decisions.

4   The fourth step is to WRITE OUT POSSIBLE ALTERNATIVE COURSES OF ACTION with the pros and cons of each, using the facts previously assembled. We suggest writing them down with the pros and cons under each alternative because this method seems to produce better decisions, probably because it forces a more disciplined, easily reviewed, method to weigh the facts and think.

5   Fifth, MAKE THE DECISIONS AND PUT THEM INTO ACTION. It is surprising to see the number of managers who are good at planning until they are called upon to make the decision. Wishy-washy, indecisive planners, afraid to act for fear of being wrong, are both poor planners and poor executives. No one can be *right* 100% of the time. However, those who continually postpone decisions can be certain of being wrong a large percentage of the time.

6   Sixth, EVALUATE AND UPDATE YOUR PLANS. The reader should note that all action plans to be really helpful must have *controls* with a *timetable* so that management, when faced with a need to change plans, can *evaluate* its previous work. The firm will also be able to extend its planning further into the future based upon the facts already learned and the mistakes planners inevitably make. It is only with controls and timetables that accomplishments and errors can be discerned and future planning can be improved.

Suppose, for example, that such a simple thing as accounts receivable planning has been done. The amount of $40,000 will be collected according to plan. It is of extreme importance to know *when* they will be collected and from whom (so that a proper bad debt allowance is set up). Similarly, a sales timetable must be forecast for *each product* so as to guide production schedules, predict cash flow, etc.

One additional thought needs mentioning before leaving this important subject of planning. Plans should be made for both the immediate future (monthly, quarterly, and for a year's duration) and for the longer-range future (three to five years). While it is true that a five-year plan will undoubtedly be changed once or many times, the advantages of long-range planning are many. It focuses attention on the possible alternative courses of action. It also concentrates thinking on pitfalls to be avoided and sets up a *disciplined structure* for problem solving.

LACK OF COMPETENT PROFESSIONAL ADVICE

A law school graduate who went into business and never practiced law, when asked what he had learned from law school said, "I learned two things: first, never to be my own lawyer, and second, to go to an attorney *before* I sign a contract, not after I've signed and gotten into trouble." This is similar to the old saying—he who is his own attorney has a fool for a client.

Many small businesspeople do not seem to realize that professionals can be hired for nominal amounts to set up their books (accountants) so that meaningful decisions can be based on good costs; to add protective clauses to contracts that will prevent surprising and often unpleasant legal actions from occurring (attorneys); to help save substantial amounts of money by buying the right insurance in the right amount (insurance advisors); and to perform or supply reliable market studies that may change the entire course of the business (market researchers).

The largest hurdle to overcome is finding and selecting truly competent professional consultants. Unfortunately, just as there are incompetent doctors, there are mediocre and poor attorneys, C.P.A.s, and other consulting specialists. They can lead to irreparable damage to your business. Our recommendation is that you talk to at least several other businesspeople who have previously used the services of the consultant. Question the consultant as to background and past technical performance just as you would when hiring a new manager. Question references closely *before* you engage them.

A highly successful businessman made these suggestions regarding hiring of professionals:

1. The best is not necessarily either the most expensive or the cheapest. Don't be timid about discussing fees.
2. Ask plenty of questions. Many professionals are specialists. Ask what their specialty is and how much they know about small business problems, tax accounting, real estate, partnership law, or whatever your problem is. Beware of the expert who is too glib or the one who constantly needs to refer to the books. Check references (previous clients) thoroughly.
3. You aren't married to the consultant. If the consultant evidences poor judgment several times—GET ANOTHER. Obviously consultants may make minor mistakes and still be valuable because basically a company seeks the skills and judgments of the consultants. Consultants who make errors in judgment can cost a company more than it can afford. When we hire a consultant, it's a business relationship and should not be an emotional relationship.
4. Above all, don't try to be your own professional—the more you know the better, but only so that you can ask good questions. If you know too much you are probably neglecting your own business which is where you make your living.
5. Lastly, look for men that are future oriented, the ones who can help prepare you for things that haven't happened yet but probably will or even just might happen.

Carl Day, a Harvard MBA, did extremely well working for a Pittsburgh firm, but wanted to return to the midwest. A former classmate and good friend, Justin Knight, told him about a steel fabricating firm, Price Brothers, Corp., in the northwest part of Chicago. Carl jumped at the chance to buy the tools, dies, spray painting booths, steel inventory, building, and good will of Price Brothers Corp. for $565,000.

After assuming the mortgage on the building, making a cash payment and giving a note to Milton Price's widow for the balance, Carl was left with $50,000 for working capital. Carl retained an attorney and a CPA recommended by his friend Knight.

Carl soon found that due to insufficient working capital he would either need to shrink his sales or sell the building. Within 60 days he found a potential buyer for the building, Schwinn Bicycle Corp. Schwinn had a nearby plant and needed the extra space as well as the railroad siding that ran behind the plant. On the day of the closing of the deal for the building, Schwinn's lawyer pointed out a clause in the deed that said the easement for the railroad siding had to be used once a week by Price Brothers or the owner of the right-of-way could revoke the easement. The Price Brothers had not used the siding at all because trucks had been favored. As a result, Schwinn refused to go through with the sale at the original price. Carl immediately replaced his attorney with a new one.

Carl's new attorney advised Carl to trade his building for a new one-story smaller building owned by Schwinn so that he would not have to pay taxes on the entire capital gain. Carl then replaced his CPA who had failed to guide him in his attempted sale.

Because Carl's original attorney had failed to point out the clause regarding the easement and had not advised means for securing the easement, Carl netted $85,000 less on the sale/trade with Schwinn.

OVEREMPHASIS ON SPEED

> "He was a young man named Bright
> Whose speed was far faster than light:
> He began business one day
> In a relative way
> And failed the previous night."

This pitfall of overemphasis on speed has three parts as discussed below.

OVEREMPHASIS ON GROWTH

The limerick just quoted pretty well tells it all. Mr. A devotes all his time and energy devising ways and means "to beat last year's figures." He wants to increase his sales and do an ever-increasing business. Even managers of middle-sized and large businesses are often affected by the concentration on the sales volume syndrome and seem to forget that profits are of more importance than sheer volume. They alibi their malady or "figure themselves rich with a pencil" by pointing out that increased sales will reduce costs and increase profits "a year from now" or at some later date. Unfortunately, the increased costs related to the sales push, or the lost-now profits are overlooked.

As we say in the accounting section of this manual, trends have a tendency to persist. Those businesses concentrating solely on sales not only show poor profits now but have a strong tendency to show small or no profits in the future.

The small businessperson solely concerned with sales stretches the resources, human and money, to the breaking point. Cash discounts are lost, bills go unpaid, the credit rating deteriorates. At this point, any small unforeseen slowdown in sales puts the business into bankruptcy. The cure is simple—sales do need pushing but only as fast and as hard as the resources will stand. Patience (not complacency) is the virtue to be cultivated with a reorientation in thinking—greater emphasis on the quality and profitability of the organization and less on *speed* of growth.

LACK OF CAPITAL

Starting a business without enough capital is given as the reason for failure of many small businesses. While lack of capital may be the *coup de grace* causing bankruptcy, the real culprit is "haste." The desire to go into business becomes so overwhelming to the would-be entrepreneur that he or she simply can't wait long enough to beg, borrow, or accumulate the capital that even the most superficial examination of the problem dictates as necessary.

Sometimes it is the desire to own 100% of the business that prevents the admission of a partner, active or inactive, with the necessary additional funds. Other small business owners refuse to admit, even to themselves, their naivete when it comes to handling figures. A major problem is their inability to forecast financial needs for the year. As a rough *rule of thumb,* the capital necessary to start a business will be equal to the amount of capital needed to maintain the business through one inventory turnover period without collecting a single dollar on sales.

Ms. A wants to start a small retail business. She estimates three turns a year on her inventory (once every four months). A rough guide to beginning capital needs might be:

6 months' rent (4 months' plus 2 months' beginning rent deposit) at $500	$3,000
Furniture and Fixtures	6,000
Inventory (beginning) at cost	9,000
Purchases (4 months) at cost	9,000
Owner's salary (4 months)	4,000
Utilities (4 months)	600
Miscellaneous expense (4 months)	1,200
Accounts receivable (none—all cash)	
	$32,800

If Ms. A has only $15,000, she would be well advised to wait to open her store. If she has $33,000 or more and everything else is favorable, then she is in a good position to begin.

A similar procedure for a small manufacturing business can be used to estimate capital needs. It should be remembered, however, that in a manufacturing business, sales of an unknown product may be slow before payment of invoices will be received from customers. All during this waiting period, the payroll must be met, raw material purchases must be paid for, machinery and tool bills paid, etc. Capital required can best be estimated by cash planning as outlined below.

Later on, after a business grows, nearly every such firm faces a second type of lack of capital—the need for *expansion capital*. Corporations at the present time pay an income tax of 15 percent on the first $25,000 of income and up to 46 percent on all earnings over $100,000. This means that it is all but impossible for small corporations, or for that matter, even the largest ones, to finance rapid growth solely from retained earnings. Similarly, sole proprietorships and partnerships also find it impossible to grow at more than a snail's pace from capital generated by the business unless they are in one of the few highly risk-prone but particularly tax-favored industries such as oil drilling or are certain types of real estate firms. In sole proprietorships and partnerships, the individuals must pay a personal income tax on all earnings of their firms regardless of whether or not the actual money is retained in the business.

Mr. Robert Lewis (a man 46 years of age) owns a three-year-old plastic manufacturing firm (a fictitious name but an actual firm). The business pays Mr. Lewis a $25,000 salary, has sales of $500,000 per year and earns $25,000 before taxes on an original investment of $100,000 to which $16,000 has been added from retained earnings. When Mr. Lewis bought the business he had to borrow $25,000 from his bank. This loan is being paid off by monthly installments of $672.44 ($8,069.28 per year). With two children in college, the loan to pay, his personal income tax ($1,504.00) plus the normal living expenses of his family, he had a difficult time on the salary he drew to make ends meet. As he said, "I didn't realize how lucky I was when I was working at Acme Manufacturing Company with a steady salary and no business loans to pay off." On the $25,000 the business earned last year, out of which he paid a corporate income tax of $3,750, he found that the $21,250 in retained earnings minus $3,500 in negative surplus that he needed to make up the net loss of his first two years in business left only $17,750 to add to his capital. This was insufficient to finance the modest expansion he had in mind. He estimated his net capital needs as follows:

Machinery	$19,000
Added Inventory (cost)	22,000
Accounts Receivable Increase	25,000
Leasehold Improvements	7,000
Miscellaneous	5,000
Total	$78,000

Not having the needed capital with which he felt certain he could greatly increase his sales and earnings, what are his alternatives? They are:

1. Plod along with what he had knowing that a 4% to 6% increase in sales was all his already stretched capital would finance.
2. Sell *common stock* which with only one year of fairly respectable earnings would mean selling the stock at bargain prices.
3. If he could arrange it, borrow $78,000 with some sort of *long-term debt*. He rented his factory building leaving only machinery which could be used as collateral. It might be possible to arrange a loan from the Small Business Administration, particularly if he could get his bank to make part of the loan using his machinery for collateral.
4. Use *short-term debt* including factoring of his accounts receivable.

After considering all of the alternatives, Mr. Lewis decided to restrain his impatience and not attempt the expansion. His reasoning was that with two more good years, earnings and his personal loan nearly paid off, he would then be in a position to borrow more personally and to sell common stock at a fair price based on three years of solid profits (one or two years of earnings are rarely enough to establish an earnings base to establish a reasonable price and still remain attractive to common stock investors—particularly after his loss during the first year and only a small profit the second year). By increasing his personal loan back to the original $25,000, he would have $19,000 in cash, his net profits for two years would amount to $21,000 above current needs. He could then sell common stock amounting to a 2% interest in the firm for possibly as much as $70,000 which give him ample funds for a major expansion.

The problems of Mr. Lewis just described point out the very real problems faced by many small business owners who have successfully passed through the perilous first few years, have a moderately profitable company, and see a real opportunity for future growth if they only had capital to expand. The alternatives open to them are few and the pitfalls many.

Banks normally lend money to small firms only on a short-term basis. Long-term loans generally require collateral, meaning solid, valuable assets such as land, buildings, or easily sold machinery, which the typical small business does not have. The sale of bonds in small amounts is next to impossible, and of course, a bond is a type of long-term debt guaranteed by pledging of assets of value just enumerated (land, buildings, etc.). If the small business owns its own building, the chances are that a mortgage already exists which rules out that avenue of approach. About the only alternatives for expansion capital are those that were open to Mr. Lewis:

1. Retained earnings patiently accumulated over a period of years. For many business owners, particularly those of a somewhat conservative nature, this is the path that allows them to sleep at night and avoid heart attacks or ulcers or both.
2. For the more venturesome and then *only after* the most careful analysis indicates long risk odds for *profitable* continuance of the

business, factoring of accounts receivable should be considered. Some of the better finance firms doing factoring (Heller International, Talcott National Corp., Commercial Credit, and C.I.T. Financial) actually lend funds with a side bonus—expert financial advice which can be extremely helpful.

3. Loans from the Small Business Administration, depending upon its funding and availability of money. The S.B.A. has had a number of policy changes. We merely mention this as a possibility for investigation by the small business owner.

4. Sale of common stock which can be accomplished through friends, direct to the public, through firms who make a business of lending capital to small and medium-sized companies and through S.B.I.C.s (Small Business Investment Companies) which are privately or publicly owned firms in business specifically to make loans up to quite a few million dollars to firms with good prospects who need capital.

5. In rare instances, some insurance companies have made debenture loans to small businesses. Generally these carry an extremely high rate of interest. In the case of the firm, a loan of $400,000 was made for 12 years at a low 7 percent interest rate but along with it was an agreement by which the insurance company could convert the debenture into enough shares of common stock at a pre-agreed upon low price to give the insurance company ownership of 35 percent of the company. The agreement in connection with this loan was 67 pages long! This will give the reader some idea of the many restrictions placed upon the company during the twelve-year period of the loan.

The point of this entire discussion is, as Mae West phrased it years ago, "I like a man who takes his time." Lack of capital planning, neglect of anticipating capital requirements, too much haste, and too little patience often lead to the downfall of the small businessowner.

LACK OF CASH PLANNING

Whether or not a businessperson is short of initial capital or wants to pace growth rate over a period of years, every business needs CASH PLANNING. (If there are any readers with unlimited funds, they can skip this section.) As we said in our comments in the section on "Lack of Competent Professional Advice" the first and cheapest investment for a new business, particularly if the owner is *not figure-minded*, is to hire a competent accountant to set up the books including a method of forecasting cash requirements. This was the case for a small manufacturer of fishing equipment. For $300, an accountant set up the books, and for a year-end fee he prepares the tax returns after reviewing the books. While it is too early to predict this manufacturer's future success, we strongly urged him to make this modest investment. The "cash needs forecast" for the first year has already resulted in a decision to conserve capital by renting space instead of buying a building and this despite the relative affluence of the owner.

Capital can be conserved in many ways and often "Cash Planning" presents facts upon which the following questions can be answered and proper decisions made. Shall we hire extra salespersonnel? Shall we spend more on advertising? Questions of this type are translated by cash planning to mean, "If we hire more salespeople or do more advertising, will we have the capital that is required by the resultant added sales (more people to manufacture the product, increased raw material, work in process, finished goods inventory, higher accounts payable)?" The question of shall we buy or rent more machinery becomes translated into, "Can we afford the extra payroll, added inventory, and accounts payable?" In other words, cash planning avoids too much concentration on growth without consideration of money constraints which have often caused dire consequences for the small businessowner (also for many large businesses, e.g., Ling-Temco-Vought). To conserve cash-one method is to slow down excessive growth. Putting it in a positive fashion, a firm should only grow as rapidly as its capital allows.

A second method of conserving cash, the need for which having been foretold by cash planning, is to avoid investments in fixed assets that can often be leased at favorable rates. It is possible to lease such diverse fixed assets as delivery trucks, store fixtures, heavy machinery, buildings, and tools.

Cash analysis and planning will also direct attention to other means of conserving cash which are luxuries the small businessperson cannot afford. For example, one of the most common errors made by many businesses is product proliferation, i.e., too many unneeded models, styles, types or even too many different products. The more widespread the line of products offered, the higher the inventory and the less is the chance for economies of scale. The loss from disposing of obsolescent products at markdown prices which invariably comes with product proliferation also increases and reduces cash supply.

Usually the balance sheet items in a small business which must be watched most carefully are accounts receivable, accounts payable, inventory, and machinery or equipment. Larger firms may take advantage of a smaller firm by paying bills late and still taking the cash discount for prompt payment. In times of a business recession, many firms will gradually slow down on the promptness with which they pay their invoices, particularly if the firm to whom the money is owed makes no effort to collect. It therefore behooves the manager of a small business to check on accounts receivable at least once or twice a month and to write *all* customers large or small requesting prompt payment.

The President of the Vulcanium Corporation of Northbrook, Illinois, recently showed us his system which seems to work very well. He has his secretary-bookkeeper post the total of his accounts receivable on the first day of each month in a loose-leaf notebook. They are posted in four columns (1) current, (2) 15 to 30 days late, (3) 31 to 50 days late, and (4) over 51 days late. Comparable figures for three previous years are also shown so that he can immediately spot overall trends.

On a separate page following the above is a list of all accounts that are overdue with the amount due and the due date. Mr. J. E. Leopold, the President of Vulcanium, says that when he is quoting prices on a new order he pulls the notebook out and reminds his customers of any overdue amounts. Often the mere reminder is enough to stimulate the customer to pay (because the customer knows that he, Mr. Leopold, is cognizant of, and acting on overdue bills). He also keeps separate pages in his notebook on accounts payable, inventory by category, and machinery purchases contemplated. By knowing his monthly cash flow (from his accountant) run-off monthly on a computer he knows exactly how much he can buy in raw materials and machinery and when he can pay for them.

Mr. Leopold said, "In my opinion the most difficult part of managing a small business is in cash budgeting. I am particularly interested in sales and the factory operation, and I suppose that's why if I'm not extremely cautious I'll overbuy when someone offers me a low price on, say, titanium tubes or sheets. It took me a long time to learn that even though the purchase may be low priced and the profit potentially large, I simply cannot afford to buy beyond my ability to pay. I've also found out that I need to remind my customers of their overdue accounts if I expect to collect in a reasonable period of time. With the records my secretary keeps for me in my little black book, I keep on top of the situation with very little effort on my part. This last year I would have been in very bad shape without my controls."

All of these methods, now made easy by the use of personal computers, suggest ways of conserving cash for managers who forecast cash requirements six to twelve months ahead. The average small business entrepreneur *must* learn to do this at the very inception of the business. If the accountant does not suggest this at the very first meeting, he or she is derelict in his or her duty and should be replaced forthwith. It is a *necessity* for business success.

MANAGERIAL PROBLEMS

It is true as we said before, that in a sense every problem, from lack of a competitive strategy, relying on "thinks" instead of facts, down to and including lack of capital, is a managerial or management problem. In this section we will devote ourselves to other specific managerial problems not previously covered which cause business heartaches time after time. They are so important as to cry out for attention. These are:

1. Lack of general management abilities.
2. Lack of specific managerial experience in the industry.
3. Inability to change managerial style as the business grows.
4. Succeeding generation management gaps.

Lack of General Management Abilities

Unfortunately, when it comes to general management abilities, there are some who seem to be born losers. Often an individual thinks he or she can be a successful manager, but lacks both a natural aptitude or realization of the personal development that will be required to learn how to become a good manager. We advise any would-be entrepreneurs to ask themselves the following soul-searching questions before they decide to start their own business.

A. Will I enjoy being my own boss, working pretty much by myself? Making my own decisions? Or, would I prefer working with others in a larger organization where the decisions are not solely on my shoulders?
B. Am I the kind of person who, if I work for myself, will ruin my personal life by taking my worries home every night?
C. Can I work extremely long hours? (Most successful small business owners put in incredibly long hours.)
D. Am I capable of carefully controlling expenses and at the same time spending money (taking the risk) when the right opportunity presents itself? Most people are either always tight with a dollar or, alternatively, gamblers. The small business owner who succeeds usually combines both attributes but senses when to apply them.
E. Has my past decision-making ability proven satisfactory? Do I make shrewd, astute decisions as a rule? Or, to the contrary, do I make mistakes fairly often because of lack of keen insight or because of poor planning?
F. Can I honestly say that I have the general management experience and know-how to run a business?

Lack of Specific Managerial Experience

In small businesses the key individual must not only have general management ability but in many fields he or she must have specific know-how for the particular industry. Whereas in a larger business, an executive with the required skill can be hired, in a small business it is often a one- or two-person-show and management either has the knowledge or doesn't have it.

Typically, in the apparel business, a combination production-financial individual will go into partnership with a sales-oriented person. The failure rate in small apparel businesses is appalling. Why? The answer often is that neither partner has the creative, innovative artistic skill to design tasteful eye-appealing merchandise. They lack the specific managerial knowhow required in the apparel business to give the firm a competitive edge.

As an illustration, two men with wide general managerial skills went into the burlap bag business. Within three years they had failed because success in that particular field is dependent upon knowledge of "hedging" in the importation of jute from India and neither man knew enough or could learn the art fast enough to perpetuate the business.

Many other illustrations come to mind but the two just mentioned will suffice to make the point. Why do otherwise bright individuals make this error? Probably for two reasons: either they think they can master the skill rapidly, or in their enthusiasm to get rich quickly (it seems so easy), they fail to identify the one most important skill that separates the winners from the "also-rans." Usually, the needed expertise is the one that gives the firm the ability to do the job better than its competitors (the competitive edge) and hence to attract customers. In the first example just cited, better styled apparel is the attraction appeal for customers to buy from the firm rather than other manufacturers. In the second example, all burlap bags are pretty much alike so that price becomes extremely important (assuming service is equal) and the determining factor in price is for how low a cost can the material be purchased. Material (jute) is not only the major component of the finished goods cost, but the market price often fluctuates rapidly. This fluctuation becomes extremely important when material must be bought many months in advance of its delivery and use.

Inability to Change Managerial Style

When a business is first begun the owner-manager does just about everything. He or she may open up early in the morning, sweep out the accumulated mess, see that the work is started, open the mail, make the bank deposits. He may take a customer to lunch, settle a dispute between employees, write an ad, help with production bottleneck and wearily lock the door at night. In short he is a *doer*. As the business progresses, however, he finds he cannot do everything himself. Gradually he hires a few people to help take part of his load. At that point, individuals take widely divergent paths. One man continues to breathe down the neck of every employee, watching over every minute detail. He remains the *doer* because he cannot delegate. With only 24 hours in the day for him to work, the business can only grow so far before the strain becomes too great. A second individual may be able to delegate—he takes in a partner or learns to concentrate his efforts on the critical parts of his management job. Unfortunately, he still hasn't got it made. Consider this situation.

Bill Starbuck started a cement block manufacturing firm in 1969. Within seven years sales had progressed to nearly $3,000,000. Profits were highly satisfactory until 1975 when they leveled off. In 1977 sales again went up but profits dropped. A management consultant firm hired in the fall of '77 after a detailed analysis put the problem succinctly.

Bill Starbuck was not a good manager! The consultants pointed out that while he did delegate some authority to those under him, he was inept in leadership qualities. His constant criticism, second guessing, and constant harping on minute details so upset his main subordinates that, despite their fancy titles, they were afraid to make decisions. Numerous opportunities to cut costs, improve operations, and satisfy customers had been lost. Bill was so furious when he received this report that he fired the consulting firm. By mid-1979, the firm's profits were nearly down to the vanishing point and sales were falling badly.

Bill would not or could not change. In fact, he could not even admit to himself that he was not a man capable of managing a medium-sized business, which meant managing a team (four key people) of executives. He was great for a small business where he made all the important decisions. He could set up systems and delegate authority to people such as an office manager who was primarily a bookkeeper, and a yard super-intendent who saw that the truck drivers picked up and delivered the concrete blocks and other building supplies. Those people were no threat to his own image of himself as a manager, his one-man authority. His downfall came after he had hired a vice-president for production, a vice-president for finance (treasurer/accountant/tax expert/cost expert/credit manager as well as financial manager), an executive vice-president who was really a glorified salesman, and a vice-president of operations (real estate, yard operations, time study, some product R & D, and computer time-sharing). These four people were a threat to his self-image. They separated him from his workers (most of whom he intimately knew), the detail which he really loved, and the feeling of being creative in all aspects of the work. His job as president called for a person who could accomplish results through leadership of others so that he could concentrate more on the crucial problems of the business such as long-range planning, diversification of products, plant expansion and financing, and sharpening of the competitive edge of the firm.

To a large extent, the head of a medium-sized business must learn to lead and motivate others and to control the operation through paperwork. For many individuals this is impossible. The previous experience and habits of a lifetime are a hindrance rather than a guide. For those people the only answer seems to be to keep the business small or sell out and start over again.

For others who can make the transition, rough though it may be, the path can be smoothed by such devices as (a) enrolling in evening classes in a nearby university (Human Resource Management is the title given to the appropriate major at some colleges of business); (b) hiring on a part-time basis an industrial psychologist; (c) enrolling in the seminars conducted by the American Management Association; (d) instituting a Board of Directors composed of individuals who have successfully made the leadership change in themselves.

Succeeding-Generation Management Gaps

"From shirtsleeves to shirtsleeves in three generations" just about sums up the problem of failure to provide for management succession. A person works diligently and long and builds a business. The son or daughter manages it with less industriousness, turning it over to his or her offspring who care even less about it. Hence the business is either sold or it fails. Without going into the psychological implications, suffice it to say that many children or grandchildren either do not have the interest or the capabilities to run "the old man's business."

The problem for the original owner becomes twofold: first, does the "next-in-line" have both the desire and the ability, and second, if not, what preparation needs to be made to insure the survival of the business?

Easy answers to this management succession question are difficult to find. That many parents would like to have their children follow in their foot-steps has been clear in the past. Equally clear is the average parent's inability to be either teacher or judge of the son's or daughter's managerial talent. Let's assume that it has been decided the son or daughter will not succeed the parent. It then becomes necessary for the protection of the founder's family, whether or not the company is a single proprietorship or a partnership, to insure the survival of the business after physical impairment or death occurs. Problems to be solved are:

1. Who will operate the business?
2. In case of death, will there be enough capital left to operate the business after paying federal and state inheritance taxes (which are far higher than most people expect) and attorney's fee (also high)?
3. How do you prevent squabbles among the heirs that will impair the earnings of the business?
4. Is the business always in condition to be sold at a fair price?

The answers to these questions are far too complex and too individual in nature, depending upon the circumstances, to be answered in a manual of this type. What must be said is that an owner or part-owner of small- and medium-sized firms must plan in advance for these eventualities, unpleasant as they may be. If the planning is done well in advance, many heartaches can be minimized or eliminated. Some of the possibilities might be:

1. Training a successor over a period of years.
2. A voting trust with a preselected person given voting control.
3. Sufficient life insurance payable to the business to insure payment of an agreed upon fair amount for the deceased's share of the business.
4. A buy-and-sell agreement with funding either through loans or insurance to prevent dilution of control.
5. A regular plan of stock gifts to family members. Currently, gift taxes are quite low in comparison to estate taxes and fees. Additionally, a married person can give away $20,000 per year to each of any number of individuals without tax.
6. A life insurance plan payable to heirs so that cash to pay taxes will be available.
7. Selling part of the stock either to investors or the public while the business is viable. Often after the death of a key individual the price of the stock will decline.

  8. Converting the owner's equity to preferred stock giving the heirs common stock which would then have a lower value but would insure voting control.

  9. Developing an outside board of directors knowledgeable and interested in the business who would then be available for help, sound advice, and possibly an investment in the business.

SUMMARY

In this portion of Chapter 5 we have attempted to point out and explain some of more important and most frequently observed management lapses that cause small business mediocrity or failure. The business policy student may wish to use the following checklist after reading a case to help identify the specific management errors which apply to the firm being studied.

In our checklist we have slightly rephrased the pitfalls so as to present them in positive fashion as caveats. Business executives will want to think about each of them in relation to their own individual business or department. While we do not cover every possible error contributing to poor business results, we venture a belief that most small business failures can be traced to one or a combination of several of the factors discussed.

A. You must have a *competitive edge*—sufficient plusses to do better than competition to motivate an ever-increasing number of customers to buy because they want and need your offering.
Competitive edge must be realistic.
Competitive edge must be based on accurate costs.
Competitive edge must be compatible with the firm's capabilities and constraints.
Competitive edge must constantly be updated.

B. Decisions must be made on facts not "thinks" (and constantly push for additional facts).

C. Management must plan in writing (be prepared for the future).
Outline every factor you intend to plan.
Determine possible sources of information.
Gather the facts and organize them.
Work out all alternative courses of action.
Make the decisions and act upon them.
Evaluate and update your planning.

D. Seek competent professional advice (don't try to be your own lawyer or accountant).

E. Have patience, don't act with undue haste.
Emphasize profits (not growth alone).
Don't start without sufficient capital.
Use cash planning.
Conserve cash.

F. If specific managerial experience is necessary, get it before you start.

Adopt your managerial style to the needs of business.

Plan management succession.

PROBLEMS IN LARGER FIRMS

The medium and large business firms are discussed together because they have common differences from, and advantages over, the small firm. First, they have an individual manager for each major function. Second, they have access to the large capital markets. Third, either the companies serve broad markets, have a diversified line of products, or both.

With the obvious speed-up of change, increased size, rapid technological advances, and the extreme complexity of modern-day organizations, any description of pitfalls preventing progress in large corporations must of necessity be somewhat simplistic in nature. To try to pinpoint this or that reason as the only, or even major, reason for mediocrity of a large firm, is somewhat absurd. Usually there will be many reasons with each contributing to the less than spectacular showing with varying degrees of importance. It should, however, be pointed out that in the final analysis, the chief executive *is responsible for all failures.* This is true for every business, large or small.

Interestingly enough, many chief executives recognize and accept this responsibility with delight. *Forbes,* in its 15 May 1971 issue, quotes the former chief of I.T.&T., Harold Geneen, as saying, "I don't care what anybody tells you, the top man is responsible for the results."[7] Charles F. Myers, Jr., Chairman of Burlington Industries, says "If you put a man in over his head and he's being torn apart by the responsibility, it is *your* (the chief executive's) fault, not his. It's *your* job to put the right man in the right job.[8] J. Irwin Miller, Chairman of Cummins (diesel) Engine puts it this way, "You can delegate decisions. You cannot delegate responsibility. If things go wrong, it's your responsibility."[9] *Forbes* itself headlines the index to their 26 interviews with top executives thusly, "The Buck Stops Here: The Role of the Chief Exeucitve." John P. Fishwick, President of Norfolk & Western says, "We have a lot of problems, yes, but I am having the time of my life."[10] To which *Forbes* comments, "Like the majority of chief executives, he's doing what he's doing because he *enjoys* solving —or trying to solve—problems."[11]

If the chief executive is responsible for success, mediocrity, or failure of both large and small firms, what are the differences requiring special treatment for the medium-sized and larger corporations? It is true that nearly every pitfall mentioned relating to small enterprises can also be important in analyzing larger firms. There are, however, additional problems which are intensified by the sheer size of the company. These pitfalls are often the result of *inherent conflicts* associated with (1) strong managerial style differences as well as viewpoints among the various important executives (and their cliques of staff members), (2) the diverse personal goals of the top executives which may not be compatible with the overall goals of the enterprise, and (3) the highly visible differences between the firm and its environment. A strong chief executive may be able to reconcile these conflicts or he or she may only succeed in submerging them so that at least temporarily they are hidden. A weaker chief may hardly be aware that they exist until they break out into the open and breed disaster.

In this chapter we will examine the more often seen problems of firms that have reached a size necessitating a full complement of executives. The pitfalls raised, together with those examined earlier, will make an excellent checklist for the student to apply when analyzing a case in business policy or for the businessperson to use in reference to his or her own company.

Our criterion for success will be substantially increased earnings per share of common stock over a period of years. To dispel the idea the reader may have that a particular industry in which the company is operating will be of overwhelming significance, note Exhibit 5.2. In each industry, one firm was able to increase earnings per share rather well between 1968 and 1978, while another firm in the same industry and the same period of time was not doing nearly so well. This is by no means an exhaustive list, but it does indicate that some chief executives found a way, regardless of industry, to achieve excellent growth in earnings even if it meant some diversification into other industries.

Exhibit 5.2 should preclude the alibis of the chief executive who may claim that the woes of his or her firm are brought about because "our particular industry is dying." It is true that in some industries, one or more limiting factors may be present which makes the chief executive's job extremely difficult. Often, however, some opportunities, some alternative options or even diversification into other industries are found to keep the company progressing. The truly great leaders as indicated in the quotations at the beginning of this section accept the challenge, "make lemonade out of lemons," and push on to greater earnings.

And now, let us examine the critical factors contributing to the success of medium-sized and large firms and the pitfalls preventing progress.

CLEARLY, FULLY, SPECIFICALLY STATED OBJECTIVES AND POLICIES

Many evenings my wife and I walk our dog. We have no set pattern. One night we may aimlessly walk up and down our neighboring streets while another night we may find ourselves by chance walking over to, and down, the ocean beach. Often we follow the dog who in actuality is the leader. Contrast that with the way we walk to the late night grocer for a loaf of bread. My wife even argues with me as to which is the shortest path! And so it is with business. Without clearly, fully, and specifically stated goals and objectives, the company may often be

EXHIBIT 5.2

Earnings Per Share, 1978 vs. 1968 for Selected Companies

Industry Company	Earnings Per Share 1978	1968	Comment On Change
Apparel			
Bobbie Brooks	$ 1.20	$ .23	420% increase!
Farah	d .68	1.15	Decrease!
Jantzen	3.16	1.48	168% increase
Air Transport			
Eastern	2.91	d 1.06	Frank Borman takes charge
National	1.68	2.51	33% decrease
Automobile			
General Motors	12.24	6.02	A contrast in management
Chrysler	d 3.54	6.19	
Chemical			
Lubrizol	3.95	.84	One-product strategy
Olin	2.82	2.35	
Computers			
Burroughs	6.21	1.32	370% increase
Data General	4.98	d .02	Take-off!
IBM	5.32	1.54	245% increase
			Is everybody winning?
Cosmetics			
Alberto	.71	1.27	44% decrease
Avon	3.92	1.24	216% increase
Faberge	1.13	1.52	26% decrease
Paper			
Hammermill Paper	3.35	2.05	increase
St. Regis Paper	3.95	1.67	136% is better
Publishing			
Prentice-Hall	2.68	1.30	106% increase
Scott-Foresman	2.40	.59	307% increase – a comer?
Steel			
Bethlehem	5.15	3.55	Increase vs. decreases.
Kaiser	1.75	4.95	Can it be the management?
U.S. Steel	2.85	3.13	
Retail Stores			
Federated Dept.	4.15	1.85	Hot competition
Allied Stores	4.10	1.50	
Tire and Rubber			
Firestone	d 2.51	2.16	Good guys finish first
Goodyear	3.12	3.08	
Petroleum			
Atlantic Richfield	6.60	1.85	257% increase
Exxon	6.20	2.97	109% increase
Texaco	3.14	3.08	2% increase, can't keep up

d – deficit

Source: *Value Line Investment Survey,* Arnold Bernhard & Co., 5 East 44 St., New York, New York 10017.

"walking the dog." It isn't going anywhere in particular and won't get there by the shortest path except by accident. On the other hand, if the company has a specific destination (goal) and an arrival time, its chances of getting there on time (of earning 20% on its equity by June 30, 1985, for example) are greatly enhanced.

The best managed firms have written objectives and policies covering:

a. The specific industries in which the firm operates.
b. The competitive edge it has and is seeking.
c. The constraints it recognizes (for example, the firm may only wish to compete in the low price, high volume markets for its products).
d. Specifics regarding its marketing posture (own brands or private brands, direct salespeople or wholesalers, national and/or international in certain areas, etc.).
e. People goals.
f. Financial objectives with a timetable (often a five-year plan).
g. New product policy.
h. Research and development goals and policies.
i. Production objectives (including degree of vertical integration).
j. The organization structure.
k. Long-range planning procedure and responsibility.
l. Accounting and control systems.
m. Inter- and intra-company communications policies.
n. A complete set of objectives and policies for each separate division.
o. The sum of the numbers for resources utilized and returns expected for the division to tie into and support the overall corporate goals.

Problems rarely arise over goals and objectives in small companies if they have thought out their competitive edges and planned for the future. This is true because the top one or two individuals of a small business have their goals and policies firmly in mind as a result of their planning. However, as a firm grows in volume, additional executives are hired. They take over important functions without being party to the planning or development of objectives and policies. Often in a family firm, with the addition of other family members, the lack of written goals brings on extremely serious problems. One brother may be ambitious, anxious for fast growth, and of a gambling nature, whereas another brother may be extremely conservative, satisfied with slow growth, and not willing to borrow capital for expansion. With the addition of a second and even a third generation, some of whom may want to participate in the management while others may want only large dividends on their stock ownership, the potential for disagreements becomes increasingly great.

In either case, the medium-sized business, family owned or not, often runs into difficulties which can only be overcome by agreement on a clearly written complete set of objectives and policies that can give direction to the entire enterprise. This will stop the almost daily, repetitious discussions and arguments about what policies are to be followed, how to handle a particular job, and who is responsible for what. These arguments can go on interminably at the vice-presidential level and below with bitter conflict and great wasting of time without the president even being aware of what is going on. It becomes even worse if the heir to the throne is not apparent and each vice-president is jockeying for position.

In the largest firms where the chain of command becomes long and communications poor and unclear, the need for written objectives and policies becomes a must. While most of the large corporations have them, some do not. Written goals are only the first step, however, and not the complete answer.

> One of the classic examples of failure which has been attributed to lack of written objectives and policies (in fact, no spelled-out corporate objectives nor even basic accounting controls) can be found in the story of Korvette, for a time the outstanding operator of discount department stores in the country. Eugene Ferkauf, the sole founder, in a comparatively few years ran the business from one small store to a chain doing several hundred million dollars. Unfortunately, he completely lost the business despite his obvious talents, when a merger became necessary to save the stores (which are still operating under the name *Korvette*).

> When one of the authors met him at the height of his success, he so detested putting anything into writing that he had neither an office nor a secretary! He appeared to think of his objectives in broad general terms such as "reduce costs, keep mark-ups below competition, take small profit margins on large volume." This worked well when he ran the business alone. When the business grew so that he had to open more stores and hire a team of executives apparently the old ways no longer worked. One of his executives remarked at the time he left the company, "I never know my responsibility nor my authority. If a particularly good buy came along, I never knew whether to take it or pass it up. Everything was a crisis and utter confusion reigned supreme. We had no policies and if we had, I wouldn't have known what they were."

Most individuals in executive positions want to be free to exercise their own judgment about how to achieve corporate goals but they need policy guidelines and specific goals to work towards. They need to know the extent of their authority in each area. For example, hiring and firing and line authority may be vested in a certain manager or may be circumscribed by the personnel manager. The person may be able to authorize the expenditure of $1,000,000 if he or she lives within a prescribed overall budget which has been previously approved.

NO UNIFIED SENSE OF DIRECTION

Lack *of a unified sense of direction* is without a doubt the most difficult, single problem of the chief executive and the total enterprise. Yet if the CEO (chief executive officer) is not an outstanding manager-administrator, he or she might well not even know the problem exists!

Objectives and policies are fine and absolutely necessary first steps, as we have just shown, but do not guarantee that the employees will pay them any more respect than mere lip service. Conflict is both endemic and epidemic whenever groups of individuals are organized as they are in any but the smallest of business firms. In medium-sized firms conflicts usually first appear because of the differences in the individuals who are the department managers. Individuals have their own personal characteristics which influence the particular way in which they view the problems as well as the objectives of the business. Further, these personal differences cause conflict which, if not properly controlled, at worst, can tear an organization apart and, at best, will leave the organization with no unified sense of direction. We are not saying that different viewpoints, different ways of viewing problems are not helpful to a firm because they are. We are saying that after discussion and consideration, the agreed-upon goals and objectives of the firm must take precedence over personal preferences. Without everyone working as a team, bending every effort to achieve the firm's objectives, the progress of the company will be greatly handicapped.

Conflicts come about for many reasons. Some of these are due to:

1. *Age differences*—An older man may want to hold on to what he has and hence be ultra-conservative, opposing expenditures for new equipment or plant whereas a younger person may be just the opposite. He may want to gamble with the entire future of the firm by proposing very large expenditures for labor-saving or faster equipment.

2. *Previous Training*—The person who has come up through sales may feel that sales volume and good customer relations are of maximum importance while the financial person views with alarm projects that might reduce profit, or return on investment.

3. *Vocational aspirations*—John Jones may be trying for the boss's job and directing his efforts toward his own political campaign, while Sue Smith is only interested in maintaining the status quo. As a result, Smith spends her time toadying up to the head man by telling him of the mistakes Jones is making.

4. *Natural Styles of Leadership*—One man hates compromisers or as he calls them "employee do-gooders." He believes in making everyone under him fear him. A second man leans over backwards to cater to the men under him, believing in a very permissive type of leadership. Personal differences of this type lead to personal animosity which often finds expression in one man automatically taking the opposite point of view from the other despite the merits of the proposition.

5. *Differing social positions, speeds of thought, technical abilities, educational backgrounds,* and many more personal characteristics lead to smoldering personal antagonisms which in turn color business decisions almost to the point that what one person says is white, the other will view as black. Consider the football team whose half-

backs continually bicker over who is going to carry the ball and whether the next play should be an end run or a smash through center. How successful could such a team possibly be? It is all too true that grown people often act like little children. Unfortunately, without a strong and wise CEO many businesses fail because they do not have a unified sense of direction.

In larger corporations this same type of problem becomes magnified many times over. Staff members of the organization line up behind their favorites to form cliques. Division heads fight for power and resources for their particular divisions and often with little or no regard for overall corporate goals. Corporate tendencies to diversify and form conglomerates have exaggerated the omnipresent conflicts described. People who have spent their entire business lives with one company in one particular industry suddenly find themselves in competition with strangers in other companies (divisions) in industries they know nothing about. Questions arise such as: Which division gets the capital to expand? Which is contributing most to the corporate earnings? How will the promotional dollars be divided up? Why do we need a central hierarchy superimposed upon us? If there are joint efforts as, for example, a central organization sales staff or a central lobbyist in Washington, then more conflicts arise, viz., why do they pay more attention to Division X than to our division? All these questions, and many more, add new potential and actual conflicts which tend to reduce the efficiency of the total enterprise.

Describing the problem (lack of a unified sense of direction) is easy. The difficult part is finding a solution. Better communications, telling all concerned at every echelon exactly *what* and *why* they were made as they were is only a partial answer at best (and what company wants to telegraph its strategy in advance to the competition, which most certainly will happen if *all* know the what and the why). The best answer seems to be a chief executive officer who can weld a team much like our best football coaches, who can inculcate "do or die" spirit in their players. At the same time the CEO must be wise enough to pick the best players, coach them in new smart plays and then call many of the signals when the team is on the playing field.

To illustrate the problem of establishing a unified sense of direction, consider the problems faced by George S. Trimble when he took over Bunker-Ramo as president and chief executive.

When Trimble came aboard, the company was a hodgepodge of operations, from knit fabrics to automobile clocks, all limping along independently. There was no central planning or financial control and little new-product development or marketing focus. Bunker-Ramo looked like a jigsaw puzzle dropped on the floor.

"For its size, it's one of the most complicated businesses I've ever seen," says Trimble. "At any company, you start with the assumption that everyone wants to work and that the boss's job is to create the right environment. But at Bunker-Ramo we were so screwed up that we couldn't even figure out what the work was."

Trimble set about studying the pieces and, in a spirit of experimentation, trying various reporting and planning systems. When something didn't work, he junked it—a process that applied to product lines, too. Faced with division chiefs used to operating alone, Trimble instituted a philosophy of teamwork (imposed, paradoxically, by his autocratic fiat) that led at first to numerous defections. He now has a 10-member executive council that meets with him monthly in no-holds-barred, shirtsleeve sessions.

Source: Adapted from *Business Week,* 15 August 1977.

Even with a clear-cut, beautifully written set of goals and policies, far too many companies flounder because the CEO flouts the objectives or policies as "the exigencies of the circumstances demand." As one CEO stated, "If I break the rules I must allow those below me to bend the rules."

A large, diversified, multi-division company after considerable study and thought decided that henceforth they would not make any acquisitions where the present volume of the firm being purchased was less than $20,000,000 annually. Furthermore they made a policy stipulating that no further acquisitions would be made in specified industries where they already did sufficient volume to put additional new company purchases under the scrutiny of the F.T.C. Within six months, the CEO went to the Board of Directors and secured approval to purchase two companies, one whose sales were well below the minimum and the other which raised "restraint of trade" problems with the F.T.C. Both of these policy infractions were noticed and remarked upon by the so-called "Management Committee" composed of eleven top executives. As a result, over a period of time, various other members of the committee each found it convenient to disregard accepted and written company policy just as though they were testing to find out how far they could go.

It seems clear that the CEO must make certain that goals and policies be clearly, fully, and specifically stated. They must be agreed upon by all *as a way of life,* including the CEO. If there are any doubts in the CEO's mind he or she either must hide them or see that the objectives and policies are changed so that he or she can wholeheartedly get behind them. It is only then that a firm can possibly have the unified sense of direction so necessary for its success.

INADEQUACY IN AN IMPORTANT FUNCTIONAL AREA

The "Law of Averages" precludes one firm having superiority in *all* functional areas over *all* of its competitors for any long (five or more years) period of time. This does not mean, however, that a Procter and Gamble cannot have a superior marketing department, which it has, and has had for many years. It does mean that marketing superiority alone or superiority in other functional areas alone cannot propel a firm to success if it is totally *inadequate* in other areas.

Suppose, for example, that Procter and Gamble had an inadequate new products department or an extremely weak financial setup, then despite its strong marketing department the long-range success of the firm would be doubtful at best.

Think about I.B.M. for a moment. Technological superiority they had. They also had a strong marketing department and good service centers all over the free world. They had strong financial controls and, more to the point, were not *inadequate* in any area of their business.

We put this rather obvious point in our list of pitfalls because so many students of business policy (and businesspeople too) often seem to have a one-track mind. They will carefully examine a company in their own particular area of competence and completely overlook one or more other areas. Chief executives have this same blind spot, this predilection to favor their particular functional area, usually the one in which they rose up through the business. The better chief executives recognize their own deficiencies and hire or appoint good employees that are strong in the areas where the chief may be weak. They do this because they know that while strength in one area will help overcome mediocrity in other areas, real inadequacy in any area can rarely if ever be completely overcome. For example, an old saying in the advertising profession is "the best advertising will not sell a bad product."

Similarly, in respect to the business as a whole, one or two strong departments will certainly help the business to forge ahead but they will not carry the weak departments indefinitely. In this era of rapidly changing consumer tastes and the speed-up of technological improvements necessitating new industrial products, the department or functional area charged with the responsibility for developing *new* products should be examined carefully. This is generally the Research and Development (R & D) department.

The output of an R & D department is not only difficult to measure, but it is a convenient department for management to starve budgetwise in order to improve the firm's profit picture. A starvation diet for R & D may not be apparent to analysts for several years. Only by looking back to see how well a company is innovating or introducing new products *vis-a-vis* competition is it possible to make a judgment as to the effectiveness of its research and development activities and/or the size of its R & D budget. Even then, an outsider finds it difficult to criticize as the company may have a good R & D department and a king-size budget only to be beaten to the market place in some instances by a lucky competitor. If this happens often, of course, then it is probably *not* a matter of luck.

The Chairman of the Board of one of America's largest and most successful companies recently said, "Immediately upon being appointed Chairman, I decided to concentrate my efforts on two areas. First, on planning, and second, on the weakest department we had which I felt was R & D. I beefed up R & D because it not only tied in with our future planning (very important) but also because I thought being weak in that area would seriously curtail the long-range success of our entire company. The stronger departments, marketing and production, obviously had strong people in them and would continue to be strong. Part of my job was to strengthen our weakest areas to achieve better overall balance. As soon as I realized why we were falling behind competition both in new products and technical improvements in the tried and true products which accounted for 74% of our profit, I forced our Board to appropriate $2,500,000 to back up the new Chief of R & D I brought in. Today, not only do we have better bread and butter basics but you see the first of our new products. I can now confidently predict we will no longer be called the sleeping giant."[12]

◆ ◆ ◆

Harry B. Cunningham, Chairman of S.S. Kresge Company, pointed out one answer to this entire question of functional department weakness when he said, "There is one thing I think every chief executive should avoid. That is, the natural tendency for you to surround yourself with men with backgrounds very similar to your own. This is a weakness because there is not a balance in top management."[13]

PEOPLE PROBLEMS

The real fundamental difference between businesses in the same field of endeavor is always *people*. A large business may have the advantages of size, greater access to capital or more natural resources, but in nearly every industry over a time span, new, young, more aggressively managed firms have sprung up, grown large, and successfully challenged the what might be called lethargic, perhaps self-satisfied or ingrown slow-moving, large, well-entrenched firms. The petroleum industry is a good example. Why have Continental Oil, Amerada-Hess and Occidental Petroleum been able to grow so rapidly (two with 1970 revenues over $2 billion and Amerada over $1 billion) in such a capital-intensive, well-matured industry? The answer, of course, is people—management people.

About the only way for an outsider to judge the effectiveness of management people is by their past results. How does the company being analyzed compare with other firms in the same industry? On sales growth? On growth of earnings per share? On return on investment? On innovations introduced?

J. C. Penney for many years did an outstanding job in selling soft goods, particularly domestics (towels, sheets, piece goods, etc.). Their growth was steady if not spectacular. Penney's was known as a great place to work. Their store managers, especially, were highly paid. No one seemed to think they had people problems, even though Sears was growing far more rapidly in sales, earnings per share, and earnings on investment. More recently, however, Penney's has become alive to changing conditions. They have extended credit which they had not done previously, they added hard lines (*a la* Sears' success), they bought a mail order catalog house and expanded it, they opened new far larger stores than before and put them in shopping centers. Today, Penney's is thought of as an aggressive, fast expanding organization. What made the difference? The answer, again, is management people. J. C. Penney Chairman, William M. Batten says, "We are thinking unaccustomed thoughts." In a memo when he was assistant to the president he bluntly told the directors that the company was more in tune with the way things *were* than the way they were *going to be.* "You never know when you do things like that," he said, "whether they will throw you out or promote you. But you don't worry about it."[14]

In thinking about people problems, it is helpful to divide the analysis into subheadings similar to the following:

Board of Directors

Is the board a perfunctory do-nothing board which meets only rarely? Is it primarily composed people looking for prestige? Who don't want to rock the boat? More interested in how things were than will be? Are they primarily devoted to their own interests rather than the interests of the company?

Chief Executive Officer

Is the CEO a dynamic, hard-hitting executive who knows where he or she wants the firm to go and provides leadership to get there? Or is the CEO a compromiser who is content to be influenced (swept along) by the various forces within the company? Does the CEO react to the environment of the firm (often too late), or does he or she anticipate changes and move earlier to make the most of them? Will the CEO accept innovative ideas from subordinates? Or, does he or she resist change particularly if it's someone else's idea? Is the CEO good at promoting the best people regardless of whether they are similar in thinking and/or background to himself or herself? What kind of climate does the CEO create for those around him or her? Relaxed? A climate ruled by fear? Or one attempting to get the best out of each subordinate?

> When Dictaphone Corp.'s new president, E. Lawrence Tabat, began arriving at the company's Rye (N.Y.) headquarters at 7 a.m., calling out, "Anyone for breakfast?" it was obvious that a new sense of urgency had gripped the ailing company.
>
> Since Tabat took charge in August, 1971, the 85-year-old office equipment company has, indeed, been undergoing a massive shakeup. Unprofitable office furniture operations have been dropped, promising new products have been rushed to market, and the company is in the black this year after posting losses because of heavy special charges in 1971 and 1970. During the first nine months of 1972, operating income increased 24% to $2.1 million on a 6% sales gain to $63.8 million. . . . "At last we have some breathing space," says Tabat.[15]

People Policy—Inbreeding—Nepotism

Do the policies of the company encourage inbreeding, i.e., everyone thinks alike, acts alike, dresses alike? (You're all right when you get hired," says a man who quit Southern Bell, "But as the years go by your head becomes more and more Bell-shaped.")[16]

Is loyalty to old-timers followed to an extreme? Do young people have an opportunity to advance? Even if their thinking is different from the accepted norm?

How about nepotism? Do relatives get promoted regardless of ability? Is favoritism an irritating or upsetting factor?

People Problems—Miscellaneous

Does the company have management in depth? Are personnel policies, the personnel department, and people themselves regarded as of maximum importance to the affairs of the company (in the firm's hierarchy)? Does leadership exist at all levels? Are new ideas embraced or viewed with suspicion? Is the firm well organized or is there constant overlapping of authority and responsibility? Are individuals encouraged to act as entrepreneurs running their own companies? Or is "passing the buck" the custom?

LACK OF LIVING BY THE MARKETING CONCEPT

To fully understand the marketing concept and its importance, read Chapter 6. The sole question we raise here is, does the firm being analyzed merely pay lip service to the marketing concept or is it a way of life which takes precedence over everything else? This question may seem to be an anachronism but unfortunately firms still exist, albeit not in the best of health, which do not realize that every continually successful company is in business to satisfy the needs and wants of its customers at a profit to itself. How well firms satisfy their customers, now and in the future, how well they anticipate customer wants, improving upon present products and introducing new products will in large part, govern their own success.

Even well-known, consumer-oriented companies are sometimes suspect, as the story below shows.

> Harley-Davidson Motor Company, a division of AMF, Inc., completely missed the motorcycle boom that swept the country in the '60s and '70s. Harley's market share fell from 50% to 3.6%, as the Japanese captured 90% of the market. While Honda and other Japanese manufacturers produced lighter, sportier, less expensive bikes that attracted the growing number of novice riders, Harley followed a do-nothing strategy of promoting the large, expensive "Harley Hog." Thanks to a declining dollar and more experienced riders trading up, Harley's market share inched up to 7% in 1978. This improvement was not based on anything Harley did but was based on favorable trends in the market. Harley's response has been to expand production capacity for modified versions of its traditional product, the large touring bike, combined with promotion of the Harley bikes' distinctive roar and macho image. In 1979, Harley faced the prospect that EPA noise limitation regulations would eliminate even this small competitive edge.

It should be pointed out the marketing concept has been generally followed by our largest corporations. Because so few of us have really original ideas, there is a strong tendency to copy the current trend (in marketing), whatever it may be. Firms that "reverse the field" some-times hit the jackpot. Volkswagen is an excellent example of revers-ing the field. Contrary to what others did, they did not bring out new models every year (which added to costs) nor did they appeal, with either their product or their promotion, to consumer desires for high speeds, high horsepower, luxurious cars. Zenith (radios and TVs) like-wise reversed the field, stressing quality at a high price when nearly every other manufacturer was opting for lower prices regardless of quality. Discount department stores made huge inroads into tradi-tional retailers' sales at a time when the marketing literature was filled stories concerning a rising taste level of consumers and their willingness to pay the price of quality and service. All these examples point out one important marketing lesson: just because everyone else says, "this is what the consumer wants" is no proof it is true. In other words, run your own marketing show based upon your own marketing research. The firm that truly practices the marketing concept best will often have a marketing competitive edge.

LACK OF GOOD CONTROLS OR TOO MANY TOO LATE

As a firm grows larger and lines of communication are stretched longer and longer, controls which were once adequate either no longer work or they take effect so late as to be meaningless. When we say, "They no longer work," we mean that any one or all of the following may happen.

a. The paperwork becomes so voluminous that the really important controls are buried in reams of electronic data processing paper that are either never studied ("I don't have time") or only barely glanced at.

b. Responsibility is passed down the line to a third-level clerk who even if he or she knew what was happening would be afraid to do anything about it.

c. The optimum level for any given control is not specifically spelled out in advance. A summary of variances should go to the person in management authorized and charged with the responsibility to do something about a breach and to *that person's* manager.

d. By the time the right person gets the report, it is too late for him or her to do much about it, including making certain it doesn't happen again.

Illustrations of control problems are numerous. Rarely ever is there a large company who at one time or another hasn't found itself with unwanted inventories of raw materials bought for products that may not ever be produced again. Someone forgets to tell someone in the purchasing department that the product's specs were being changed. The writer has even seen an order for 1000 written as 10,000 and be passed along and be acted upon by personnel in the order department, the sales department, production control, purchasing, inventory con-trol, credit, the production department, shipping and through the customer's entire organization. This, despite the fact that single orders for $400,000 were very uncommon!

Each functional area has need for only a few but highly important controls. The credit department needs to know, for example, (1) What is the daily or weekly total amount of credit being extended? (2) How does this relate to sales? (turnover) (3) What is the percentage of the total that is overdue and how long? (4) Which individual accounts are late so that action can be taken to collect?

The person in charge, in this case, the credit manager, needs to get this information on a daily or weekly basis, promptly in either event, and have the responsibility and authority to take appropriate action. Controls or information that are not going to be acted upon should not be allowed to accumulate nor be gathered.

In this electronic age where computers can turn out literally thousands of pages of data per day, the tendency in modern business is to have too much in the way of controls rather than too little. Too much often is similar to having none because no one ever gets around to doing anything about them. The recent losing of over 400 railroad cars by Penn-Central is a perfect example of information indigestion.

Sperry Rand was put together in one of the biggest mergers of the 1950s. It was perhaps the top office systems and equipment company, it had a unique head start in the computer field, and a top-notch technical division in Sperry. Every few years it was touted on Wall Street as a turn-around company and then it fizzled.

"Our problem is that Sperry Rand is a multicylinder organization," says chairman and CEO J. Paul Lyet, "but the cylinders never functioned at the same time."

Apparently Lyet was able to establish balanced coordination and control based on the strong revitalized organization built by his predecessor, J. Frank Forster (hit fatally by a car in New York in July 1972). Lyet accelerated Forster's drive toward centralized monitoring, strengthened marketing forces, formal long-range planning, and quarterly in-depth reviews of divisions. The results were record earnings for the fiscal year ending March 31, 1973.

LACK OF AN INTERNATIONAL MENTALITY

This pitfall has relevance for many medium-sized firms. Fear of the unknown is strong in all of us whether we be CEOs or plumbers. This fear of international business has been so strong that many firms did not even try to establish an overseas branch of their business, or if they did try, it was such a half-hearted attempt that it often invited its own defeat. Unfortunately, our own government did not make it easier, nor encourage companies to expand abroad as other nations did.

Competition today is worldwide as our steel, electronics, and automobile companies know only too well. Many of our largest corporations are very happy that they expanded their horizons when they did.

They may be doing 20% to 50% of their entire volume with commensurate profits in foreign countries. Rapid changes and higher risks must be considered, though, as discussed in Chapter 12.

VISIONS OF GRANDEUR

One of the most common problems of large companies is the psychotic desire for rapid growth. When a company is sinking fast, it hires a new dynamic president who will "turn the company around in a year." The new president goes on a diversification spree by product proliferation and acquisition of companies, like the frog in the fable who tries to puff himself up to the size of a cow and explodes.

With the same false vision of grandeur, a new president may take over a healthy company and attempt to expand it far too rapidly.

Some instances of this pitfall are given below with sources for more details.

After failing in attempts to diversify out of traditional areas of strength and facing intense competition from rivals, the CEO of the Gillette Company established the policy that, in the future, Gillette will concentrate only on products that fit its marketing expertise.

Clark Equipment Company had visions of grandeur with a planned growth of 20% per year through diversification. The company got in over its head and has recently completed a return to its traditional business of making lift trucks and construction machinery. Clark has sold off most of its diversification ventures and launched a $300 million expansion of its basic business. As a result, Clark's profits are up 36%.

An illustration which shows that a company that avoids the mania for growth through diversification can prosper greatly is given below.

Readers Digest is the only mass-circulation, general-interest magazine to have survived television. The *Digest* continues to prosper as the world's most widely read magazine, even though it sticks to an editorial formula that has scarcely changed in over fifty years. As a result, Reader's Digest Association, Inc., was expected to have 1979 sales of over $1 billion and net earnings of at least $100 million.

SUMMARY OF PITFALLS TO PROGRESS IN LARGE CORPORATIONS

Progress in large firms is very spotty; some do well, others stagnate. Sheer size alone is no guarantee of success. In the final analysis the major roadblock in the way of prosperity as well as the prime mover behind those firms who are unusually successful is the chief exeuctive officer. It is his or her responsibility.

While we have not mentioned every pitfall, we have covered the big ones. Omitted are such obvious problems as funny arithmetic (accounting manipulation or figuring yourself rich with a pencil) and conglomerate accounting (pooling of interests).

We suggest that an analyst attempting to dissect a large company start with the points covered in this section and then use those discussed in relation to small firms.

The questions we raised in this section are:

1. Are both objectives and policies of the firm clearly, fully, and specifically stated in writing?
2. Does the firm have a unified sense of direction understood and followed by all?
3. Are there any obvious inadequacies in any functional area? Good R & D?
4. What are the people problems? Board of Directors, Chief Executive Officer? Is there too much inbreeding? Nepotism evidence? Do they have management in depth? Good leadership at all levels?
5. Does the firm live by the marketing concept? Are they innovative? Do they ever reverse the field?
6. Have they an international mentality?
7. Is the company attempting to expand by acquisition beyond its financial and managerial capabilities?
8. Does the company lack formal strategic planning?
9. How good is the total control system? Is there too much control of detail and not enough measurement against key performance objectives? (See Chapter 4.)

ENDNOTES

1. *Problems of Small Firm Growth and Survival,* Small Business Research Series 2, Washington, D.C.: Small Business Administration, 1961.
2. A comprehensive analysis was made by Joseph D. Philips, *Little Business in the American Economy,* Urbana, Ill.: University of Illinois Press, 1958.
3. Robert B. Buchele. *Business Policy in Growing Firms,* San Francisco: Chandler Publishing Company, 1967, p. 111.
4. Or write their headquarters, Small Business Administration, Washington, D.C., 20416.
5. For a list of trade associations, write *Directory of National Trade Associations,* U.S. Government Printing Office, Washington, D.C.
6. *Sales Management,* 630 Third Avenue, New York, New York, 10016.
7. Forbes, Inc., May 15, 1971.
8. *Ibid.,* p. 191.
9. *Ibid.,* p. 50.
10. *Ibid.,* p. 5.
11. *Ibid.,* p. 195.
12. Name withheld by request.
13. *Forbes,* May 15, 1971.
14. *Ibid.,* p. 66.
15. "The Man Behind Dictaphone's Turnaround," *Business Week,* December 16, 1972.
16. *Fortune,* May 1970, p. 159.

SELECTED BIBLIOGRAPHY ON
MANAGING SMALL BUSINESS

Broom, H.N. *Small Business Management* (5th ed.). Cincinnati: South-Western Publishing Co., 1979.
Justis, Robert T. *Managing Your Small Business*. Englewood Cliffs, N.J.: Prentice-Hall, Inc., 1981.
Kline, John B.; Stegall, Donald P.; and Steinmetz, Lawrence L. *Managing the Small Business* (3d ed.). Homewood, Ill.: Richard D. Irwin, 1982.
Steinhoff, Dan. *Small Business Management Fundamentals* (3rd ed.). New York: McGraw-Hill, 1982.

SELECTED BIBLIOGRAPHY ON
MEDIUM AND LARGE COMPANIES

Diveley, George S. *The Power of Professional Management*. New York: American Management Association, 1971.
Murdick, Robert G. *Management Information Systems: Concepts and Design*. Englewood Cliffs, N.J.: Prentice-Hall, Inc., 1980.
Ross, Joel E., and Kami, Michael. *Corporate Management in Crisis: Why the Mighty Fall*. Englewood Cliffs, N.J.: Prentice-Hall, Inc., 1973.
Votaw, Dow, and Sethi, S. Prakash. *The Corporate Dilemma*. Englewood Cliffs, N.J.: Prentice-Hall, Inc., 1973.

SELECTED BIBLIOGRAPHY ON
CORPORATE CONTROL

Horngren, Charles T. *Introduction to Management Accounting* (5th ed.). Englewood Cliffs, N.J.: Prentice-Hall, Inc., 1981.
Lindberg, Roy A., and Cohn, Theodore. *Operations Auditing*. New York: AMACOM, 1972.
Murdick, Robert G. Managerial Control: Concepts and Practice. *Advanced Management Journal,* January, 1970.
———. *Management Information Systems: Concepts and Design*. Englewood Cliffs, N.J.: Prentice-Hall, Inc., 1980.
Santocki, J. Meaning and Scope of Management Audit. *Accounting and Business Research,* Winter, 1976.

6

FUNCTIONAL AREA— MARKETING

That marketing managers are highly paid is well known. Top-notch salespersons are often among the most highly paid people in a company. The reasons for compensating marketing managers and salespersons well are not hard to find. First, good marketing men and women and good salespeople are scarce and difficult to obtain. The law of supply and demand immediately comes into play. It has often been estimated that on the average sales force, the top 25 percent of the sales people produce 75 percent of the sales and conversely 75 percent of the sales force produces only 25 percent of the sales. Finding those top producers is not easy; the supply is thin. Second, marketing is both an art and a science. You may read many books on marketing, but this won't guarantee you'll be a top marketer any more than reading all the books on golf will make you a well-known pro.

In this section, therefore, we point out that simply going through the mechanics of marketing is not enough. The art as well as the science of marketing must be mastered. We emphasize further that the *entire personnel* of the firm must be *marketing oriented*. The success or failure of a company hinges on its application of these two basic ideas and applying the marketing concept outlined below in the analysis of cases. The signs that a company does not understand or apply the marketing concept may be subtle or they may be obvious. We will present the approach to analysis of marketing activities from a philosophical rather than a mechanistic framework so that the student may detect the subtle as well as the obvious symptoms that a firm is heading for a crisis. We start with the *marketing concept* which underlies all of marketing.

WHAT IS THE MARKETING CONCEPT?

The *marketing concept* is a philosophy which, when applied, guides the attitude of every individual in the firm. It combines the concept of the total marketing job in terms of employees, customers, and business objectives. The marketing concept is described more specifically as follows.

TREAT THE CUSTOMER AS ALL-IMPORTANT

The entire firm must be devoted to stimulating and satisfying the wants and needs of customers. Too often, only the sales department subscribes to this philosophy so that a rude truck driver or insolent or careless clerk may undo months of effort by marketing and management.

> A good contrast might be some of the railroad passenger lines and the Bell Telephone system. All employees of the Bell System have been trained to be courteous under extremely provocative conditions. As a result, the companies have, by and large, retained the favor of the public and avoided government ownership. At the time when bus companies began to upgrade their service after the Second World War, the conductors on trains were often abrupt, curt, or even rude to passengers. There has been a great change in recent years, but it is possible that such treatment of customers in the face of new competition was another factor in the disintegration of the railroad passenger business.

A marketing-minded organization sees the business as providing products and services to people. If there is a manufacturing manager who believes his or her job is only to produce goods to meet specifications according to a schedule, that manager is not focusing correctly. The manager's job is to produce goods for *customers,* and he or she should be thinking of *customers,* not just plant operations and efficiency reports. This is true for the V.P. of finance, the engineer, and the clerk.

> A secretary in the sales office of a large soft goods manufacturer received a call from a customer complaining about his last shipment. She connected him with the salesman but forgot to turn off her desk communications system. Then she said to a coworker, "The old b_____ is complaining again." The customer heard this, and the company lost one of its largest accounts. No amount of apologizing could bring him back.

The *attitude* of each employee, in viewing himself or herself as being paid to service the customer and help him or her with problems, must be evaluated in a real-life case. In policy case courses, we can only look for attitudes in the event clues are given in a particular case problem.

PINPOINT A TARGET MARKET

Under the marketing concept, the firm must specify what market it is aiming at. Very few products are universally desired. A product which a company designs to fulfill the desires of a very specifically defined group of people has an edge over the product whose design is a compromise to suit widely divergent tastes. The total market (potential buyers) is like the color spectrum. At each end are the extremes in colors (tastes of buyers) with a slowly changing or merging of colors from one extreme to the other. From the spectrum of potential buyers, a *segment* must be defined in terms of numerous characteristics such as economic status, age, education, occupation, and location (discussed later in Chapter 6).

One of the common mistakes made by business firms and students in business policy is the failure to recognize the need to segment the market. It is a common occurrence, for example, to see a retailer trying to sell high quality and low quality merchandise in an attempt to straddle the total market. As a result, he carries a little of everything, he has no good selection of anything, and customers cannot identify his store clearly with respect to their needs.

The automobile manufacturers provide an excellent example of market segmentation. The student, without thinking, is apt to think of millions of cars for millions of people. Actually, each manufacturer has carefully researched the market and developed classes of cars priced to reach clearly defined economic groups. Each has then developed special styles, such as sedans, economy, or high-performance cars to match clearly defined segments of the market in terms of their self-image or ego needs. Finally, each car manufacturer produces a range of options to segment the market further to an extremely high degree.

The soap manufacturers offer another familiar example of defining target markets. The contrast between them and car manufacturers is the price of the products. Economic segmentation and image segmentation are more difficult to work out.

The opportunity for the small manufacturer, wholesaler, or retailer is to identify a market segment which is not well served by other companies. In fact, such segments may be too small for the big company. By designing its product and marketing services especially for this group of buyers, a company may carve out a comfortable niche in the market.

Marketing means finding and filling real needs of customers; it is *not* forcing a product on people by advertising and gimmicks. The only reason a company should be in business is that it fills some need in the market better than any other company.

The Stanley Works was the first tool company to correctly read the 1970s trend toward increasing do-it-yourself remodeling and repairs. Seizing this opportunity, Stanley transformed itself from a sleepy toolmaker into the leading firm in the hand-tool industry by following the marketing concept. The company redesigned many of its hand tools for the amateur market and achieved production economies through longer runs. A costly television and print advertising campaign both promoted its tools and helped attract more people into do-it-yourself activity. Stanley pulled out of garden and power tools to concentrate on its strength in hand tools. As a result, Stanley's sales rose 18 percent in 1978, while earnings rose 27 percent. The company expects to ride a rising wave of expansion in the do-it-yourself market to a growth rate of 15 percent per year.

GET A COMPETITIVE EDGE

The firm must concentrate on a "competitive edge" to fulfill the marketing concept. This means that a company must seek to develop products or services which are better than its competitors'. It must also make customers aware that such products or services satisfy their needs better than competitive products.

Gerber Products Co., the country's largest baby-food maker, realized several years ago that the declining birth rate meant the total market for baby products would steadily shrink. Gerber made several abortive attempts at diversification, including catsup and single-serving adult foods. The company simply could not develop a competitive edge outside its traditional baby market. Gerber is now trying to build on its strength in baby food to develop a line of non-food juvenile products to be sold to the same people who use their baby food.

♦ ♦ ♦

Bausch & Lomb's share of the rapidly growing soft contact lens market fell from 100 percent in 1974 to not quite 50 percent in 1978. Since then, Bausch has employed superior marketing tactics and has developed its competitive edge to recapture a strong market position. Bausch has become a competitive pricer and has introduced better fitting and longer lasting lenses. It has instituted support service programs such as sending bills to patients. Bausch sells its lenses on consignment to both the commercial and professional retail markets, thus warehousing its lenses conveniently close to the consumer.

FOCUS ON PROFITS

An excellent way to go out of business is to act as if increasing sales is the goal of business instead of increasing profits. There have been numerous company presidents who have enlarged their companies by greatly increasing sales. They have thereby attained larger salaries for managing such expanding firms. The unfortunate part is that they were not *accountable* to an alert independent board of directors who asked, "What about profits?" Good marketing focuses on profits, not just sales volume. This policy and implementation should be checked in studying case problems.

Examples abound of companies that have apparently concentrated on increasing sales without sufficient emphasis on profit to keep the firm growing in a healthy way. This shows up most clearly when we look at the increase in profit/share-of-stock. This ratio is all-important to the owners (stockholders) who invest their money in the company when buying stock in the hope of either long-term capital gains or increased dividends. Note the following few illustrations.

Company	Sales ($ million)		$ Earnings/Share	
	1970	1978	1970	1978
Bell & Howell	298.6	567.5	2.02	2.20
Damon Corp.	34.5	131.9	.71	.03
Recognition Equipment	34.7	86.7	1.04	.80
Seatrain Lines	100.6	555.5	1.12	.77
Greyhound Corp.	2,740.0	4,351.2	1.40	1.33

We hear much today about the social responsibilities of companies and some people conclude that companies should even operate unprofitably if it is necessary to carry out such responsibilities. The simple truth is that companies which do not make a profit won't be around long. If social and ecological responsibilities are also required, then companies that don't both make a profit and fulfill societal responsibilities won't be in business.

WHAT DISTINGUISHES THE GOOD MARKETER?

The *best marketers* are those who possess the creative art of envisioning the key factors of the total complex business, of foreseeing the key factors in the future, and of creating superior strategies involving these factors. The *best marketers* are those who satisfy best the largest number of buyers at the greatest profit to their firms over *a number of years*. A "number of years" means at least ten years. There are many quick-buck operators, managers who ride the wave of an industrial expansion, or marketers who have found themselves with a good technical product who do not qualify as *good marketers* under our definition.

The good marketer recognizes that marketing is both an art and a science, and probably more art than science. Yet he or she does not hesitate to draw upon scientific methods to help whenever he or she can.

The "science" of marketing lies in making use of systematic procedures and utilizing knowledge from the more developed disciplines of mathematics, economics, sociology, psychology, anthropology, finance, accounting, and others.

Thus, Eastman Kodak Co. applies systematic research procedures to analyze its competitive position and to identify changing markets. The "art" of marketing determines the future of the company. It involves identifying reasons for lack of growth, identifying opportunities for the future, and conceptualizing the whole range of activities. This is not a mere mechanical procedure. Some companies such as GAF Corp., West Germany's Agfa-Gavaert, and Britain's Ilford Group Ltd., for example, have been unsuccessful in matching Kodak's appeal or products. Consequently, Kodak continues to dominate the market as its competitors struggle to survive.

Eastman Kodak Co. has been in a superior position in the market for photographic equipment for 101 years. Although it has remained strong, there are indicators of a tough challenge emerging. Like many other U.S. corporations. Kodak is having to deal with Japanese competition.

In order to deal with this competition effectively, Kodak is assessing its marketing techniques and competitive position—making adjustments where necessary. First of all, a new position has been created called the "chief of market intelligence," whose job it is to coordinate worldwide market research. Indications are that there will be heavy emphasis on demographic information in analyzing markets. Additionally, a team of strategic planners has been formed to look at potential for growth in areas outside of Kodak's traditional product range. Within the traditional lines however, efforts are being made to coordinate marketing and manufacturing functions. Consequently, the Photographic Division has been reorganized into one unit for all operations.

One of Kodak's strongest points has always been the uniqueness of its products. A good marketing concept thrives on this advantage, and Kodak is working to maintain it. Kodak currently has about 65 percent of the conventional film market and 40 percent of the world's color paper business. Both of these will continue to be areas of growth, but mainly in foreign countries. Kodak is also introducing new lines to encourage growth, such as small and inexpensive cameras that use discs instead of film rolled cartridges. Electronic cameras that use tape instead of film are the next proposed additions.

Kodak is introducing several unique nonphotographic products, too. A fast new office copier/duplicator that could replace offset printing for many uses, medical instruments such as Ektachem, a dry-slide blood analyzer, and a high speed electronic motion analysis system are examples. Areas of growth also include growth through acquisition. Kodak has already purchased Atex, Inc., one of the biggest suppliers of computer-based text editing systems to publishers.

According to Chairman Walter A. Fallon, Kodak doesn't want unlimited expansion. Its new growth and diversification is a response to a changing market. "I'll tell you what the real change has been at Kodak," Fallon states. "It has been in awareness."

In evaluating the marketing activities of a company, therefore, the good marketer will ask:

1. Is the art of marketing inherent in all activities of the company? That is, are innovative strategies and techniques sought and applied, or is all change resisted because of risk, fear, and inappropriate analysis?
2. Are scientific systematic procedures being employed where appropriate? Or is the company trying to create new concepts and strategies by mechanistic methods alone?
3. Is the marketing concept being applied in its totality?

ANALYZE THE MARKETING PHILOSOPHY, POLICIES, STRATEGY, AND OPERATIONS

If a company is in trouble or its marketing obviously isn't functioning well, the tendency is to start looking at sales reports, distribution, or some other functional subarea. This is often futile because any improvements made may just mean doing the wrong thing better.

For a firm which is stagnating or is heading for trouble, the priority of questions is:

1. Is the firm truly adhering to the *marketing concept?*
2. Have broad marketing policies been established?
3. Has the marketing strategy of the firm been well defined within the framework of broad policy?
4. Are the marketing operations being carried out effectively and efficiently?

We have already covered the marketing concept because of its importance to the whole business function. In order to help the case analyst, we will next point out examples of broad marketing policies and the need to tailor these individually to each company. Then we will discuss possible marketing strategies and factors in their selection. Finally, we will review marketing operations from the viewpoint of the marketing mix framework. A checklist of typical problems, weaknesses in implementing marketing activities, and possible corrective actions will be given.

The ability to change basic product and customer policy and strategy to meet a rapid fundamental change in the environment is critical to a company's prosperity. B.F. Goodrich Co., which has been selling primarily tires for 112 years, hit a long recession, highlighted by declining car sales and the switch by consumers from traditional bias-ply tires to long-lasting radials. John D. Ong, chief executive of Goodrich, recognized the potentially devasting effects of this trend, and B.F. Goodrich is switching from tires to chemicals as a main business. As Ong put it, "To stand still is to deteriorate. This is less risky than doing nothing."

Goodrich is placing the most emphasis on production of PVC—polyvinyl chloride. Developed by a Goodrich scientist, PVC is a versatile plastic used for everything from wire coating to upholstery to pipes. Goodrich still plans to make tires, but only the most profitable types. This will enable them to sell businesses not contributing to the new growth and use the proceeds from those sales to build new businesses instead of refitting the old ones. Goodrich currently holds world leadership in PVC and is in the process of more than doubling its production.

♦ ♦ ♦

Another company applying a strategy similar to Goodrich is Sears, Roebuck & Co. Sears has been in the retailing business for many years; however, recent revenue has not been encouraging, and profits have been declining since 1977—mainly because of marketing operations. While profits might come back up in the 1980s, Sears is expanding its operations into other areas including: specialty retailing, real estate, stock brokerage, and other financial services.

Sears has already opened business products stores featuring computer and electronic office products. There are plans for 200 stores to be opened by 1984. Sears current financial services include insurance (property, casualty, and life), auto and boat installment loans, savings and loan operations in California, commercial realty, and store leasing. Space for H & R Block and dental clinics, for example, is leased within Sears stores. Acquisition of Dean Witter Reynolds Organization Inc. and Coldwell Banker & Co. are further evidence of the growth process in stock brokerage and realty, respectively. Chairman of Sears, Edward R. Telling, plainly states that Sears plans to become "the largest consumer-oriented financial service entity."

MARKETING POLICIES FOR COMPANY STRATEGY

Top level marketing policies are directed to top managers who formulate company strategy and perform top level planning. These policies are called strategic marketing policies. Strategic marketing policies may cover seven areas:

1. Morality and public service,
2. Products,
3. Markets,
4. Profits,
5. Personal selling,
6. Customer relations,
7. Promotion.

MORALITY AND PUBLIC SERVICE

Policies on morality and public service may be general statements on the company's desire to be honest in its dealings with the public and its customers. At the end of the range such policies may be intended to avoid foreseeable hazards. For example, the president of General Electric in the 1950s foresaw the hazards of G. E. executives meeting with competitors to split up the turbine-generator market and fixing prices. He issued a policy designed to forestall such collusion which, unfortunately, was not followed. In some cases this led to criminal convictions of executives.

PRODUCT POLICIES

Policies on products may be designed to indicate the direction in which the firm will grow in the future, or they may be designed to keep the company from running off in all directions. Companies such as Xerox and IBM maintain policies of producing and marketing products in the information field. As a result of such broad policies, despite the fact that each started with completely different types of products, they have each expanded their products until they now overlap. It now appears that these two giants will become engaged in a major competitive struggle.

Product policies are also important at the retail level. Some department chains deal in low quality, low price goods while others are guided by a policy of providing high-quality, high price goods. A store may have a policy which limits its growth to only soft goods or only to durable goods. A manufacturer may limit its products to high-volume assembly-line classes of products, or the firm may be guided by a policy which restricts its products to more custom manufactured low-volume products with less competition. In evaluating a company, the analyst must determine if the company has policies, or is following policies, which are appropriate for the character and resources of the company and its potential markets. Are such policies consistent and clear? Are all people in the company aware of them?

MARKET POLICIES

Market policies are designed to clarify the geographic, customer, and other characteristics of the market as appropriate for the firm. Some examples of market policy concepts are as follows:

1. We will remain a local business (or a regional business or a multiregional business or a national business).
2. Our policy is to expand from regional markets to the national market.
3. Our policy is to reach all appropriate markets throughout the world.
4. We will market only in the consumer or the industrial or the defense goods markets. (Or a combination of these markets.)
5. We will sell only at retail (wholesale or to manufacturers).
6. We will avoid entering markets where any one firm holds more than 25% of the market.

7. No business will be conducted in a specified regional market until adequate outlets (or service centers or warehouses) have been established.
8. We will restrict ourselves to the high-technology markets.

PROFIT POLICIES

Policies with regard to profits place a large burden on marketing in two ways. They may require that sales goals be specified which will provide a large enough sales volume to provide a sizable *dollar* profit future. At the same time, a minimum profit as a *percentage* of sales may be specified which calls for low marketing costs. Marketing, therefore, must be involved in formulating such general market policies as well as in screening potential *new* products from the profit viewpoint.

Some questions the case analyst might ask are:

1. Are there profit policies stated which will affect the selection of new products and dropping of old ones?
2. Are profit policies stated for profits as a percent of sales and profits as a return on investment?
3. Do profit policies permit variations in profit by product group? By the phase of the life cycle of a product? For temporary competitive reasons?

PERSONAL-SELLING POLICIES

Personal-selling policies may be wide-ranging from those guiding the structure of the sales organization to those covering behavior of salesrepresentatives on the job. Because of the sensitivity of the salesperson-customer relationship, top management may be more concerned about this than other aspects of the business. Examples of possible policies are:

1. Only one representative of the company may call upon an account.
2. "House sales" will (or will not) be credited to the company instead of the salesperson in the territory.
3. Commissions accruing to a salesperson because of sales he or she closed will be paid to him or her in the event the salesperson separates from the company.
4. No "hard sell" will be permitted. The salesperson will only accept an order if it is in the best interest of the customer.
5. No deceptive practices will be employed to contact the customer or make the sale. Some years ago the producers of an encyclopedia were charged with using deceptive practices to gain entry to a home. Salespersons allegedly posed as researchers taking a survey.
6. No "kickbacks" will be given to customers. (These amount to price reductions or bribes.)
7. No bribery of foreign customs officials is permitted, despite general practices in the trade.

8. Salespeople will not be permitted to work the rest of the day after drinking alcohol.
9. Salespeople who do not bring in a minimum specified volume of sales each year will be separated if they have been with the company five years or less or reassigned or retrained if they have been with the company over five years.
10. All salespeople must complete a factory training program before their first assignment.

Other sales policies may relate to qualifications of salespeople, compensation, or constraints on sales managers.

CUSTOMER RELATIONS

Marketing policies covering the company's relations with customers may often be unwritten, especially those that take a hard line toward a small number of disgruntled customers. The analyst should look at actions of the firm which suggest policies it follows, such as:

1. The customer is always right. (Is this a written policy which is *not* followed or is it an unwritten policy which *is* followed?)
2. We (a large industrial firm making capital goods) will serve our customers night and day and provide emergency service on our equipment without regard to cost.
3. We will deal with our customers fairly but "at arm's length," purely on a legal or contractual basis.
4. Since our only customer is the government, we can recoup all costs of obtaining contracts. Therefore, we will spare no expense in entertaining official personnel.

PROMOTION

Broad company-wide promotion policies are not usually written, but the pattern of the advertisements reveals the underlying philosophy of management. Often top management plays a passive role condoning the copy which the advertising agency prepares or the schemes of some creative promoter within. Because the effects of advertising and sales promotion are difficult to measure, management has little to guide it. Some policies which companies have followed in the past and some which are followed today are:

1. We will not advertise; our product speaks for itself. (Hershey Co. followed this for many years, but changed its mind as competition grew.)
2. We will advertise big discounts by overstating the list prices. (Policy of a chain of appliance stores).
3. We will follow a policy of tasteful advertising at all times.
4. We will advertise our product in any legal way.
5. We will restrict our promotion to trade shows (or to industrial publications or to TV, etc.).
6. We will maintain a public service program as a part of promoting our company's name. (Xerox, General Electric, and other large

companies have sponsored public information and education programs on TV and taken part in movements to improve our environment.)

7. We will advertise *competitively,* i.e., we will spend as much (or more) of the total industry's advertising as a percentage as is our share of the market.
8. In good years we will reduce the percentage of advertising-to-sales cost in order to increase the percentage in poor years (when our competitors will be doing the opposite, lowering their advertising expenditures).
9. Policies regarding co-op advertising.
10. Policies regarding institutional advertising.

SUMMARY

The analysis of a case and the recommendations for action to be followed by the company under consideration requires a look at the philosophical policies of the company. These basic policies are revealed in the areas of morality and public service, product policies, market policies, profit policies, customer relations, and promotional policies. These policies must be examined relative to strategic marketing plans of the company. Are the policies consistent with marketing plans of the company. Are the policies consistent with marketing strategies? Should either, or both, basic marketing policies and marketing strategies be changed? *What* changes might benefit the company in the long run? In order to answer such questions, the student must be able to identify strategies and pitfalls in the area of marketing strategy. We will touch on some high points of this problem next.

MARKETING POLICY—WHAT TO DO

A company may innovate in product design, marketing, or manufacturing to obtain a competitive edge. A combination of innovation in each area may be used, but many firms find it necessary to adopt the innovations in two areas and concentrate on innovating in one activity.

The three basic policy options in marketing are:

1. Expand sales into new classes of customers.
2. Increase penetration in market segments corresponding to existing customers.
3. Make no marketing innovations; simply copy new marketing techniques and attempt to hold the present market share by product design and manufacturing innovations.

EXPANDING SALES INTO NEW MARKETS

While "expanding sales into new markets" may be a grand marketing strategy, specific "what to do" and "how-to-do" plans must be developed. To reach new markets, the firm may:

1. Expand geographically into new regions or new countries. The trend toward multinational giant corporations started with marketing expansion abroad.
2. Develop additional related products or models within its product line to reach clearly defined market segments not yet tapped. Jantzen's entry into the sportswear field from its base as a bathing suit manufacturer or Gillette's entry into the women's and eventually family's toiletry products are examples. Owens-Corning Fiberglass Corp. is an outstanding example of a company which has consistently expanded by finding many new fiberglass products and uses to compete against more basic materials such as wood, aluminum, or steel.
3. Develop completely new products unrelated to its present line. The Singer Company, which started with sewing machines, a consumer product, has expanded into a whole new line of products such as small computers. The thread which related this growth was Singer's experience in light manufacturing precision products.
4. Find new applications in new markets for the same product. The telephone companies reached new markets by arranging for data communication over existing transmission lines. Some rug dealers have found that there is a market for covering the walls as well as the floor of conference rooms. TV broadcasting stations are reaching a new market by means of educational programs.
5. Develop customized products. Companies which developed portable dishwashers and refrigerators on wheels reached a market of young apartment dwellers whose careers depended upon their moving from city to city or to new and larger residences at periods of several years.

   The opposite strategy is that of the custom manufacturer who attempts to expand into a mass market. This is difficult to achieve because of the new channels of distribution, different promotion techniques, and, generally, entrenched competitors.

   More commonly, a producer of low-cost, low-quality goods may be successful in upgrading to medium-quality goods. The problem is to overcome the reputation of the inferior goods. The Japanese manufacturers have been successful in this strategy.
6. Find a price-promotion mix which opens up new economic-class markets. RCA's introduction of color television is a classic case. By getting its price down to a certain threshhold and promoting color TV by subsidizing programs, RCA finally reached a broad middle-income class.

INCREASING PENETRATION OF PRESENT MARKET

Marketing has its most difficult task when it is directed toward increasing the penetration of a firm's product in a highly competitive marketplace. Consider such products as gasoline, peanut butter, cigarettes, and aspirin. The product differences in most cases are negligible. The major way to sell more product is to take customers away from well-entrenched competitors through superior marketing, although in some instances the total market can be expanded. Some major strategies which have been used successfully are listed below.

1. Develop competing products in a "product overlap" strategy. Procter & Gamble, Colgate-Palmolive-Peet, and the cigarette companies are examples of firms which try to reach new markets with competing variations of their products. Manufacturers may produce under their own label and under private labels different quality merchandise. The typewriter manufacturers, for example, produce their own brands and produce Sears Roebuck and Montgomery Ward brands.

   Another strategy is to sell a replacement part, primarily, but attempt to expand by selling to the manufactuer of the entire assembly (O.E.M. or original equipment manufacturer). The automobile tire manufacturers, spark plug makers, and producers of automotive air conditioning units are typical.

2. Product customization may be possible, to some extent, even in mass consumer markets. Automobiles, cigarettes, and soft drinks represent attempts along these lines. The true custom product is designed for one customer only. In the clothing business, some manufacturers who own retail outlets for men's suits attempt to sell "custom suits." The measurements taken at the retail store would be sent to the factory and the suit tailored to fit with final alterations at the store.

   More typically, tailors, nursery companies, interior decorating firms, and custom furniture manufacturers are illustrative of custom products and services.

3. Sell a product system concept instead of just the product. Remington Rand has long been known for selling office systems which if the customer bought the system, he or she also bought the products. Office furniture firms try to sell a complete furniture system including efficiency of operation, decor, layout, wall partitions, desk, files, and furniture.

4. Find a pricing and service mix which gives you a competitive edge. In some cases, the customers may want more service then your competitors are giving, even at a little higher price. This has been a successful strategy of large companies such as Sears Roebuck, IBM, and General Electric. The discount retail stores followed the opposite strategy of practically no service but low prices. Adjustment of warranty periods which add little cost may provide an attractive price-service combination.

   A number of companies, including retail stores, lease their products or complementary products in order to lower the investment of the user. For example, a hardware store may lease lawn care equipment, rug cleaning equipment, or power tools.

5. Seek promotional techniques which will drown out competitors' advertising or find unique distribution techniques which will cut costs and improve service.

6. Pinpoint markets by reducing variety of products and models. By concentrating on fewer but much better defined market segments, gains may be made against competitors who seek to cover broad market segments. Control Data Corporation originally competed against IBM by defining its customers as high technology firms which .had sophisticated programmers among their employees. CDC therefore sold specialized large computers at low competitive prices to customers who did not require much servicing or software from the supplier.

—MAKE NO MARKETING INNOVATIONS

The policy of adopting current marketing practices without trying to innovate is perhaps suitable for small firms whose strength lies in their technical competence. Rather than sinking money into untried marketing tactics, these firms depend simply on quality of product and innovations. Industrial firms such as these depend upon their being "known in the trade" because of the high quality, personal selling, and perhaps modest trade advertising programs.

In the retail business, there are frequently retail store managers who should follow this strategy, but instead they succumb to the pitfall of constantly attempting marketing innovations. They switch between high-price and low-price merchandise, they attempt promotional sales without any special lasting purpose; they embark on contests; and they increase variety beyond the optimum for their market and type of store. The result is that they project no clear image which will attract people to specific products and classes of goods.

SUMMARY

We have discussed the three basic "what-to-do" marketing policies. These are broad in concept. In analyzing cases, the student should determine which of these policies are appropriate for a company. It should be noted that different policies may be appropriate for different divisions of the same company.

Over the long term, a firm may follow one strategy for a number of years with the intent to switch after certain marketing goals have been achieved.

Once the basic strategic objectives have been determined, the next step for the analyst is to evaluate current "means" or plans. Considerable ingenuity is prized in developing plans and tactics of "how-to-do-it" in marketing. However, a systematic approach is useful for suggesting possibilities.

"HOW-TO-DO-IT" PLANS AND TACTICS

The "means" to strategic objectives involve marketing subfunctions. While we may analyze each subfunction separately, the final total strategy must be reviewed for consistency and unified sense of direction. In evaluating a company's plans for operations, the student may utilize the checklists which follow. We note that any particular means for achieving some single goal is not necessarily good or poor in itself; it's the whole complex of means which must be evaluated in total. In most case studies, only a small portion of the "means" will be described adequately for evaluation. On the other hand, the student is usually required to formulate *recommended* means for accomplishing the basic strategy of the company.

GAINING AND HOLDING A COMPETITIVE EDGE

1. Does the company have a competitive edge? If not, what is it doing about it?
2. Has the company defined its market? (Location, sex, age, education, occupation, socioeconomic quality, ethnic group, personal habits, leisure activities, and lifestyle.)
3. Is the product strategy clearly formulated and matched to the defined market and the company's special skills to give a competitive edge?
4. Has the company really measured the potential market in terms of both units and dollars? Has it considered a replacement market? A repair market?
5. Has a sales forecast been prepared, both long and short range, which takes into account the degree of competitive edge?
6. Has a breakeven point been computed for both old products and new products to determine if the expected sales volume will be adequate?
7. Has the breakeven analysis suggested ways of gaining a competitive edge by price reductions in different markets or for large purchasers?
8. Is the firm considering what competitors are doing to reduce its competitive edge? Are the competitors known and studied? Is the firm on the lookout for new competitors edging into the market or potentially threatening new products?
9. Is the firm closely following market changes due to shifts in the make-up of customers, their locations, and their values and preferences? Failure to do this may result in the competitive edge vanishing in a very short time.
10. Despite a competitive edge, is there some drawback such as (a) lack of wholehearted marketing attitude by all employees, (b) some product weakness, or (c) lack of vitality in promotion or distribution which may cause a disastrous loss of position to a new competitor?
11. Is the company coming into the market early in the life cycles of new products and switching to new products as profits begin a rapid decline in the maturity phase of the cycle?

12. Is the company clearly segmenting markets, matching product models (or lines) to segments and yet avoiding offering *overchoice* through *variety control* to maximize profits?

Often the strongest competitive edge is obtained through product superiority. This may be obtained by carefully segmenting the market and differentiating the product to suit that segment better than any competitor does. Here are some questions which help in analyzing the product relative to others on the market.

1. What are the physical attributes of the product? (size, shape, color, strength, smell, transparency, weight, consisting of liquid or powder, sound or tone, etc.) Which are better and which are worse compared with each competitive product?
2. What are the functional characteristics? For example, toothpaste is supposed to clean teeth, make the breath sweeter, toughen gums. A pen is supposed to write on specified surfaces, in a certain color, with a certain width of line for a specified minimum time.
3. What is the reliability, serviceability, maintainability, and functional life of the product? How do these functional characteristics compare with competing products?
4. How does the packaging improve the appearance of the product or serve as a bonus product. For example, for some brands of jelly, the jars can be used as glasses.
5. What attributes are really both *unique* and *important to the purchaser?*

HOW GOOD IS THE MARKETING RESEARCH?

1. Is the company conducting marketing research or just guessing at marketing decisions? Is there a formal marketing research organization or responsible person?
2. Does the company appear to be doing research on the right questions? No company can afford to do all the research it would like, so companies must select projects where the payoff is greatest.
3. Are the objectives of each research project carefully specified?
4. Is the company applying good judgment in its selection of techniques? That is, is simple library research being used or expensive experimentation as appropriate in terms of cost and the value of the decisions to be based on the research?
5. Are market tests made before national introduction of new products?
6. Is the research carefully designed with appropriate control of variables?
7. Are inferences and extrapolations logical? For example, advertising based around a TV sports program in New York City may be a success, but the same campaign in Dallas, Texas, might be expected to be a flop. The inference that both markets are similar would likely be illogical for many products and many marketing activities.

WHAT ADVERTISING AND SALES PROMOTION POLICIES ARE BEST?

1. Is advertising and sales promotion used to back up the salespeople or in place of them? For mail-order selling, advertising is extremely critical and sales should be measured directly against ads with carefully designed research studies.

   To back up the salespeople, the ad must prepare the way so that the product and the company are well known and have a clearly defined image.

2. For "mass" consumer markets, is there a carefully prepared advertising campaign? Are the theme, the copy, the media, the timing and the frequency of ads, and the duration appropriate? We notice that fur coats are now advertised in May to clear out goods and in August to lengthen the season. This has become the case with many style goods. With a limited ad budget, would this make sense for the company being studied?

3. Is the company logotype, trademark, or name tied into all products of affiliate companies or divisions?

4. How is the advertising budget developed? If it is a percent of projected sales, then the less you sell, the less you advertise when you need most to increase sales. On the other hand, there are diminishing returns from advertising so that we may expect that profits will be maximized for some calculated value of sales and advertising.

   Is the budget developed with the goal of obtaining a certain share of the market within a specified time? This represents a long-range view of profits since it will usually be expensive to make market gains if there are any strong competitors.

   Are ad budgets just haphazardly made to meet variations in competitor's advertising?

5. Are retail promotions employed to obtain brand switching? Stamps? Two for the price of one? Premiums? Are these really effective in obtaining new customers or are profits reduced?

   Are store demonstrations useful? Beauty aid manufacturers have found these work well when used selectively. Does it pay to use them for inexpensive novelty household products?

6. Are trade shows important if the firm produces industrial products? For what kind of products are trade shows especially important? Machine tool producers and toy manufacturers, for example, both use trade show promotion because the potential buyers are widely scattered geographically, not always identifiable, and because there are significant innovations each year.

7. Can the firm do enough advertising to make a real impact on the market? Promotion below a certain threshold is completely wasted from a consumer viewpoint, but can be profitable because of the impact on the dealer.

8. Do the salespeople have good sales kits, good *up-to-date* promotional materials, and quality catalogs?

9. Should the firm's products be promoted jointly or separately?
10. What unique innovative promotional techniques could this firm use to gain a strong competitive edge, at least temporarily? "Which twin has the Toni?" became a unique classic promotional theme for home permanents. Amoco gasoline jumped on the antipollution bandwagon as nonleaded gasoline. For years it had bucked advertising of other companies which promoted their lead in gasoline.

PERSONAL SELLING

1. Are company salespeople, agents, or brokers most appropriate?
2. Should sales offices be decentralized or should salespeople work out of corporate headquarters?
3. Should salespeople be matched to industry, government, and institutional customers or divided by product category?
4. Is there a basic sales strategy which takes into account:
   a. Number of accounts per salesperson and average account size.
   b. Compensation plan—salary, commission, salary and commission, salary or commission with bonus. The method of payment of expenses as reimbursement or built into the salary plan?
   c. Cost of obtaining new accounts vs. cost of holding old accounts. This determines how much time a salesperson should spend servicing accounts of a given size.
   d. Are overlapping territories or exclusive territories better?
   e. Should large accounts be serviced by headquarters to reduce commission expenses (called "house accounts")?
   f. Are the salespeople to be specialists in one product or line so that several salespeople may call on some customers? Or will the salespeople be generalists and handle the entire line with backup from, say, company engineers? Remember that specialists are easier to train and provide greater on-the-spot impact. Generalists must be trained well enough in all product areas so that they can handle most situations. One generalist to a customer leaves less confusion than when several specialists keep contacting the customer. What about the quality/quantity relationship? Would high-quality, high-paid salespeople be better than a larger number of less competent ones?
   g. How are older and decreasingly productive salespeople treated?
5. Are there regularly scheduled meetings of all salespeople each year?
6. Is there a continuous or special training program for salespeople?
7. Are there contests tied into promotions which stimulate salespeople several times a year?
8. Are salespeople given an opportunity to be trained and promoted into management positions?
9. Is there a good working relationship between the sales organiza-

tion and the marketing research group? This is important for sales forecasting and new product development.

10. Is the sales organization working closely and cooperatively with manufacturing? Are the salespeople getting into the factory to undercut production planners on orders? Is the factory cognizant of the need to expedite some orders? Are salesperson's promises and the factory's capability and willingness matched, or are customers not getting promised deliveries?

11. Is the sales organization putting its best effort and best salespeople in the most lucrative markets where it must meet the best competition head-on? Or does it seek unsuspected and untapped markets?

12. Does the vice-president or president come to the support of a salesperson who is struggling to land a big account?

CHANNELS OF DISTRIBUTION AND LOGISTICS STRATEGIES

The choice of channels of distribution is not a simple one, although it is often treated thoughtlessly as such. The tendency is to observe what other firms in the industry do and then copy them. If a firm is a manufacturer of hardware, it is apt to sell to wholesalers who sell to retail outlets. If a firm manufactures large appliances, it is apt to sell directly to dealers who sell to consumers.

The basic idea is to avoid competition at the many levels in the distribution chain, yet it is desirable to reduce logistics costs. For example, General Electric tried the concept of having dealers take orders for large appliances which were shipped directly to the purchaser-consumer in a few days from the wholesaler (who also did the servicing).

A very frequent problem occurs when a company uses two parallel channels of distribution in competition. For example, a manufacturer of shoes may have its own outlets and compete against retailers who buy its brand. The owned store may even undersell its competition. A manufacturer may sell to wholesalers as a general practice but sell to large retail stores or chains directly. Again, this is a problem because the wholesalers may drop the products in favor of competitors' products. Each manufacturer must resolve this conflict in his own way.

Another problem is whether to ship directly from the factory or establish regional warehouses. Regional warehouses mean more rapid service of both new items and *replacement parts*. At the same time, inventory carrying costs are likely to be higher because of the need to carry more inventory. However, shipments among warehouses may permit lower inventories. Such a strategy depends on the nature of the demand, relative location of warehouses, warehouse costs, the type of product, and transportation costs.

The selection of the ultimate outlet is very important because these outlets must be willing to work closely with the manufacturer on promotion of the products. If mass-type outlets such as drug chains, grocery chains, or supermarket chains are used, the product will have to fight for shelf space and position. If selected outlets such as retail carpeting stores, are chosen, particularly if there is territorial overlap, the firm's products may not receive the attention they would if exclusive territories were granted. Many products require the "pull" through the channel from the retail level helped by exclusive arrangements as well as the "push" by the manufacturer.

Whatever channels are selected, the firm should specify in advance criteria for selection of outlets and apply the criteria in practice.

PRICING STRATEGIES

A surprising number of companies, particularly those small one-person ventures, believe that there are only two pricing steps: add a profit on to cost and then charge anything above this that the market will bear. The student who has studied economics is well aware that for many products, the lower the price, the larger the volume. The goal is really to find the price-volume combination which will maximize profits. Since costs vary in some fashion with volume, the cost-volume relationship must also be accounted for. Those students with some quantitative background may estimate the shape of the revenue curve and cost curve as a function of units and thus find approximately the optimum volume to be sold per year.

Even this more advanced breakeven/profit graph does not represent the complexities of pricing in most real-life situations. Exhibit 6.1 summarizes the various pricing strategies the student has covered in previous course work. The case analyst must take into account, when setting a strategy:

1. The customer and channel of distribution
2. Competitive and legal forces
3. Annual volume and life cycle volume
4. Opportunities for innovative strategies over the life cycle or for special market promotions
5. Product group prices. The object is not to make a profit on each model, but to win customers so that profits on some models, and losses on supporting models, yield maximum *total* profits.

The marketing approach to pricing views price as only one aspect of selling a "satisfaction." It is the product itself, the price, the delivery, service, and fulfilling psychological needs which form the total package which the customer buys. *A lower price does not necessarily mean more units will be sold.* The price must be consistent with the product image. Consumers often perceive the quality of unknown products by the price (hence raising prices may increase sales).

It also should be noted that true prices are not always the stated price. By adding extra service, warranties, or paying transportation costs, a firm may sometimes effectively lower price without suffering the retaliation of lower prices by competitors with no resulting volume gains.

EXHIBIT 6.1

Pricing in Practice

Consultants—Professionals
  Hourly and daily rate
  Per consultation
  Per job - fixed fee
  Cost plus - fixed fee (CPFF)

Industry—Government
  Average Cost + Markup or Total Cost Pricing
  Target return on investment (ROI)
  Usual trade discounts
  Meeting competition
  Charging what the traffic will bear - monopoly pricing
  Marginal pricing
  Incremental pricing
  Marketing penetration pricing - Promotive pricing on new products, stay-out
    pricing
  Skimming pricing; life cycle pricing; high initial prices, sliding down the de-
    mand curve
  Maintenance of market share
  Put-out pricing; price low to eliminate weak competitors
  "Fair return" pricing - as high as you can get without exciting anybody and
    never low enough so that profits drop enough to excite stockholders
  "Administered" prices
  Stabilization pricing (prices to be kept from fluctuating)
  Follow the leader - national or in each market area
  Product-line pricing: carry full line even if some items are sold at a loss

Retail
  Odd number and round pricing: $3.95 vs. $4.00; $1.99 vs. $2.00
  Imitative pricing
  Discount (house) pricing
  Price lining - limited set of prices to cover all qualities
  Promotional pricing - cents off, stamps, coupons
  Loss-leader pricing

Price Differentials
  1. Quality - standard vs. deluxe
  2. Size specials - family size vs. economy vs. giant size
  3. Use differentials - milk for drinking vs. milk for cheese making - phones
      for business vs. residences
  4. Load factor differentials - movie prices afternoon vs. evening, peak and
      off-peak electric rates - phone rates
  5. Trial discounts
  6. Style cycle progressions - book editions, merchandise markdowns
  7. Trade discounts - prices vary at different points in the channel of distribu-
      tion
  8. Geographical discounts or differentials
  9. Customer discrimination discounts (professional services) (office equip-
      ment to industry, 15% off)

THE MARKETING MIX—A SUMMARY

The marketing mix consists of the combination of activities selected to achieve the marketing goals. This includes the allocation of resources to each activity. It is, perhaps, helpful to analyze each activity or very closely related groups of activities by the checklists, questions, and alternatives we have presented. The difficult task is to develop alternative feasible total programs or integrated strategies which fit the company's potential and its current resources.

The student, after developing such an integrated strategy, should check by asking:

1. Do all activities point toward unified objectives? That is, are marketing research, personal selling, advertising and promotion, distribution, and pricing all directed toward selling the same product and product image?
2. Are tradeoffs made so that each activity contributes the same net marginal benefit? That is, if dollars are taken away from the sales organization to be used in marketing research, are profits apt to fall?
3. Are programs, budgets, and schedules prepared on a formal basis at regular intervals (yearly, quarterly, etc.)?

Finally, we emphasize here a pitfall into which students constantly stumble. If advertising is weak, if the sales force appears to be too small, if the training program could be improved by a major expansion, the student advises a go-ahead. For each additional cost incurred, the student should be required to estimate the cost and the result on revenues and profits after taxes. For example, if he or she recommends setting up a new sales office on the West Coast with ten salespeople and a manager, the student should list likely salaries, rent, office furniture, clerical and communication costs, and anticipated revenue. Often he or she will be shocked to find that expansion to overcome current deficiencies results in a greater loss. *It is new systems, better procedures, better people, better management, and innovative ideas which make marketing pay off more.* If the marginal net benefit from one more marketing dollar spent is less than that for engineering or production, then that dollar should not go to marketing!

SUMMARY—MARKETING PITFALLS

There are some mistakes in marketing, which occur in so many companies in trouble, that the skilled consultant or analyst especially looks for these. Although these have been covered systematically in this chapter, we highlight these so-common problems here as *pitfalls:*

1. Overexpansion of sales when manufacturing cannot expand production rapidly enough to satisfy customers.

2. Too much favoritism to larger customers to the neglect of smaller customers. Associated with this pitfall is the failure to establish a policy with regard to maintaining a large number of small but, perhaps, profitless customer accounts.
3. Failure to keep up with changes in technology, consumer behavior patterns, environmental constraints. A producer of wooden boats was five years late in shifting to fiberglass. Electronic component manufacturers failed to shift to integrated circuits. Many *component* manufacturers are even today failing to recognize that customers are seeking *total systems* from a single producer who will install them and start them up.
4. Failure to recognize that every customer is all-important, *particularly during a sellers' market.*
5. Too much hunch in marketing decisions and not enough research and analysis. Lack of internal records is an associated pitfall.
6. Failure to establish a competitive edge *as seen by potential customers,* not the company's management.
7. Proliferation of models and items so that customers are confused, and sales, engineering, and production costs are excessive.
8. Lack of a clear-cut image. Lack of policy on objectives of the firm. A firm might try to produce both high-quality and low-quality clothing, for example. In one case, an elite resort hired a mediocre maitre d' and installed only a nine-hole golf course.
9. Constant drive towards cutting the price instead of improving the value. Related to this is the fear of raising prices along with quality or service.
10. The marketing team is constantly fighting with the production department rather than working as a team on design and packaging, forecasting and inventory control, and customer service.
11. Failure to coordinate personal selling, advertising, and promotion.
12. Failure to invest in salespeople as long-term valuable assets. This pitfall is reflected in poor compensation plans, lack of total company support of the salespeople in the field, lack of development plans for salespeople and treatment of long-service salespeople.

SELECTED BIBLIOGRAPHY ON MARKETING

Bailey, Earl L. (ed.). *Pricing Practices and Strategies.* New York: The Conference Board, 1978.

Brion, John M. *Corporate Marketing Planning.* New York: John Wiley & Sons, 1967.

Cravens, David W., and Hills, Gerald E. *Marketing Decision Making.* Rev. ed. Homewood, Ill.: Richard D. Irwin, 1980.

Kotler, Philip. *Marketing Management: Analysis, Planning, and Control.* 4th ed. Englewood Cliffs, N.J.: Prentice-Hall, 1980.

Lazer, William and Culley, James D. *Marketing Management: Foundations and Practices.* Boston: Houghton Mifflin, 1983.

McCarthy, E. Jerome. *Basic Marketing: A Managerial Approach.* 7th ed. Homewood, Ill.: Richard D. Irwin, 1981.

McDaniel, Jr., Carl. *Marketing*. 2d ed. New York: Harper & Row, 1982.

Pride, William M., and Ferrell, O. C. *Marketing: Basic Concepts and Decisions*. 2nd ed. Boston: Houghton Mifflin, 1980.

Stanton, William J. *Fundamentals of Marketing*. 6th ed. New York: McGraw-Hill, 1981.

Sullivan, William F., and Claycombe, W. Wayne. *Fundamentals of Forecasting*. Reston, Va.: Reston Publishing Co., 1977.

7

FUNCTIONAL AREA— ACCOUNTING AND FINANCE

FINANCIAL ANALYSIS FOR NON-FINANCIERS

This chapter is written for people who must operate businesses but are not seeking to become financial wizards. These people fall into one of two groups:

1. The large group of students and businesspeople who say, "I had some accounting and finance courses in school, but frankly I never liked them."
2. A large segment of the business population who know something about the subject but want to learn more. While they are "rusty," they realize that financial analysis is a worthwhile tool for determining strengths and weaknesses of a firm *or* one of its divisions *or* one of its departments.

Included in both groups will be (1) students in business policy courses who are required to evaluate firms by the "case method" of study; (2) people working in enterprises who have risen to management positions and want to be able to pinpoint problem areas in their own departments or better understand the interrelationship between all departments of a business; (3) entrepreneurs running their own firms who need to know the pitfalls to be avoided, or how a banker when approached for a loan, might analyze a business; and, (4) investors in securities to whom much of the analysis on "tout sheets" of brokerage houses is so much gobbledygook.

We assume that the reader has a little background in accounting, a minimum facility with arithmetic, and an ability to read a balance sheet and profit and loss statement. If the reader is uncertain about his or her skills in these areas, we suggest study of the appendices to this Chapter 7. Appendix A gives a simple review of business arithmetic, Appendix B covers breakeven analysis, and Appendix C provides simple definitions of common accounting terms.

We will not touch on the more advanced techniques of financial analysis. This is *not* to say they do not have their place, but we have chosen to show the simpler forms of analysis that are commonly used and can be mastered by the average person. Those who wish to delve deeper should refer to one of the many good specialized texts on the subject.

WHY BOTHER TO LEARN FINANCIAL ANALYSIS?

Financial analysis is one of the most important tools for analyzing the health of a business firm in its entirety or of subdivisions of the firm. Just as a physician asks you many questions about the symptoms of your poor health in order to determine your real sickness, so does a financial analysis point up *symptoms* that help to diagnose or pinpoint the real problems.

A doctor is not concerned about your headache (symptoms) per se, but rather the cause. For example, what causes your headache? Is it eye strain (real problem)? Is it from a stomach ulcer or a brain tumor (real problem)? Similarly, suppose a business manager making a financial analysis notices a rising trend in the ratio of long-term debt to invested capital. This could be a symptom of a serious underlying problem such as mismanagement of inventories or poor expense controls. On the other hand, the rising debt could be properly explained as a necessary increase needed to buy a new single-floor factory building that will increase efficiency and lower costs far more than the extra cost or added risk of the increased debt.

A good financial analyst can often (but not always) recognize the symptoms by knowing the right questions to ask, diagnose the real problems, and suggest the alternative courses of action that can be taken to improve or correct the situation. To help you recognize symptoms, diagnose problems, and suggest solutions we have included a section entitled *How to Improve Your Analytical Skills*.

JUST HOW GOOD IS FINANCIAL ANALYSIS?

Bankers, professional investors, and securities analysts, to name a few, have historically used financial analysis as the beginning point in their investigations. A typical approach would be a study of operating statements for five or ten years, including a trend analysis of sales, earnings, profits per share, debt/equity, etc., plus a ratio study comparing the firm being reviewed with published industry standards.

Despite the many years during which serious analysts have based many or most of their decisions primarily on the results of their financial investigation, there are *serious drawbacks*.

The LIMITATIONS to financial analysis are:

1. Accountants (those who are not good financial analysts) tend to focus on the *past*. Often they do not even prepare reports promptly enough to be useful. Rarely do they look at *future problems*.
2. Financial trends may or may not portend the future. Managers today must constantly have one eye on the present, one eye in the back of the head looking at the past, and two more eyes must be future oriented. This four-eyed monster portrays today's "promotable manager." How well a person can foresee and prepare in advance for future turns in the marketplace, the moves competitors will make, and the postures the company must take for next month, next year, and five years hence is vital. The future is rarely seen from financial analysis alone. Problems often can be sensed long before the figures reflect them. A new revolutionary process may make Company A's future extremely black and yet their statements will show only a long history of profitability.
3. In many industries, due to either rapid technological changes or fashion obsolescence, the figures tend to jump up and down like a yo-yo. These wide fluctuations prevent the ratios from being useful or meaningful.
4. Accounting data represent what the accountants believe, or interpret as true. In the big salad oil scandal of 1963, salad oil was moved from full tanks to empty tanks as inventory was taken so that assets were greatly overvalued.

In a 1977 court fight over a takeover bid, a federal judge found that Sharon Steel Corporation had used accounting methods which inflated its earnings. Sharon was forced to restate its earnings, lowering them 45%. Among his findings, the judge noted that Sharon:
1. Wrote up its iron ore inventory by $4.7 million.
2. Increased shipments to an affiliate and reported the resulting accounts receivable as income.
3. Paid an excess $1.2 million to its pension fund one year and reported the money as income the following year.
4. Reduced its inventories of some products which, under LIFO (Last-in/First-out) accounting, reduced its cost of goods sold and increased reported profits. A Sharon executive referred to such practices as "profit enhancement opportunities."

Source: adapted from *Business Week,* 9 May 1977, pp. 34–35.

---

5. Few people are good enough financial analysts to make figures really "sing." Financial analysis is an art mastered by few. For this reason much that is represented as financial analysis not only is superficial but actually leads to wrong conclusions.

The ADVANTAGES of financial analysis are:

1. *Trends do persist.* Management that can increase profits consistently in good or bad times is often very excellent management and will continue to operate well over a long period of years.
2. Financial analysis will often point up *symptoms* of basic problems that need to be improved. Good managers will therefore study accounting statements ever on the alert for the symptoms which point up serious problems to be solved.
3. Perhaps most important of all, to manage successfully one department or an entire business, a quantitative appraisal of the odds favoring differing courses of action is usually a "must." To make this appraisal requires at least a minimum of financial analytical skill. The rewards to the individual who improves quantitative proficiency will be large. If you work on mastering this section, you will be surprised and pleased with the results.
4. For those companies seeking outside capital, financial analysis is the method *most frequently used* by the sources of capital (bankers, investment firms, insurance companies) and hence will help the company raise the needed funds.
5. *Figures are more precise than words* and can often help the manager *pinpoint exactly where problems lie.* For example, the vice-president in charge of production of a firm was constantly being criticized for high production costs. It was only after costs had been studied for a period of time that he realized that small runs and increased employee turnover were increasing his make-up pay and hence his production costs. Fewer but longer runs were achieved after a concerted push on selected products by salespeople, reduced employee turnover, lowered make-up pay, and resulted in substantially reduced production costs.

Financial analysis can therefore be said to be a vital tool for analyzing the health of a business, but it must be used carefully and intelligently with a knowledge of its limitations.

MAJOR SOURCES OF FINANCIAL INFORMATION

GENERAL SOURCES

Some very useful general sources of financial information are:

1. *Moody's Manuals* which are available in most libraries. The annual manuals are published in five separate volumes according to types of business and present financial statements in detail.
2. *Standard & Poor's Manuals and Surveys* which are similar to Moody's (financial statements) but additionally, its Industry Surveys are compilations of group data on a number of industries.
3. *Major brokerage houses* (Merrill, Lynch, Pierce, Fenner & Smith; Dean Witter Reynolds, Inc., E. F. Hutton & Co., etc.) which often provide detailed reports both on individual companies and on industries.

4. *Annual reports sent to stockholders* of most larger firms which are available in libraries, from the firm itself, or from stockbrokers. Also helpful may be the prospectuses from firms required by the S.E.C. when new stock is being sold.

5. *Trade Associations* which often publish yearly industry data and statistics, for example, National Retail Merchants Association, American Iron & Steel Institute, National Retail Hardware Association. Such associations and their addresses are listed in the *Encyclopedia of Associations* (Detroit: Gale Research Co.) or *Directory of National Trade Associations,* U.S. Government Printing Office.

6. Publications by *Federal government agencies* (Department of Commerce) *Facts for Industry, Industry Reports, Statistical Abstract, Census of Business,* Small Business Administration (S.B.A.) books, and trade publications.[1]

RATIO REPORTS

It is very helpful to the businessperson, banker, or financial analyst to compare the key financial ratios for the company under study to the corresponding ones for the industry. Robert Morris Associates and Dun & Bradstreet are two financial services firms which supply industry-wide ratios for manufacturing, wholesaling, and retailing firms.

Leo Troy's *Almanac of Business and Industrial Ratios,* Prentice-Hall (current edition), also provides industry financial ratios over a range of 12 companies classified by size of assets.

The *Annual Statement Studies* published by Robert Morris Associates each September is primarily used by bankers. The data provide benchmarks to evaluate the financial health of a firm when a businessperson comes in for advice or a loan. Exhibit 7.1 shows the format of the data in this report.

Dun & Bradstreet have for many years provided the business community with 14 key ratios by means of which a businessperson or analyst can compare a specific business with other *like* businesses. Besides a complete annual report, parts of the annual report appear in the October, November, and December issues of *Dun's Review.* Sample pages of the annual report are shown in Exhibit 7.2.

Disclaimer Statement—Exhibit 7.1

RMA cannot emphasize too strongly that their composite figures for each industry may *not* be representative of that entire industry (except by coincidence), for the following reasons:

1. The only companies with a chance of being included in their study in the first place are those for whom their submitting banks have recent figures.

2. Even from this restricted group of potentially includable companies, those which are chosen, and the total number chosen, are not determined in any random or otherwise statistically reliable manner.

EXHIBIT 7.1

Manufacturers-Miscellaneous Fabricated Wire Products

SIC# 3496

	Current Data						Comparative Historical Data				
	62(6/30-9/30/80)			66(10/1/80-3/31/81)			6/30/76-3/31/77	6/30/77-3/31/78	6/30/78-3/31/79	6/30/79-3/31/80	6/30/80-3/31/81
	0-1MM	1-10MM	10-50MM	50-100MM	ALL		ALL	ALL	ALL	ALL	ALL
NUMBER OF STATEMENTS	42	60	27	1	130	ASSET SIZE	88	107	117	123	130
ASSETS	%	%	%	%	%		%	%	%	%	%
Cash & Equivalents	7.9	7.6	5.3		7.2		6.9	7.9	6.6	6.4	7.2
Accts & Notes Rec Trade(net)	27.5	23.3	23.1		24.7		25.5	25.3	28.1	27.6	24.7
Inventory	30.7	32.2	26.3		30.6		28.1	30.3	32.3	31.4	30.6
All Other Current	.8	1.8	2.3		1.6		1.3	1.1	1.3	1.6	1.6
Total Current	66.8	65.0	57.0		64.0		61.9	64.6	68.4	67.1	64.0
Fixed Assets (net)	27.2	27.6	34.9		28.8		30.5	26.9	24.8	26.3	28.8
Intangibles (net)	.7	.4	.1		.4		.5	.9	.3	1.0	.4
All Other Non-Current	5.3	7.0	8.0		6.7		7.2	7.6	6.5	5.7	6.7
Total	100.0	100.0	100.0		100.0		100.0	100.0	100.0	100.0	100.0
LIABILITIES											
Notes Payable-Short Term	7.8	11.4	4.5		8.8		8.9	7.8	10.7	9.3	8.8
Cur. Mat-L/T/D	5.3	2.5	2.5		3.4		3.5	2.7	3.2	2.9	3.4
Accts & Notes Payable-Trade	16.2	15.1	11.9		14.9		14.1	15.4	16.1	17.5	14.9
Accrued Expenses	6.9	7.0	5.3		6.6		6.8	6.3	6.4	6.4	6.6
All Other Current	2.8	4.2	3.1		3.5		4.2	2.8	3.8	3.7	3.5
Total Current	39.0	40.2	27.4		37.1		37.4	35.1	40.1	39.7	37.1
Long Term Debt	16.4	11.3	21.0		15.0		14.0	13.4	12.8	13.0	15.0
All Other Non-Current	4.4	.1	2.1		2.4		2.0	1.9	1.7	1.6	2.4
Net Worth	40.1	47.3	49.6		45.5		46.6	49.7	45.4	45.7	45.5
Total Liabilities & Net Worth	100.0	100.0	100.0		100.0		100.0	100.0	100.0	100.0	100.0
INCOME DATA											
Net Sales	100.0	100.0	100.0		100.0		100.0	100.0	100.0	100.0	100.0
Cost Of Sales	72.1	74.9	74.8		74.1		77.3	76.4	75.7	74.2	74.1
Gross Profit	27.9	25.1	25.2		25.9		22.7	23.6	24.3	25.8	25.9
Operating Expenses	22.9	18.3	17.3		19.5		17.2	18.1	17.8	19.1	19.5
Operating Profit	5.0	6.8	7.8		6.4		5.6	5.5	6.5	6.7	6.4
All Other Expenses (net)	1.4	1.5	2.4		1.6		1.0	.9	1.3	1.6	1.6
Profit Before Taxes	3.5	5.3	5.5		4.8		4.6	4.6	5.2	5.1	4.8
RATIOS											
Current	2.1	2.4	2.8		2.4		2.6	3.2	2.6	2.5	2.4
	1.8	1.6	2.1		1.8		1.7	1.9	1.7	1.7	1.8
	1.3	1.2	1.8		1.3		1.3	1.4	1.3	1.4	1.3
Quick	1.2	1.3	1.3		1.3		1.3	1.7	1.3	1.4	1.3
	.9	.9	1.1		.9		1.0	.9	.9	.9	.9
	.6	.6	.9		.6		.6	.6	.6	.6	.6
Sales/Receivables	27 13.3	30 12.1	39 9.3		31 11.7		31 11.9	34 10.8	36 10.1	34 10.6	31 11.7
	37 9.9	39 9.3	48 7.6		40 9.2		42 8.7	45 8.2	46 7.9	44 8.3	40 9.2
	49 7.5	44 8.0	59 6.2		50 7.3		53 6.9	53 6.9	56 6.5	54 6.7	50 7.3
Cost of Sales/Inventory	27 13.6	43 8.5	54 6.7		41 8.9		41 9.0	45 8.2	38 9.6	42 8.6	41 8.9
	64 5.7	69 5.3	91 4.0		69 5.3		64 5.7	69 5.3	72 5.1	68 5.4	69 5.3
	94 3.9	104 3.5	104 3.5		104 3.5		87 4.2	96 3.8	107 3.4	111 3.3	104 3.5
Sales/Working Capital	5.9	5.3	4.2		5.1		5.0	4.3	5.1	5.2	5.1
	9.8	8.4	6.3		7.9		8.1	7.0	7.9	7.8	7.9
	17.1	34.3	7.5		16.2		21.2	13.7	15.1	15.9	16.2
EBIT/Interest	(37) 5.5	(48) 10.4	(26) 7.7		(112) 7.7		(65) 13.9	(82) 12.1	(95) 9.5	(105) 10.0	(112) 7.7
	3.1	3.6	3.0		3.2		3.8	5.2	5.0	5.0	3.2
	1.8	1.5	1.1		1.6		2.1	2.1	2.5	2.2	1.6
Cash Flow/Cur. Mat. L/T/D	(26) 4.2	(40) 11.6	(24) 8.5		(91) 9.1		(53) 15.4	(63) 8.2	(75) 7.1	(81) 9.6	(91) 9.1
	2.6	6.9	3.8		3.8		3.2	3.8	3.6	3.8	3.8
	1.0	2.4	3.0		1.9		2.1	1.7	1.9	1.9	1.9
Fixed/Worth	.3	.4	.4		.4		.3	.3	.3	.3	.4
	.6	.6	.8		.6		.7	.6	.5	.6	.6
	1.2	.9	.9		1.0		1.1	.9	.9	1.0	1.0
Debt/Worth	1.0	.6	.6		.7		.6	.6	.7	.7	.7
	1.7	1.2	1.0		1.3		1.1	1.0	1.4	1.3	1.3
	2.7	2.2	1.5		2.3		2.6	2.0	2.5	2.2	2.3
% Profit Before Taxes/Tangible Net Worth	(41) 45.3	34.7	28.6		(129) 36.0		(87) 37.2	(105) 32.7	(116) 38.6	(121) 36.3	(129) 36.0
	24.9	18.2	17.6		19.0		20.3	20.0	23.4	24.2	19.0
	10.5	8.2	2.3		8.9		7.4	7.8	11.7	12.8	8.9
% Profit Before Taxes-Total Assets	14.8	15.4	17.6		15.0		16.9	15.2	16.7	16.3	15.0
	8.5	8.3	8.7		8.6		9.3	8.7	9.8	9.4	8.6
	4.3	2.7	.7		3.2		2.9	4.4	5.2	5.4	3.2
Sales/Net Fixed Assets	19.9	13.5	5.9		15.6		13.1	15.5	18.5	15.5	15.6
	13.1	8.6	4.7		7.9		7.2	8.2	10.7	9.1	7.9
	5.7	5.9	3.7		4.9		4.4	5.2	5.6	5.6	4.9
Sales/Total Assets	3.2	2.6	2.0		2.7		2.6	2.5	2.6	2.6	2.7
	2.5	2.2	1.6		2.7		2.0	2.1	2.1	2.1	2.2
	2.2	1.7	1.2		1.7		1.6	1.6	1.7	1.7	1.7
% Depr.,Dep.,Amort./Sales	(40) 1.1	(56) 1.1	(26) 2.1		(173) 1.3		(82) 1.6	1.2	1.1	1.2	1.3
	1.7	1.9	2.8		2.1		2.3 (100)	2.0 (105)	1.8	1.9 (123)	2.1
	3.1	2.9	3.9		3.7		3.2	2.7	2.6	2.5	3.7
% Lease & Rental Exp/Sales	(26) .4	(28) .3			(61) .5		(37) .3	.4	.4	.5	.5
	1.1	1.1			1.7		1.3 (50)	1.3 (53)	1.1 (56)	1.0 (61)	1.2
	2.4	2.1			2.7		2.1	2.2	2.3	2.0	2.2
% Officers Comp/Sales	(24) 3.3	(25) 1.8			(54) 1.9		(37) 1.7	1.6	1.7	2.0	1.9
	3.3	2.7			3.6		3.3 (52)	3.0 (52)	3.7 (49)	3.6 (54)	3.6
	11.3	6.3			8.1		5.7	5.7	6.6	5.9	8.1
Net Sales ($)	61135M	398148M	981891M	179286M	1620489M		688920M	901332M	1227497M	1459771M	1620459M
Total Assets ($)	23765M	183138M	683627M	61913M	952433M		367921M	475888M	648628M	703330M	952433M

© Robert Morris Associates 1981

M – $thousand   MM $million
See Pages 1 through 11 for Explanation of Ratios and Data

EXHIBIT 7.1 (Continued)

Manufacturers-Paperboard Containers & Boxes

SIC# 2651 (52,53,54,55)

	Current Data 94(6/30-9/30/80)				131(10/1/80-3/31/81)		Comparative Historical Data				
ASSET SIZE / NUMBER OF STATEMENTS	0-1MM 94	1-10MM 108	10-50MM 18	50-100MM 5	ALL 225		6/30/76-3/31/77 ALL 199	6/30/77-3/31/78 ALL 206	6/30/78-3/31/79 ALL 187	6/30/79-3/31/80 ALL 227	6/30/80-3/31/81 ALL 225
ASSETS	%	%	%	%	%		%	%	%	%	%
Cash & Equivalents	8.5	5.9	8.0		7.2		6.8	7.0	6.1	5.8	7.2
Accts. & Notes Rec.-Trade(net)	29.7	23.8	18.6		25.8		26.4	26.2	26.7	26.5	25.8
Inventory	23.0	24.6	18.5		23.5		24.4	23.6	25.0	24.1	23.5
All Other Current	1.7	1.2	.9		1.4		1.8	1.4	1.5	1.4	1.4
Total Current	62.9	55.5	46.0		57.8		59.3	58.2	59.3	57.3	57.8
Fixed Assets (net)	30.4	37.0	43.7		34.6		33.4	33.9	33.4	34.9	34.8
Intangibles (net)	.3	.8	.4		.6		.5	.6	.6	.6	.6
All Other Non-Current	6.4	6.7	9.9		7.0		6.7	7.1	6.7	7.2	7.0
Total	100.0	100.0	100.0		100.0		100.0	100.0	100.0	100.0	100.0
LIABILITIES											
Notes Payable-Short Term	7.9	6.8	2.3		6.9		8.6	8.1	7.3	6.9	6.9
Cur. Mat.-L/T/D	3.9	4.4	2.5		4.0		3.3	3.7	4.5	4.5	4.0
Accts. & Notes Payable-Trade	18.7	15.0	12.0		16.2		15.4	16.9	16.3	16.2	16.2
Accrued Expenses	6.1	5.5	5.4		5.8		6.5	6.3	6.2	5.7	5.8
All Other Current	2.3	2.9	1.9		2.5		5.3	3.4	2.6	2.3	2.5
Total Current	38.9	34.7	24.2		35.3		39.2	38.4	36.9	35.6	35.3
Long Term Debt	16.9	22.9	26.2		20.6		16.5	17.3	18.2	21.0	20.6
All Other Non-Current	1.2	2.2	2.3		1.8		2.3	1.7	2.2	2.6	1.8
Net Worth	42.9	40.2	47.4		42.2		42.0	42.6	42.8	40.8	42.2
Total Liabilities & Net Worth	100.0	100.0	100.0		100.0		100.0	100.0	100.0	100.0	100.0
INCOME DATA											
Net Sales	100.0	100.0	100.0		100.0		100.0	100.0	100.0	100.0	100.0
Cost Of Sales	72.6	76.7	74.4		74.9		74.3	75.4	75.9	75.7	74.9
Gross Profit	27.4	23.3	25.6		25.1		25.7	24.6	24.1	24.3	25.1
Operating Expenses	23.7	18.3	21.3		20.7		20.4	20.1	20.1	19.8	20.7
Operating Profit	3.8	5.0	4.3		4.5		5.3	4.5	4.0	4.5	4.5
All Other Expenses (net)	.9	1.5	.6		1.1		1.1	1.6	1.0	1.4	1.1
Profit Before Taxes	2.9	3.5	3.7		3.3		4.2	2.9	2.9	3.2	3.3
RATIOS											
Current	2.4	2.4	2.2		2.4		2.4	2.3	2.4	2.3	2.4
	1.7	1.7	1.8		1.7		1.7	1.6	1.7	1.7	1.7
	1.2	1.2	1.7		1.2		1.2	1.2	1.2	1.2	1.2
Quick	1.6	1.3	1.2		1.4		1.3	1.3	1.4	1.3	1.4
	1.0	.9	1.0		1.0		.9	.9	.9	.9	1.0
	.7	.6	.8		.7		.6	.6	.6	.6	.7
Sales/Receivables	27 13.5	31 11.6	29 12.8		29 12.7		28 12.9	28 13.0	30 12.2	30 12.0	29 12.7
	35 10.5	38 9.5	30 12.1		37 9.9		35 10.3	37 9.9	37 9.9	38 9.5	37 9.9
	46 7.9	46 7.9	41 9.0		46 8.0		46 8.0	45 8.2	47 7.7	46 7.9	46 8.0
Cost of Sales/Inventory	17 21.0	28 12.9	33 11.1		24 15.4		26 14.3	26 14.1	27 13.4	24 13.4	26 14.3
	37 9.9	52 7.0	40 9.2		47 7.7		45 8.1	46 8.0	47 7.7	51 7.2	47 7.7
	62 5.9	79 4.6	66 5.5		72 5.1		74 4.9	66 5.5	76 4.8	70 5.2	72 5.1
Sales/Working Capital	7.0	6.3	7.2		6.6		6.6	7.2	6.5	6.6	6.6
	11.6	10.1	9.1		10.2		11.5	10.9	9.8	10.8	10.2
	31.5	35.9	14.7		29.6		26.9	34.8	26.8	24.0	29.6
EBIT/Interest	(77) 5.6	(97) 4.7	(17) 7.1		(195) 5.3		(159) 13.5	(165) 10.3	(144) 6.4	(191) 6.8	(195) 5.3
	3.0	2.6	2.9		2.9		5.2	4.9	3.2	3.1	2.9
	1.2	1.5	1.7		1.5		2.2	2.1	1.8	1.6	1.5
Cash Flow/Cur. Mat. L/T/D	(55) 6.2	(81) 4.1	(17) 7.7		(158) 5.6		(124) 6.0	(126) 4.6	(126) 3.7	(162) 5.2	(158) 5.6
	2.8	2.4	4.2		2.7		2.8	2.4	2.4	2.4	2.7
	1.1	1.3	2.6		1.4		1.4	1.4	1.4	1.3	1.4
Fixed/Worth	.3	.6	.7		.5		.5	.5	.4	.5	.5
	.7	1.0	1.0		.8		.7	.8	.8	.9	.8
	1.4	1.6	1.3		1.5		1.3	1.4	1.3	1.6	1.5
Debt/Worth	.7	.9	.8		.8		.6	.7	.8	.8	.8
	1.3	1.6	1.2		1.3		1.3	1.3	1.3	1.4	1.3
	2.6	2.8	2.0		2.6		2.6	3.1	2.6	3.0	2.6
% Profit Before Taxes/Tangible Net Worth	(86) 32.2	28.9	23.9		(215) 29.0		(191) 35.9	(199) 36.6	(182) 32.3	(220) 31.6	(215) 29.0
	18.5 (106)	16.4	16.8		17.4		20.5	19.4	16.9	18.2	17.4
	7.4	7.9	6.2		8.1		9.1	7.9	6.8	8.8	8.1
% Profit Before Taxes/Total Assets	15.7	11.5	10.5		13.2		17.0	14.9	12.9	13.7	13.2
	8.0	6.2	7.1		7.2		7.9	7.8	6.7	7.0	7.2
	1.9	2.7	3.4		2.7		3.9	2.3	2.3	2.0	2.7
Sales/Net Fixed Assets	17.6	9.5	6.1		11.9		13.0	13.5	13.4	10.9	11.9
	10.4	5.8	4.8		6.8		7.6	7.1	7.6	7.1	6.8
	5.6	3.9	3.7		4.3		4.4	4.7	4.6	4.4	4.3
Sales/Total Assets	3.7	2.7	2.2		3.1		3.1	3.1	3.1	3.0	3.1
	2.9	2.0	2.0		2.2		2.3	2.4	2.3	2.3	2.2
	2.0	1.7	1.8		1.8		1.9	1.9	1.8	1.8	1.8
% Depr. Dep. Amort./Sales	1.2	1.8	1.7		1.6		1.3	1.5	1.5	1.5	1.6
	(90) 1.8	(102) 2.5	2.8		(215) 2.2		(187) 2.1	(189) 2.1	(177) 2.2	(210) 2.2	(215) 2.2
	2.6	3.3	3.8		3.1		2.8	2.9	3.0	3.2	3.1
% Lease & Rental Exp/Sales	1.5	.4			.8		1.0	1.1	1.4	1.2	.8
	(54) 2.6	(56) 1.6			(116) 2.0		(108) 2.2	(108) 2.2	(92) 2.3	(117) 1.9	(116) 2.0
	3.6	2.4			3.2		3.1	3.2	3.2	3.3	3.2
% Officers' Comp/Sales	3.0	1.5			2.1		2.3	2.2	2.2	2.0	2.1
	(49) 4.8	(50) 2.6			(101) 3.3		(98) 3.9	(106) 3.5	(92) 3.4	(107) 3.1	(101) 3.3
	7.3	4.0			5.7		5.9	5.9	6.2	5.7	5.9
Net Sales ($)	137896M	767337M	720714M	558942M	2184889M		1342409M	1143204M	1090135M	1702648M	2184889M
Total Assets ($)	48576M	354708M	351481M	343259M	1098024M		664296M	559288M	546480M	816709M	1098024M

‹ Robert Morris Associates 1981

M = $thousand   MM = $million

See Pages 1 through 11 for Explanation of Ratios and Data

Source: *Annual Statement Studies,* 1981 ed., Philadelphia, Pa.: The Robert Morris Associates, 1981, pp. 135 and 141.

Disclaimer Statement—Exhibit 7.1 (*Continued*)

3. Many companies in their study have *varied* product lines; they are "miniconglomerates," if you will. All they can do in these cases is categorize them by their *primary* product line, and be willing to tolerate any "impurity" thereby introduced.

In a word, don't automatically consider their figures as representative norms and don't attach any more or less significance to them than is indicated by the unique aspects of the data collection.

Dun's figures are gathered from as many firms of a particular category as possible. Let us take women's ready-to-wear retail stores as an example to demonstrate the meaning of the three figures in each box of the report (see exhibit 7.2). Suppose data on net profit/net sales have been gathered on 9558 stores. The ratios are arranged in order on a list with the best ratio at the top and the poorest ratio at the bottom. On inspection, the ratio in the middle is called the MEDIAN of the group. It is also called the MIDDLE QUARTILE figure. In our case, it can be seen to be 5.00 percent in Exhibit 7.2.

The ratio halfway between the median and the top figures is the UPPER QUARTILE ratio. In our case, this ratio is 10.71 percent. That is, exactly one fourth of the firms have a net profits/net sales ratio better than 10.71 percent. On the other hand, exactly one fourth of the firms have a value for net profit/net sales below 1.68 percent as shown in Exhibit 7.2. Note in some cases such as fixed assets/net worth, smallest ratios are best.

Most businesspeople are *not satisfied* if they are doing only average or close to the median (middle quartile) because this means to them if they have 100 competitors, they are ranked about 50th! As a result, many top business firms attempt to be near the top of the range or at the top unless for some specific competitive reason they decide to pay no attention to the particular ratio. For example, a firm may feel that excellent deliveries are more important to its business success than any other single factor. In this case it may decide that even with the best forecasting and inventory management, it will still need a larger inventory than many of its competitors. Hence, it will be satisfied with less than the best inventory turnover.

RATIO COMPARISONS

Conglomerates can only be compared when figures for divisions of the conglomerate are shown separately. Then the comparison must be on the basis of each division. If, however, you have a case where a large preponderance of the firm's business is in one area which is shown in Dun's, *use it* and make the necessary suppositions or adjustments.

Warning: Be sure to use the category in Dun's most like the business you are examining. Note, for example, there are separate figures shown for electrical industrial apparatus and for electronic components and accessories. Another example might be paints and

EXHIBIT 7.2

How the Ratios are Figured

Although terms like "median" and "quartile" are everyday working language to statisticians, their precise meaning may be vague to some businessmen.

In the various ratio tables, three figures appear under each ratio heading. The center figure in bold type is the **median;** the figures immediately above and below the median are, respectively, the **upper** and **lower quartiles.** To understand their use, the reader should also know how they are calculated.

First, year-end financial statements from concerns in the survey (almost exclusively corporations with a tangible net worth over $100,000) are analyzed by Dun & Bradstreet statisticians. Then each of 14 ratios is calculated individually for every concern in the sample.

These individual ratio figures, entered on data-processing cards, are segregated by line of business, and then arranged in order of size—the best ratio at the top, the weakest at the bottom. The figure that falls in the middle of this series becomes the **median** for that ratio in that line of business. The figure halfway between the median and the top of the series is the **upper quartile;** the number halfway between the median and the bottom of the series is the **lower quartile.**

In a statistical sense, each median then is the **typical ratio figure** for all concerns studied in a given line. The upper and lower quartile figures typify the experience of firms in the top and bottom halves of the sample respectively.

CURRENT ASSETS TO CURRENT DEBT
Current Assets are divided by total Current Debt. Current Assets are the sum of cash, notes and accounts receivable (less reserves for bad debt), advances on merchandise, merchandise inventories, and Listed, Federal, State and Municipal securities not in excess of market value. Current Debt is the total of all liabilities falling due within one year. This is one test of solvency.

NET PROFITS ON NET SALES
Obtained by dividing the net earnings of the business, after taxes, by net sales (the dollar volume less returns, allowances, and cash discounts). This important yardstick in measuring profitability should be related to the ratio which follows.

NET PROFITS ON TANGIBLE NET WORTH
Tangible Net Worth is the equity of stockholders in the business, as obtained by subtracting total liabilities from total assets, and then deducting intangibles. The ratio is obtained by dividing Net Profits after taxes by Tangible Net Worth. Tendency is to look increasingly to this ratio as a final criterion of profitability.

Generally, a relationship of at least 10 per cent is regarded as a desirable objective for providing dividends plus funds for future growth.

NET PROFITS ON NET WORKING CAPITAL
Net Working Capital represents the excess of Current Assets over Current Debt. This margin represents the cushion available to the business for carrying inventories and receivables, and for financing day-to-day operations. The ratio is obtained by dividing Net Profits, after taxes, by Net Working Capital.

NET SALES TO TANGIBLE NET WORTH
Net Sales are divided by Tangible Net Worth. This gives a measure of relative turnover of invested capital.

NET SALES TO NET WORKING CAPITAL
Net Sales are divided by Net Working Capital. This provides a guide as to the extent the company is turning its working capital and the margin of operating funds.

EXHIBIT 7.2 (Continued)

COLLECTION PERIOD
Annual net sales are divided by 365 days to obtain average daily credit sales and then the average daily credit sales are divided into notes and accounts receivable, including any discounted. This ratio is helpful in analyzing the collectibility of receivables. Many feel the collection period should not exceed the net maturity indicated by selling terms by more than 10 to 15 days. When comparing the collection period of one concern with that of another, allowances should be made for possible variations in selling terms.

NET SALES TO INVENTORY
Dividing annual Net Sales by Merchandise Inventory as carried on the balance sheet. This quotient does not yield an actual physical turnover. It provides a yardstick for comparing stock-to-sales ratios of one concern with another or with those for the industry.

FIXED ASSETS TO TANGIBLE NET WORTH
Fixed Assets are divided by Tangible Net Worth. Fixed Assets represent depreciated book values of building, leasehold improvements, machinery, furniture, fixtures, tools, and other physical equipment, plus land, if any, and valued at cost or appraised market value. Ordinarily, this relationship should not exceed 100 percent for a manufacturer, and 75 percent for a wholesaler or retailer.

CURRENT DEBT TO TANGIBLE NET WORTH
Derived by dividing Current Debt by Tangible Net Worth. Ordinarily, a business begins to pile up trouble when this relationship exceeds 80 percent.

TOTAL DEBT TO TANGIBLE NET WORTH
Obtained by dividing total current plus long term debts by Tangible Net Worth. When this relationship exceeds 100 percent, the equity of creditors in the assets of the business exceeds that of owners.

INVENTORY TO NET WORKING CAPITAL
Merchandise inventory is divided by Net Working Capital. This is an additional measure of inventory balance. Ordinarily, the relationship should not exceed 80 percent.

CURRENT DEBT TO INVENTORY
Dividing the Current Debt by Inventory yields yet another indication of the extent to which the business relies on funds from disposal of unsold inventories to meet its debts.

FUNDED DEBTS TO WORKING CAPITAL
Funded Debts are all long term obligations, as represented by mortgages, bonds, debentures, term loans, serial notes, and other types of liabilities maturing more than one year from statement date. This ratio is obtained by dividing Funded Debt by Net Working Capital. Analysts tend to compare Funded Debts with Net Working Capital in determining whether or not long term debts are in proper proportion. Ordinarily, this relationship should not exceed 100 percent.

ECONOMIC SECTOR: RETAIL

	SIC: 5599 AUTOMOTIVE DEALERS, NEC				SIC: 5611 MEN'S & BOYS' CLOTHING & FURNISHINGS				SIC: 5621 WOMEN'S READY TO WEAR STORES				SIC: 5631 WOMEN'S ACCESSORY AND SPECIALTY STORES			
	TO 50M	50-2MM	2MM+	TOTAL	TO 50M	50-2MM	2MM	TOTAL	TO 50M	50-2MM	2MM	TOTAL	TO 50M	50-2MM	2MM	TOTAL
	(122)	(157)	(66)	(345)	(2097)	(2798)	(757)	(5652)	(5032)	(3659)	(867)	(9558)	(495)	(241)	(41)	(777)
CURRENT ASSETS TO CURRENT DEBT (TIMES)	2.45	3.29	3.95	3.16	4.68	6.92	6.43	5.89	6.47	7.71	6.22	7.08	6.70	8.98	9.27	7.65
	1.34	1.80	2.38	1.65	2.31	3.28	3.03	2.91	2.92	4.00	3.20	3.32	3.00	4.19	3.21	3.27
	1.05	1.29	1.27	1.14	1.43	2.07	2.02	1.81	1.62	2.25	1.98	1.88	1.57	2.15	1.80	1.80
NET PROFITS ON NET SALES (PERCENT)	5.06	5.16	7.01	5.25	8.81	9.92	6.72	9.11	11.05	10.55	8.62	10.71	12.42	12.30	8.32	12.04
	2.18	2.99	3.09	2.83	3.70	4.43	3.48	4.05	4.77	5.56	5.00	5.00	5.32	4.52	3.70	4.96
	.53	1.28	2.22	1.22	.92	1.70	1.95	1.48	1.32	2.21	1.74	1.68	1.48	2.17	1.62	1.87
PROFITS ON NET WORTH (PERCENT)	61.02	42.63	28.00	46.66	57.80	29.32	17.92	34.70	54.45	29.66	18.20	40.62	60.75	31.33	35.43	45.12
	29.60	28.88	12.90	22.31	24.19	15.21	11.19	16.60	25.94	15.70	10.18	18.77	27.83	14.44	14.55	19.78
	9.46	10.20	6.74	8.85	6.01	6.40	6.09	6.19	7.52	6.62	5.36	6.72	7.09	5.41	3.72	6.35

EXHIBIT 7.2 (*Continued*)

PROFITS ON WORKING CAPITAL (PERCENT)																	
55.21	52.98	45.82	53.54	54.74	35.00	24.05	38.50	54.43	39.04	31.23	45.64	51.61	37.2	58.42	4 93
22.28	19.03	10.77	18.96	21.49	17.94	13.89	18.04	23.49	21.20	17.20	21.73	26 24	16.87	22.22	21.93
.83	4.60	1.17	4.29	4.40	6.61	7.10	6.00	5.49	8.29	8.46	6.96	4.59	7.29	11.20	5 04

SALES TO NET WORTH (TIMES)

18.36	11.94	9.40	12.01	9.85	4.78	4.37	6.21	8.03	4.51	4.11	6.11	8.07	4.44	4.86	6 38
7.76	5.68	5.56	5.97	5.40	3.14	2.64	3.53	4.36	2.77	2.07	3.42	4.50	2.55	3.20	3.80
2.44	1.98	1.25	1.93	2.94	2.01	1.52	2.16	2.55	1.59	.79	1.95	2.65	1.58	1.5	2.11

SALES TO WORKING CAPITAL (TIMES)

13.70	11.57	12.19	12.27	7.93	5.38	5.38	6.26	7.24	5.64	5.73	6.49	7.81	5.99	7.2	7.13
6.12	5.76	4.62	5.67	4.54	3.49	3.23	3.75	4.27	3.47	3.15	3.86	4.32	3.51	4.35	4.11
.73	2.50	1.78	1.82	2.66	2.32	2.07	2.38	2.55	2.22	1.77	2.33	2.67	2.00	1.95	2.36

COLLECTION PERIOD (DAYS)

18	16	36	22
7	7	23	10
2	3	11	3

SALES TO INVENTORY (TIMES)

7.1	10.8	7.8	9.7	5.5	5.1	5.9	5.3	6.4	7.1	9.3	6.9	6.8	6.7	8.3	6.8
3.2	5.2	4.7	4.4	3.6	3.6	4.2	3.6	4.3	4.6	5.8	4.5	3.9	4.3	4.7	4.0
2.6	2.9	2.1	2.7	2.5	2.5	2.9	2.6	2.9	3.1	3.7	3.0	2.8	3.2	3.8	2.9

FIXED ASSETS TO NET WORTH (PERCENT)

135.3	87.4	96.9	106.9	59.5	28.8	34.1	38.7	49.6	36.1	40.8	43.1	39.6	36.6	55.5	39.6
36.5	31.6	35.8	33.3	24.5	12.8	16.4	16.4	22.8	16.3	17.1	19.8	19.0	17.1	19.0	18.4
10.1	11.4	9.2	10.3	9.0	5.4	6.5	6.5	9.6	6.7	6.2	7.6	8.9	6.4	5.5	8.0

CURRENT DEBT TO NET WORTH (PERCENT)

453.9	184.2	149.7	229.4	191.6	77.0	73.5	104.2	124.6	58.9	60.2	84.6	140.3	48.8	83.2	94.6
121.1	82.1	75.2	92.4	74.8	36.6	36.7	45.3	46.6	25.2	28.1	34.0	45.9	21.4	30.3	34.1
17.8	29.5	15.5	20.6	23.7	14.3	13.6	16.7	13.7	10.4	10.8	12.0	14.5	10.3	6.1	11.7

TOTAL DEBT TO NET WORTH (PERCENT)

607.3	242.1	243.9	350.6	305.1	105.7	99.1	153.8	204.0	86.3	85.6	131.7	196.6	80.2	111.7	134.7
212.2	126.0	92.4	137.4	126.4	50.1	46.0	62.4	74.7	40.4	39.0	52.0	66.1	31.3	42.4	49.1
27.3	55.6	26.3	34.7	35.3	20.1	19.8	22.8	19.2	16.2	16.7	17.5	19.2	13.2	13.7	15.9

INVENTORY TO WORKING CAPITAL (PERCENT)

330.0	217.6	159.9	238.1	189.9	135.9	124.7	149.1	140.4	110.1	100.3	124.3	138.4	116.6	144.1	133.6
106.4	114.6	107.4	108.2	115.1	97.4	84.0	101.7	95.2	78.9	62.9	87.8	96.0	81.8	76.6	92.2
29.6	53.9	57.5	45.8	81.5	69.5	54.3	70.9	69.9	50.5	36.1	57.8	69.4	49.0	44.3	61.3

CURRENT DEBT TO INVENTORY (PERCENT)

136.0	124.9	120.3	126.3	91.1	70.7	90.0	81.1	88.2	84.0	122.3	89.8	83.8	85.4	111.5	85.2
96.4	79.8	59.5	87.4	56.6	43.8	55.8	49.8	48.7	47.3	75.8	50.0	47.3	39.4	69.6	46.5
62.7	51.0	35.8	50.8	28.5	21.9	29.5	25.1	21.6	22.4	40.3	23.0	20.1	17.7	27.1	20.0

FUNDED DEBTS TO WORKING CAPITAL (PERCENT)

249.6	173.1	93.6	175.4	117.9	68.0	60.4	90.2	119.8	95.3	84.2	108.1	127.3	111.4	100.5	118.4
91.4	69.0	42.9	69.0	76.2	35.7	25.5	46.6	71.0	43.9	35.8	56.6	71.9	49.4	45.0	65.1
10.0	14.2	15.4	14.1	36.6	16.0	7.6	18.6	35.5	17.8	11.2	21.8	28.4	14.0	13.1	20.5

Source: Key Business Ratios, Statistics in Over 800 Lines of Business, 1979, New York: Dun & Bradstreet, Inc. 1979, pp. 62, 65, 158–9.

varnishes (wholesaling) and paints, varnishes, lacquers, and enamels (manufacturing and construction). *Choose the category carefully.*

Industry comparisons must be used with restraint. Individual companies as indicated above, in order to attain a competitive edge or for any of a dozen other reasons, may choose to "look bad" in comparison with the industry figures. Before drawing conclusions, it is wise to ask, "Is there a good reason for the discrepancy?"

Why do so many analysts use industry figures in comparison with the company being analyzed? Primarily because industry figures are relatively easy to get and can be used as benchmarks to give added meaning to the analysis of a particular company.

For example, if you were analyzing the financial data of Deere and Co., you would look at the following information (Exhibit 7.3).

EXHIBIT 7.3

Deere & Co. Financial Data

	1973	1975	1977	1979	1981
Operating Margin %	14.9	12.3	14.3	12.7	11.1
Working Capital $M	754	929.7	1140.2	1281.6	1326
Long-Term Debt $M	199.5	422.9	507.8	640.2	696.6
Net Profit $M	168.5	179.1	255.6	310.6	251.0
Earnings/Share $	2.88	3.02	4.24	5.12	3.79

Source: Value Line Investment Survey, August 27, 1982.

Close examination of the data seems to indicate that these are the figures of a declining company. However, when compared with those of other companies in the agricultural equipment industry, a different picture develops. International Harvester, for example, had an operating margin of 7.5 percent in 1973, which fell to 0.2 percent in 1981. Their long-term debt increased from $497 million in 1970 to $1985 million in 1981. Looking at the industry as a whole, the operating margin was 3.8 percent in 1981 compared with 11.1 percent in 1981 for Deere and Co. Furthermore, if other factors are considered, Deere and Co.'s relative strength is reinforced. The current excess supply of grain, which generates low prices, gives a lower income to the farmer. This reduced income coupled with high interest rates in the economy make it difficult for farmers to cover the cost of production, much less purchase new equipment. With these facts in perspective, Deere and Co. appears to be a different company than a first glance at its data suggests.

While we strongly recommend the use of industry standards, other writers deplore their use. It is true that if you only use the *averages* you will be comparing your performance with mediocrity. It is also true that such wide variations exist that comparisons may be absolutely meaningless. We believe, however, that comparisons intelligently interpreted as suggested herein can be *one* easily obtained additional measuring device that can be used as a *starting* point for analysis. If the figuring does nothing more than suggest additional questions to the analyst, it will be worthwhile.

HOW CAN ACCOUNTING HELP PEOPLE IN BUSINESS MAKE DECISIONS?

Depending upon the identity of the financial analyst, the purpose of financial analysis may be quite different. For example, a banker asked to lend a business $1 million for one year will be interested solely in how certain the chances are that the loan will be repaid. An insurance company about to make a 20-year mortgage loan will be primarily concerned with the long-term value of the building and land. The owner or president of a business may want to answer very basic key questions relating to the policies of the business whereas a functional area manager may be interested primarily in (a) reducing departmental expenses in comparison with competition, (b) understanding the effect of decisions made in other areas on his or her department or (c) improving the controls (systems) of the department and forecasting costs or savings and its OVERALL MANAGEMENT EFFECTIVENESS.

At the top management level, financial accounting should provide answers to the following five basic questions:

1. How is the enterprise doing, in total? This requires a report on profits, return on investment, growth of assets and growth of equity, market share, and growth of market share.

In small businesses, accounting will answer such questions fairly well, although supplementary information *not shown* will also need to be used. For example, a large and growing backlog of unfilled orders, customarily not shown on accounting statements, may be extremely important and can be good or bad. It is good if the backlog means the product is in demand by the customers and/or economies of scale are about to be realized. It is bad if the increased backlog means poor deliveries, dissatisfied customers, poor production scheduling, etc.

Other examples of needed additional information may be the valuation of assets and the method of treating types of "investments," i.e., charging them off as expenses or capitalizing them as assets. A perfectly good building, old though it may be, can have been depreciated for a long period of years to the point where it is worth far more than the stated book value and hence represents a hidden asset of substantial proportion. On the other hand, an asset listed as "goodwill" may be an R & D expense that has been capitalized and yet be worthless.

2. Which alternative plan is most attractive?

Accounting should help managers choose between alternatives.

Since plans should be future oriented and accounting tends to focus on past events, *budgets* and *cost predictions* should be prepared that will bridge the gap and help at least partially to answer questions of alternative future courses of action. Both budgets and cost predictions will be predicated on past accounting changed to portray the predicted future.

— 3. What is going wrong? Where? How do you remedy it?

Accounting materially aids managers to control operations by looking at financial comparisons of what should have happened with what actually did happen. Past emphasis has been on what *went wrong;* present-day emphasis is on what is *going wrong.* If differences show up promptly as they should on monthly operating statements (or even daily or weekly for key figures such as sales, returns from customers, etc.) remedial action can be instigated quickly to prevent crises and disasters.

A different aspect of control which is becoming increasingly important is illustrated by the "custodian" aspect of accounting—for example, the control of valuable property susceptible to theft. Theft of computer time and of information stored in company computer files are two new concerns. Proper accounting procedures which can *quickly* bring losses to light may be extremely valuable.

— 4. How can all activities be coordinated?

Accounting procedures provide for the transmittal of much of the information needed to coordinate activities and direct them to common goals. It provides reports for managerial appraisal of results, for instituting remedial action, and predicting consequences of proposed plans. And *if* the goals of the firm are understood at every level, it will help the individual know whether or not he or she is helping or hindering the firm in meeting its goals. One example should make this accounting function clear.

Suppose one of a firm's goals is a 15 percent ROI (return on investment). This goal is based on certain expense factors for each department—sales, engineering, production, etc. Accounting reports will quickly tell each manager how well he or she is contributing to the common goal. Profit Center Accounting which measures separately the contribution toward the common goal of each separate function or factor has indeed been set up for this very purpose (and is growing in usage because it has proven effective).

— 5. How well does the firm deal with its environment?

Accounting information is, often, absolutely essential to effective managerial dealing with its environment. This includes such federal agencies as the Internal Revenue Service and the S.E.C. as well as many other outside groups. Examples are plentiful: banks when negotiating a loan, unions when settling labor rates, insurance companies when asked for a mortgage, and brokers or investment bankers when establishing a better market climate for stock, and even for a prospective executive who needs convincing before accepting a position. In all these cases, and many more, accounting information is required to help the firm deal with, or be understood better by, outside entities.

HOW DO I START MY ANALYSIS?

Every business activity is derived from the interlocking sales forecast and business plan. To analyze the past, present, and the trends, start with the financial reports for the most recent 10 years. For analysis of the *profit-and-loss statement* items, each dollar value is converted to a *ratio of net sales* (net sales therefore equals 100 percent). *Indicators* of the state of the business or business activity are given by certain ratios formed from *balance sheet* values alone or in combination with profit-and-loss statement items.

Suppose you see a spread sheet for a company such as the one often shown near the end in an annual report and it looks like this (all figures shown are in millions of dollars).

	19X7	19X8	19X9	19Y0	19Y1	19Y2	19Y3	19Y4	19Y5
Sales	100	110	121	133	146	161	177	195	215

(10% Compound Rate of Growth)

It is rather obvious that this firm's sales are compounding up at a rate of about 10 percent per year. There have been no setbacks, which is quite remarkable for a span of nine years, and unless outside influences change the situation, it is likely that the future outlook for this firm is bright. Why? Because trends have a tendency to persist— whether up or down or sideways.

We can't guarantee that this upward trend will continue but we can say it is likely. Many things could happen to reverse the trend. For example, the entire management team could be wiped out in an airplane accident (unlikely because good management policy forbids company executives from traveling together) or a new invention or process could obsolete this firm's product or process. Again, this is not likely because good management would probably foresee this possibility and provide against it. However, part of both catastrophes might happen which would materially slow their progress. Therefore, conclusions based on trends do have *limitations*. When used with other judgmental analysis factors such as supplementary information regarding the industry, market analysis, quality and performance in the industrial relations area, R & D effectiveness, etc., these trends can be pregnant with meaning.

We will now provide a list of questions to be asked in analyzing any business firm from analysis of the 10-year financial reports. In order to answer these questions, you must have a clear understanding of the meaning of the terms. An appendix at the end of this chapter provides these definitions for your convenient review.

KEY QUESTIONS TO BE ANSWERED FOR THE PROFIT-AND-LOSS STATEMENT

There are a number of key questions that should be answered with respect to the profit-and-loss statement.

1. What is the sales trend? Compound rate of growth compared with industry figures? Fast growth, slow growth, or erratic? Is there any explanation of the trends available from written material in the annual reports or other outside sources? How convincing is the explanatory material? Have sales and earnings forecasts by executives of the company been on target? (An indication of the soundness of management judgment.)

How does the trend in sales compare with inflation (higher price) in the firm's particular industry? If the industry as a whole has been raising prices rapidly, it is entirely possible for a firm to show good sales increases with no growth in real product output. Wherever possible, sales trends should be compared with the industry's sales and trends to show growth or loss of share of the market.

2. What is the trend of cost-of-goods-sold expressed as a percentage of sales? Note that in using sales as 100%, the cost-of-goods-sold percentage plus gross-margin percentage equals 100%. In other words, if cost of goods percentage has risen, the gross margin (opportunity for profit) will go down. Does this indicate effective control of costs? Improving production efficiency? Ability to raise prices in keeping with rising costs? Is any supplementary material available? For example, from even a gross breakdown of cost of goods sold (material cost, direct labor cost, markup cost and manufacturing overhead) a better analysis can be made. How does the company being analyzed compare with competition?

Unfortunately, much of the above kind of financial information is available only to insiders. Occasionally annual reports will comment on the situation as will published analyses in periodicals.

3. What is the trend in operating expenses as a percentage of sales? Can a further breakdown of operating expense be made, e.g., sales expense, advertising, general and administrative, R & D, etc.? Can these be compared with industry averages? Do these trends give any clue to management's ability to control expenses? Keep down overhead? Effectively use advertising (does this expense bear a relationship to sales)? Manage a sales force? Does the firm use departmental budgets? How accurate is its forecasting technique? How great is management's determination to abide by its budgeting?

4. Most important, in fact, the outstanding question is "What is the trend in profits?" From the profit-and-loss statement alone you can figure profit percentage on sales for each of the past years. Is the trend up, down, or level? How does it compare with similar sized, larger, or smaller firms in the same industry? What does the comparison suggest? (In some industries just as in some retail stores, a certain minimum sales volume seems to be necessary before a satisfactory profit percentage can be attained. In other words, economies of scale require a volume of sales.) Is the percentage of profit high enough to preclude disaster in the face of rapidly changing product obsolescence in the industry? For example, a 2% net profit may be OK for supermarkets because of the relative stability of the food business, but 6% is very poor for an integrated circuit manufacturer where risk of obso-

lescence is extremely high. A spread sheet showing profit on sales, profit per share of common stock, and net profit to net worth (see following section) will tell a great deal about management's policies, its aggressiveness, use of the marketing concept, and overall performance.

RATIOS FROM THE BALANCE SHEET OR BOTH THE BALANCE SHEET AND P & L STATEMENT

1. *PROFITABILITY?*

What do the following ratios tell you about management's performance?

Net profit to sales

Net profit per share of common stock

Net profit to net worth

Company profit ratios (above) relative to industry ratios or ratios of top performers in the industry.

Net profit to net worth is a highly important ratio. It indicates the percentage of return (profit) on the amount the stockholders (owners) earn on their investment. It would be rather foolish for an investor to buy stock in a company for a return of less than he or she might get from an investment in completely secure government bonds (6% to 7% at this writing). Why should someone take the risk (inherent in every business) unless he or she receives a greater return now or the expectation of a far greater return in the future? The question then becomes, "How good are the chances of the future high yield?" This is the same question a business owner asks before he commits himself to purchasing a new asset. Will the added investment or added cost produce a good return (better than safer investments outside of the business)? How quickly will he or she get that return? How much risk is involved?

Note: Be careful of changing tax rates over which management may have little or no control. Net profit before taxes may be a more useful figure than profits after taxes.

2. *LIQUIDITY?*

Liquidity ratios tell whether management can meet its debts as they come due. These are:

Current assets to current liabilities

Acid or quick-asset ratio

Fixed assets to net worth

Funded debt to net working capital

From these ratios we can judge the answers to such key questions as:

Will short-term loans be available from banks? How well can the firm pay its bills under adverse conditions? Is the firm technically bankrupt? Can the firm raise additional capital for expansion?

3. *LEVERAGE?*

Current debt to net worth?

Total debt to net worth?

Is the firm leveraged to the point that small increases in sales may bring large increases in return on equity?

How much of the business do the stockholders own? If the business has too much leverage (too high a ratio of debt to equity) a small decrease in sales may change a profit to a loss. Unfortunately, this ratio is a matter of judgment depending on the risk odds of the firm and its industry. Stable businesses like electric utilities may properly have fairly high ratios whereas the same ratio may be a quick road to bankruptcy for a high risk firm in an unstable industry.

4. *TURNOVER?*

Inventory Turnover? If possible, analyze by raw materials, work in process and finished goods. Your analysis may allow you to make an evaluation of production management, purchasing management and market management. How good are their controls and systems?

Accounts receivable? (Expressed in days, see Definitions in the Appendix.)

How about bad debts?

Net sales/net worth?

5. *OTHER PERTINENT QUESTIONS*

Is it possible to do a breakeven study? Is profit center or cost center accounting being used? Is it possible to determine sales and profit trends by product line and market (government, industry, etc.)? This is very important in multi-product companies to determine management's ability to delete unprofitable lines or products. This may also shed light on how good the company's acquisition program is.

WHEN IS BREAKEVEN ANALYSIS IMPORTANT?

Quite often the best way for management to determine (1) whether or not to add sales or advertising expense in order to increase volume, (2) the relative merits of decreasing prices to increase volume, (3) the advisability of borrowing for capital improvements needed to increase capacity, or (4) the wisdom of automating production or office work is by means of a breakeven analysis after dividing costs into:

Fixed costs—those costs which are constant in amount regardless of volume and

Variable costs—those that vary in close proportion to unit volume.

Consider the following situations where a good breakeven analysis will point to a solution of maximum impact on the policies of the company.

1. When fixed costs (machinery, buildings, overhead, etc., which do not rise with increased production) are high in relation to variable costs, emphasis must be on volume if profit is to be maximized. Often volume can be increased by, for example, increasing the size of the sales force or adding to advertising pressure which may in-

crease sales or advertising costs. It may add substantially in comparison with previous costs but add *not* at all to fixed costs and hence improve profits considerably.

2. On the other hand, if fixed costs are low in relation to variable costs, then increased sales volume may add little to profit, or actually decrease profit when extra costs or lower prices are required to secure the added volume. In this type of situation the remedy for *improved profit* may be raising prices by adding fashion, quality, design improvements or perhaps actually adding to fixed costs by installing automatic machines that will *reduce* such variable costs as direct labor more than will be added to fixed costs.

It should be noted that even for an insider, breakeven analysis can be incredibly complicated. Costs, volume, and price for a single product can change rapidly and when a factory manufactures many products in the same plant, the interrelationship can indeed be difficult to determine. Despite the difficulties described, breakeven analysis is a standard procedure in manufacturing enterprises because of its ability to shed light on many management problems. We have included a brief how-to-do-it discussion in an appendix in this chapter.

DEPRECIATION AND VALUATION OF INVENTORIES

While sometimes little can be found out about a firm's depreciation accounting, it should be recognized that whatever figure a company takes for depreciation of its assets is a direct deduction from profits. Consider the case of two identical firms—Company A takes rapid depreciation on its machinery, equipment, and buildings while Company B depreciates the same assets very slowly. The result is that Company A may understate its profits and Company B overstates them. Moreover, if Company A changes its method of depreciation from fast to slow, comparisons of profit trends from year to year can be very misleading.

Similarly, a high valuation on year-end inventories which may only be salable at far less than the book value will reduce cost of goods sold and increase profits. Conversely, understating the value of inventories increases cost of goods sold and reduces net profits and income taxes. We point this out to indicate the opportunities for "swinging" stated profits from year to year which undeniably complicates the financial analyst's problems. The particular accounting practices of the firm will make a substantial difference in reported profits. Some of the more important practices are in respect to (a) long-term contracts —for example, if you have an expensive piece of equipment which you manufacture and lease for a term of years, do you take all the profit in one year or over the entire term?; (b) expensing or capitalizing research; (c) depreciation, amortization, and valuation of inventories. These make a substantial difference in stated profits.

One important means for conserving cash in this inflationary era is changing the way the firm accounts for inventory. Since 1974, scores of firms have switched to the Last-in, First-out (LIFO) formula for inventory accounting from the First-in, First-out (FIFO) method. The switch to LIFO may deflate the company's reported earnings substantially, but it also cuts the firm's income taxes so the company keeps more cash.

FUNDS FLOW CONCEPT

Management of nearly every firm is constantly required to make decisions as to (1) if and when to invest additional funds to help the business grow and (2) where to obtain the funds. Example of investment decisions are: Should we buy, build, or lease a new plant? Should we add to our inventories? Should we buy new machinery? If we answer any of these questions affirmatively, we need to know where the money is coming from. Generally, the sources of funds are (1) sale of assets we no longer need, (2) selling of stock or bonds, (3) borrowing from a bank, (4) reduction in assets such as inventories or accounts receivable, (5) increase in retained earnings.

The decisions as to increasing and decreasing of assets and the need to know where funds are coming from is a continual problem. Equally important is a judgment as to how well funds were used. Were the funds used proportionately to the various needs of the business so as to improve profitability in the best possible manner? To assist the analyst in answering these questions, one of the best techniques is to employ the commonly called "where-got, where-gone" statement: Source and Application of Funds. This statement shows how management shifts its resources over a period of time.

SOURCE AND APPLICATION OF FUNDS
PURPOSE:

1. To trace and account for cash receipts and expenditures.
2. To show the movement of funds within the business.
3. To indicate what purchasing power was available, its sources and uses.

FUNDS MAY BE PROVIDED BY:

1. Additional investment by owners.
2. Profits.
3. Sale of fixed assets or investments owned by firm.
4. Increasing long-term liabilities.
5. Decreasing "net working capital" (look this up to be sure you understand).

FUNDS MAY BE USED TO:

1. Decrease net worth (by paying dividends) or repurchase of outstanding stock, or losses during a period of time.
2. Purchase of fixed assets or investments.
3. Decrease long-term liabilities.
4. *Increase* net working capital.

Consider the simplified balance sheets for years:

	19Y1	19Y2	Change
Assets of the Company			
Net current assets	$210	$240	+ $30
Fixed Assets	500	450	— 50
Debt and Equity Claims			
Stock	500	500	0
Long-Term Debt	200	175	— 25
Retained Earnings	10	15	+ 5

The Funds Flow table below summarizes how funds were generated and applied for the one-year period.

Sources of Funds	
Decrease in Fixed Assets	$50
Increase in Retained Earnings	5
	$55

Uses of Funds	
Increase in Net Current Assets	$30
Decrease in Long-Term Debt	25
	$55

A brief guide for classifying changes in balances into flow of funds is provided below.

SOURCES	USES
Decrease in assets	Increase in assets
Increase in liabilities	Decrease in liabilities
Increase in equity	Decrease in equity
Decrease in cash	Increase in cash
Decrease in accounts receivable	Increase in accounts receivable
Decrease in inventory	Increase in inventory
Decrease in prepaid expenses	Increase in prepaid expenses
Increase in current liabilities	Decrease in current liabilities

Increase in deferred taxes	Decrease in deferred taxes
Increase in stock	Decrease in stock
Increase in long-term debt	Decrease in long-term debt
Increase in retained earnings	Decrease in retained earnings

PRO-FORMA STATEMENTS

Overall company plans are reflected ultimately in income statements and balance sheets for future years which are called *pro forma* statements. Status and trends based on past data provide a check on the reasonableness of company plans. For the evaluation of alternative decisions about basic strategy, the pro-forma statement resulting from each alternative is a valuable tool.

BUDGETS

Budgets, if well prepared, provide perhaps the best criteria for evaluating management performance. Budgets are in reality a representation of the future, a picture of things to come, a portrayal of the total of all the planning of the firm. Budgeting can answer all of the following:

1. How well do we expect to do in the future? As has been said, "We should be interested in the future. After all, we live the rest of our lives in it!"
2. How good was our planning? Did we stay within our budget? Exceed it? Do a poor or realistic job of estimating? Deviate from our plans? If so, why? In other words, budgeting can show our triumphs and our disasters. Furthermore, based upon our past experiences with budgeting (or in a broader sense, planning) we should improve in the future.
3. Which of several alternatives should we choose? Budgets are versatile, flexible, comprehensive, and relevant. By making a budget based on each major alternative, the most attractive alternative becomes clear.
4. What went wrong? Where? Monitoring performance and reporting deviations between plan and actual result (feedback) allows management to immediately detect problems and pinpoint what went wrong and where. Most importantly, management can then make the necessary changes to correct and improve the operation or prevent the recurrence of failures. Budgets act as a communicating and motivating device. They spell out in financial terms what is expected of each managerial subunit. If the manager has been consulted and has participated (as he or she should) in the estimating process, the manager has a commitment to deliver what he or she helped plan. After receiving the comparison of budget with actual, the manager is in a position to plan remedial action.

HOW TO IMPROVE YOUR ANALYTICAL SKILLS

We have purposely omitted in depth, how-to-do-it details on break-even analysis, specific depreciation and inventory valuation guide-lines, and funds flow concepts because this is a manual for evaluating the policies of a business, not a book on management accounting. Previous footnotes indicate books that will more than adequately help the beginner master the accounting techniques mentioned. For those without specialized training in accounting, whom we believe to be the vast majority in business, the most important steps are to get your feet wet; to begin to try to answer the simple questions asked in the preceding sections of this chapter; to discover for yourself that you can do at least rudimentary financial analysis.

Start with the trends and ratio analysis. Analyze them, and then compare them with industry ratios as benchmarks. Then use the symptom charts that follow. It's not only fun but very rewarding. As one of our readers recently wrote, "You know, I didn't realize at first how little I know. Now I know how little I know, but more important, I can really do a useful financial analysis. It's a source of satisfaction for me and a stimulant to learn more of what I previously thought was boring and unimportant." For an example of a simple analysis of a firm, see Chapter 15 of this book.

To help you to interpret the meaning of symptoms appearing on the income statement, we have introduced Exhibit 7.4 showing symptoms, some of the possible *real problems* (indicated by typical symptoms), and lastly, the management action that is indicated. These problems often cross the usual departmental functional lines of authority.

Exhibit 7.4 by no means gives a complete listing, but it does indicate lines of thought not previously recognized by the beginning financial analyst. It also suggests questions to be asked of management insiders so that a more meaningful study can be made. As the years go by, it is our belief that more and more detail will be published by larger companies either because they want to woo their stockholders or are forced into it by such agencies as the S.E.C.

ENDNOTES

1. Your regional offices of the Department of Commerce located in most major cities and the Small Business Administration can often be most helpful in supplying data.
2. *Value Line Investment Survey,* Edition 8, December 4, 1970 (alphabetical listing).
3. Actual figures were $90.1 million.
4. Available from American Iron & Steel Institute, Washington, D.C.
5. *Wall Street Journal,* January 26, 1971, pp. 1, 8, 22.
6. See Robert G. Murdick and Donald D. Deming, *The Management of Capital Expenditures,* New York: McGraw-Hill Book Co., 1968.

EXHIBIT 7.4

Symptoms	Possible Problems	Needed Action
1. Poor sale trend	a. Ineffectual marketing b. Competitively poor products c. Poor systems and/or controls resulting in high prices d. No unified sense of direction e. Problems caused by undercapitalization or engineering f. Production difficulties	a. Improve marketing b. New and improved products c. Improved systems and controls d. Change or improve management e. Secure additional capital f. Pinpoint areas and improve
2. Rising percentage of return goods	a. Poor delivery or quality, or basis on which sales are made	a. Pinpoint problem and rectify
3. Increasing trend of cost of goods sold percentage	a. Insufficient attention to buying (markup in a retail store or wholesaler)	a. Set up policies on markup and adhere to them
4. Material cost increasing	a. Inefficient material usage in cutting or fabricating. Process waste or pilferage b. Material price increase c. Reduction in price received for scrap material d. Increased transportation charges	a. Find specific problem and change system or control b. Increase finished goods price if unable to increase productivity c. Explore alternatives for increasing selling price of scrap or increase finished goods price d. Improve controls or order in larger quantities, etc.
5. Increased percentage for packaging	a. Buying high cost packaging with resulting insufficient increase in sales	a. Change packages to either improve sales results or decrease packaging cost

EXHIBIT 7.4 (Continued)

Symptoms	Possible Problems	Needed Action
6. Increasing percentage of direct labor	a. Problems in methods used (pinpoint area—cutting, welding, sewing, or wherever)	a-1. Improve supervision 2. Improve methods 3. Strive for economics of scale 4. Introduce engineering changes 5. Obtain better tools or machinery for faster processing
	b. Proliferation of products causing loss of economies of scale	b-1. Reduce number of products 2. Change direction of sales force toward higher profit items 1. Increase inventories to be able to produce in larger lots
	c. Increased wages without increased productivity	c-1. If impossible to increase productivity, increase prices 2. Increase labor efficiency through better training or simplifying job
	d. Too many intricate product specifications	d. Reduce or raise prices but remain competitive
	e. Too much down time on machines	e. Use better machine servicing methods
	f. Poor labor market	f-1. Relocate plant 2. Improve production flow
7. Increased makeup pay in work plants	a. Excessive labor turnover requiring hiring of apprentices or learners	a-1. Improve personnel hiring techniques 2. Improve working conditions and/or fringe benefits
	b. Too many switches to hourly pay from piecework	b-1. Decrease product proliferation to increase length of runs

EXHIBIT 7.4 (Continued)

Symptoms	Possible Problems	Needed Action
		2. Decrease "custom made" products requiring time work (change marketing policy)
		3. Improve production scheduling system
		4. Increase inventory of made-up stock or partially finished goods stock
		5. "Buy" instead of "make" components or finished goods with limited sales
		6. Increase prices on losing items
8. Increasing manufacturing expense percentage	a. Supervisory problems	a-1. Reduce number of supervisors
		2. Improve training for supervisors
		3. Improve plant layout
	b. Loss of control of nonproductive labor	b. Improve control and supervision
	c. High occupancy expense	c-1. Lease out unneeded space
		2. Examine lower cost alternatives
9. Increasing sales expense	a. Sales management problems	a-1. Check hiring, compensation method, training and supervision of sales force and improve
		2. Change territorial or product breakdown. Check alternatives. Look for backtracking, number of product lines handled, etc. for improvement
	b. High advertising cost	b-1. Set up controls, measure effectiveness, change advertising manager or agency, etc.

EXHIBIT 7.4 (*continued*)

Symptoms	Possible Problems	Needed Action
	c. Increased warehouse or shipping expense	c-1. Call in consultant to improve warehouse techniques 2. Improve order handling system 3. Investigate transportation expense (traffic control) 4. Improve physical set-up
10. Increasing inventory percentage to sales (turnover) on raw materials work-in-process of finished goods and/or increasing markdowns on finished goods	a. Poor marketing policy	a-1. Decrease assortments of products proliferation 2. Watch for obsolescence and discontinue items faster 3. Improve new product introduction control 4. Improve salespeople's supervision and/or incentives 5. Check and improve order scheduling procedures
	b. Poor manuacturing-marketing coordination	b. Set up clearly defined policies, authority and penalties
	c. Poor manufacturing policy	c-1. Too much concentration on economy of scale, set up controls 2. Improve material flow (purchasing included) 3. Reduce in-process time 4. Reduce raw material inventory 5. Improve production scheduling to improve deliveries

SELECTED BIBLIOGRAPHY ON
ACCOUNTING AND FINANCE

Anthony, Robert N., and Welsch, Glenn A. *Fundamentals of Management Accounting.* 3rd ed. Homewood, Ill.: Richard D. Irwin, 1981.

Corporate Profiles for Executives and Investors (1976–77 ed.) Chicago: Rand McNally.

Horngren, Charles T. *Introduction to Management Accounting.* 5th ed. Englewood Cliffs, N.J.: Prentice-Hall, 1981.

————. *Cost Accounting: A Managerial Emphasis.* 5th ed. Englewood Cliffs, N.J.: PrenticeHall, 1982.

Lynch, Richard, and Williamson, Robert. *Accounting for Management: Planning and Control.* 2nd ed. New York: McGraw-Hill, 1975.

Raby, William L. *Income Tax and Business Decisions: An Introductory Tax Text.* 4th ed. Englewood Cliffs, N.J.: Prentice-Hall, 1978.

Sweeny, Allen. *Accounting Fundamentals for Nonfinancial Executives and Managers.* New York: McGraw-Hill, 1977.

APPENDIX A:
HOW TO USE YOUR HEAD IN COMPUTING

To avoid large and stupid arithmetic errors (which some of us make far too often) *you should always mentally check the reasonableness of your answer.* You can do this "in your head" with a reasonable degree of accuracy with just a little practice, try it a few times and you will discover how easy it is.

FIGURING WITH PERCENTS

Let's first review the meaning of percent, fractions, and decimals and their interrelationships. *A percent means the number of parts in 100 parts.*

To find a given percent of a number, there are several simple methods as shown in the box.

Rule 1 for large numbers.
To find 22% of the number 13,572 approximately, drop the last two digits of the number and multiply by 22:
$$22 \times 135 = 2,970$$

Rule 2 for large numbers.
To find 22% of the number 13,572 (accurately) move the decimal point two places in the left (i.e., divide by 100) and multiply by 22:
$$22 \times 135.72 = 2,985.84$$

Rule 3 for any size number.
To find 22% of 1,357, drop the percent sign, shift the decimal point of the multiplier two places to the left, and then multiply:
$$.22 \times 1,357 = 298.54$$

Rule 4 for any size number.
To find 22% of 135,720, convert the percentage to a decimal (.22) or fraction (22/100) and multiply:
$$.22 \times 135,720 = 29,858.4$$

Percent	Fraction	Decimal
.001%	$\dfrac{1}{(1,000)\,(100)} = \dfrac{1}{100,000}$	.000 01
.01%	$\dfrac{1}{(100)\,(100)} = \dfrac{1}{10,000}$	.000 1
.1%	$\dfrac{1}{(10)\,(100)} = \dfrac{1}{1,000}$	.001
1%	$\dfrac{1}{100}$	.01
10%	$\dfrac{10}{100} = \dfrac{1}{10}$	.10
100%	$\dfrac{100}{100} = 1$	1.00
1,000%	$\dfrac{1,000}{100} = 10$	10.00

Now let's try out the rules with examples. Suppose that we want to find 1% of 1,300. Remember that 1% = 1/100th. Therefore 1% of 1,300 = 1/100 of 1,300 = 13.

In the above example, read 1,300 as thirteen hundred, not as one thousand three hundred. A second way to do this is by remembering that to find 1/100th of a number, you merely set the decimal point over two places to the left. Thus 1/100th of 1,300 becomes 13.00 or thirteen.

Now suppose that we wish to find 1% of a large number and great accuracy is not required. We simply strike off the last two digits:

1% of 13,456,789 = 134,567

Now suppose you want to find 10% of 241:

10% = 10/100th or 1/10th

10% of 241 = 10/100th × 241 = 1/10th × 241 = 24.1

Note that to take 1/10th of a number it is only necessary to move the decimal point one place to the left; 241 becomes 24.1. For fast figuring just drop off the last digit of whole numbers (no decimal point); 10% of 241 or 1/100th of 241 becomes 24 which is reasonably close.

25% = 25/100th = 1/4   25% of 2000 = 1/4 of 2000 = 500
50% = 50/100ths = 1/2   50% of 21,000 = 1/2 of 21,000 = 10,500
200% = 200/100ths = 2   200% of 80 = 2 × 80 = 160
.1% = 1/10th of 1% = .1 × 1/100 = .001 = 1/1000

Percentages can be written as whole numbers or parts of whole numbers, *viz.*, 10%, 27% or 27.1%, or .9%, or 123% or 123.9%. The meanings are:

```
 10%  = 10/100ths = 1/10
 27%  = 27/100ths
27.1% = 27.1/100ths or 271/1000ths
 .9%  = .9/100ths or 9/10th of 1% (less than 1%) = 9/1000
123%  = 123/100ths = (more than 100%)
123.9% = 123.9/100ths = (nearly 125% which is 1 1/4)
```

COMPUTING RATIOS

A *ratio* is simply a number that expresses the result of dividing one quantity (number) by another.

$$\text{Example:} \quad \frac{\text{Profit}}{\text{Sales}} = \text{Ratio} \qquad \frac{5000}{50,000} = 1/10\text{th} = 0.1$$

Note that when we are talking or writing about percentages .1% = 1/10th of 1%, whereas in ratios 0.1 = 1/10th of 100% = 10%. The difference is whether or not there is a percentage (%) sign after the number. 1% is 1/100th as the *percentage* sign means "parts of a hundred" when there is no decimal point, 1.0 used as a *ratio* is the same as 100%. Thus:

$$0.8 = \quad 8/10\text{ths of } 100\% \text{ or } 80\%$$
$$3.1 = \quad 31/10\text{ths of } 100\% \text{ or } 310\%$$
$$43.6 = 436/10\text{ths of } 100\% \text{ or } 4360\%$$

In other words the decimal point in the ratios above marked the dividing line between 100% and a part of 100%, for example 0.81 = 81%.

```
Sales=$100   Inventory=$25
100÷25=4.0  (meaning sales are 4 times or 400% of
             inventory).
```

Another ratio example:

$$\frac{\text{Debt}}{\text{Equity}} = \text{Ratio} \qquad \frac{231,700}{745,000} = \frac{2317}{7450} = 0.31 \qquad \text{(meaning debt is 31\% of equity)}$$

Ratios are usually expressed as whole numbers with decimal points although it is perfectly proper to use fractions. However, it is usually easier to compare whole and decimal values rather than fractions. Which is easier for you?

$$\frac{471}{23} \qquad \text{compared with} \qquad \frac{876}{55}$$

or

$$20.43 \qquad \text{versus} \qquad 15.91?$$

COMMON SENSE IN USING PERCENTS AND RATIOS

Now that you understand percentages and ratios, here are a few suggestions to use when you are working with numbers as on a balance sheet or a production estimate.

1. After you have calculated percentages or ratios, *check them in your head* to make certain you are reasonably close. For example, if you come up with 15% for net earnings on equity, the earnings being $27,000 and the equity $1,800,000, ask yourself, "Is it right or wrong?" Don't write it out on paper! Check the figure in your head like this:

Mentally (you think to yourself) you say 27 thousand divided by 1800 thousand is just about the same as 30 divided by 2000 which is the same as 3 divided by 200.

$$\frac{27,000}{1,800,000} \text{ about the same as } \frac{30}{2000} \text{ which is the same as } \frac{3}{200}$$

$$\text{which is the same as} \frac{1\frac{1}{2}}{100} = \frac{1.5}{100} = 0.015 \text{ (When you divide by}$$

100, move decimal point two places to left, thus 1.5 becomes 0.015).

2. Another way of doing this that may be easier for you is illustrated here. Suppose that a character in a case says that net earnings on equity are 15%. Equity is $1,800,000 and earnings $27,000. You want to give this a quick close mental check:

   (a) 10% of $1,800,000 is $180,000 (to take 10% of a number, drop off the last digit). Since $180,000 is much larger than $27,000, try 1%.

   (b) 1% of 1,800,000 is $18,000

½% of 1,800,000 is ½ of $18,000 or $9,000

Therefore, if earnings are $27,000, the ROI is really 1.5%, not 15%.

In this case, we hit the nail on the head. Usually you will not be able to estimate so exactly in your head. Try 3.25% of 13,000,000.

1% of 13,000,000 = 13,000,000 ÷ 100 = 130,000

3% is then, 130,000 × 3 = 390,000

¼th of 1% = $\dfrac{130,000}{4}$ = 32,500

3.25% = 3¼% = 390,000 + 32,500 = 422,500

Or, another way of doing 3.25% of 13,000 is:

3 × 13 = 39

¼ of 13 = 3¼

39 + 3¼ = 42¼ or 42.25

but is it 4225? 42,250? or 422,500?

1% of 13,000,000 = 130,000

Hence 3.25% must be 3¼ × 130,000 = 422,500

3. Suppose you are asked to figure earnings on equity but you have forgotten just exactly what "equity" means. OK, this manual makes it easy for you. Just turn back to the list of definitions in Appendix C and look up the meaning. You see it is the same as Net Worth which

is defined as the ownership capital of the business or the total of all assets minus all liabilities. Now you know for sure what equity means and can readily figure it. If you are at all uncertain of the meaning of an accounting term, *look it up in the* definition appendix.

4. But you say, "I always forgot whether you divide earnings by net worth or divide net worth by earnings in order to find the percentage return." To quickly find out, try some small numbers in your head. For example, earnings are $15, equity is $60. Is it

$$
\begin{array}{r}
.25 \\
60 \overline{\smash{)}15.00} \\
120 \\
\hline
300 \\
300 \\
\hline
\end{array}
\qquad \text{or} \qquad
\begin{array}{r}
4 \\
15 \overline{\smash{)}60} \\
60 \\
\hline
\end{array}
$$

You know that $15 is about ¼th of $60 or 25% so obviously you divide $15, the earnings, by $60, the equity.

APPENDIX B: BREAKEVEN ANALYSIS

If a company sells a unit of a product for $2.50 and the direct (variable) cost is $2.00, then the difference of $.50 is called the *variable profit* or *contribution margin*. For a one-product company which sells all it buys (or makes), the company must sell enough units to cover its fixed costs (period costs). If in this instance:

Fixed Costs = $4,000/year
Variable Profit = $.50/unit

then the company just breaks even if income equals costs. If Q^* is the number of units that must be sold to break even, then:

$.50 Q^* = $4,000
Q^* = 8000 units

That the company must sell 8000 units before it covers its fixed costs is important information for management. Small businessmen, without knowledge of breakeven (BE) techniques, may forecast sales of 6000 units and believe that this will yield a profit.

Second, in selecting products for production or for buy and sell, the small business manager may use BE analysis to compare the alternative products. A product with a higher breakeven point may require a greater marketing effort and expenditure.

Third, a manager may wish to choose between a manual method and the purchase of an expensive machine. The anticipated sales as related to the breakeven point is a useful decision guide.

Fourth, although BE analysis is based upon the assumption of a single product company, it can be used for a multiproduct company:

(a) If revenues and costs are developed for each product and (usually) related graphically to determine the breakeven point and profits, or

(b) If the product mix is relatively constant.

Small companies which do not have good cost accounting systems may use past earnings statements to deduce the approximate value of its fixed costs and its breakeven dollar volume. The company can then prepare plans and budgets for adequate sales or elect to go out of business.

ELEMENTARY BREAKEVEN ANALYSIS

We know that if

P = profit

p = price/unit

v = variable cost/unit

F = fixed costs

Q = number of units produced and sold

then   Profit = (Margin $\times$ Quantity − Fixed Costs

so that $P = (p - v) Q - F$

The BE volume occurs when $P = 0$ or $(p-v) Q - F = 0$

Hence $Q_{BE} = \dfrac{F}{p - v}$ units   (See Example)

In dollars, $BE = pQ_{BE} = \dfrac{F}{1 - v/p}$

DETERMINING THE BREAKEVEN CHART
FROM PAST EARNINGS STATEMENTS

If a multiproduct company has not, or cannot, segregate fixed and variable costs, the analyst may make a crude approximation based upon previous earnings statements. Suppose that sales and total costs are determined from earnings statements for the past five years. If we plot sales vs. sales as shown in Exhibit 7.5, we obtain the 45-degree line which passes through the origin. This is labeled "Net Sales" in the Exhibit.

Next we plot costs for 1970 ($1.2 million) against sales ($1.0 million) from the 1970 earnings statement. This point is labeled 1970 in

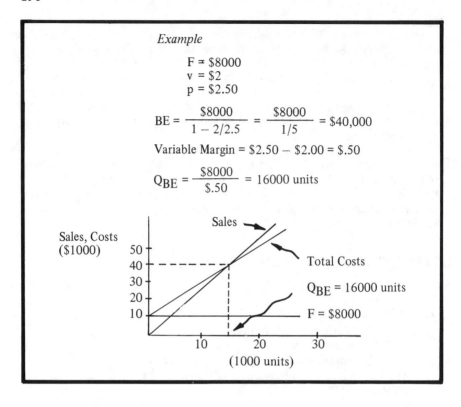

Example

$$F = \$8000$$
$$v = \$2$$
$$p = \$2.50$$

$$BE = \frac{\$8000}{1 - 2/2.5} = \frac{\$8000}{1/5} = \$40,000$$

Variable Margin = $2.50 - $2.00 = $.50

$$Q_{BE} = \frac{\$8000}{\$.50} = 16000 \text{ units}$$

the Exhibit. We then plot total cost vs. net sales for the other four years. We have drawn a line by eye to fit the five cost points. (The more sophisticated student may step to the computer terminal and run off a least squares line to fit the data).

From our crude graph, we estimate that fixed costs for the company are $.70 million and the breakeven point is $1.6 million in sales. In this representation for a multiproduct company, note that we can only obtain a dollar (not quantity in units) estimate of the breakeven point.

MARGIN OF SAFETY

The Margin of Safety index indicates how closely the company is operating to the breakeven point. It is possible for a company to be making a large profit and yet have a low Margin of Safety. A small drop in volume of units sold will then plunge the company into a loss position. The Margin of Safety (MS) is:

$$MS = \frac{\text{Actual Sales—Breakeven Sales}}{\text{Actual Sales}}$$

EXHIBIT 7.5

Break-even Analysis for Past Data

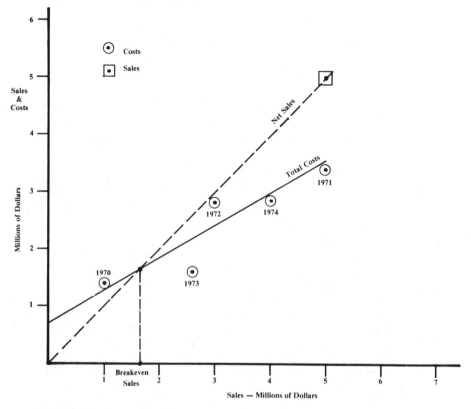

In Exhibit 7.5, sales for 1974 are $4.0 million, the breakeven point is $1.6 million, so that

$$MS = \frac{4.0 - 1.6}{4.0} = 60\%$$

Thus, sales must drop 60% before the company sustains a loss.

APPENDIX C: DEFINITIONS

ACCOUNTS PAYABLE—Money owed by a company for materials or services bought. The financial report that Dun & Bradstreet sells (available at low cost for banks and for business firms) often indicates whether or not a firm is paying its bills on time. This information is gathered from the firm's creditors and shows the amounts owed, the normal credit terms in days, and the dates the actual bills were paid (or if overdue, how many days overdue).

ACCOUNTS RECEIVABLE—Money owed *to* a company for materials or services sold. It is important to know how well we are collecting amounts owed to us. An analysis of Accounts Receivable (A/R) should be made monthly in one of two ways:

1. By classifying Accounts Receivable in terms of the number of days bills are owed to the firm and evaluating the results. For example:

0 to 30 days	—$10,000
31 to 60 days	—$90,000
61 to 90 days	—$30,000
Over 90 days	—$11,000

   We might conclude that $11,000 of debts are turning bad and that "slow" collection of $30,000 is too high.
2. By determining the average number of days all Accounts Receivable are outstanding. This average number is also known as the *collection period*. This measure can then be compared to the credit terms granted to customers (by the firm or industry). Deviations from this norm are both a warning signal and a measurement of the effectiveness of the firm's credit department. (Also, it may be an indication of the value and/or quality of the Accounts Receivable). Care must be taken, however, to prevent credit policies from becoming so strict as to restrict sales (and profits).
   To find *days* of sales represented by Receivables:
   a. Calculate receivables as a percentage of sales for the period. For example, on a year-ending statement—Sales $200,000, Accounts Receivable $50,000. The A/R to Sales ratio is 25%.
   b. Apply this percentage to the number of days in the period. In this example, 25% of 365 days equals 91.25 days. Some firms use 30 days for a month, 90 days for a quarter, and 360 days for a year. (*Note:* This is *not* applicable for some seasonal business, e.g., toys.)

ACCRUED EXPENSES (same as *Accrued Liabilities*)—Amounts currently owed. For example, sometimes the end of an accounting period will come at a time not concurrent with a payroll date so that money is owed to certain employees for work performed for say three days. This amount could then be shown as Accrued Expenses (the amount will be estimated from previous payrolls). Other types of accrued expenses are taxes, depreciation, bond interest, etc.

ACID RATIO—Often called the "quick ratio" because it is a ratio comparison of the current assets, minus inventories, with current liabilities. To find the "quick ratio" divide the current assets minus inventories (which may not be quickly converted into cash) by the current liabilities.

AMORTIZATION—Intangible noncurrent assets such as patents, copyrights, goodwill, organization costs, or leaseholds must be written off over a period of years. They depreciate just as do physical assets. Amortization is the accounting process of writing off such intangibles just as depreciation is the writing off of physical assets.

ASSETS—Everything of value owned by a firm.

BALANCE SHEET—A typical balance sheet shows, as of a certain date, all the assets (everything of value owned by a firm) classified into categories such as cash, securities owned, accounts receivable, inventories, machinery and equipment, land and buildings, etc. The balance sheet also shows all of the liabilities (debts or obligations of the company) such as accounts payable, notes payable, payroll money owed, etc. The difference between assets (what is owned) and the liabilities (what is owed) is also shown on the balance sheet as the equity or ownership capital (net worth).

BOOK VALUE—The value of the company as shown on the books as *net* assets, all assets minus all liabilities. The book value is *not* likely to be the value of the company if it were liquidated. Book value provides a *benchmark* for evaluating the worth of a company.

BOOK VALUE/SHARE OF STOCK—The value for each class of stock divided by the paid-in capital and surplus applicable to that class of stock. Suppose that the following data are given:

6% preferred stock $1,000 par	$1,000,000
Common Stock, $10 par, 40,000 shares	400,000
Paid-in capital in excess of par	500,000
Retained earnings	100,000
Total Capital	$2,000,000
Less: Preferred stock	1,000,000
Equity of common stockholders	$1,000,000

$$\text{Book value/share} = \frac{\$1,000,000}{40,000} = \$25$$

CAPITALIZATION RATIOS—The proportion of each kind of security (bonds, debentures, preferred stock, and common stock) to the total equity. Interest on bonds and debentures usually must be paid before dividends on preferred stock and dividends on preferred stock in turn must be paid before dividends on common stock. Too high ratios for bonds or debentures reduce the attractiveness of preferreds. Similarly, too high a preferred stock ratio reduces the attractiveness of the common.

Generally, an industrial company should have a bond ratio of less than 25%, and the common stock ratio should be at least as much as the total of the bond and preferred stock ratios.

CAPITAL SURPLUS—The net assets minus the value of common and preferred stocks at their par values. The AICPA has recommended that the term *surplus* be discontinued and the following terms be used:

1. Paid-in capital in excess of par. Common stock often has a no-par or low-par value (issued face value) to reduce certain taxes. The

	Computation of Ratios	
	Amount	Ratio
Bonds	$ 3,000,000	30%
Preferred stock	500,000	5%
Common stock, capital surplus and retained earnings	6,500,000	65%
Total	$10,000,000	

amount it is sold for originally minus the par value provides the "excess capital" paid in.

2. Retained earnings (earned surplus) are the accumulated earnings less dividends paid from the date of incorporation. If a company has heavy losses, retained earnings may be wiped out and even the original capital may be reduced.

CASH FLOW ANALYSIS—An analysis of cash received and cash disbursed to show net cash on hand or cash required for each month (or other period such as quarter or week) of the year ahead. The purpose is to assure that the company will be able to pay current bills and to invest cash surpluses wisely.

A cash flow analysis is also used to aid decision makers in evaluating major alternative capital investments. In this case, the discounted cash flow for each investment may be compared. More complicated techniques, internal rate of return or MAPI, are sometimes applied to cash flow analysis for decision making.[6]

COLLECTION PERIOD—See Accounts Receivable. Too long a collection period may indicate:

1. Poor controls—allowing customers to pay at their discretion.
2. Poor marketing policies—selling to second-rate customers.
3. Poor credit policies—passing credits for companies in financial difficulties resulting in a large percentage of bad debt losses. Too short a collection period may indicate lost sales through overly stringent credit policies.

To calculate, see Accounts Receivable.

COMPOUND RATE OF GROWTH—If a firm's sales increase at 10% a year, they will not double in 10 years but in approximately 7.2 years. If sales doubled in 7.2 years, their compound rate of growth would be 10%, meaning sales increased at a rate of 10% each year over the previous year.

To find the number of years it will take for a number to double at any given rate of increase, divide 72 by the rate. For example, given a 6% rate of increase 72 ÷ 6 = 12. It will take approximately 12 years for the original amount to double.

CONSOLIDATED STATEMENT OF INCOME—See Profit-&-Loss

Statement. *Consolidated* means the inclusion of all companies owned over 50% by the parent company unless otherwise stated.

CONTRIBUTION MARGIN—The excess of sales over variable costs expressed as a fraction or percentage of sales. Any product which has a positive contribution margin makes a contribution towards paying overhead expenses or increasing profit or both. (*Note:* Often a share of fixed costs is arbitrarily assigned to a product which makes it appear that the product should be dropped when actually it has a positive contribution margin).

COST OF GOODS SOLD—See Cost of Sales.

COST OF SALES—The total of materials used in the manufacturing process (beginning inventory plus purchases, minus ending inventory) plus labor cost for manufacturing, plus production overhead. In retail stores, cost of goods sold is acquisition cost of merchandise, plus the transportation cost and sometimes minus the cash discount. (Other adjustments may be made depending upon trade practice). Cost of sales or cost of goods manufactured is used to show the manufacturing costs and the *gross profit* (Sales minus manufacturing costs) which can then be used for comparative purposes (year to year or period to period) with all operating expense (sales, advertising, administrative, etc.) segregated. In retail stores, sales minus cost of goods sold is called gross margin—See also gross revenue. Gross margin also is expressed as a percentage. The formula is gross profit divided by sales.

CURRENT ASSETS—All assets readily convertible into cash within a reasonably short time—not over one year.

CURRENT ASSETS/CURRENT LIABILITIES—This is one of the tests of solvency used in analyzing a firm's balance sheet. This is the common so-called "Current Ratio" and is one measurement of the firm's ability to pay its debts. The higher the ratio the greater its "liquidity." To find this ratio, divide current assets by current liabilities. Too high a ratio may indicate inefficient use of working capital, i.e., stagnant cash, slow collections, poor inventory turnover.

CURRENT DEBT—See Current Liabilities.

CURRENT DEBT/NET WORTH and TOTAL DEBT/NET WORTH—These two ratios indicate the proportion of total debt and current debt to the equity (money put in by the owners including retained earnings) of the owners (stockholders). If the ratio of debt to ownership is high then the leverage is high. If it is too high, additional funds will be difficult or impossible to raise. While some go-go financial people say that the higher the leverage, the greater the chance of gain for the owners, more conservative analysts will not invest in companies where total debt to net worth is greater than 100%, or net worth exceeds a certain percentage they deem proper for the particular type of business. To calculate, divide total debt or current debt by net worth.

CURRENT LIABILITIES—Money owed which must be paid within one year or less. Current debt is the portion of the total debt payable within one year and including *current matures on long-term debt.*

CURRENT RATIO—Found by dividing current assets by current liabilities.

DEBT—See Current Debt and Long-Term Debt.

DEPLETION—Used primarily by mining and oil companies. Depletion means the exhausting of the underground assets or a part of them, which the company no longer owns (as they have been used).

DEPRECIATION—An allocation made on the books to record the cost of the use of an asset during an accounting period. For example, an automobile purchased new for $3,000 may only be worth $2,400 at the end of the first year. The $600 difference ($3,000 − $2,400) is a reduction in value and *a cost of doing business* called depreciation. Depreciation, therefore, is a true expense of doing business. Purchase of an asset can be thought of as the purchase of a "fund of usefulness" used in the operation of the business. A portion of the "fund" is consumed or expires until it has no value and must be replaced. If the automobile mentioned above is needed to operate the business and can be used for five years, at which time it can be traded in for $500 on a new car, then the depreciation cost per year is $500 ($3,000 original price minus $500 trade-in value equals $2,500 divided by five years equals $500 per year depreciation cost). Depreciation is a direct charge against profit and if it is not taken, or too little is taken, profit will be overstated. Conversely, if too much (very rapid) depreciation is taken, profits will be understated. Financial analysts are well advised, therefore, to investigate depreciation charges as thoroughly as possible. Annual statements generally have footnotes indicating depreciation policies. The methods firms use in depreciating assets, whether they be on materials, machinery, buildings, etc., can make a *very substantial difference* in a firm's reported *profit*.

EARNINGS RETAINED IN THE BUSINESS—See Capital Surplus.

EARNED SURPLUS—See Capital Surplus.

EARNINGS PER SHARE—Figured by taking the profit of the company and deducting dividends on preferred stock, if any, and dividing by the number of shares of common stock.

EXPENSE—See Cost of Sales, Fixed Costs, Accrued Expenses.

EXTRAORDINARY INCOME (or loss)—Income or losses that are unusual, i.e., nonrecurring. Usually a footnote will specifically identify them.

FIXED ASSETS—Assets such as buildings, machinery, etc., used in the business that are not intended to nor can be readily convertible into cash.

FIXED ASSETS TO NET WORTH—As with other "liquidity" ratios, the purpose of this ratio is to determine the firm's ability to weather times of stress—to meet its obligations—to pay off its creditors. If the ratio is high, the firm may be unable or at least find it difficult to increase its long-term debt, raising additional funds with which to pay creditors and operate its business. *Note:* This ratio varies considerably from industry to industry, often high in capital intensive industries. If the ratio is too low, some analysts feel that firms are not making enough use of the leverage provided by using the funds of others. Other analysts think that a low ratio is indicative of good management because the company can borrow and offset temporarily business mistakes or adverse conditions requiring extra cash. To calculate this ratio, divide fixed assets by net worth.

FIXED COSTS—Expenses that are relatively fixed in amount regardless of sales volume as opposed to *variable costs* which vary in close proportion to changes in sales volume. (Some costs are fixed or partly fixed under certain conditions and variable under other conditions making them difficult to categorize). Also see *operating leverage.*

FIXED LIABILITIES—Long-term liabilities. Debts not anticipated to be paid off in less than a year. For example, five-year notes or long-term bonds.

FUNDED DEBT—Long-term debt (bonds, notes, debentures) with specific future dates at which time the loan will be paid.

FUNDED DEBT/NET WORKING CAPITAL—This ratio is used in conjunction with other liquidity ratios to determine first whether or not long- or short-term debt is in proper proportion to net working capital and second, if it is not in proportion where it is faulty. To calculate, divide funded debt by working capital.

GOODWILL—If one firm buys another and pays more for its stock than the net value of the assets, it may show the difference as goodwill. At this writing, the purchasing firm must write off the goodwill over a 40-year term. Accountants often look with jaundiced eye on goodwill. Corporate practice varies widely in assigning value to goodwill. Also see Intangibles.

GROSS MARGIN—Net sales minus cost of sales (same as cost of goods sold) can be expressed as a percentage of sales or in dollars. See cost of goods sold. Gross margin is the amount of dollars left from sales after cost of goods sold has been deducted with which *all* other expenses (selling and administrative, for example) can be paid, and from which the profit is realized.

GROSS REVENUE—Same as sales, merchandise shipped or professional services rendered.

INCOME STATEMENT—See Profit-and-Loss Statement.

INTANGIBLES—Also see Goodwill. Intangibles refers to the value of nonphysical assets such as trademarks, patents, goodwill, or franchise value. Some companies have reduced the value of intangibles to $1, others continue to assign large amounts to their value.

INVENTORY—Stock on hand. In manufacturing firms generally there are three types of inventory: (a) raw materials, (b) work in process including an allocation for production and other costs already in the partially finished goods, and (c) finished goods. While supplies of stationery, pens, and pencils are in an inventory of office supplies (prepaid office expense), generally the term *inventory* refers only to materials used in the manufacturing process or the finished goods offered for sale. The inventory value is stated at cost or market value, whichever is lower. Market value must take into account obsolescence, deterioration, decline in prices, etc., in order to be a conservative valuation.

LEVERAGE—The use of borrowed money to increase profit and hence increase the rate of return on the owners' invested capital. The Debt/Equity ratio (see Current Debt/Net Worth) measures the leverage. Usually a value of 50 percent is considered quite high for a company. A value of zero to 20 percent may indicate the company is not maximizing its growth opportunities.

LIABILITIES—The debts or obligations of the company which must eventually be paid off. See Current Liabilites, Fixed Liabilities, Funded Debt.

MARKETABLE SECURITES—An asset, usually an investment of funds not needed immediately in the operation of the business which can quickly be converted into cash with a minimum of market fluctuation (short-term government notes, commercial paper, bonds, etc.).

NET PROFIT—The amount of profit earned by the firm after paying *all* expenses, including taxes.

NET PROFITS/NET SALES—A measure of profitability and good management. This ratio must be high for the industry and accompanied by a stable or growing market share to be considered good. For example, 2 percent or 3 percent might be very good for a retail food chain with its high volume, *provided* the chain was not pricing so high as to decrease its market share. On the other hand, in a high technology manufacturing industry, 20 percent to 30 percent might be a more typical range. To calculate, divide profit by net sales.

NET PROFITS/NET WORTH (ROI)—The measure of the business relative to other opportunities for investing money.

If a firm is not earning sufficient profit on the money that the stockholders have invested in the business to pay out dividends and put more money back in the business so that it will grow and remain competitive, then there isn't much sense in continuing the business. Many firms have as an objective a certain return on net worth. The exact figure is based on the type of business, degree of risk involved, etc., but rarely is the objective less than 8 percent (utilities) and often is as high as 20 percent or more (high risk airplane manufacturers or retail stores where turnover is high so that investment can be as low as in discount stores). As with profit percentage on sales, if this ratio is too high, growth may be inhibited by too high selling prices. To calculate, divide profit by net worth.

NET SALES/INVENTORY—A very important *ratio* inasmuch as comparison with other companies in the same type of business often tells a great deal about the effectiveness of management's policies and control.

If inventory turnover is poor, any or all of the following may be indicated:

1. Marketing policies are poor. Too many items in the assortment offered. Trying to be all things to all people. Not enough market

research to have a "sense of direction." May be selling through wrong channels or to too many unprofitable customers.

2. No policies at all—allowing the customer and/or the market to dictate policy or allowing production to say to marketing, "you must sell everything or anything we produce" or conversely, "you in production must produce everything our customers need" or "competition requires that we have a complete (meaning too full) line."

3. Controls of the company are poor or not enforced or both. Objectives are not clearly spelled out or not known or not followed.

Inventories that are too large:

1. Tie up money needlessly, reduce return on investment, and/or require additional capital which may be better used elsewhere.
2. Often result in excessive losses because large inventories:
   a. Increase obsolescence
   b. Result in product deterioration
   c. If funds are needed elsewhere or in a forced liquidation are sold at heavy markdowns.

Inventories that are too low:

1. Increase stockouts which may slow down or shut processing for lack of parts or materials and/or lose customers.
2. Increase cost of manufacturing due to small or broken lots, or excessive expediting because of short runs.

To calculate, divide net sales by inventory.

NET SALES/NET WORTH—This ratio (expressed in numbers or times rather than percentages) indicates the turnover relationship between sales and equity (ownership funds). Generally, the higher the turnover the higher the profit is likely to be. Sometimes high turnover may indicate an under-capitalized company (which is the major cause of early failure in new businesses). Use this ratio with other ratios to get the full meaning, e.g., current ratio, debt to net worth, etc. To calculate, divide net sales by equity (same as net worth).

NET WORKING CAPITAL—Current assets minus current liabilities (sometimes called working capital). Analysts refer to the net working capital position because it represents the excess of assets readily convertible into cash with which to pay current moneys owed.

NET WORTH—The total of all assets minus all liabilities. This means the total of preferred stock, common stock, and all surplus; or, in other words, the ownership capital of the business (equity).

NOTES PAYABLE—A loan to the business usually payable on certain specified dates, on which interest is usually paid, and evidenced by a written "note." Notes can be guaranteed by collateral or merely backed by the general credit of the company.

OPERATING EXPENSES—Costs directly related to the running of the business (selling and administrative expense) but not including cost of goods (manufacturing expense) and not such things as income taxes or costs not directly related (charitable contributions, for example).

OPERATING LEVERAGE—When a *more* than proportional increase in profits results from increased sales volume. Operating leverage is sometimes used by marketing managers as a reason to shade the selling price on large volume orders. A complete study of fixed and variable expenses, the breakeven point, etc., is generally advisable *before* such action is taken as well as applicable federal law which may specifically restrict or prohibit such cutting of prices.

OPERATING PROFIT—Profit before other income and before taxes. See Other Income.

OTHER ASSETS—May be prepaid expense, patents, goodwill, etc.

OTHER EXPENSES—Expenses other than those normally shown as cost of goods sold or selling, administrative and general expenses. Accrued liabilities or small interest expenses are sometimes included in other expenses.

OTHER INCOME—May be income from rents, securities owned, etc., that is income not directly related to the principal business of the firm.

PREPAID EXPENSE—Expenses paid before the full service has been rendered. For example, insurance premiums may be paid a year ahead of time and at the time the statement period was ended may have been paid for six months into the future.

PRIMARY EARNINGS (per share)—Dividing earnings by the number of shares outstanding plus the number that would be outstanding if all convertible securities (including stock options and warrants) were converted into common stock.

PROFIT—The amount left after all operating expenses have been paid or accounted for. Often shown before taxes have been deducted. Also, see Net Profit and Operating Profit.

PROFIT-AND-LOSS STATEMENT—A financial summary of the operations of a company by sales, costs, expenses, income, etc., for a specified period of time—usually for three, six, nine, or twelve months, although most companies' accountants make estimated profit and loss statements each month.

PROFIT MARGIN—Earnings before interest and taxes divided by sales and usually expressed as a percentage.

PRO-FORMA STATEMENTS—Income and balance sheet statements for future years which are part of the company's plan. They are also prepared for consideration of special plans such as mergers or new ventures.

QUICK ASSETS—See Acid Ratio. Quick assets equal current assets minus inventories.

RETAINED EARNINGS—The accumulation of earnings (not paid out in dividends) which is kept in the business for day-to-day operation and/or expansion of the business.

RETURN ON EQUITY—A very important percentage indicating the money earned (net profit) on the net worth (money put into the business or later added). See Net Profit/Net Worth. To find, divide net profit by net worth.

ROI—Return on Investment. See Return on Equity and Net Profits/ Net Worth.

REVENUE—All income, regardless of the source.

SINKING FUND—An accumulation of money established by setting aside a specified amount of cash at regular intervals for the purpose of providing funds at a specific future date. For example, funds may be needed to pay off a bond issue or replace a capital asset.

SURPLUS—See Capital Surplus.

TANGIBLE NET WORTH—Net Worth (see above) minus intangible items included in the assets, such as patents, goodwill, trademarks, leaseholds, mailing lists, organization expenses, etc.

TURNOVER (INVENTORY)—The number of times per year that average inventory (in dollar value) is sold (or moved). If sales are $100 and the average inventory selling price is $25, the turnover is 100 divided by 25 or 4 *times* per year. See Net Sales/Inventory.

Warning: In figuring inventory turnover, be sure to use either sales at selling price and average inventory at selling price *or* sales at *cost* (cost of goods sold) divided by average inventory at cost.

Turnover is best compared with turnover of companies in similar lines of business as slow turnover or fast turnover is often a characteristic of the particular type of business, i.e., slow turnover is characteristic of piano manufacturing, aged whiskey, expensive antiques, etc.

8

FUNCTIONAL AREA— PRODUCTION

THE BIG IDEAS

"Production" activities are not confined just to manufacturing of a tangible product. Rather, production is the process of converting any *design of product or service* into the *actual* product or service.

In any production system, the most immediate goals are getting out the *right quantity* of the product at the *right time* at the lowest cost. These aims *tend to take precedence over quality,* but not in all companies. Because the marketing organization desires the highest quality possible, in addition to the preceding requirements, there are often conflicts between manufacturing and marketing which much be resolved by formulation and implementation of policies. Such policies may require levels of quality control varying from none (all risk passed on to the purchaser) to a very high level (most risk assumed by the manufacturer). The need for policies dealing with manufacturing aims once again shows the need for spelling out a unified sense of direction.

An illustration of the importance of efficient production may be found in the major appliance industry. Over the last few years, several major corporations, including Westinghouse, Ford, American Motors and General Motors, have abandoned the industry because they could not handle the intense price competition. All these firms sold their plants and brand names to White Consolidated Industries—a former sewing machine manufacturer which entered the major appliance field in 1967. White succeeded where bigger firms failed by careful attention to production efficiency. White didn't do anything fancy—just a fanatical devotion to cost cutting combined with a profit-centered organization that places great pressure on each plant manager and allows precise accountability for results.

The principal external factor which produces a problem in hundreds of thousands of small firms is their operation below "critical mass." That is, the firms have such a small share of the market that they do not reach a level of operation where economies of scale are great. As a result, they often have idle machine time and employees who must perform a variety of jobs on constantly varying planning schedules. The solutions to these problems are more technical than management based, except insofar as management can expand sales.

One further big idea to consider in evaluating the production activity of a company is the nature of the company. Production of hardware may pose many problems different from those of production of life insurance plans, advertising campaigns, or telephone and telegraph services. Labor relations, work assignment and control, equipment maintenance, quality control, and inventory control must be viewed quite differently in different types of industries. Often, industry practices place varied restrictions on production practices. This means that the student should make an industry study as described in Chapter 13 in order to derive workable, realistic solutions to production problems.

The differences in emphasis on the various production activities of a factory and an insurance company are indicated in the following listing.

Activity	Importance	
	Factory	Insurance Company
1. Equipment and process	Very important	Not dominant
2. Plant layout, work flow, and work environment	Very important	Very important
3. Material procurement	Very important	Little importance
4. Personnel management	Fairly important	Very important
5. Work methods and measurement	Very important	Important
6. Equipment maintenance and replacement	Very important	Some importance
7. Production planning and scheduling	Very important	Little importance because mostly routine once established
8. Assigning and dispatching work	Very important	Generally routine
9. Controlling inventories	Very important	Negligible
10. Controlling quality, cost, time	Critical	Very important
11. Landlord operations	Some importance	Some importance

POLICIES

Many of the policies associated with manufacturing are beyond the control of the manager of manufacturing. For example, while he or she may make recommendations, the following policies are usually made by top management.

1. Plant location, plant additions, or plant renovation
2. Major equipment purchases and capital budgeting
3. Purchasing policies such as single vendor or multiple vendor source alternatives
4. Transportation of raw materials in and storage and transportation of finished goods
5. Trans-shipments of materials among plants within the company
6. Centralization or decentralization of the manufacturing management information system. Will the plant establish it and run it or will corporate staff?
7. Inventory policy for finished goods
8. Quality level of products to be maintained. Should quality be dominant or sacrificed to cost reduction in manufacturing backed by customer service on faulty products?
9. Union recognition
10. Disciplinary policies and rules
11. Training
12. Hiring, promotions, transfers, and terminations

In analyzing a company policy case, we should clarify who has responsibility for establishing manufacturing policies, particularly those policies which are at the root of company problems.

TYPICAL GENERAL MANUFACTURING PROBLEMS

There are certain general problems which the student will find occur fairly frequently in real life, and hence in case problems. A number of these are listed below.

1. The manufacturing plant consists of an antiquated, multistory building, with a restricted undesirable floor shape. Problems of material handling and work flow are critical.
2. The plant construction was modified when it was built because of undercapitalization of the company. Equipment, processes, and material handling costs are excessive because of the retrenchment.
3. Equipment for the plant has become obsolete. Numerical controlled machines, automation of assembly work, and completely new production process and quality control techniques have left the plant far behind.
4. Orders are produced far behind schedule, bottlenecks in production exist, work-in-process is accumulating, and material move-

ment is hampered. Unbalanced production due to lack of an adequate number of machines of a certain type or poor production planning may be the cause.

5. Sales fluctuate greatly producing a widely varying demand on the factory. The production manager and marketing manager are in constant conflict.

6. Problems in obtaining raw materials arise because of a single-source policy. Costs of raw materials vary because of multiple-source policy. Problems of quality may occur in either case.

7. It is difficult to accumulate accurate time and cost on production operations for a wide variety of reasons, one of which is a poor production system.

8. Daywork and piecework pay are both used in the plant and this is causing employee dissatisfaction or high costs for some operations.

9. Shoddy quality products are reaching consumers, or the factory is shipping sizes and models to customers which do not match the salespeople's orders.

10. Historical labor practices are preventing the introduction of new equipment and preventing new methods which will reduce costs.

11. Absenteeism and turnover are high because of specific policies of the company dealing with such topics as wages, working conditions, safety, etc.

12. A wide variety of models, "specials" for customers, and rush jobs are creating constant conflict between the manufacturing and the marketing departments.

13. A wide variety of reports on production status is required. Many of these reports appear not to be used, or even read, by many recipients. These reports are taking up a lot of the time of supervisors and production control people.

14. Sales personnel keep requesting immediate delivery on items which must be produced from expensive materials or subassemblies which must be purchased on a long lead-time basis.

15. There are large scrap and rework losses.

16. Manufacturing methods seem unduly involved and no work methods studies or time studies are conducted.

FIVE MAJOR SYSTEMS FOR ANALYSIS

Five systems which form a basis for analysis of production policies and problems are:

1. The manufacturing organization,
2. Production planning,
3. Production operations,
4. Production control,
5. Relationships between the manufacturing organization and other organizational components of the company.

MANUFACTURING ORGANIZATION

The traditional manufacturing organization structure is shown in Exhibit 8.1. Internal control problems often arise because of unclear division of responsibility in the foreperson's area of activity. This may be seen from the list of responsibilities and impinging staff activities shown below.

Foreperson's Prime Activities	Staff Responsibility
1. Direct supervision of labor	
2. Set up work places	
3. Train shop employees	Personnel
4. Schedule at the detail level	Production Planning
5. Dispatch	Production Control
6. Move material	Production Control
7. Plan operations	Manufacturing Engineering
8. Apply methods and time standards	Manufacturing Engineering
9. Test	Quality Control
10. Inspect	Quality Control
11. Maintain equipment	Facilities
12. Supervise housekeeping	Facilities

PRODUCTION PLANNING AND CONTROL

A typical organization for production planning and control is shown in Exhibit 8.2. This organization is the center of the manufacturing information system.

PRODUCTION OPERATIONS

Production operations consist of the work actually performed on the product in process. They form the line activity at the lowest level in the working hierarchy. They involve the processes, work methods, transportation, and temporary storage necessary to change the form of the material in process. These operations depend heavily on the nature of the basic manufacturing process.

RELATIONSHIPS WITH OTHER COMPONENTS

Manufacturing activities are closely tied to engineering and marketing activities and are affected by staff personnel in training and industrial relations. The information system for a particular company shown in Exhibit 8.3 suggests many of these relationships.

BASIC TYPES OF PRODUCTION

Some of the problems in manufacturing arise because management does not recognize the basic type of production called for in the manufacture of its products. It may therefore apply policies and techniques which are inappropriate for its correct production form. The basic processes are:

1. Product-based. Equipment and people are fixed according to the order of operations required by the product.
2. Process-based. Process departments and groupings of like machines are established and the goods in process must be transported to the proper department.
3. Material-based. People and equipment must be brought to the materials in process so that the materials do not move.

A comparison of some aspects of these is shown in Table 8.1.

CHECKLIST FOR ANALYSIS

Demand

1. Is demand constant, seasonal, or highly irregular?
2. Are too high or too low sales forecasts constantly causing increased production costs?
3. Are there a wide variety of products and many orders which are difficult to forecast?
4. Is manufacturing trying to second-guess the sales department on forecasts of demand?

Plant

1. Are manufacturing facilities centralized or dispersed as appropriate to the many factors such as market, transportation, and raw materials sources?
2. What are the problems with present locations?
3. Is there a lack of space or is there unused space?
4. Is there room for expansion?
5. Are facilities owned or leased?
6. What is the total cost and the cost/square foot?
7. Is single story or multistory appropriate?
8. Is there adequate high-bay area?
9. What are the conditions of the buildings, grounds, waste disposal system, security system, access roads, and parking?
10. How is the lighting, air conditioning, and noise suppression?
11. What is the climate, appearance, pollution, and general livability of the area?
12. Will the plant be adequate five years hence?

Equipment

1. Is the equipment general purpose, special purpose, or both, as appropriate?
2. Is a modernization program in force which results in a good trade-off between capital costs and labor costs?

3. Is the equipment capable of maintaining process control within the limits of tolerances usually specified?
4. What is the maintenance policy—preventive by periodic service, breakdown maintenance or continuous inspection?
5. Are there equipment replacement policies and procedures in effect?
6. What is the average life of the equipment? Are records kept on the age and condition of each machine?
7. Is there an accumulation of idle, long unused equipment?
8. What is the ratio of maintenance expense to direct labor and how does this compare with the ratio for the industry?
9. Is equipment properly equipped for operator safety?

Plant Layout, Work Flow, and Work Environment

1. Is the plant layout appropriate for the basic type of production process and products?
2. Is the work flow designed to minimize transportation and handling costs?
3. What is the space utilization efficiency ratio? (SUE = cubic feet usefully occupied/net usable cubic feet.) Average for fabricating industries is 0.53 and for process industries, 0.63.
4. Are there aisle space problems?
5. Are there storage space problems?
6. Are there safety problems due to overhead cranes, conveyors, protruding equipment, etc.?
7. Can goods-in-process and finished goods be stored safely without fear of damage or theft?
8. Are electrical outlets, compressed air, gas, and other utility outlets conveniently located for the equipment and the workers?
9. Are building codes and local and state fire laws being complied with?
10. Is mobile or fixed material handling appropriate?
11. How are the temperature, colors, lighting, noise level, dust, floor surface, lunch facilities, rest facilities, safety, and other factors of the work environment?

Material Procurement

1. Is there a policy on single-source vs. multiple-source procurement?
2. Is procurement planned to minimize inventory system costs in terms of holding costs, procurement costs, shortage costs, and quantity discounts?
3. Is procurement lead-time constant and short?
4. Are there adequate controls on maximum amounts of each material which is ordered?
5. Is there control of quality and quantity of incoming shipments?

EXHIBIT 8.1

Traditional Manufacturing Organization

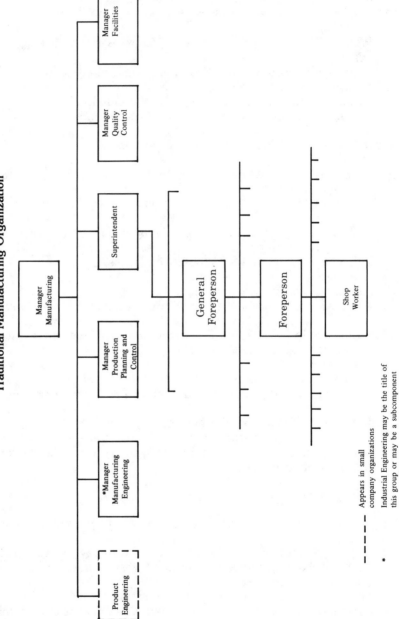

- - - - -   Appears in small
                company organizations

    *   Industrial Engineering may be the title of
             this group or may be a subcomponent

EXHIBIT 8.2

Traditional Production Planning and Control Organization

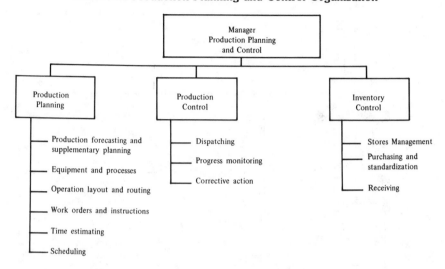

Personnel Management

1. Are there clearly stated policies in hiring, promotion, layoff, discharge, disciplinary action, seniority, and fringe benefits?
2. What are the policies on piecework, daywork, and overtime?
3. Are fair-employment practices followed and equal pay for equal work given?
4. What is the turnover rate?
5. What is the relationship between management and the employees? Between management and the union?
6. Are all aspects of working conditions and compensation comparable to local standards and industry standards?
7. Are there any differences or inequities in the treatment of employees among different plants?
8. What relationship and responsibility problems face the foreperson due to company personnel policies?

Work Methods and Measurement

1. Are work methods developed for each operation?
2. What method of work measurement is employed?
3. What is the union's attitude toward work methods and measurement?

Equipment Maintenance and Replacement

1. Is there a policy on equipment maintenance which specified the method for each equipment group?

EXHIBIT 8.3

Job Lot Production System

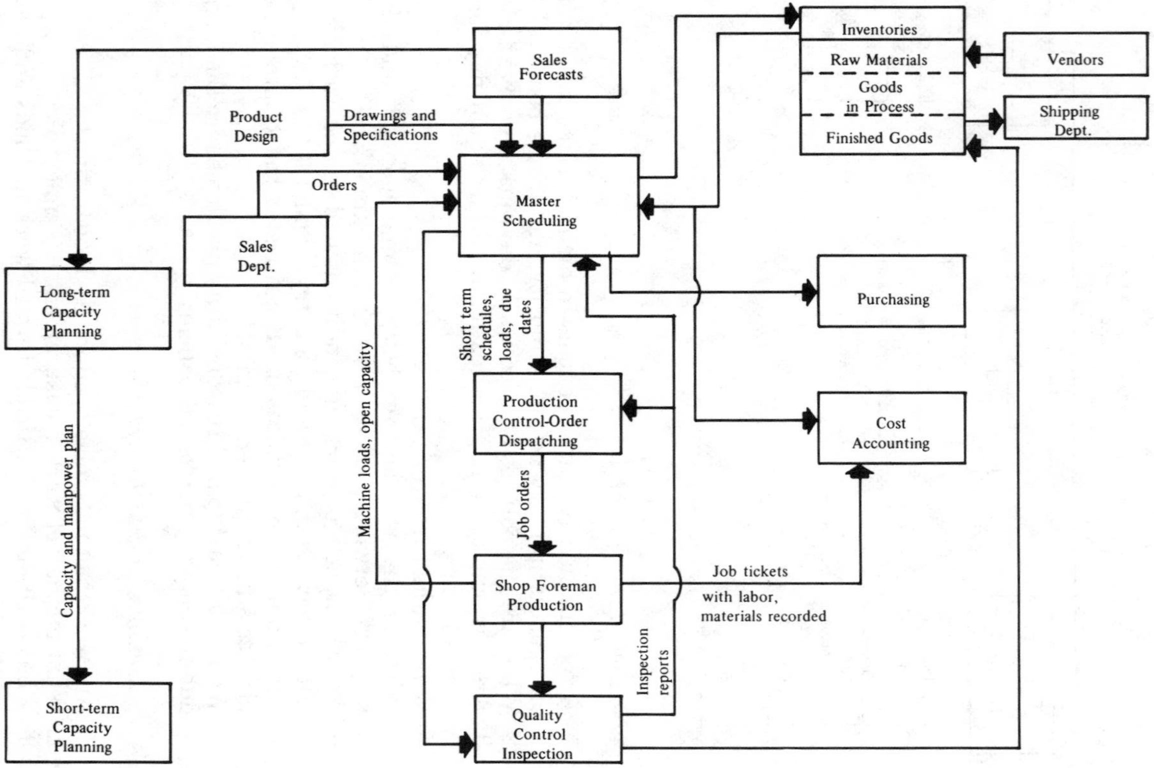

2. Are records maintained for each machine?
3. Is there a replacement policy and is it implemented?
4. Is the size of the maintenance crew balanced against the cost of downtime?
5. Is there a policy as to what maintenance may be performed by the equipment operator?

Production Planning and Scheduling

1. Is there a formal system for production planning and scheduling of orders?
2. Is there a policy to handle "rush" and priority orders?
3. Does the planning smooth the demand requirements?
4. Is overtime minimized or is additional plant capacity needed?
5. Are there bottlenecks in production?
6. Is worker productivity high?
7. Does the company use an incentive system?
8. Are materials available and machine time available as the orders are dispatched to the foreperson?
9. Is the line balanced well if mass production is the mode?
10. What is the make-or-buy policy?

Assigning and Dispatching Work

1. Are work orders assigned in accordance with known availability of machines and manpower?
2. Are priorities indicated?
3. Is there a formal system for dispatching work (start production) orders to forepersons?
4. Could a centralized computer provide efficient dispatching of orders throughout the plant?

Controlling Inventories

1. What is the ratio of goods-in-process inventory (dollars) to cost of goods produced per period?
2. Are goods-in-process piled up at storage areas on the plant floor?
3. Are production runs based on economic lot size calculations?
4. Is control concentrated on high cost items as in the ABC inventory control policy?
5. Are finished goods inventories kept at the plant or sent?
6. Is statistical sampling of lots employed to minimize system costs?
7. Are customer returns for faulty goods excessive?
8. Are reorders based on Economic Order Quantity (EOQ)?
9. Are budgets employed effectively?
10. Is there a well-organized incentive-based cost reduction program?
11. Are costs increasing or decreasing and why?
12. If there is a sudden decline in demand, could costs be quickly reduced?
13. Is indirect expense carefully monitored and tightly controlled?

TABLE 8.1

Comparison of Basic Types of Production

Characteristic	Product-based	Process-based	Material-based
1. Other terminology	Mass Production Standard	Batch or job shop	Project
2. Product or standard variant	standard variants	Nonstandard, but usually within a general class of process type	Unique, standard, or standard variant
3. Quantity produced	Large	Small or large	Small, often only one
4. Type of equipment	Special purpose	General purpose	Both general purpose and special purpose
5. Material flow	No back-tracking	As required by the sequence of processes	Fixed position
6. In process inventory	Low	High	Low (ordered as needed)
7. Relative worker skill level	Low	High	Medium to high
8. Difficulty of supervision	Easy	Difficult	Easy to difficult
9. Job instructions	Very few	Very many	Usually many and often very detailed
10. Planning	Difficult and complex but only done once	Complex and often	Relatively easy to complex
11. Control	Very easy	Difficult	Difficult for custom projects
12. Flexibility in changing the process	Very difficult	Easy	Easy
13. Examples	Radios, light bulbs, automobiles	Aircraft, men's suits, pressure gauges	Steam turbines, ships, homes, prestressed concrete panels

14. Have standard operating ratios been established and used as control devices?
15. Is the manufacturing cycle time known and controlled?
16. Is the progress of orders through manufacturing monitored and corrective action taken if they fall behind schedule?
17. What is the record of meeting delivery promises?

Housekeeping

1. Is the plant painted regularly, the windows cleaned, and the floor cleaned daily?
2. Are the barrels of trash, scrap, oily rags, and cigarette butts visible?
3. Are warning signs clear?
4. Is plant fire and other protective equipment checked regularly?
5. Are the grounds, roads, and parking areas kept up?

SELECTED BIBLIOGRAPHY ON PRODUCTION MANAGEMENT

Aljian, George W. *Purchasing Handbook.* 3rd ed. New York: McGraw-Hill, 1973.

Buffa, Elwood S., and Miller, Jeffrey G. *Production-Inventory Systems: Planning and Control.* 3rd ed. Homewood, Ill.: Richard D. Irwin, 1979.

Chase, Richard B., and Aquilano, Nicholas J. *Production and Operations Management: A Life Cycle Approach.* 3rd ed. Homewood, Ill.: Richard D. Irwin, 1981.

Holstein, William K. Production Planning and Control Integrated. *Harvard Business Review,* May-June, 1968.

Lewis, Bernard T. *Management Handbook for Plant Engineers.* New York: McGraw-Hill, 1976.

Mills, Peter K., and Moberg, Dennis J. Perspectives on the Technology of Service Operations. *Academy of Management Review,* July, 1982.

Moore, Harry D., and Kibbey, Donald R. *Manufacturing: Materials and Processes.* 3rd ed. Columbus, Ohio: Grid Publishing, Inc., 1982.

Skinner, Wickham. *Manufacturing in the Corporate Strategy.* New York: John Wiley & Sons, 1978.

Snyder, Charles A.; Cox, James F.; and Jesse, Richard R., Jr. A Dependent Demand Approach to Service Organization Planning and Control. *Academy of Management Review,* July, 1982.

9

FUNCTIONAL AREA— ENGINEERING AND R & D

WHAT ARE RESEARCH AND DEVELOPMENT AND ENGINEERING

There are many people living today in the United States who in their early childhood never saw a radio, an electric light bulb, an automobile, or an airplane. Technical research, development, and engineering have provided us with thousands of new products to make life less arduous and more enjoyable.

There is considerable vagueness in the terminology of technological development so that we give the following as guides:

1. *Fundamental or basic research* is the search for new knowledge regardless of possible applications. Practically none of this type of investigation is carried out by industry, although Bell laboratory and General Electric's R & D Center work in relatively broad areas. Universities are the principal source of this work.
2. *Applied research* is research directed towards a particular product line or particular product. It is the search for new knowledge needed to solve a current practical problem. An example would be metallurgical research oriented toward finding a material which could be used as a coating to prevent the burning up of spacecraft reentering the atmosphere.
3. *Development,* advance development, or advance engineering is concerned with examining new conceptual designs or the development of performance specifications. Generally it is concerned with the application of new knowledge and requires some support from applied research. The end result is a gross system design which speci-

223

fies the performance expected of the system and the components of the system.

4. *Design engineering* starts with the desired performance specifications as given and ends with a set of design specifications. Design specifications consist of drawings and reports which describe the product in sufficient detail so that it may be manufactured.
5. *Production equipment engineering* is the design of unique or specialized equipment used to produce a particular part.
6. *Process* or *manufacturing engineering* consists of the specification of equipment and processes to be used in production. It is also concerned with translating engineering drawings into manufacturing drawings and instructions.
7. *Industrial engineering* is a broad term for the technical-economic problem solving required for manufacturing.

ROLE OF ENGINEERING AND RESEARCH (E & R)

The role of E & R within the company is to contribute to the profitability of the business by providing technical support to the formulation and implementation of the organization's objectives. In brief, it supplies technical advice and designs products which can be produced economically to meet market needs.

In 1970, $26.1 billion was spent on what the government defines as research and development. In 1983, approximately $85.0 billion was spent. About 50% of these funds are provided by the United States government. The implication is that firms which point their products towards government areas of interest will be able to conduct more research and development work.

One of the major functions of the E & R organization is to determine the direction and the degree of technological advances for up to 25 years in the future. This is called *technological forecasting*. It involves technical trends, government policy, social pressures, environmental states, and economic growth. Small companies are not likely to indulge in such long-range forecasting, but they should keep themselves aware of developments just on the horizon for their own products.

BASIC STEPS IN THE DESIGN PROCESS

The design process may be put into action by one of three events:

1. A customer of the firm transmits to the firm a general need, a particular problem, or a particular requirement.
2. The marketing or the E & R department identifies a problem which calls for the design of a new or improved product.
3. E & R makes a technical advance which has a practical application. Market research and economic analysis indicate that a new product resulting from the technical advance has a good commercial possibility.

The design process is basically an information production and processing process. An idea for a product is developed by setting the characteristics which the product should possess. These are often called performance specifications. These product characteristics are listed below:

1. Performance of basic and subsidiary functions
2. Accuracy of performance
3. Speed of performance
4. Cost
5. Reliability
6. Environmental adaptability
7. Maintainability
8. Replaceability by successive models
9. Safety and fail-safe features
10. Producibility
11. Optimum materials and process for size of manufacturing run
12. Simplification, standardization, preferred sizes, and modular construction
13. Weight
14. Size and shape
15. Styling and packaging
16. Compatibility with other systems or auxiliary equipment
17. Ease of operation (human engineering)
18. Balanced design through tradeoffs
19. Ease of transporting and installing
20. Legality
21. Social aspects (pollution, radiation, sound blasts, etc.)

Information is produced by two methods based upon the economics and the risk involved. These methods are analysis (quantitative applications of scientific principles and available data) and experiments. Analysis and experiments are like the right foot and the left foot, each advancing one step at a time. The iterative or feedback nature of the design process and the process itself are shown in Exhibit 9.1.

Some of the terms in the diagram require further explanation for the non-technical manager. The term "conceptual design" is a rough or gross design usually developed by means of sketches and preliminary calculations. The purpose of conceptual designs is to develop a number of different approaches before selecting a particular one.

The "reference design" gives the assumed performance specifications and other assumptions about characteristics of various components. This permits the engineer to design a component to fit with the other components. At certain times, the reference design has to be changed and everyone concerned must be notified.

The "prototype model" is the first unit of the product to be made which is supposed to be exactly like those to be sold. Actually, after field tests and a production run of a few models, some modifications are usually made.

EXHIBIT 9.1

Graphic Portrayal of the Product Design System

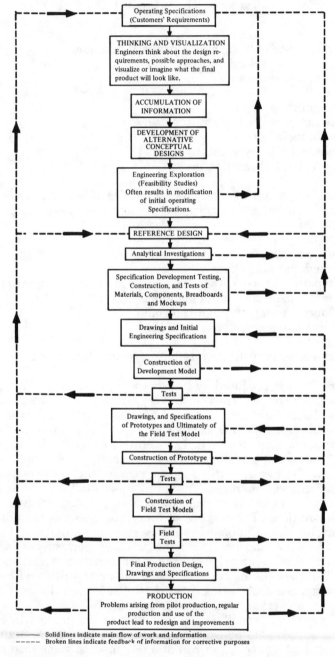

Solid lines indicate main flow of work and information
Broken lines indicate feedback of information for corrective purposes

Source: D. W. Karger and R. G. Murdick, *Managing Engineering and Research,* adapted from 3rd ed. New York: Industrial Press, Inc., 1980.

UNIFIED SENSE OF DIRECTION

Engineering and research must be considered from a business viewpoint, not as a shop where technical people carry out pet projects of their own choice. E & R is the source of new products, and often of new product ideas. As such, it plays a key role in the continuing existence of the firm. It must work with marketing to make new products fulfill needs. It must work with manufacturing to achieve the optimum quality/cost mix.

In 1977, the new president of RCA, Edgar H. Griffiths, was placing new emphasis on profitability. RCA was for many years a firm which was unable to turn its superior technology into substantial profits. To turn the situation around, Griffiths re-ordered RCA's goals, identified markets, segmented them, and directed RCA's research and development towards products which serve specific market segments.

POLICIES

Typical major policies which might be established for E & R are as follows:

1. The budget for E & R shall be based on sales volume.
2. E & R shall be restricted to specific products rather than broad product areas. The contrary policy or variations of such restrictions may be formulated.
3. E & R must be represented on all product development committees.
4. E & R performed by the company shall be kept to a specified limited amount and outside E & R will be purchased when needed. The contrary policy or variations of this may be in force instead.
5. Model construction and engineering tests may be required to be performed by the company or outside the company as stated in policies.
6. Policies may specify or restrict the work of technical people. For example, engineers may be prohibited from doing any drafting or operating of test equipment. However, it may be a company policy that an average of two technical supporting personnel be assigned to each engineer.
7. Policies with regard to information flow are extremely important in E & R. Who gets various types of technical reports, who establishes reference design data, how drawings and drawing changes are processed, who gets test results, and who gets financial information and approvals.

8. Policies for authorization of new projects require specified information and approvals.
9. Engineering will be decentralized but research will be centralized (in a multidivision company).
10. Only commercial or nonclassified (defense) research and engineering projects will be carried out.
11. A tuition refund program and other incentives may implement a company's basic policy to continually develop its technical personnel.
12. Policies with regard to publication of technical articles and books, as well as with regard to talks at technical society meetings may be either supportive or restrictive.

TYPICAL GENERAL E & R PROBLEMS

Common problems related to research and engineering are as follows:

1. Failure to set basic objectives is evidenced by uncompleted projects, bootleg projects, pet projects, projects unrelated to company areas, feelings of frustration in the organizations, and lack of any methods of measurement.
2. E & R is attempting to develop products which *it* thinks are proper but which are not considered appropriate by the marketing organization.
3. E & R is always falling behind schedule and exceeding budgets and costs because:
   (a) it has not separated research from engineering so that the feasible accomplishments are delayed by the unknowns of research, or,
   (b) there is no planning and control system for interrelating and controlling cost/time performance.
4. E & R is inefficient because its budget is based on a fixed percentage of the sales budget. The result is repeated retrenchment and expansion. Further, when sales are low, new products are needed the most, but E & R effort is cut back at just this time.
5. Lack of effective and timely drawing-change notification system, or lack of establishment and timely distribution of each reference design creates chaotic design conditions.
6. Obsolescence of the engineering and research personnel causes the company to lag behind its competition in terms of new products and improvements.
7. A staff-type of project management system is producing friction between project program managers and the functional line engineering managers.
8. No responsibility for industrial design is delegated so that the

company's products are unattractive in appearance and in packaging.

9. Engineering disclaims responsibility for defective items on the basis that these are a manufacturing problem. No field service organization exists where it would be appropriate to correct initial problems that customers experience.

10. The E & R organization has a poor mix of scientists, engineers, technicians, and drafting personnel. Depending on the mix, bottlenecks may occur or work may be done by overqualified or by underqualified people.

11. Failure of engineering to design products with producibility in mind. Expensive manufacturing costs due to close tolerances, special material requirements, and nondesirable characteristics of form and detail result.

12. The E & R organization is dealing directly with customers and bypassing the marketing organization. Commitments are made on service and price which the company cannot adhere to. Internal illwill or loss of customers or profits results.

13. In a multiproject organization with line project managers, top E & R management is weak so that conflicts between project managers for resources are debilitating the company.

14. In a multiproject organization, new projects are coming in at peak periods of activity so that the E & R organization is far overloaded at times and largely idle at other times.

15. A company is organized so that it has a research organization separate from its engineering organization. The research organization is working on projects which have little relation to future economic exploitation by the company. The opposite situation is one where the research organization becomes so involved with engineering crises that it never has time to carry out long-range investigations which form the basis for new products or improvements.

16. Computer-aided design is not being used because of the cost of computer time, the procedures of the computer service center, or the resistance to computer use by the engineers. The results are poorer designs and slower and more costly engineering.

MAJOR SYSTEMS FOR ANALYSIS

Five systems which form a basis for analysis of E & R policies are:

1. Commitment of the company to creativity and innovation,
2. The E & R organization,
3. The planning and control system,
4. The design process,
5. Relationships between the E & R organization and other company components, particularly manufacturing and marketing.

COMMITMENT TO CREATIVITY

The degree of control, the assignment of clerical and nontechnical tasks, the facilities and test equipment available, the relative rewards and sanctions for originality and failure, and the general work climate indicate the commitment of the company to a program of innovation. These and other factors, often subtle and difficult to measure, are characteristic of organizations whose functions are based upon a high level of intellectual effort.

E & R ORGANIZATION

Although various types of E & R organization may work in a given company, some provide inherent difficulties in a given situation. Generally, research, applied research, and engineering should be separated. This is because it is possible to plan and control engineering tasks fairly well unless research is incorporated with them.

It is generally more economical and effective to have centralized research facilities rather than decentralized research. However, the size of the company and the diversity of its products are important considerations.

There are four basic organizational structures for engineering and development (Exhibit 9.2):

1. Organization by technical *discipline*. For example, mechanical engineering, electrical engineering, metallurgy, and optics might be the components of an engineering organization. This is also called a *functional* type of organization.
2. Organization by systems and components. In a simple case, there might be a manager of electrical systems designs, a manager of mechanical systems design, a manager of electrical components design, and a manager of mechanical components design.
3. Line project organization. When a company's output is based upon a continuing inflow of unique, and often complex, projects, it may establish a project or program manager for each project. The project manager is given the people and funds required to perform the job. His or her organization functions like any other line organization in that he or she is responsible for the evaluation, promotion, transfer, and performance of individuals in the project.

    The project organization itself is usually based on a structure of tasks required to design the final project. Some tasks may be the design of systems, the design of components, the conduct of specific tests, or the conduct of specific mechanical, thermal, electrical, hydraulic, etc., analyses.
4. Matrix or staff project organization. A special group of project managers is established which reports to the manager of E & R. The remainder of the organization is functionally structured as in 1 above. When a project is started, it is assigned to a project manager who must then plan for the work, manpower, and funds needed. He or she then "contracts" with the line managers for the service of such of their people as can be agreed upon.

EXHIBIT 9.2

Simplified E & R Organization Structures

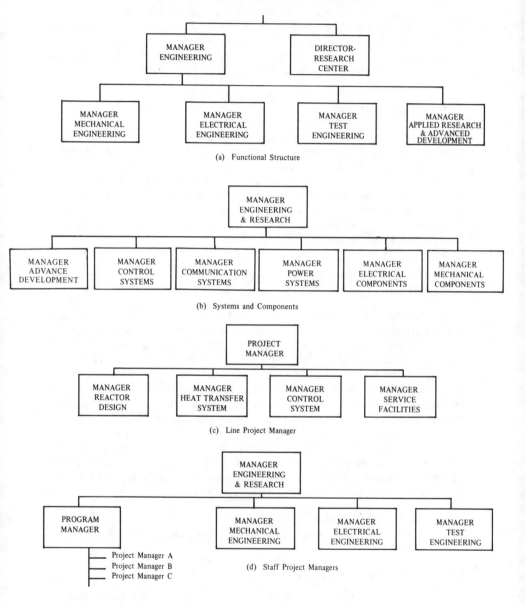

(a) Functional Structure

(b) Systems and Components

(c) Line Project Manager

(d) Staff Project Managers

THE PLANNING AND CONTROL SYSTEM

In large engineering development projects, special planning and control systems are essential to get the projects completed on time without large cost overruns. Time, cost, and performance are the basic factors which must be synchronized and controlled. The usual approach is to break the project into tasks by means of a hierarchical work breakdown structure. Control over the system of tasks is attempted by means of a critical path method such as PERT. Special progress charts are developed to monitor cumulative and monthly performance and costs for each task and the project as a whole. Performance is the most difficult factor to measure.

THE DESIGN PROCESS

Is there a systematic approach to the design process? Is management balancing the economic considerations involved for the manpower mix, analysis vs. testing, and information flow? These are the fundamental areas for evaluation of the design process itself. The design process is analogous to the manufacturing process. Manufacturing adds value by adding materials and labor to change the form of raw materials. Engineering adds value by adding creative thought and analysis to produce a new form of ideas.

RELATIONSHIPS BETWEEN E & R
AND OTHER COMPONENTS

The relationship between E & R and marketing is determined to a great extent by the technical content of the product. Marketing has certain fundamental responsibilities such as preparing quotations, making delivery schedules, and assuring customer service which should not be taken over by E & R for even the most technical products. Marketing represents the *business* policy of the firm, even though E & R may have to deal directly with the customer to obtain technical agreement prior to formal company contracts.

E & R is also a close working partner with the manufacturing organization. Close informal working relationships do much to reduce design costs and expedite manufacture of prototypes and production units. Procedures and information systems should be established which bind these two components closely together.

CHECKLIST FOR ANALYSIS

Demand for Engineering Services

1. Is the inflow of work stable, seasonal, cyclical, or "feast or famine"?
2. Is the demand for constant small improvements or for handling large and complex projects close to the state-of-the-art?
3. Is the company policy one of start-and-stop, or is there recognition of the need for stability of funding, regardless of the ups and downs of demand?

Plant and Layout

1. Are private offices, semiprivate offices, or "bull pens" provided for engineers and scientists?
2. Are the offices modern, well-decorated, well-lighted, air conditioned, and quiet?
3. Is there a good company technical library convenient?
4. Is there a well-equipped and staffed laboratory?
5. Is the engineering location convenient to the marketing offices and plant?
6. Is the computer center conveniently located?
7. Are well-equipped conference rooms and lecture rooms available?
8. Are the dining facilities appropriate?

Equipment

1. Is the central computer fast enough? Is the storage adequate? Is there adequate peripheral equipment? Is there time sharing? Are there automatic plotters? Is the service readily available?
2. Are there small computers and individual desk computers available?
3. Is there a video information system for calling out drawings and making hard copies?
4. Is the test equipment and instrumentation modern?
5. Are there good reproduction facilities available? Photographic services?
6. Is there a telephone on every engineer's desk?

Procurement

1. Are policies for procurement of equipment, materials, and subcontracts clear and are they simple for the engineers to implement?
2. Do engineers have budgets and responsibility for approval and control of purchases within a reasonable latitude?

Personnel Management

1. Do the salary, work restrictions, fringe benefits, and incentive system form an attractive package for the high type of professional desired?
2. What is the turnover rate, and what type of people tend to leave?
3. Does management provide freedom for originality along with responsibility and accountability, or is restrictive administrative control exercised?

Engineering and Research Planning and Scheduling

1. Is there an annual and monthly performance, time, and cost plan?
2. Are projects and assignments clearly defined?

Assigning and Dispatching Work

1. Are assignments clearly stated when they are assigned so as to permit management by objectives?
2. Does each engineer report to only one person?

Controlling Quality, Cost, and Time

1. Is there a work breakdown structure for each project with costs and schedules tied into it?
2. Is there a title and number for each job or project?
3. Is the shop order system set up to permit control and analysis of expenditures?
4. Is there a cost reduction program with an annual target?
5. Are as many accounts as possible, such as training costs, travel costs, and drafting costs, charged as direct labor costs to appropriate tasks?
6. Is quality of output defined and measured?
7. Is a single individual held accountable for each defined and assigned task?
8. Is there a cost reporting system giving monthly, year-to-date and budgeted costs within one week after the end of each fiscal month?

SELECTED BIBLIOGRAPHY ON ENGINEERING AND R & D

Blanchard, Benjamin S. *Engineering Organization and Management.* Englewood Cliffs, N.J.: Prentice-Hall, 1976.

Chase, Wilton P. *Management of System Engineering.* New York: John Wiley & Sons, 1974.

Cleland, David I., and King, William R. *Systems Analysis and Project Management.* 2nd ed. New York: McGraw-Hill, 1975.

Coutinho, John De S. *Advanced Systems Development Management.* New York: John Wiley & Sons, 1977.

Hall, Arthur D. *A Methodology for Systems Engineering.* Princeton, N.J.: D. Van Nostrand, 1962.

Karger, D.W., and Murdick, R.G. *Managing Engineering and Research.* 3rd ed. New York: Industrial Press, 1980.

Preston, William D. Industrial Research from 1975 to 2050. *Research Management,* November, 1974.

Samaras, T., and Czerwinski, Frank L. *Fundamentals of Configuration Management.* New York: John Wiley & Sons, 1971.

Science Resources Studies Highlights. Washington, D.C.: National Science Foundation, NSF 73-320 and 321, 1975.

U.S. Bureau of the Census, *Statistical Abstract of the United States: 1981* (102nd ed.) Washington, D.C., 1981.

10

HUMAN RESOURCES: PROBLEMS AND POLICIES

MOST PROBLEMS ARE ULTIMATELY PEOPLE-PROBLEMS

The president of one of the country's leading management consulting firms says:

1. Most business problems stem from having misplaced people in management positions, often in top management.
2. Human Resources Management is probably less understood and more poorly executed than all other management functions combined.
3. The first step, if we are to improve the operation of the business, is to identify the people who are causing the problems.
4. Once identified, such misplaced people must be shifted to positions where the firm can build on their strengths and work to improve their weaknesses, or they must be terminated.
5. Management training in most companies is best conducted by on-the-job coaching and occasional brief in-plant or outside seminars. Larger companies can afford broad management development programs which pay off.

When we analyze a company or a case, we usually search for functional problems and recommend policies, systems, procedures, and corrective action to prevent repetition of the problems. Too often we fail to examine the weak links, the individuals who originally failed to recognize an operating or a strategy problem. Can we depend upon the same individual to forestall future problems? To recognize when a new installed system eventually must be changed or how to change it?

In the last analysis, almost all problems are attributable to individuals in the company. As a consultant, if we devise a technical solution which solves a business problem, we have really only provided half the solution. The other half is dealing with those responsible for the problem in the first place.

The president of a management consulting firm said that the following points up the often-met confusion between *functional business problems and human resources problems:*

Several years ago we were called in to improve a firm's order processing system. Our mission appeared to be straightforward, to reduce costs and improve inventories. During the orientation phase, it became apparent that high costs and high inventories were symptoms of other problems.

Sure, we could save a modest amount by improved systems, but we could never substantially increase profits unless we faced up to the real problems. These were excessive product proliferation and poor sales forecasting which generated short factory runs, frequent schedule changes, large inventories of slow moving items, and constant back orders on fast moving, wanted merchandise. As a consequence, manufacturing and order handling costs were high. Approximately 70% of the orders had to be handled four to eight times before finally completed.

Excessive product proliferation and poor sales forecasts led us directly to the vice-president in charge of marketing—who incidentally was a protege of the president.

What became readily apparent was the fact that the vice-president of marketing was the *wrong person* for the job. Although he had been a tremendous success in sales and possibly the reason for the firm's position of dominance in the market, he was not familiar with the managerial aspects of marketing. The vice-president had no experience in product development or cost analysis. Because he had been the best salesman the firm had ever had, it was assumed he would be the best choice for vice-president of marketing. Sales forecasts became extremely inaccurate and new products proliferated with the result that inventory cost soared. No amount of sales pitches seemed to reverse the trend.

The president had to make a serious decision—demote his friend back to sales, or continue to suffer poor forecasts and high inventory costs, or find help immediately for his vice-president of marketing. These decisions weighed heavily on his head.

HOW TO ASSOCIATE PROBLEMS AND PEOPLE

In a consulting assignment, there are three approaches which should be used to make sure people who are performing inadequately are identified:

1. Conduct in-depth interviews with key people apparently connected with a particular problem area. Sometimes it will be immediately obvious who the weak link is. At other times, several or all of those concerned may lack competence. In some cases, personal conflicts will surface that have resulted in lack of cooperation, blocking of communication, or just plain sabotage.

Company X, a manufacturing concern, was a fair-sized division of a billion dollar corporation which had fallen on hard times. Despite increased sales in five out of the last eight years, profits had vanished. Each of the six vice-presidents blamed their problems on one or more of the others. From in-depth interviews lasting about two to four hours each, it became evident that the first and most important problem was the president of the firm. When our confidential report was given to the chief executive officer of the parent organization, and verified by two V.P.s of his own group, replacements were made. Not only the division president but also two of his V.P.s were moved out. Within one year profits were up substantially.

---

2. Start with the symptoms of problems as they appear in the operating statements. Work backward until the individuals ultimately responsible are identified.

A large retail store was selling $1.5 million annually in women's shoes, far higher as a percent of total shoe sales than the National Retail Merchants Association figures for stores of similar size. The problems were lower-than-average turnover, higher markups, and such high markdowns and high advertising costs that contribution to store profit was extremely low. Both the store controller and the merchandise manager admitted the buyer was a genius at promotion, had the wanted merchandise at the right time, and inspired the sales force. However, he was unable to control his operations, as profit and loss statements proved. The general merchandise manager decided not to fire the buyer—he merely placed the department under the control of another merchandise manager who was a lavish man with praise for a job well done. While the new man was tough and figure conscious, he was a fine leader, and within a reasonable time, had the buyer eating out of his hand. The important improved turnover and profit added to the buyer's bonus but more importantly, to his self-esteem—"I can master figures that formerly were a deep mystery to me."

The sales figures proved the buyer knew his business. He could promote and sell. At the same time, the slow turnover and large markdowns proved the buyer needed a good controller which led the general merchandise manager to the real culprit, the buyer's boss—the merchandise manager who had failed to manage!

— 3. Evaluate the background and apparent performance of each executive, major decisions or contributions and goofs he or she has made, and the general operation of his organization. Any statements which reflect the executive's views and philosophy should also be considered. This is the approach which business policy students must usually follow.

Since this method is so important to the business policy case study method, we will show one possible format for analysis of the individuals relative to major company problems. We will use the material from the Vogue case in Chapter 15. Since we are only demonstrating format, there is no necessity for reading the case at this point.

We first identify key decision makers and "influencers" in a company and list these in a column as shown in Exhibit 10.1. We then determine the capabilities of each individual and appraise his or her performance in general. We also relate the individuals to all problem areas with which he or she has any connection. After subsequent analysis of the problems, we may then recommend action of each individual as indicated by the last column of Exhibit 10.1. Incidental problems, such as lack of management depth, may be uncovered.

The tendency of many students of business policy, and even of some consultants, when they discover that a person is doing an inadequate job is to say, "Fire him!" The capabilities, experience, and dedication of individuals in business cover a wide range. If all the "not-great" workers were fired, it is probable that we would only replace them with not-great workers. The cost of continually replacing employees would be great. Each individual should be appraised in terms of his or her *potential* to the company with proper training and guidance. From a practical standpoint, unions, civil service regulations, company traditions, or legal problems, may knock out firing as a means of disposing of problem workers.

The most serious problem is the president of the company who is not performing well. The president has no leader to guide and train him or her. Past success and advanced age combine to produce some resistance to change. Pride will likely stand in the way of perception and admission of poor performance. For the business policy student to recommend the president's dismissal is simply unrealistic. If the board of directors has not taken such action, it is unlikely that it will. Approaches taken by one management consultation firm are to ask some basic questions and proceed as follows:

1. Does the president have (a) real skill in at least two areas, (b) a desire and willingness to learn, and (c) the motivation and ability to work hard? If so, we work with the president on an ongoing basis trying to support him where he is weak. We also try to suggest positive action steps to be taken within time limits.
2. If the first approach does not work out, we may suggest that he consider a new appointment as chairman of the board or chief ex-

ecutive officer and bring in a new president with complementary skills as chief operating officer.

3. If neither of the first two suggestions is feasible, and the president is a major stockholder, we try as diplomatically as possible to get him to recognize his own limitations as a constraint on the success of the company. After all, it's his money, and if he is willing to plod along, it's OK with us.

4. If, on the other hand, he is not very bright or isn't willing to work, we admit defeat and terminate our contract. So look for the telltale signs.

Too many unprofitable statistical indicators—that's the first clue. Look for indecisive leadership. Look for such clues as too many bosses, too much internal bickering, lack of a sense of direction in one or more managers. Try listening intently to both what is said, and *what is omitted.* Look for lack of risk taking, no entrepreneurship, a policy of managerial no hits, no runs, no errors. That's the real old-fashioned disease of conservative mediocrity, the greatest killer of all.

THE VALUE OF PEOPLE— YOUR HUMAN RESOURCES

Of all the resources at the disposal of management, only people have infinite ability to vary their productivity. A machine can only perform its task within the limits of its capacity. The machine lacks creativity, cannot be motivated to better performance by excellence of leadership, and can only perform the task its designer intended. People, on the other hand, have *performance capabilities* which are almost limitless; they can be motivated to superhuman efforts by proper leadership; they can be innovative and adaptive; and in short can think and vary their behavior by adapting to changing circumstances.

Every manager, irrespective of the size or nature of his or her business, manages people. How well, or how poorly he or she manages people, is without question a major cause for the rise or fall of the business. Unfortunately, there are no six quick easy lessons to teach a manager how to manage. No two people in the world of humans are alike. Each has encountered different experiences, grown and developed in cultures different from each other, received education and training unique to him or her alone, has differing mental and physical abilities, and huge differences in the level of aspiration and drive.

Recently, an area of study, human resources accounting, has attempted to demonstrate the true value of each employee. Although it seems callous to attempt to calculate the value of an employee in terms of dollars and cents, it does bring to light much more clearly than other techniques the worth of the individual. Many business people only respect that which is valuable and expensive.

The amount of money invested in each employee, plus the cost of replacing him or her, are shockingly high and bring a new awareness of the value of an employee. Recruiting, selection, and training costs, plus the time required to bring the employee up to the level of productivity of an experienced person, will vary from firm to firm. Learning requires mistakes and mistakes cost money. If a manager were told that these costs and losses totaled $10,000 per employee, which in many firms might be true, there is no doubt that the manager would take much better care and interest in management techniques. No manager would take a $10,000 piece of equipment down to the dock and drop it into the sea. Yet, that is exactly what some managers do when they ride roughshod over their employees.

Despite their uniqueness, people in business must be managed in aggregates (groups) and not just as individuals. The balance of this section is devoted to the means by which human resources can be better managed despite the problems enumerated above. We shall also examine the methods by which successful firms attempt to utilize their human resources to the maximum.

MANAGERIAL LEADERSHIP

The quality of any business leadership sets the tone of business operations. The elements which comprise leadership are many and complementary.

Leadership is the ongoing process of influencing the behavior of an individual, or group, in efforts toward goal achievement in a given situation. Effective managers must thoroughly understand all elements of the total environment: themselves, their followers, and the situation. Only when these elements are understood, can true leadership exist.

An example can be given of a situation in which a successful manager in one functional area of the business was transferred with new responsibilities to another area. The result was failure, not because of lack of technological skills but because the man lacked the ability to adapt to a new situation. The employees and tasks in the new job were unlike his previous assignment, and his leadership style was inappropriate in the new situation.

A simple but important distinction should be made at this point between successful and effective leadership. A leader may coerce his or her employees into completing all assigned duties successfully, but in the process create resentment and anxiety. The *effective* leader succeeds in the task while maintaining employee morale. The workers accept their assigned tasks and willingly perform them. This creates a climate for long-run success.

There seems to be no single "leadership type." That is, selection of leaders based upon traits is not possible. This means that leaders are developed through experience and training. Such training should be

EXHIBIT 10.1

Name and Title	Actual Responsibilities	Age	Experience Years and Kind	Educational Qualifications	Summary of How Well Qualified	Philosophy and Views of the Business
Walter White Executive V.P.	Sales and order processing Merchandising	62	25 years with Vogue		Appears to be well qualified by experience	Cut out reports. Cut prices. Cast out merchandising and advertising people and contract out advertising. Believes quotas, Industry potentials are worthless. Increase finished goods inventory. Get out the goods and stop worrying about control. Wants to broaden line further.
B. H. Winslow V.P.-Production	Production except for production control	61	25 years with Vogue	At least high school but not a college degree	Appears to understand his job well and be doing a good job	Feels need for strong president to get a unified sense of direction for the company.
Robert Kelley V.P.-Operations	Accounting real estate Secretary-treasurer, purchasing, production control	59	25 years with public accounting firms. V.P. in charge of loans for a bank. About 5-10 years with Vogue	College degree in accounting. C.P.A.	Extremely well qualified	Recognizes limitations in merchandising and production.
Paul Trout Advertising Manager	Advertising and sales promotion	54	J & J Apparel Salesman-4 years Advertising Mgr. 3 years Asst Sales Mgr. P.L. Brooks Sales mgr-8 years. V.P.-Marketing 10 years	M.B.A. U of Chicago	Very strong qualifications for his job Overqualified	Sees need for management team with unified sense of direction. Believes strongly in marketing concept and integration of all activities.

EXHIBIT 10.1 (*Continued*)

Name and Title	Actual Responsibilities	Age	Experience Years and Kind	Educational Qualifications	Summary of How Well Qualified	Philosophy and Views of the Business
Sam Chapman Merchandise Manager	Implementing merchandising decisions of Walter White	39	3 years as merchandise manager with Vogue plus unmentioned experience	Not known	Seems OK	Understands market segmentation. Desire to reduce styles and price lines. Concentrates on medium quality, mass market in 20-45 age group.
Tom Evans V.P.-Systems	EDP systems	48	Apparently broad business and systems experience	Not known	Appears qualified	Believes EDP could be expanded for management decision making.
Toni DeMarco Head Designer	Designs the apparel	34	13 years of designing for Vogue	Graduate School of Design	Well qualified	Believes design is more important than production modifications to reduce cost.
Richard Roberts Chief Engineer	Manufacturing equipment design	32	7-10 years with Vogue	Mechanical Engineering degree Graduate work in wide range of subjects including management	Very well qualified	Believes in concentrating on his own job, despite his broad academic qualifications.
Harry Thomas Personnel Manager	Routine personnel activities	41	Not mentioned	Not mentioned	Unknown	Likes prestige of reporting to the president.

directed toward improving the manager's skill in analyzing the nature of organizational situations. The manager must then be able to adjust his or her style to the situations as they arise.

Motivation is the individual's inner will to perform. It is the reason why workers will give freely of their human energies. Three major theories used to explain motivation are (1) needs models, (2) expectancy models, and (3) operant conditioning. Needs models hypothesize that people act to fulfill certain needs inherent or learned. Expectancy models hypothesize that individuals look ahead to certain goals and the means to achieve goals and act according to likelihood of achieving such goals and to the value of the goals. Operant conditioning views people as acting according to past rewards for a particular act. If certain types of behavior have been rewarded, the individual will act accordingly in the future.

Whatever theory is subscribed to, the manager takes the same action. The manager creates an environment of opportunities and rewards which cause the individual to act in the interests of the organization as well as in his or her own. A manager must know each subordinate well enough so that he or she can create the appropriate working climate and reward system for the work situation. Each person is different from one another so that no general program will be as effective as individual attention. Performance is a function of both abilities and motivation.

Clarence Francis, a former Chairman of the Board of General Foods, is quoted as saying:

> You can buy a man's time; you can buy a man's physical presence at a given place; you can even buy a measured number of skilled muscular motions per hour, or day; but you cannot buy enthusiasm. You cannot buy initiative; you cannot buy loyalty; you cannot buy devotion of hearts, minds, and souls. You have to earn these things.

Leadership effectiveness has been found from research to be determined by (a) the leadership style, (b) the nature of the work group, and (c) the task to be performed. Fred Fiedler developed the Least Preferred Coworker (LPC) index to measure leadership style from task centered to people oriented. He then defined the work situation in terms of:

1. Leader-member relations—extent to which the leader "gets along" with subordinates,
2. Task structure—well-defined jobs are high-structure jobs,
3. Position power—power inherent in the position held by the leader.

These three items in various combinations produce various degrees of "situational favorableness." The most effective leadership style can be determined for various situations.[1] Exhibit 10.2 depicts this "contingency" model in abbreviated form.

244

EXHIBIT 10.2

Leader Effectiveness

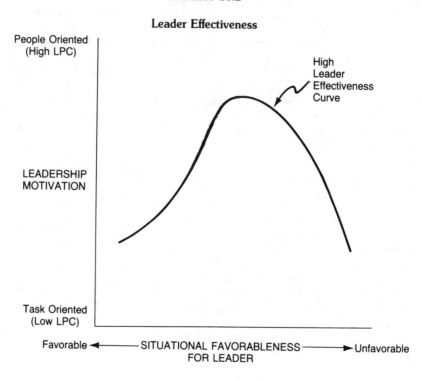

"Growers" vs. "Undertakers"

At G.E., an adherent of product portfolio analysis, strategic objectives for the company's wide-ranging products are defined as "grow," "defend," and "harvest," depending on the product life cycle. Now its general managers are being classified by personal style or orientation as "growers," "caretakers," and—tongue-in-cheek—as "undertakers" to match managerial style with the product's status. Notes one consultant and G.E.-watcher: "I hear they have a shortage of growers, but they are making great efforts to remove the undertaker types who are heading up growth businesses."[2]

Effective leadership can take many forms.

1. In a crisis situation, where failure is imminent and risks are high, an authoritarian leadership style might well be most effective.
2. In situations where workers are not capable of constructive contributions, authoritarian leadership must prevail.
3. Where exact and uniform procedures must be followed, a bureaucrat is best.

4. When workers are sufficiently skilled to contribute creatively, and where a variety of complicated tasks are simultaneously being carried out, a more consultive leadership style is generally appropriate.
5. The type of leadership style displayed should be a function of the maturity of behavior of the followers. The more mature the followers' behavior, the more consultive the leader's style.
6. Don't confuse consultive style with the use of committees. Committee management is seldom effective because it does not allow fixing of responsibility for poor decisions.
7. Managers lead through more than their formal authority. Effective leaders identify the informal group and its leaders and work to cultivate communication networks and obtain more honest feedbacks.
8. Effective leadership requires frequent face-to-face contact to reinforce the leadership role. Managers cannot lead from afar. To be effective the leadership quality must come in contact with the followers on a continuing basis and at close range so that the manager's personal leadership style and image are repeatedly reinforced.
9. Effective leaders set high production standards—high, but fair and reasonable. Employees know that quality work of merit will be recognized and rewarded. Effective leaders praise superior performance.
10. Effective leaders are honest and fair. Their word is their bond even to the loss of their own prestige. A person who is willing to stand up for employees when he or she thinks that they are right will gain their respect. When you are wrong, admit your mistake.
11. Never retain poor managers. Work with a man or woman as best you can, but if the person does not have a desire for growth, responsibility, and an empathy toward people, he or she is not going to make it. If training fails, help the employee find another position. Such a person reflects on you as a manager. (Furthermore, subordinates will be suffering under his or her poor management.)

PROBLEM AREAS IN HUMAN RESOURCE MANAGEMENT

POLICY MODEL FOR ACTION

A student of business policy in the area should ask some basic questions:

1. What type and quantity of personnel does the firm have and what will it need in the future?
2. Where will the firm's personnel come from?
3. Where will the firm lose managers and at what cost to the firm?
4. How can the firm improve its managers?

5. How well are personnel performing?
6. What and how should employees be compensated?

The answers to these questions will guide the student in an appraisal of the most commonly encountered problems in personnel. The sequence of analysis is important because policy decisions at one point often affect subsequent decisions. (See Exhibit 10.3.)

PERSON-POWER PLANNING—WHAT TYPE AND QUALITY OF PERSONNEL DOES THE FIRM HAVE AND WHAT WILL IT NEED IN THE FUTURE?

Person-power planning begins with a determination of where the firm presently is. Questions to ask and things to do are:

1. What is the competence of our present top executives? List their strengths and weaknesses.
2. What are their ages? Look for loss due to retirement.
3. Collect and analyze industry growth data. Attempt to determine the "why" behind the trends.
4. Study your own firm's growth data. Does it follow the industry growth pattern? If not, where and why does it deviate.
5. Develop contingency plans as shown in Exhibit 10.4. Person-power plans should be detailed by job classification or skill in order to be useful in identifying critical shortages.
6. Inventory the skills of your present staff. Such an inventory should include all personnel. Areas to be covered would include an objective appraisal of their managerial talents, technical skills, and trades.
7. Compare your contingency plans with your person-power inventory in order to identify serious shortages.
8. Reminder: both quantity and quality of work force are important.
9. Be flexible and update your plan at least semi-annually.

RECRUIT OR PROMOTE DECISIONS: FROM WHERE WILL THE FIRM'S PERSONNEL COME?

Once your person-power needs are identified, the next step is acquiring personnel. Entry-level positions, by definition, are filled through recruiting. However, policy problems arise at all levels above entry positions. The typical hangup occurs when a firm commits itself to only one policy, i.e., promote only from within.

The following are some advantages and disadvantages of each method.

Promote From Within

Advantages:

1. Employees perceive that productive efforts will result in promotion. Excellent for morale.

EXHIBIT 10.3

Policy Model—How to Appraise Human Resources Management

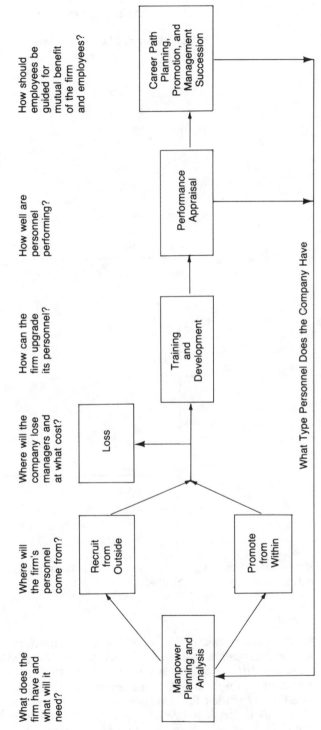

EXHIBIT 10.4

Contingency Manpower Plans

A. FIRM

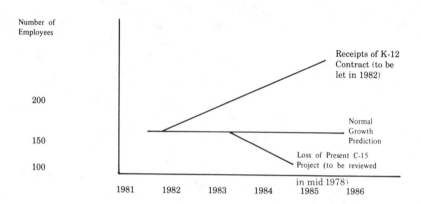

B. ELECTRICAL ENGINEERS

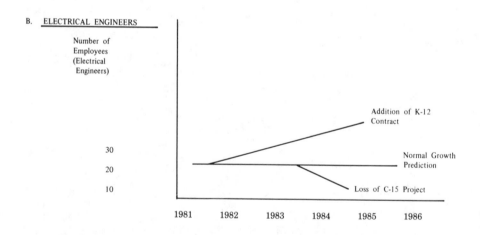

2. Promotion, when it comes, is seen as a form of achievement recognition and reinforces above.
3. Employees can identify those with whom they are competing.

Disadvantages:

1. It puts the company in an awkward position if there is no one whom management deems promotable in the positions below the one to be filed. This is especially critical in a growth situation.
2. For a promote-from-within policy to be effective, time and money must be expended for training.
3. It is more difficult to predict the potential of a recent college graduate than to recruit proven managerial talent.

4. In small firms nepotism in promotion can destroy any of the above-mentioned advantages.

Recruit Exclusively

Advantages:

1. Allows the firm to examine a wide variety of proven and experienced people and select the one which best fits their needs.
2. Training costs are very low or nonexistent.

Disadvantages:

1. Normally ambitious workers will leave if they do not see a chance for advancement into responsible positions. High turnover rate among good employees at lower levels is a trouble sign.
2. Company morale is generally low because of lack of reinforcement through promotion for productive work.

Balanced Program:

In every sense, a balanced program is superior to either policy taken separately.

The following are some questions to ask and things to do.

1. Are we wed to an either/or policy? If so, give yourself some flexibility through a balanced policy of promotion from within and recruiting from outside when the need arises.
2. Can our present policy attract and keep qualified employees without discrimination on the basis of sex or other basis?
3. Are we reviewing our personnel inventory periodically in order to identify promotable persons and those who need training?

MANAGEMENT TURNOVER AND SUCCESSION—WHERE WILL THE FIRM LOSE MANAGERS AND AT WHAT COST TO THE FIRM?

Loss of management talent can be an important sign of greater troubles. All firms experience some degree of managerial turnover. People die, become disabled, retire, or just quit. Some types can be predicted, others not. The voluntary separations, or quits, is a key indicator. When this is unusually high look for reasons.

Often it is a poor manager. Other times a dead-end job can cause good managers to quit. The faster you uncover the reason why, the less your loss in qualified men. Replacing qualified managers with experience in your firm is always a costly proposition.

For small and medium-size firms a related problem is management succession. Some small and medium-size firms are as good as the one, two, or maybe three key personnel. No one really plans on dying or becoming disabled but when it happens in a firm of this size, failure is not unusual. The reason is simply that no provisions were made for training a successor. "It was a one-man business and when he died unexpectedly we didn't know what to do." Comments like this are commonplace. Just as one buys insurance to protect one's family in case of an untimely demise, so one should train one or more trusted employees in the total working of the firm.

The following are some questions to ask and things to do:

1. Analyze the cost of losing a single middle manager—the figure will shock you.
2. Study turnover statistics of your firm looking for extremes—too high or too low. Pinpoint where they are coming from and then ask why. Remember that no turnover is a sign of a stagnate organization. Some turnover possibly indicates that you are developing good people and other divisions want them.
3. Always compare yourself with the trade averages—it's a good benchmark.
4. Is turnover a statistic you study at management meetings? If not, add it to the agenda.
5. Do you have a key person problem? A person without replacement? If something would happen to him or her, would the operations of the business be impaired? If yes, begin to train a replacement.

MANAGEMENT TRAINING—HOW CAN A FIRM IMPROVE ITS MANAGERS?

Management training is not accidental. It requires a thoughtful plan beginning with the selection of who will train and who will be trained. The best training is realistic and meaningful. On-the-job training programs which are highly structured and well supervised are of greatest value.

The following are some key points of a well-managed training program.

1. Careful selection of the trainer. Just because a person is a good manager does not mean he or she can convey the skills of management to another.
2. Careful selection of those to be trained. Training for any skill requires timing. Don't bring a person along too quickly—faster than he or she can absorb the training and demonstrate the skills—or stagnate a person in the program.
3. Make the training program action-oriented. Have objectives which must be achieved. Establish milestones as benchmarks along the way to accomplish the goal. If the training program is lengthy, establish reward for reinforcement at key milestones.
4. Require multidirectional feedback of performance. The trainer should periodically report results both to the trainees and top management. The trainees should be required to submit written reports of their progress quarterly to top management.
5. When a trainee finishes a lengthy or major training and development program, have a new and challenging assignment for him or her. Don't send the graduate back to the original job. Training should be a stepping-stone to greater responsibility.

PERFORMANCE APPRAISAL—HOW WELL ARE PERSONNEL PERFORMING?

Does your present appraisal system really measure performance or is it simply an exercise performed by your managers to comply with company procedures? In many cases no relationship can be found between employee appraisals and either performance or promotions.

1. For performance appraisal to be effective, what we are rating must be identical with the criteria for promotion.
2. Both performance appraisal and promotions serve as a means of recognizing the superior employee. Your performance appraisal system should also identify the marginal employees and point up areas of improvement and possible training needs.
3. In order to reinforce the concept of management-by-objectives and the maintenance of a good communication system, each individual manager should be responsible for the establishment of written performance criteria used for promotion.

Management-by-objectives has, as a key element, the establishment of mutually acceptable performance criteria. Manager and employee agree on what the employee is going to attempt to perform during the rating period and the objectives and subsequent performance serves as measure of success.

COMPENSATION—WHAT AND HOW SHOULD EMPLOYEES BE COMPENSATED?

Once evaluated, the next question becomes one of compensation of the work force. There are some general guidelines which should be considered in determining wage and salary levels. They are:

1. Government regulation—federal and state minimum wage laws.
2. Industry wage levels—check with your trade association for this information.
3. Area wages—what similar skills are receiving in the area. This is how the law of supply and demand comes into play.
4. The patterns established through collective bargaining, whether your firm is unionized or not, will affect your wage rates.
5. The standard and cost of living of the area go hand in hand. There are more things to do in New York City (standard of living) and prices are higher there than other parts of the country (cost of living).
6. The firm's ability to pay—often overlooked—is a key factor to consider early in your analysis. Study your cost structure very carefully.
7. The productivity of your employees. Some firms are blessed, through good management, with employees who produce more than others. Consequently, these firms are more able to grant wage and salary incentives.
8. Compensate managers on the basis of short-term results for har-

vest/divest businesses and for long-range plans and benefits for entrepreneurial businesses.

Not all of the above guidelines are appropriate in every situation, but the combination of most of the items listed above will give the reader some direction in setting general wage and salary levels.

How employees should be paid for their contribution in a relatively new field of study. Behavioral research indicates that for employees above a subsistence level, an increase in wages of one dollar does not result in an increase of productive effort of one dollar. The standard wage payment form is just not motivating the majority of American workers as we believed it once did. However, some programs have been successful in relating productivity to compensation. Two of these programs are outlined below.

1. Cafeteria approach to fringe benefits—under such a system every employee receives a statement of the amount, (in dollars), they are entitled to in fringe benefits and then are required to allocate yearly the money between a variety of programs as they see fit. Research indicated that less than 3% of employees really know what the value of their fringe benefits are, and subsequently their present value as motivator is highly questionable. The cafeteria approach makes the employee aware of the value of part of his or her compensation—the fringe benefits—and shows him or her the freedom of choice he or she had. This approach is personalized and tends to provide a source of motivation.
2. Bonus awards for outstanding performance.

The concept of this program is not new, but with some alterations it can serve as a vital motivation in a firm. The present bonus program culminates in the award of some number of dollars to the outstanding employees. They, in turn, purchase what they want. However, this separation between performance and desired reward can be brought closer through the awarding of the gifts the employees were going to buy with their bonus money. The closer the reward is to the productivity, the greater its impact on motivation.

GOVERNMENTAL IMPACT

The federal government, and later state government, has increasingly affected the way companies treat employees since the 1900s. Companies have resisted laws and regulations by both illegal and legal means. Sometimes policies which forestall the impact of a particular law will give a company a tremendous advantage. For example, IBM's treatment of its employees has been so liberal that unions have not been able to gain a foothold in this giant company. Other companies have fought rearguard actions to delay the impact and costs of some of the legislation and regulations. Many companies have been trapped in no-win situations due to recent affirmative action and antidiscrimination laws. Policies must be developed quickly to make adjustments and minimize large fines. AT&T made, in 1973, $15,000,000 in back payments to women who were allegedly discriminated against in compensation and employment. In January 1979, Sears, Roebuck & Co. sued 10 federal agencies including the contract compliance agency. Its purpose was to resolve what it called conflicting laws and regulations restricting jobs and promotions for minorities and women.

It is apparent that policy makers must take into account both the main thrust of legislation and the particular points involved in making a variety of decisions on human resource problems. Exhibit 10.5 provides a brief guide for the policy course. Company EEO and Affirmative Action plans are clearly long-range in nature. Companies must prepare goals and time tables for recruitment, training, and progression up the ranks for men and women: handicapped, Vietnam veterans, and minorities classified as black, Asian, and Hispanic. An availability analysis and a utilization plan of the general form shown in Exhibit 10.6 is required. The volume of data that must be processed to maintain up-to-date status and plans is such that a computer is a requirement.

AUTOMATION IN HUMAN RESOURCE MANAGEMENT

The rapid increase in the power of small computers accompanied by an equally rapid decrease in cost per operation is revolutionizing the management of human resources. Managers may now obtain, upon request, all sorts of analyses and performance indicators relating to organizations and individuals. They may track easily the progress of subordinates in their careers from hiring to death. In addition, the burden of keeping accurate maintenance records (vacation time, sick leave, insurance, pensions, etc.) and producing required government reports is greatly lightened.

Current policy problems deal with such questions as:

1. Shall we maintain a piecemeal (independent subsystems) approach to automation of personnel record keeping?
2. Shall we pursue a modular approach to automation whereby we automate and test one system at a time and eventually link them together? This is also called the "application program" approach.
3. Shall we plunge ahead with development of a DBMS (Data Base Management System), which provides a unified, nonredundant data base but is much more complex to develop? The associated development costs and risks are higher than with the application approach.

Regardless of the approach taken, it appears that personnel subsystems may be defined and related in terms of data as depicted in Exhibit 10.7.[3]

SOME SPECIFIC POLICY QUESTIONS FOR EVALUATING SMALL BUSINESSES

1. If there are to be only two or three key people, should work be divided by skill, or should all key people be assigned tasks as each is free to take them on?

EXHIBIT 10.5

Impact of Legislation on Human Resource Management*

	Year	Main Thrust	Policy Implications
Sherman Anti-Trust Act	1890	Designed to limit business combinations in restraint of trade, it was also applied against union activities interfering with interstate commerce.	Legal constraints imposed on management and unions in use of power to provide for selfdetermination by an employer and employees, with procedures of collective bargaining for negotiating differences over wages and conditions, to promote peaceful settlement of disputes. Management policy as to organizing efforts of unions must be within limits established by the anti-trust and the labor relations acts and consistent with leadership philosophy, its personal values and economics of situations.
Clayton Act	1914	Exemption of union activities from anti-trust actions except when in combination with business group to restrain competition by affecting labor outside of the bargaining unit.	
Railway Labor Act (amended in 1934, 1936, 1966)	1926	Established unionization rights of employees and collective bargaining procedures for airline and railroad managements and unions selected by majority of employees in appropriate unit as determined by National Mediation Board; outlaws yellow dog contracts.	
Federal Anti-Injunction Act (Norris-La Guardia Act)	1932	Restricted federal courts from enjoining or restraining legal labor organizing, picketing or strike activities, or from holding legal yellow dog contracts by which employees agreed not to join unions.	
National Labor Relations Act (Wagner Act)	1935	Business activities affecting interstate commerce subject to management unfair labor practices prohibiting interference in employees freedom to organize and to bargain collectively; majority in appropriate unit can select a union, as determined by the National Labor Relations Board; which enforces unfair labor practices.	

EXHIBIT 10.5 (*Continued*)

	Year	Main Thrust	Policy Implications
Davis-Bacon Act	1931	Provides minimum wages and conditions of overtime for construction and for other contracts with U.S. Government.	
Walsh-Healy Act	1936		
Fair Labor Standards Act	1938	Provides minimum wages and overtime conditions, with child labor prohibitions, or industries producing goods for interstate commerce; amended to prohibit lower wage for females than males on work requiring similar skill, effort and responsibility or exclusion of females from highly paid jobs.	Management, subject to coverage, must meet statute requirements in employment, compensation, overtime, promotion and record-keeping practices or be subject to penalties; expert human resource staff is essential.
(Wage-Hour Act) (amended by Equal Pay Act of 1963)			
Labor-Management Relations Act (Taft-Hartley Act) (Includes National Labor Relations Act provisions)	1947	Adds to NLRA union unfair labor practices restricting interference with management or employee freedom, prohibits certain union economic action against management or affecting public health and welfare, allows suits in federal court against violation of labor agreements, establishes the Federal Mediation and Conciliation Service.	Management has to make decisions regarding its attitude toward unionization efforts and type of bargaining with union, to contain its power or for accommodation with cooperation in administration of contract and grievance processing; necessary legal and labor relations advisors for management.
Labor-Management Reporting and Disclosure act (Langrum-Griffing Act)	1959	Covers in detail a Bill of Rights for union members with the responsibility and liability of members, officials, and unions for unlawful conduct; employer and union reports required as to management payments to influence unions or agents or employees on collective bargaining matters.	Management must maintain financial as well as administrative separation from internal union affairs and employee-union matters.

EXHIBIT 10.5 (Continued)

Executive Order 11246	1963	Applied only to contractors and subcontractors on federal work.	Same impact as Civil Rights Act. Title VII.
Civil Rights Act, Title VII amended by Age Discrimination in Employment Act of 1967 and Equal Employment Opportunities Act of 1972.	1964	Elimination of employer and union discrimination against applicants and employees on basis of race, color, religion, sex, age or national origin, with regard to hire, terms of employment, compensation or union membership or apprentice programs; administered by Equal Employment Opportunities Commission with individual right to court suit.	Burden placed on all employers, including state and local government management with 15 or more employees; all subject to injunction and affirmative action orders including hiring with back pay for prohibiting discrimination unless based on bona fide occupational qualification necessary to normal operation; any job test or qualification may cause reverse discrimination order and cost.
Occupational Safety and Health Act	1970	Requires employment free of recognized hazards to employees, subject to severe penalties.	Cost of meeting OSHA requirements; consideration of reasonableness of standards and regulations for acceptance or to legally oppose.
Vocational Rehabilitation Act	1973	Affirmative action to employ and promote qualified handicapped persons.	Revisions of recruitment and hiring and medical programs; effect on productivity, labor cost, work procedures, promotions, and layoff policy.
Employment Retirement Insurance Security Act	1974	Required standards for pension programs to protect employee benefits and fringes established by company or by collective bargaining.	Name fiduciaries within company; long-range and immediate costs; pension and benefit plan changes; impact on turnover, productivity, recruitment, on acquisitions or mergers.
Civil Service Reform Act	1978	Statutory standards for Federal Service Labor Relations under a Federal Labor Relations Authority, similar to private labor-management standards (except no right to strike); established an Office of Personnel Management and a Merit System Protection Board.	Expansion of grievance arbitration and compulsory arbitration for disputes over new agreements in public sector may affect policies toward strike substitutes (like basic steel industry Experimental Negotiation Agreement).

*Prepared by Professor A. Howard Myers

EXHIBIT 10.6

EEO WORK FORCE ANALYSIS

By Job Title Within Department

Department _____

Page _____ of _____

As of _____ 19 _____
(Date)

JOB GROUP NO.	JOB TITLE	EEO-1 CATEGORY	SALARY CODE	ALL EMPLOYEES			MINORITY EMPLOYEES									TOTAL	PROGRESSION LINES
							MALE				FEMALE						
				TOTAL	MALE	FEMALE	BLK.	ASIAN	HISP.	N.AMER.	BLK.	ASIAN	HISP.	N.AMER.			

TOTAL - THIS PAGE

GRAND TOTAL - LAST PAGE

BLK. - BLACK   HISP. - HISPANIC   N.AMER. - NATIVE AMERICAN

FOR PROGRESSION LINES INDICATE 1,2,3,4,ETC.

EXHIBIT 10.7

Subsystems and Their Relationship in Computerized Human Resource
Management Systems

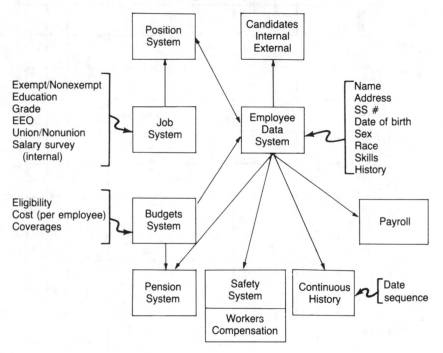

2. Is it a better policy to pay low salaries to key managers to keep expenses down or pay high salaries to obtain better individuals?
3. What compensation plan will best motivate key managers to produce profits?
4. Should the business be based on a few key people who own a significant part of the business?
5. There are action-oriented men and women and analytical (staff) type men and women. Is the work divided upon this basis? For example, if there is only one analytical key person, he or she might be assigned sales forecasting, production planning, budgeting and financial control. An action-oriented sales manager and an action-oriented supervisor might complete the staff.
6. Despite all formal training, there is generally no substitute for the entrepreneurial person who is aggressive, a risk taker, and a good profit maker. Such a person might be used in product development, in manufacturing, or in merchandising or retailing. Is there such an individual in the firm? Is this person given wide latitude of action? Is this person in the right organization spot?

7. Is expansion being *planned* for by having one or two trainees, interns, or key people being given an opportunity to learn both details and broad problems of the firm? Is attention being given to develop these people and keep them informed of their prospects so they don't leave the company just before you go to promote them?

8. Is there a good, simple, inexpensive training and review procedure for all employees to ensure that they make friends and customers for the company?

9. Is the company organized to keep out unions or does it welcome unions for stability? Does it use constructive policies of leadership in employee salaries, working conditions, etc., to keep out unions? Does it organize itself primarily with professional people?

10. If the small company is subject to seasonal layoffs, does it hire people who desire only seasonal work or does it have some policy for taking care of laid-off employees?

11. Are there a few inexpensive controls to prevent embezzlement or other employee misfeasance?

12. In very small companies, if the owner is ill for a week or month, can the company function? Is there someone in the family or some key employee who can run it?

13. Does the company have a clearcut policy as to what business it will, and will not, engage in?

14. Are safety rules established and safety procedures maintained in the production shop, in the office, on the floor of the retail store, or on walks and drives leading to buildings?

SOME SPECIFIC POLICY QUESTIONS FOR EVALUATING LARGE BUSINESSES

1. Are person-power plans established which are based on realistic long-range estimates of the business?

2. Is the tradeoff between overtime and a larger work force evaluated?

3. Have policies been established for hiring, training, promotion, and compensation?

4. Are good individuals promoted promptly within the organization or do negative factors hold all people to bureaucratic progression?

5. Can the company truly fit the eccentric genius into a spot where he or she will make a large contribution to profit with minimum disruption? Does it do so?

6. Does the company have risk-taking components with wide latitude for the development of products from concept to market success? Are the risk takers rewarded or removed according to their "batting averages?"

7. Is the organization periodically restructured to stimulate new relationships, uncover possible hidden talent, and break up vested interest groups?

8. Does management keep employees informed regularly of major objectives and major problems of the company?

9. Do managers demand high level performance and associated high rewards? Do those who perform poorly receive training or opportunities in different types of work?
10. What is the attitude of the company toward unionization?
11. Do employees have a channel for presenting possible unfair treatment?
12. How should long-term company career employees be treated if their performance declines with age in later years?

SUMMARY

The policy analyst or consultant should not concentrate on purely technical solutions to general management and functional problems and issues. It is extremely important to pay attention to the *people* in the organization for it is people who cause problems, correct problems, and prevent future problems. The staffing, training, and motivating activities are of utmost importance to the success of the firm.

We may analyze a company and develop recommendations relative to human resources by:

1. Examining long-range planning and control of human resource management.
2. Examining in detail the capabilities and performance of each manager and key individual and relating them to problems throughout the company.
3. Utilizing checklists of common policies and problems which too often go unrecognized.

ENDNOTES

1. Bernard, Bass, *Stogdill's Handbook of Leadership,* rev. ed., Riverside, N.J.: The Free Press, 1982.
2. Wanted: A Manager to Fit Each Strategy. *Business Week,* February 25, 1980, p. 166.
3. A company which specializes in human resource computer application systems and services is InSci, 95 Chestnut Ridge Road, Montvale, New Jersey 07654.

SELECTED BIBLIOGRAPHY ON HUMAN RESOURCES

Barrow, Jeffrey C. The Variables of Leadership: A Review and Conceptual Framework. *Academy of Management Review,* April, 1977.

Bass, Bernard. *Stogdill's Handbook of Leadership.* Rev. ed. New York: The Free Press, 1981.

Burns, James McGregor. *Leadership.* New York: Harper & Row, 1978.

Cascio, Wayne F., and Awad, Elias M. *Human Resources Management.* Reston, Va.: Reston Publishing Co. Inc., 1981.

French, Wendell L. *The Personnel Management Process*. 4th ed. Boston: Houghton Mifflin, 1978.

Hersey, Paul, and Blanchard, Kenneth H. *Management of Organizational Behavior*. 3rd ed. Englewood Cliffs, N.J.: Prentice-Hall, 1977.

Kelleher, Edward J., and Cotter, Kay Lillig. An Integrative Model for Human Resource Planning and Strategic Planning. *Human Resource Planning*, Vol. 5, No. 1, 1982.

Mathis, Robert L., and Jackson, John H. *Personnel: Contemporary Perspectives and Applications*. St. Paul, Minn.: West Publishing Co., 1982.

Personnel Management: Policies and Practices (loose-leaf). Englewood Cliffs, N.J.: Prentice-Hall, 1976.

Schneider, Benjamin. *Staffing Organizations*. Englewood Cliffs, N.J.: Prentice-Hall, 1976.

Stead, Bette Ann. *Women in Management*. Englewood Cliffs, N.J.: Prentice-Hall, 1978.

Steers, Richard M. *Organizational Effectiveness: A Behavioral View*. Englewood Cliffs, N.J.: Prentice-Hall, 1977.

Walker, James W. *Human Resource Planning*. New York: McGraw Hill, 1980.

Zaltman, Gerald; Duncan, Robert; and Holbek, John. *Innovations and Organizations*. New York: John Wiley & Sons, 1973.

11

MANAGEMENT INFORMATION SYSTEMS, DATA PROCESSING, AND THE COMPUTER

IMPORTANCE OF MANAGEMENT INFORMATION SYSTEMS (MIS) IN BUSINESS POLICY

Baffled by Snow Job

I've seen the ablest and toughest of executives insist on increased productivity by a plant manager, lean on accounting for improved performance, and lay it on purchasing in no uncertain terms to cut its staff. But when these same executives turn to EDP they stumble to an uncertain halt, baffled by the snow job and the blizzard of computer jargon. They accept the presumed sophistication and differences that are said to make EDP activities somehow immune from normal management demands. They are stopped by all this nonsense, uncertain about what's reasonable to expect, what they can insist upon. They become confused and then retreat, muttering about how to get a handle on this blasted situation.[1]

ADVANCES IN COMPUTER SYSTEMS

It has been said that if Detroit had done for the auto industry what the computer industry has done for the computer, cars would cost $1 and travel at the speed of light. Today, computers can perform over 2,000,000 multiplications per second compared with 2000 per second in 1952. In 1952, the cost of 100,000 multiplications on an IBM computer was $1.26. Today, the cost is less than $.006.

The computer has transformed decision making, planning, and control by making more and better quality information available to executives on a more timely basis. The development of the MIS has provided computer-assisted decision making as well as programmed decisions. The typical office has been revolutionized as video terminals with built-in computers talk to other computers. Paper and files are beginning to disappear as data are stored in computer discs and tapes and retrieved on the video terminals. Typewriters are being replaced with computerized word processors. All these changes require revolutionary changes in business operations, structure, procedures, and human skills.

ALLOCATION OF RESOURCES

The introduction or redesign of an MIS may represent a very large expenditure for equipment and services for a service whose benefits are very difficult to measure. The magnitude of these expenditures and the cost of failures may run in the millions of dollars. In one study, John V. Soden reported an original cost estimate for a utility company's information system as $2.5 million. The development cost when the project was abandoned was $7.0 million. The estimate for completion at time of abandonment was $15.0 million.[2]

INCORPORATION IN THE COMPANY STRATEGIC PLAN

As the costs and benefits of an MIS have increased, the time required to develop and implement the MIS has increased correspondingly. These factors have made it necessary to make MIS planning a part of the strategic plan.

MANAGEMENT AND COMPUTER SYSTEMS

Although managers need not be computer experts, they need to have some basic understanding of computerized MIS and data processing. From a systems view, the manager should be familiar with the following:

1. MIS,
2. Computer system,
3. Data processing.

The *MIS* is a system which monitors and retrieves data from the environment, which captures data from transactions and operations within the firm, which filters, organizes, and selects data, and which arranges and presents such data as information to managers. The four principal subsystems of MIS are the management system, the operating systems, the data-base system, and the computer system. A major mistake that companies make is to start with the computer system in designing the MIS. There must be a concept of a management system and operating systems before the computer system is developed.

The *computer system* consists of three major subsystems identified as follows:

1. Hardware—if you kick it you will hurt your toe,
2. Software—instructions telling the computer what to do,
3. People—to do the things that the particular computer and available software can't do.

Within limits, the functions of these subsystems are interchangeable. For example, if we increase the hardware, we may need less software or fewer people. Or, if we add more software, we may require less hardware and fewer people.

Data Processing is the recording, manipulating, storing, and retrieving of data. It provides the underlying basis of the MIS. The computer system has made possible mass processing of data to an awesome degree.

At the *lowest level* use of the computer are *application programs* which are software packages, often available commercially. These programs process data for repetitive standard situations. An accounts receivable program is an example. At the *highest level* of computer usage are special models, management judgment inputs, query systems (user-computer interaction), computer "learning," and associated software. The incorporation of a computer system in the MIS for the purpose of supporting management's formulation of strategy is an example. See Exhibit 11.1.

COMPUTER HARDWARE

A brief discussion of computer hardware will remove the mystique associated with the computer. For those who have toured through computer hardware centers and been awed by big cabinets hiding unknown electronics, take heart. All kinds of devices may be in a box with combinations of devices. Even a computer expert has to examine the system to know what is inside. Therefore, if we understand the basic concepts of computers, we don't need to worry about packaging to make *management* decisions about the system. With this in mind, we will simply identify the hardware components and their principal functions.

We may simplify the picture in advance by noting that hardware may be divided into two classes:

1. Basic input, processing, storage, and output equipment
2. Data communications equipment

The Basic Hardware

The central processor unit (CPU) is the most important, and generally the most expensive, computer system component. It performs the arithmetic and logic activities, and utilizes a main memory to work with directly. Data from a larger, secondary, memory may be fed to

EXHIBIT 11.1

MIS Role in Corporate Strategic Development System

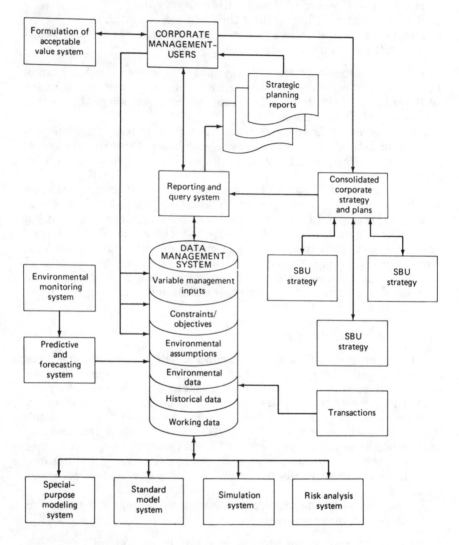

the main memory. Input devices and output devices are required to instruct the computer. Exhibit 11.2 shows alternative forms of the various components.

Data Communication Equipment

When data are to be transmitted from terminals remote from the CPU, both technical and economic problems are posed. A technical

EXHIBIT 11.2

Computer Components (except for data transmission equipment)

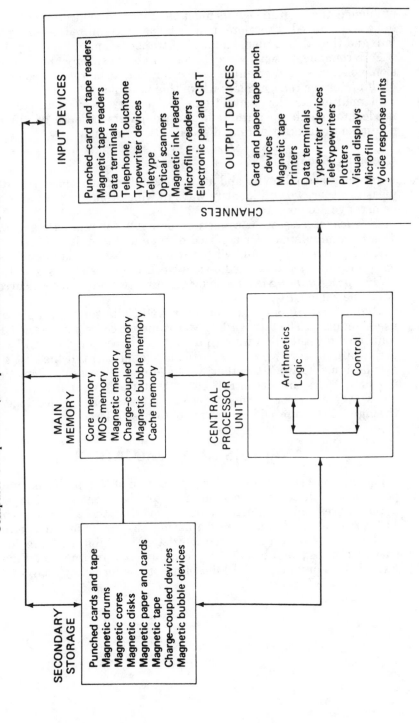

problem is that digital signals must be converted to modulated signals to be transmitted. Therefore, two *modems* are required, one to modulate and the other to demodulate the transmissions.

For economic reasons, we also would like to use only one transmission when several terminals are connected to a remote computer. *Multiplexors* or *concentrators* make this possible.

In addition to the above items, various types of *controllers* are needed to match up terminals and computers because of different equipment characteristics and speeds of operation.

Operating Modes

For purposes of brevity and at the risk of lumping somewhat unlike ideas together, we will identify ways in which computer systems may be arranged to operate.

In *batch processing,* a collection, or batch, of related transaction data is accumulated over a period of time and then is processed. For example, additions to, and withdrawals from, stock may be recorded on forms and then processed once a week to give a status report.

Multiprogramming is a mode for running two programs concurrently on the same CPU.

Multiprocessing is the use of several CPUs to service a number of users' requests. The total CPU power is increased by having the CPUs connected together this way. In *distributed* processing, the CPUs are decentralized, each serving a particular set of users. If the CPUs are also designed to work together, we have multiprocessing. Sometimes the data bases are decentralized so that we have *distributed data bases*. Again, in one version, these data bases may be tied together through CPUs to provide a central data base effect.

ANALYSIS AND EVALUATION

For the analysis of case studies, evaluation of MIS problems may be performed at three levels: computer system performance, MIS system performances, and company policies covering these areas. Exhibit 11.3 provides guidelines for evaluating the computer in operation (rather than the technical characteristics). Exhibit 11.4 provides a checklist of costs and benefits of a computerized information. Finally, Exhibit 11.5 provides a checklist of questions for policy analysis.

EXHIBIT 11.3

Characteristic Performance Indicators

Activity		Dominant Issues	Example MOE's (Measures of Effectiveness)
Clerical	Function:	cost displacement, task execution	Units per labor hour, backlog
	System:	efficiency, speed of operation, economy	Throughput, capacity utilization, data preparation cost per unit
	Information:	accuracy	Percent error transactions
Operational	Function:	monitoring and control over activity and resources	Inventory level, yield rate, messages delivered/received, missed shipping dates
	System:	maintainability, sustainability, availability, sensitivity	Percent down time, time between failures, frequency of service, percent requests with special handling
	Information:	timeliness, reliability	Response time
Tactical	Function:	decision quality, functional objectives	Return on investment, volume orders per district unit cost, overtime/regular hours, percent returned product, delivery time
	System:	auditability, compatibility, flexibility, security, scope	Actual users vs. intended users, percent service of total cost, reports returned vs. delivered
	Information:	sufficiency, conciseness, discovery	Percent file used when appropriate, volume of inquiries
Strategic	Function:	organizational mission, planning outcome of decisions	Share of market, new products, earnings/share, change in risk, percent R&D of total expense
	System:	user satisfaction[a]	Number of accesses per inquiry, time to formulate inquiry, percent compliments vs. complaints
	Information:	relevance	Percent responses appropriate

[a]Access ease, available period, dependable source, suitability to purpose, personal convenience.

Source: W.A. Smith, Jr. *Effectiveness of Information Systems*. Reprinted with permission from the Monograph, Planning Guide for Information System Evaluation Studies. Copyright © Institute of Industrial Engineers, Inc., 25 Technology Park/Atlanta, Norcross, GA 30092.

EXHIBIT 11.4

Proposed List of Costs and Benefits for
Information Systems Evaluation

Possible Information System Costs

Procurement costs
   Consulting costs
   Actual equipment purchase or lease costs
   Equipment installation costs
   Costs for modifying the equipment site (air conditioning, security, etc.)
   Cost of capital
   Cost of management and staff dealing with procurement

Start-up costs
   Cost of operating system software
   Cost of communications equipment installation (telephone lines, data lines, ect.)
   Cost of start-up personnel
   Cost of personnel searches and hiring activities
   Cost of disruption to the rest of the organization
   Cost of management required to direct start-up activity

Project-related costs
   Cost of applications software purchased
   Cost of software modifications to fit local systems
   Cost of personnel, overhead, etc., from in-house application development
   Cost for interacting with users during development
   Cost for training user personnel in application use
   Cost of data collection and installing data collection procedures
   Cost of preparing documentation
   Cost of development management

Ongoing costs
   System maintenance costs (hardware, software, and facilities)
   Rental costs (electricity, telephones, etc.)
   Depreciation costs on hardware
   Cost of staff involved in information systems management, operation, and planning activities

EXHIBIT 11.4 *(Continued)*

Possible Information System Benefits[a]

Benefits from contributions of calculating and printing tasks
  Reduction in per-unit costs of calculating and printing (CR)
  Improved accuracy in calculating tasks (ER)
  Ability to quickly change varibles and values in calculation programs (IF)
  Greatly increased speed in calculating and printing (IS)

Benefits from contributions to record-keeping tasks
  Ability to "automatically" collect and store data for records (CR, IS, ER)
  More complete and systematic keeping of records (CR, ER)
  Increased capacity for recordkeeping in terms of space and cost (CR)
  Standardization of recordkeeping (CR, IS)
  Increase in amount of data that can be stored per record (CR, IS)
  Improved security in records storage (ER, CR, MC)
  Improved portability of records (IF, CR, IS)

Benefits from contributions to record searching tasks
  Faster retrieval of records (IS)
  Improved ability to access records in databases (IF, CR)
  Improved ability to change records in databases (IF, CR)
  Ability to link sites that need search capability through telecommunications
    (IF, IS)
  Improved ability to create records of records accessed and by whom (ER, MC)
  Ability to audit and analyze record searching activity (MC, ER)

Benefits from contributions to system restructuring capability
  Ability to simultaneously change entire classes of records (IS, IF, CR)
  Ability to move large files of data about (IS, IF)
  Ability to create new files by merging aspects of other files (IS, IF)

Benefits from contributions of analysis and simulation capability
  Ability to perform complex, simultaneous calculations quickly (IS, IF, ER)
  Ability to create simulations of complex phenomena in order to answer "what
    if?" questions (MC, IF)
  Ability to aggregate large amounts of data in various ways useful for planning
    and decision making (MC, IF)

Benefits from contributions to process and resource control
  Reduction of need for manpower in process and resource control (CR)
  Improved ability to "fine tune" processes such as assembly lines (R, MC, IS,
    ER)
  Improved ability to maintain continuous monitoring of processes and available
    resources (MC, ER, IF)

---

[a]CR = Cost reduction or avoidance; ER = Error reduction; IF = Increased flexibility; IS = Increased speed of activity; MC = Improvement in management planning or control. The classification of tasks is adapted from K. L. Kraemer, W. H. Dutton and J. R. Mathews. Municipal Computers: Growth, Usage, and Management. *Urban Data Service Reports* 7, 11 (1975), 8.

Source: John Leslie King and Edward L. Schrems. Cost Benefit Analysis of Information Systems Development and Operation. *ACM Computing Surveys,* March 1978. Copyright © 1978, Association for Computing Machinery, Inc., reprinted by permission.

EXHIBIT 11.5

Checklist of Questions For Policy Analysis

1. Is the MIS manager high enough in the organization to deal effectively with line managers?
2. What characteristics should the MIS have 5 years from now?
3. What will be the state of the art of computer systems 5 years hence, and is the company building its system in this direction?
4. What strategic plan is required for the development of MIS data processing systems?
5. Should we lease computer services or develop our inhouse capability?
6. Are management and users the prime decision makers in computer and MIS decisions or are the technicians in control?
7. Is the MIS supporting management's decisions, or is it in fact simply an automated data processing system?
8. Is the structure of company reports appropriate in terms of (a) numbers of reports, (b) types of reports, (c) detail at each level of management, and (d) cross-functional information?
9. Are we smothering executives with data instead of selective information?
10. Have we realistically evaluated the cost of hardware, the cost of software, and system maintenance?
11. What are the benefits of the MIS and how can we measure them?
12. What are our data security objectives, and have we planned for them in the development of the computer data base and information system?
13. What will be the impact of the MIS on the organization? Consider restructuring the organization, new procedures, new decision methods, and resistance to change.

ENDNOTES

1. Harry T. Larson. EDP, a 20-Year Ripoff. *Infosystems,* November, 1974, p. 27.
2. John V. Soden. Understanding MIS Failures. *Data Management,* July, 1975, p. 31.

SELECTED BIBLIOGRAPHY ON
MIS, DATA PROCESSING, AND THE COMPUTER

Asten, K.J. *Data Communications for Business Information Systems.* New York: Macmillan, 1973.

Burch, Jr., John G.; Strater, Felix; and Grudmitski, Gary. *Information Systems: Theory and Practice.* New York: John Wiley & Sons, 1979.

International Business Machines Corporation. *Business Systems Planning* (GE20-0527-2) 2nd ed. White Plains, N.Y.: IBM, 1978.

Kraus, Leonard I., and MacGahan, Aileen. *Computer Fraud and Counter Measures.* Englewood Cliffs, N.J.: Prentice-Hall, Inc., 1980.

Murdick, Robert G. *MIS: Concepts and Design.* Englewood Cliffs, N.J.: Prentice-Hall, Inc., 1980.

Sprague, Ralph H., Jr., and Carlson, Eric D. *Building on Effective Decision Support System* Englewood Cliffs, N.J.: Prentice-Hall, 1982.

12

ANALYZING MULTINATIONAL BUSINESS

INTRODUCTION

In this chapter we will take a look at some of the special features of business policy in multinational business operations. This chapter should not be used in isolation to solve a case in multinational business but should be combined with the techniques of business administration appropriate to the case under consideration. For example, a case in international marketing will require the combination of the contents of this chapter with good marketing practices.

The principle of the marketing concept takes on even greater significance when business goes international. Multinational business involves attempts to enter markets in which the situation may be radically different from that in the United States. Multinational business operations involve more than simply extending the techniques of domestic enterprise. When business goes international, the entire framework of economic, political, social, and cultural features will be different from that in the United States and will also be different from country to country. This requires special attention to one step in the problem solving process: the specification of constraints and assumptions under which the problem must be solved. Without this step, a completely erroneous solution may be adopted.

For years, the International Petroleum Corporation in Peru asserted ownership of the petroleum which it extracted and refined. This assertion seems quite correct to Americans, who are accustomed to private ownership of mineral resources. However, in Peru, as in most of the rest of the world, mineral rights reside with the state and private firms act only as concessionaires in extracting and refining the minerals. The battle between IPC and the Peruvian government over this issue culminated in the nationalization of IPC by Peru.

The IPC example is but one of the many possible illustrations of the classic mistake that United States based firms make over and over again—attempting to run a foreign operation the same way that it would be run in the United States. We shall see other examples of this basic type of error later on.

Business administration, as conventionally taught in the United States, is implicitly based on the American economic structure, social system, cultural values, and political system. When business goes international, the game must be played by altogether different rules (see Exhibit 12.1). The purpose of this chapter is to point out the major differences which are likely to cause trouble. We will not dwell on specific situations, but rather will look at the types of policies, problems, and pitfalls to expect in multinational business problems. You will then be in a position to seek out timely specific facts on the country and industry under consideration.

Although this chapter emphasizes *problems* in multinational business, we should not overlook the fact that there are also a multitude of opportunities. In fact, the problems which we will consider will usually only occur when a firm is pursuing a profit opportunity outside the home country. The material contained in this chapter is not intended to discourage the firm from pursuing these opportunities, but rather to help the firm avoid the common pitfalls which may prevent it from doing so successfully.

THE ORGANIZATION OF MULTINATIONAL BUSINESS

In multinational business, as in domestic enterprise, organizational structure is determined by corporate strategy. The organization provides the vehicle for implementing strategic plans. The international segment of the strategic plan may range from simple export to worldwide operations. Thus, the organizational form used to carry out this plan may range from an export department to a worldwide structure based on geography, function, or product.

The problems faced by a firm engaged in export are different from those of a firm engaged in multinational production. The decision of whether and when to expand into multinational production is a major policy issue in large domestic firms with substantial export markets.

EXPORT

Export problems are usually marketing-centered. The establishment of channels of distribution and the effects of trade barriers are major concerns, as is the design of an effective marketing mix abroad.

EXHIBIT 12.1

Differences Between U.S. and International Operations

Factor	U.S. Operations	International Operations
Language	English used almost universally	Local language must be used in many situations
Culture	Relatively homogeneous	Quite diverse, both between countries and within a country
Politics	Stable and relatively unimportant	Often volatile and of decisive importance
Economy	Relatively uniform	Wide variations among countries and between regions within countries
Government Interference	Minimal and reasonably predictable	Extensive and subject to rapid change
Labor	Skilled labor available	Skilled labor often scarce, requiring training or redesign of production methods
Financing	Well-developed financial markets	Poorly developed financial markets. Capital flows subject to government control
Market Research	Data easy to collect	Data difficult and expensive to collect
Advertising	Many media available; few restrictions	Media limited; many restrictions; low literacy rates rule out print media in some countries
Money	U.S. dollar used universally	Must change from one currency to another; changing exchange rates and government restrictions are problems
Transportation/ Communication	Among the best in the world	Often inadequate
Control	Always a problem. Centralized control will work	A worse problem. Centralized control won't work. Must walk a tightrope between overcentralizing and losing control through overdecentralizing
Contracts	Once signed, are binding on both parties, even if one party makes a bad deal	Are subject to being voided and renegotiated if one party becomes dissatisfied
Labor Relations	Collective bargaining; can lay off workers easily	Often cannot lay off workers; may have mandatory worker participation in management; workers may seek change through political process rather than collective bargaining
Trade Barriers	Nonexistent	Extensive and very important

The major pitfall to be avoided is failure to design the marketing mix to fit the target market.

The major means of export which a firm may consider are:

A. Deal through an Export Management Company (EMC). This is the simplest means because all foreign problems are handled by the export house. This is often a good way to begin exporting but consideration should be given to other potentially more profitable channels as the market grows.

B. Deal through a foreign import house. This is also a good way to break into export. The trick is to find a reliable importer who will effectively market your product. The information services available through the regional offices of the U.S. Department of Commerce and the international departments of major banks can be very helpful in this regard.

C. Deal through a manufacturer's representative abroad. This is a similar situation to the import house, but you may expect more individual effort on your product. The nature of the product may well determine which is better.

D. Set up a marketing subsidiary abroad (either wholly owned or a joint venture). This course is not usually undertaken unless the market potential has been established through export or careful market research. The exception to this is firms with considerable multinational experience. The marketing subsidiary provides maximum sales potential, but considerable volume is required to make it profitable.

E. Set up a Domestic International Sales Corporation (DISC). This is a wholly owned domestic subsidiary which enables the parent firm to shelter export earnings from federal income taxes. The tax incentive is provided to encourage domestic firms to pursue export opportunities. The DISC will usually be used in conjunction with one of the four options above.

MULTINATIONAL PRODUCTION

Multinational production often evolves to service a market which has previously been serviced by export. In this case, channels of distribution will already exist, and the extent of the market can usually be estimated. A policy decision must be made as to the form of organization to utilize. The organization must be appropriate for the firm's strategic plan and for its present stage of international involvement and level of sophistication. There are several ways to get into multinational production. Among them are:

A. Wholly owned subsidiary. In this form, the U.S. parent owns 100% of the overseas production facility. This is the most popular form for U.S. based multinational companies. The major advantages are the lack of complications introduced by foreign partners and the fact that the U.S. parent receives 100% of the profits. This form of organization is prohibited in some countries, and other factors may outweigh these advantages and suggest one of the other forms.

B. Joint venture. In this form, the U.S. parent only owns a part (presumably majority) interest in a manufacturing subsidiary. The major advantage is that local partners may be able to provide special assistance, such as knowledge of the market, political contacts, etc. The major disadvantage is that foreign partners are often a source of conflict, and the interests of minority shareholders constitute a reduction of the profitability of the venture to the parent firm and often interfere with the parent's investment and divided policy decisions. A certain percentage of local participation is required by law in some countries.

C. Minority participation with a management contract. This form may be used in those countries which require majority local ownership. The U.S. firm owns a minority interest but manages the venture under the terms of a management contract with the majority owners. This form is not popular with U.S. firms, but is often the best available means of entering a market.

In December 1978, Cleveland-based Tower International Corporation signed an agreement to build a $60 million luxury hotel in Leningrad. Tower is not actually doing any construction—Finnish subcontractors are doing that—but Tower arranged the financing, put together the whole package, and sold it to the Soviet bureaucracy. Since "profit" on the project is not allowed in the U.S.S.R., Tower will receive a straight, guaranteed "fee"—certainly a lucrative way of entering an otherwise closed market.

D. Licensing. Licensing may be used to generate profits from a market which cannot be effectively tapped through export or one of the previous forms of organization. It involves granting a license to a foreign firm to produce and market a product, for which the foreign firm pays royalties to the U.S. parent firm. This often generates quality control problems and can prevent the U.S. parent from effectively entering the foreign market at a later date. The U.S. parent may also be creating its own competitor in markets in third countries.

MULTINATIONAL ORGANIZATION: THE SYSTEMS APPROACH

Once the proper methods of servicing individual foreign markets have been found, a crucial policy area still remains: How to organize the diverse divisions into an integrated whole with the parent company. This is a far more complex problem internationally than domestically because it is extremely difficult to direct the goals of the individual subsidiaries towards the parent company's primary goal. This primary goal is maximizing profit for the company as a whole by tradeoffs among goals of subsidiaries. The goals of the subsidiaries will be influenced by host government policy and pressure, views of local national stockholders, and the natural desire of local management to optimize the performance of the subsidiaries. Add cultural differences and communications breakdown and you have a difficult problem in system optimization. These problems affect all firms, large or small.

A major U.S. automobile manufacturer, Ford, has attempted to integrate its European operations by performing different segments of the production process in different countries. The objective was to achieve cost savings and economies of scale. This effort has been plagued by nationalism, strikes, communications gaps, delivery problems, and a decline in market share.

Performance maximization for the multinational firm requires that the organization structure be appropriate for the firm's strategy and stage of international operation. Some typical organization structures are shown in Exhibit 12.2 as they are likely to evolve when a firm goes multinational.

Typically, the multinational firm evolves its international organization in a series of stages depending on strategy. The most clear-cut jump in organization, and the one where loss of control is most likely, is the initial shift from export to multinational production. After the firm is well into multinational production, the most difficult problem is system optimization in an environment where almost all forces lead to subsidiary suboptimization.

EXHIBIT 12.2

Typical Evolution of Organization Structure

Early Export: Identifying Foreign Distributors

EXHIBIT 12.2 (*Continued*)

Later Export: Establishing Own Sales Office and Distribution in Host Countries

Early International Production: Establishing Production in Host Countries

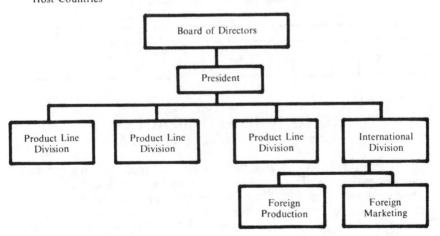

EXHIBIT 12.2 (*Continued*)

Later International Production: Establishing Subsidiary Companies in Host Countries

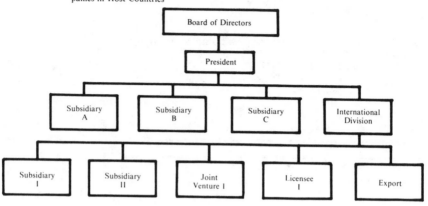

Trans-National Company: Establishing Global Philosophy and Operation

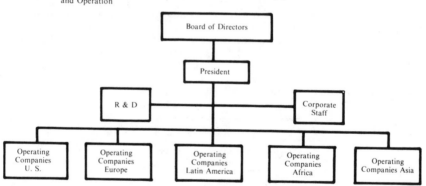

THE NATURE AND IMPACT OF
U.S. GOVERNMENT POLICY

U.S. Government policy affects international business through two important programs. These are export promotion and export control.

These appear to be contradictory, and they are to some extent. Export promotion efforts are centered in the Bureau of International Commerce of the United States Department of Commerce. The Bureau of International Commerce channels information on export opportunities to businesses through the Field Offices of the Department of Commerce. A visit to the nearest field office will produce a wealth of information on potential customers, channels of distribution, sources of export financing, and the paperwork involved in export. For a firm new to exporting, a visit to the nearest field office is a *must*.

The U.S. Government controls exports to certain countries for foreign policy purposes. This limits the opportunities for domestic firms to export to those countries. More important for multinational businesses, however, is the fact that the controls are extended to cover exports of subsidiaries abroad and exports to other countries which may subsequently re-export the goods to countries subject to the controls. The western European nations do have such controls, but exports by U.S. firms to these western European nations may not be allowed if they may subsequently end up as part of exports destined for countries subject to the controls. This becomes a particular problem in the case of the export subassemblies which go into finished goods which are sold worldwide by western European nations.

The English subsidiary of a U.S. company was providing the electrical connectors for an aircraft being constructed by a British aircraft manufacturer. Some of these aircraft were intended for sale to the People's Republic of China. The U.S. government prohibited the English subsidiary from supplying the needed connectors on the basis that they would ultimately be sold to China. The result was a multimillion dollar sales loss for the U.S. firm and its English subsidiary because the British aircraft manufacturer substituted a European supplier, not only for the parts for the aircraft destined for China, but for all other aircraft as well.

U.S. export controls are subject to frequent changes based on changes in the U.S. foreign policy objectives. As the U.S. government's attitude toward a foreign regime changes, export controls will reflect the new attitude.

In 1982, Fiat Allis North America Inc. lost a lucrative contract for the sale of bulldozer technology to the U.S.S.R. because of U.S. sanctions. Fiat Allis is a joint venture of Fiat (Italy) and Allis-Chalmers, 90% owned by Fiat. The loss of the technology contract was severe enough, by itself, but the Fiat Allis contract was part of a much larger contract negotiation between Fiat Allis' parent, Fiat, and the U.S.S.R. The U.S. sanctions had the effect of jeopardizing not only the continued operation and existence of Fiat Allis, but also the much larger potential contract between Fiat and the U.S.S.R.

The existence of export controls does not pose much of a problem for most potential exporters. This is because the vast majority of goods shipped to the major world markets require only a self-authorized export license—simply a matter of filling out a form—which *does not* require a wait for approval by any government agency.

U.S. business managers are deeply divided in their attitudes toward export controls. Hard-liners on trade call for more stringent export curbs that would keep sensitive technologies out of unfriendly hands. Makers of computers, machine tools, scientific and process control instruments, and other products are distressed over sales they are losing, even to non-Communist countries. They point out that sales they lose are made by other Western nations and that U.S. trade embargoes have been unsuccessful in changing the behavior of unfriendly regimes.

Exhibit 12.3 summarizes the ways in which the U.S. Government helps and hinders exports.

EXHIBIT 12.3

How the U.S. Government Helps and Hinders Exports

Helps	What They Do
Export-Import Bank	Finances big-ticket items
Commerce Department Export promotion	Helps small and/or new exporters enter foreign markets
Trade Negotiations	Bargain reductions in tariffs and nontariff barriers

Hindrances	What They Do
Anti-Arab boycott rules	U.S. exporters must forego contracts that require them to comply with the ban on Israeli-made goods.
Trade Act of 1974	Bars Export-Import bank credit to Communist Countries.
Lack of Most-Favored Nation Status for many Communist Countries	Prevents these countries from earning dollars with which to buy U.S. goods.
Foreign Corrupt Practices Act of 1977	Imposes jail terms and fines for foreign payoffs.
Antitrust Laws	Prevent U.S. firms from working together in overseas markets.
Trade Embargoes	Ban exports to specified countries
Export Controls	Ban exports of specified classes of goods
Human Rights Legislation	Bans Export-Import Bank credit to selected countries.

THE NATURE AND IMPACT OF
HOST GOVERNMENT POLICY

The relationship between a U.S. based multinational firm and the host government will probably be substantially different from the relationship between a domestic firm and the U.S. government. In most cases, this difference is reflected in substantial restriction of the firm's freedom of action, as compared with the U.S. domestic environment. There are several reasons for more restrictive government policies abroad. If the U.S. firm understands these reasons, it will be much more likely to operate successfully in the foreign environment.

A. *Nationalism:* Foreign governments are following policies which are designed to further the interests of the country concerned. This may sound like a trival point, but many Americans assume that foreign governments are (or should be) following policies designed to further the interests of the United States. If the interests of the United States, or a U.S. based firm, come into conflict with the interests of the host country, the host country government may be expected to resolve the issue in favor of the host country. It is therefore wise for a foreign firm to be very careful to keep its operations in harmony with host government policy because there is no neutral court to which the firm can appeal.

Sometimes, in its nationalistic or dogmatic zeal, a host country government may undertake policies which an outsider may view as irrational. The manager of an MNC cannot assume that host country regimes will *always* act rationally.

As a result of the Iranian Revolution, U.S. companies doing business with that country were exposed to approximately $1 billion in losses.

In December 1977 GTE signed a contract worth over $500 million with Iran. A condition of this communication equipment deal was GTE's advancement of $94 million in open letters of credit to Iran. The contract did not specify grounds on which the Iranian government could call the letters of credit.

GTE carried no insurance to cover its risk. The company was negotiating with the Iranian government up to the day the American embassy was seized. GTE's losses were estimated to be over $50 million.

B. *Economic Goals:* The major area of host government interest in which the foreign firm is directly involved is the area of economic goals. In underdeveloped countries, the overriding goal is economic growth. In the developed countries, the goals of growth, full employment, price stability, and exchange rate stability will be pursued simultaneously. Which goal has priority will vary from time-to-time and country-to-country. Whatever the economic goals of the country, foreign-owned firms will be expected to assist in achieving them.

If actions of the firm are directly counter to the economic goals of the host government, the firm may expect regulations or punitive action. Usually it is possible for a firm to find a way to exploit a good business opportunity without generating conflict with the host country's economic goals. The firm must seek out this method, however, because the policy which is the most profitable on paper may simply result in regulation or punitive action by the host government.

The basic mistake of IPC, mentioned on page 273, was in following dogmatically a policy which was most profitable to the firm, but in direct opposition to the economic goals of Peru. As we have seen, the ultimate outcome was expropriation. Other foreign oil companies have found profitable opportunities in Peru in joint ventures with the state-owned oil company.

C. *The Host Government's View of Multinational Business:* Host governments generally view multinational business with mixed emotions. At best, it is a source of investment, growth, employment, higher incomes, and prosperity. At worst, it is economic exploitation which seeks to drain the host country of its resources while providing nothing in return. Which view prevails depends to a large extent on how business conducts itself abroad. Excessive pursuit of short-run profits can leave the firm vulnerable to strong criticism and possible punitive action. A more enlightened approach can possibly secure tax concessions, foreign exchange availability, tariff protection, and greater long-run profit potential.

D. *Host Policies:* The specific policies encountered in a particular country at a particular point in time vary too much to be enumerated. A list of host government policies or policy areas which should be checked prior to committing the firm to a course of action are:

1. Tariffs,
2. Quotas,
3. Foreign exchange control,
4. Taxation,
5. The provision of utilities and transportation facilities,
6. Domestic equity participation required?
7. Restrictions on repatriation of earnings?
8. Labor relations, particularly restrictions on layoffs and reassignment.
9. Are cartels permitted and if so is there one in your industry?
10. One policy which must be anticipated is that all of the above policies are subject to change. An attempt must be made to evaluate current host government policy in the light of projected future developments. ASK: What is the policy in this area now, and what is it likely to be during the payback period of the projected investment?

Some policies are subject to negotiation between the firm and the host government. If the firm has done its homework, it will be able to show advantages to the host country which will result from the proposed venture. This approach greatly improves the chances of negotiating favorable terms.

Unlike the situation in the United States, a contract with a host-country government is not necessarily binding on the government. If the government finds that it has made a bad agreement, it may require that the agreement be renegotiated. The firm has little choice but to renegotiate because there is no neutral court in which it can sue the host government for breach of contract.

THE IMPACT OF SOCIOCULTURAL AND ECONOMIC FORCES

Sociocultural and economic forces in the host country will have important and sometimes bizarre effects on the operation of multinational business. Management must anticipate these effects if it is to successfully implement a multinational business venture. Problem areas to be expected in management and marketing are outlined below.

MANAGEMENT

The major impact on management results from differences in the quality of the work force and differences in management's relationship with the work force.

A. In less developed countries (LDCs) the bulk of the work force may be illiterate or semiliterate. There will likely be a severe shortage of local skilled labor and supervisory personnel. This places a definite constraint on the degree of sophistication which may be used in the design of production operations.

A major American soft drink bottler opened a bottling plant in the Middle East. The plant manager, who had opened many similar plants in the U.S., hired the best available technicians to operate the plant. Because of political and legal constraints, most of the employees were local nationals. Within a week the main conveyor broke down. The cause was that the main bearings had not been greased upon installation. Luckily the machine came with an extra set of bearings. These were installed and the plant manager instructed the machine custodian to pack them with grease. A week later, the bearings burned out again—the custodian had used the wrong kind of grease. The machine custodian said that he was not at fault because "if Allah wanted the machine to break, it would break, grease or no grease."

Incidents such as this were common at this plant in the Middle East. During the first year over 100 working days were lost because of accidents and down time.

B. In many less developed countries the sociocultural and economic values are not yet adapted to industrialization. Management may have difficulty getting the work force to adapt properly to the demands of modern factory operations. Higher wages are often an insufficient motivating tool, because the work force may be trying to achieve a certain money income and not interested in increasing their income if greater effort is involved.

C. In both the developed and less developed countries, management may be constrained in its relationship with its work force. In many countries it is extremely difficult to discharge an unsatisfactory employee (this is often a legal constraint, not a result of U.S. style collective bargaining). Given that it will probably be difficult to discharge unsatisfactory employees, and given that there may be many employees who are unsuited to U.S. style factory operations for sociocultural reasons, it is necessary that management carefully tailor production operations to the capabilities of the local work force.

MARKETING

The sociocultural and economic situation in the host country will have important effects on the design of an effective marketing mix for that country. The marketing mix which was effective in the U.S. will likely have to be changed to be effective in a foreign country. This is true because an effective marketing mix in the U.S. is tailored to the U.S. market, and that market is not duplicated abroad. Some of the important components of an effective marketing mix are considered below, and likely problem areas are outlined.

A. *Product:* Product design will often have to be tailored to the foreign market. In all cases, however, the gains to be made from tailoring the product to the specific market must be weighed against the loss in production efficiency resulting from the lack of standardization. The current world trend seems to be toward greater standardization because of economies of scale in manufacturing.

B. *Packaging:* This will almost always require changes, for language reasons if for no other. Differences in buying habits, literacy, and color appeals will dictate differences in package size and design.

C. *Distribution system:* Major changes in the distribution system are to be expected. First, the available distribution channels will be quite different abroad, and a choice must usually be made among the available channels. Second, the product will likely be in a different stage of the product life cycle in the foreign country, thus possibly requiring a different distribution system from that utilized in the U.S.

D. *Advertising:* Advertising appeals are heavily culturally determined. What appeals to the U.S. consumer will not necessarily appeal to the foreign consumer. Media customarily used in the U.S. may not be available abroad (newspapers are unsuitable for advertising to an illiterate market; television may be state-owned and not permit commercial advertising, etc.). The firm must be particularly careful to choose an advertising agency whose organizational structure, location of offices, and "style" suit the needs of the advertiser.

E. *Price:* Economic considerations are important here. Lower living standards abroad lead to relatively high price elasticities of demand for products other than basic necessities. This constrains management's flexibility in pricing policy. Also, the host government may intervene to prevent full exploitation of the firm's monopoly power in the market. The temptation is to attempt to skim the market, but penetration pricing often yields better long-term results.

Japan is often accused of keeping U.S. products out of Japan through nontariff barriers (NTBs). In 1981, the U.S. sold fewer than 8,000 cars in Japan, while 1.8 million Japanese cars were exported to the U.S. Detroit executives blame the NTBs, but the Japanese think there may be another explanation: In Japan, motorists drive on the left, as they do in Great Britain. Japanese cars for domestic sale are manufactured with the steering wheel on the right-hand side. The American cars shipped to Japan have the steering wheel on the left as they do in the U.S. Is it any wonder that U.S. cars are not popular in Japan? Japanese executives say this "left-hand-drive syndrome" is common in American industry and is one of the main causes of the trade imbalance between the U.S. and Japan.

FINANCIAL MANAGEMENT

Financial management in foreign operations is a particularly tricky business. The major problem areas are discussed below.

A. Inflation in many countries runs substantially higher than in the U.S. Internal financial policy must be restructured to protect the firm as much as possible from windfall losses resulting from inflation. For example, cash balances must be minimized; credit terms must be restricted; and pricing policy must be reviewed often.

B. Balance of payments problems in the host country have particularly important financial effects on the firm.

   1. The firm may find that its access to foreign exchange (dollars or other convertible currency) may be severely restricted. This limits its ability to import machinery, subassemblies, or raw materials. It also limits the firm's ability to repatriate earnings to the home country, to transfer capital to another sub-

sidiary, or to pay interest on Eurodollar or Eurobond borrowings.

2. Balance of payments problems in the host country also raise the possibility of currency devaluation. This would cause the firm to take large windfall losses in the book value of its assets in terms of the home country currency. It also reduces the home country value of the earnings stream generated by the subsidiary. This is a particularly difficult problem to hedge against, but some precautions can be taken. Among them are:

a) Incurring as much indebtedness as possible in the host country currency rather than in the home country currency.

b) Hedging in the forward exchange market (selling the host country currency forward).

c) Minimizing the use of capital in foreign operations through the use of leasing, agency arrangements, etc.

3. In evaluating the reported profits of an overseas operation, you must be careful to separate profits or losses resulting from *operations* from "profits" or "losses" generated by changes in the exchange rate of the dollar versus the foreign currency. The floating dollar can make reported earnings of a foreign operation bob up and down when earnings from operations are quite stable.

The Financial Accounting Standards Board (FASB) is working on an improved version of its controversial rule on reporting the results of foreign operations, FASB-8. While details of the proposed new rule are too complex to discuss here, the reader should be aware that the rules for translating foreign results into U.S. dollars are admittedly imperfect and subject to change.

Gillette gets over half its revenues from foreign sales. In one recent year, 85% of the currencies Gillette deals in moved down against the dollar. One devaluation of the Mexican peso cost Gillette over $2 million in one quarter. As a result, the head of Gillette's international division moved aggressively to cope with future devaluations. Among the techniques Gillette is using are reducing inventories, reducing accounts receivable, increasing intracompany financing, and increasing foreign borrowings.

C. Uncertainty about the movements in relative exchange rates clouds financial planning in both exporting and multinational firms. This further complicates the integration of overseas operations. Some financial intermediaries are coping with this problem by offering money substitutes made up of a "basket" of major currencies. Obligations denominated in these "baskets" would, hopefully, maintain a fairly stable total value, even if relative exchange rates changed with the "basket" itself.

All of these precautions involve costs, and may reduce the profitability of the venture. This must be weighed against the foreign exchange risk.

TRADE BARRIERS AND
INTERNATIONAL AGREEMENTS

Trade barriers and the changing pattern of trade barriers resulting from international agreements are important factors in determining the market potential facing a domestic exporter or a foreign subsidiary. Often, the pattern of trade barriers will be the major determinant of whether a market is serviced by export from the U.S., serviced by foreign production, or abandoned altogether. Therefore, the pattern of trade barriers and relevant international agreements affecting a particular foreign market area must be known before committing the firm to a course of action in that market area. The nature and impact of trade barriers and the major international agreements and trading blocs are presented below. The nature of international agreements and the membership in trading blocs are subject to change, so they are discussed below in general terms only. The specific situation in a particular country should always be researched by the firm.

A. *Trade barriers:* Trade barriers take four major forms:
   1. Tariffs, which result in an increase in the delivered price of imported commodities.
   2. Quotas, which limit the quantity of a commodity which may be imported.
   3. Exchange control, which limits the cost and availability of foreign currency, which is necessary to purchase imports.
   4. Nontariff barriers: health, safety, design, or quality restrictions which have the effect of keeping out imports.

U.S. Government regulations requiring each auto maker to attain certain fleet-average fuel economy standards are a powerful nontariff barrier to imported cars. The regulations require that each auto maker average only the cars it *makes* in the U.S., not the cars it *sells*. This means that Ford cannot use a Fiesta (made in Germany) to offset the gas consumption of a Continental. These regulations are expected to wipe out the so-called "captive imports," imported from subsidiaries of major U.S. manufacturers. Foreign manufacturers of luxury cars are also in trouble. Mercedes-Benz, for example, may have to develop and market a subcompact to bring its fleet average MPG up to U.S. requirements.

The nature and extent of use of these barriers by a country limits the ability of an exporter to market his product in that country. In order to avoid these barriers, it is necessary to produce the product inside the country, or in a country with which it has a free-trade agreement. Even in a free-trade situation, exchange control may still be an obstacle.

B. The General Agreement on Tariffs and Trade (GATT) is the major international agreement among the non-Communist countries. Negotiations under GATT have resulted in general tariff reductions and therefore changed competitive positions for exporting firms and for firms which manufacture and sell domestically to compete against importing firms. Prohibitive tariff rates still apply to countries which are not GATT members.

> The Tokyo Round of GATT trade negotiations, completed in 1979, produced both winners and losers among U.S. firms. Aerospace, agriculture, automotive equipment, and electronics expect major new export opportunities. Industries such as steel and textiles face intensified competition, but also new opportunities resulting from codes designed to reduce nontariff barriers in markets such as Japan.

The several rounds of tariff reductions negotiated under GATT have been so successful that tariffs are no longer the main barrier to market entry by U.S. firms. The intricate web of nontariff barriers (NTBs) that persists in spite of codes in the 1979 GATT agreements designed to remove them is the most serious problem U.S. exporters face. Many NTBs are unwritten, so firms do not learn of them until it is too late.

C. *Trading Blocs:* The best known and most important trading bloc is the European Economic Community (EEC). This bloc has a common external tariff, and free trade internally. Much U.S. direct investment in Europe has been motivated by the benefits of servicing this vast market from inside the common external tariff.

This is the most powerful economic bloc and the largest market in the world. The impact of the expansion of the EEC will be strongly felt by both U.S. exporters and multinational companies. The overall impact cannot be predicted with certainty, but economic expansion in the enlarged EEC should open new opportunities for both categories of firms. U.S. exporters in particular should follow developments carefully in search of new opportunities.

There are several other regional trading blocs which have tried with little success to match the EEC's performance. These blocs influence market conditions in member countries. You should always check a country's membership in trading blocs before entering the market.

While not a trading bloc *per se,* the Organization of Petroleum Exporting Countries (OPEC) has dramatically emerged as a major market. OPEC has replaced the EEC as the market of most rapid growth for U.S. based MNCs.

SUMMARY

The solution of a problem in multinational business involves applying techniques of business administration in areas for which these techniques were not designed to be used. The special considerations and constraints of the multinational situation must be uncovered and worked into the analysis. As noted earlier, the most common mistake of U.S. firms is to try to apply the same techniques abroad that are used in the United States. The successful firm will always seek out the *facts* on the situation in the foreign market and will adapt its strategies to those facts. After reading this chapter, you now have an idea of what types of facts are needed and many pitfalls to avoid.

SELECTED BIBLIOGRAPHY ON MULTINATIONAL BUSINESS

Ball, Donald A. and Wendell H. McCulloch, Jr. *International Business: Introduction and Essentials*. Plano, TX: Business Publications, Inc., 1982.

Capon, Noel; John U. Farley; and James Hulbert, "International Diffusion of Corporate and Strategic Planning Practices," *Columbia Journal of World Business* 15 (Fall 1980): 5–13.

Cateora, Philip R., and Hess, John M. *International Marketing*. 4th ed. Homewood, Ill.: Richard D. Irwin, 1979.

Coleman, William T., Jr., "Government Regulation of Foreign Business Practices—A Reassessment," *Financial Executive*, September, 1980, pp 36–40.

Davidson, William H. *Global Strategic Management*. New York: John Wiley and Sons, 1982.

Doz, Yves L., and C. K. Prahalad, "How MNCs Cope With Host Government Intervention," *Harvard Business Review* 58 (March/April 1980): 149–57.

Fayerweather, John. *International Business Strategy and Administration*. Cambridge, Mass.: Ballinger Publishing Co., 1979.

Ricks, David. *Big Business Blunders: Mistakes in Multinational Marketing*. Homewood, IL: Dow Jones-Irwin, 1983.

Terpstra, Vern; with contributions by Ian H. Giddy [and others]. *The Cultural Environment of International Business*. Cincinnati, Oh: South-Western Publishing Co., 1978.

13

HOW TO MAKE AN INDUSTRY STUDY

RELEVANCE OF THE INDUSTRY STUDY

Every company is one of a group of companies producing similar or substitute products. Such a group is called an *industry*. It is obvious that the policies, strategies, and actions of one company within such a group will affect the others in the group. As a result, the other companies often react, and their reactions must be anticipated. Further, the degree to which companies cooperate (legally) through trade associations and technical interchange affects the growth and efficiency of the industry. For example, the Machinery and Allied Products Institute produces technical reports and books to aid companies supporting it to make better capital investment decisions.

The practices, trends, and the general health of an industry affect the individual companies within the industry. For these reasons, analysis of a company without knowledge of the industry may lead to completely unrealistic conclusions. In addition, a company's problems may often be traced back to industry problems. Therefore an industry study is useful to the management consultant, to the business student developing a solution to a case problem, to the new employee in business, or to an executive changing jobs to enter a different industry.

WHAT IS AN INDUSTRY?

What companies constitute an industry is not often well defined. In fact, it is often convenient to speak of the industry to which our company belongs as those companies we view as our competitors. The U.S.

Government has established standard industrial classifications (SIC) so that much reference material on a particular industry is tied in to these particular classifications. The major divisions are listed below with the manufacturing division expanded in Exhibit 13.1 to show two-digit classifications. Actually there are subclassifications of up to seven digits. Such references as *Moody's Manuals* employ four-digit breakdowns.

EXHIBIT 13.1

SIC Divisions

DIVISION A – AGRICULTURE, FORESTRY AND FISHERIES

DIVISION B – MINING

DIVISION C – CONTRACT CONSTRUCTION

DIVISION D – MANUFACTURING

19	ordnance and accessories
20	tobacco manufacturers
21	tobacco manufacturers
22	textile mill products
23	apparel and other finished products made from fabrics and other similar materials
24	lumber and wood products except furniture
25	furniture and fixtures
26	paper and allied products
27	printing, publishing and allied industries
28	chemicals and allied industries
29	petroleum refining and related industries
30	rubber and miscellaneous plastic products
31	leather and leather products
32	stone, clay and glass products
33	primary metal industries
34	fabricated metal products, except ordnance, machinery and transportation equipment
35	machinery, except electrical
36	electrical machinery, equipment
37	transportation equipment
38	professional, scientific, and controlling instruments – photographic, optical watches and clocks
39	miscellaneous manufacturing industries

DIVISION E – TRANSPORTATION, COMMUNICATION, ELECTRICAL, GAS AND SANITARY SERVICES

DIVISION F – WHOLESALE AND RETAIL TRADE

DIVISION G – FINANCE, INSURANCE AND REAL ESTATE

DIVISION H – SERVICES

DIVISION I – GOVERNMENT

DIVISION J – NONCLASSIFIABLE ESTABLISHMENTS

MAJOR CONCEPTS IN AN INDUSTRY ANALYSIS

There are seven major facets which should be investigated for an industry background study. An analysis of these major facets will allow us to evaluate the status, growth, and future of the industry. We also learn the "form" of the industry and its interaction with its environment. A brief discussion of the common major facets follows.

DETERMINE THE IMPACT OF THE ECONOMY AND THE INDUSTRY ON EACH OTHER

For large oligopolistic industries such as the automobile, steel, or copper industries, the fate of the industry and the entire country's economy are closely intertwined. This often imposes indirect or direct pressures on the industry to avoid price raises, to avoid strikes, or to cut back on the flow of dollars for overseas expansion. Slumps and unemployment in such an industry may produce adverse affects on the entire economy.

Smaller industries such as leather tanning or the fiber box industry may have little impact on the overall economy because of substitute products available and smaller total employment. Companies in such industries may therefore have more freedom of choice of strategy and action.

FIND THE SALES TREND AND SALES POTENTIAL OF THE INDUSTRY

Have the industry sales been declining steadily over the past ten years? Buggy whip manufacturers and steam-driven auto manufacturers would have been well advised to ask this question. Managements in the tannery industry, the steel industry, and the watch and defense product industries in the U.S. should follow industry sales trends and potentials closely in these rapidly changing times. The fertilizer industry suffered severely in recent years because of overexpansion which led to extremely low prices and great losses.

The forecast of a company's sales is usually based upon share of the total industry market. This is a very important figure because strategy should be related to market share.

IDENTIFY THE NUMBER AND CHARACTERISTICS OF FIRMS IN THE INDUSTRY

The structure of the industry has a significant impact on any one company's actions. We all know that if U.S. Steel cuts its prices, other steel companies will follow suit. On the other hand, a department store in the boondocks may maintain high prices because the alternative is for the consumer to drive perhaps 150 miles to the nearest big city. We know that high technology companies must match each other's research. Small competitors must seek to supply specialized products or services if there are giants in the industry. In some industries such as the airline industry, each company's strategy appears to be a strong reflection of the personality heading the company.

In appraising an industry, the analyst should categorize it as illustrated below:

Class	Possible Implications
1. A few giants (oligopolistic) Examples: Aluminum producers Cigarette manufacturers	Price cutting is fruitless Antitrust action is a hazard Concerted action leads to a monopolistic situation facing the customers Very high capital costs to enter the industry.
2. A few giants and a relatively small number of "independents" Examples: Auto industry Oil industry Tire industry Meat processors	Price cutting by smaller companies may bring strong retaliation by giants Follow-the-leader pricing Antitrust action against the giants is a hazard Monopolistic practices Squeeze on the independents High capital costs to enter the industry.
3. Many small independent firms Examples: Food brokers Sales reps Auto supply parts Kitchen cabinet manufacturers Real estate firms Tanneries	Cost of entry is low Special services Usually Local market Threat of regional or national linking into a major competitor Sophisticated business practices often lacking.
4. Professional service firms Examples: CPA firms Management consultants Marketing research firms Advertising agencies	Confusion of standards Easy entry (and exit) Secretive pricing, often based on what the traffic will bear.
5. Government regulated to a great degree Examples: Banking Stock brokerages Rail industry Communications industry	Entry is usually difficult Government provides a semimonopoly which may lead to high profits or inability to survive in a changing world.

The analyst will find other ways of classifying firms in an industry, each with its own set of implications. Other characteristics to be considered are (1) size of firms in terms of number of employees, number of customers, assets, sales, ROI, (2) whether the industry is a manufacturing, wholesaling, retailing, or service industry, (3) extent of local, state and federal regulation, and (4) state of managerial and technological advance within the industry. Multinational firms and conglomerate firms confuse the definition of "firms making up an industry" so that judgment must be used for purposes of analysis.

IDENTIFY TRADE ASSOCIATIONS, TRADE PRACTICES, AND STANDARDS

The nature of an industry may be indicated by the number, size, and kind of trade associations. Trade associations may be primarily lobbying groups or primarily information processors. The *Encyclopedia of Trade Associations* published by Gale Research Company, Detroit, Michigan 48226, or *Directory of National Trade Associations,* U.S. Government Printing Office, will provide the students with leads to the number of associations in the industry.

Industry trade practices such as pricing, work practices (six-hour day in the rubber industry), seasonal sales, warranties (auto industry and tire industry are familiar ones), minimum wages, and employment procedures (hiring halls for longshoremen) are examples. Trade standards may relate to sizes and shapes (plumbing and electrical industries), models (auto industry), or magnetic tape characteristics (computer and radio/recorder industries).

Practices and standards are important to know about because they pose both *restrictions* and *opportunities.* The opportunities arise when a company develops a practice different from that of the industry as a whole which is then accepted by customers of the industry. For example, the plumbing industry has historically used metal piping. Now companies are following the pioneering use of plastic piping. Historically tennis rackets were made of wood until Wilson Manufacturing Company bucked the trend to produce a highly successful steel racket.

EVALUATE THE PAST GROWTH OF THE COMPANY RELATIVE TO THE INDUSTRY

The growth of the industry provides a measure for the performance of a particular company. If the company is getting an ever-diminishing share of growing industry sales, then despite possible increasing profits of the company, something may be wrong. In the long run, it may be getting squeezed out of the market.

The contrary situation where a company appears healthy because of increasing market share and profits may also be hazardous because the industry sales are diminishing steadily. This could happen because of new and better substitute products or changes in consumer preferences.

EVALUATE THE POTENTIAL GROWTH OF THE COMPANY RELATIVE TO THE INDUSTRY

The technical, economic, marketing, and financial strengths of a company should be compared to competitors. Special strengths (a single technical genius, unique location, established market, or patented product) should be identified, if any exist. Strategies and strengths of competitors should be examined and the future of the company relative to the industry should be forecast.

IDENTIFY CHARACTERISTICS OF THE MOST SUCCESSFUL AND LEAST SUCCESSFUL COMPANIES IN THE INDUSTRY

By contrasting the most successful and least successful firms in the industry, an astute management may learn good and poor practices. Those strategies and practices which are different for successful and unsuccessful firms should provide the clues.

EXHIBIT 13.2

Quality Analysis
Eastman Kodak (highest grade) versus Bausch & Lomb (lowest grade)

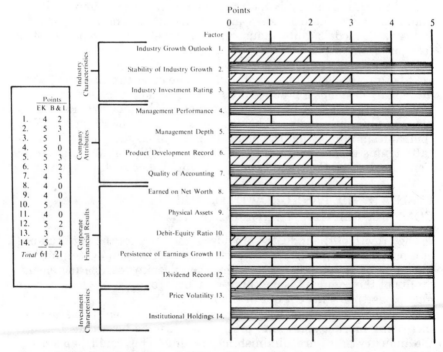

Source: Frank C. McLaughlin and William H. Kent, Use Fundamentals to Avoid Fads in Pension Fund Investment. *Financial Executive,* May 1973.

Exhibit 13.2 may suggest graphic methods for summarizing such a comparison. Obviously many more aspects should be compared in more detail in most industry studies.

A CHECKLIST OF SPECIFIC ITEMS

The organization of a report on an industry may be developed from the list of topics in Exhibit 13.3.

EXHIBIT 13.3

Industry Study Outline

a. Definition of the industry
   1. By SIC number, or
   2. Description of firms and products which comprise a group of competitors
b. History of the industry
   1. Cause of its formation
   2. Development of its production, marketing, and technology
   3. Social, legal and political influences which shaped its development
   4. Role in the U.S. (and world) economy over its history
c. Technology
   1. Level
   2. Rate of change
   3. Technological threats to the industry
d. Resources
   1. Raw materials availability, now and projected
   2. Energy requirements
   3. Managerial, specialized skills, and general labor requirements
   4. Subassembly sources
   5. Future mixes of capital and labor inputs
e. Investment
   1. Cost of entry
   2. Percent of firms failing annually
   3. Capital renewal requirements
   4. Working capital required
   5. Trends for the above items
   6. Nonfinancial barriers such as brand recognition or government licenses
f. Marketing
   1. Market areas
   2. Methods of selling and promoting
   3. Channels of distribution including trends
   4. Pricing methods
   5. Trade associations
g. Market structure
   1. Dominance, concentration, and market shares, present and forecasted
   2. Characteristics of successful firms and unsuccessful firms
h. Political-Legal-Social influences
   1. Trends in government controls
   2. Effect of trends in consumer tastes and behavior patterns
   3. Pressures for assumption of social responsibilities.

SOURCES FOR OBTAINING OR DEVELOPING AN INDUSTRY STUDY

An industry study may be developed by researching sources such as:

A Technological Assessment Methodology, Vol. 1–7 (prepared by MITRE Corp. and distributed by the National Technical Information Service, U.S. Dept. of Commerce, 1971).

Adams, Walter, ed. *The Structure of American Industry.* 5th ed. New York: Macmillan, 1977.

Industry Surveys. New York: Standard and Poor's Corp.

Investors Management Sciences, Inc. (subsidiary of Standard & Poor's), supplies custom reports on company screenings and rankings, company and industry comparisons, and 40,000 predefined ratios. 1221 Avenue of the Americas, New York, New York 10020.

Predicasts, Inc., 11001 Cedar Avenue, Cleveland, Ohio 44106, produces and markets a wide variety of industry studies.

Sumner, N. Levine, ed. *The Dow Jones-Irwin Business Almanac.* Homewood, Ill.: Dow Jones-Irwin, 1977.

Textbooks on business policy.

Trade publications and trade associations (See *Encyclopedia of Associations* published by Gale Research, Detroit, Mich.), *Forbes, Fortune, Business Week,* and other general business publications which publish occasional special reports on an industry.

U.S. Census of Manufacturers (U.S. Department of Commerce).

U.S. Industrial Outlook and *Growth Pace Setters in American Industry* (U.S. Department of Commerce).

14

HOW TO ANALYZE
A CASE

HOW TO STRUCTURE THE ANALYSIS

THE ROLE OF THE CASE ANALYST

In analyzing a case and preparing a case report, the student must clearly establish his or her role. The student may, for example, be assigned the role of consultant. In such event, he or she must make the analysis and recommendations with due regard for the views and values of the management of the company. He or she should be somewhat cautious about suggesting that the president fire his son, for example. If the president has a personal desire for keeping the company small but profitable, an expansion policy probably should not be recommended.

A second role which the student may be assigned is that of president. Assume that the current president dies or retires, and the student is elected to this office through some miracle (such as a rich uncle who owns the controlling stock). Now in his or her analysis and recommendations, the student may freely include personal values in the selection of strategy and policy. Even in this case, the student must realize that instant-policies are not possible. He or she must be realistic and realize that time will be required, in most cases, to win over the lower levels of management to changes, or time required to replace the recalcitrants.

While allowable as an analytical game, the student may be asked to "make everything right" in the analysis and report. This would be a rational (?) role which neglects the human factors of enterprise. Too often students take this position in course work and only learn the consequences at a later point in their careers.

BASIC CONCEPTS

The output of a case study is a set of recommendations for *action*. Such recommendations must be derived from the case material, material on the environment which the student may bring in, and the student's knowledge of business practice gained from other courses. Recommendations must be made with regard to corporate objectives, strategy, policies, issues, operating problems, and *implementation* of all these.

The output of the case study is the *case report*. The case report assumes that the reader is familiar with the case itself and has the case data at hand. Therefore, the student *should not rehash material or repeat tables and data* except in the case where he or she manipulates the data, makes comparison, or points out facts of the case to substantiate arguments. This differs from the *business report* in which a section or appendix must be devoted to giving data. In business, an analyst cannot assume that everyone to whom his or her report is directed has all the data.

Although the case problem method is often called *case analysis*, a case study must also include a *synthesis*. Analysis consists of (1) breaking the problem into parts, (2) determining the facts which are significant to each component of the problem, and (3) classifying the component problems and facts in some form which expedites a synthesis, and (4) interpreting the significance of the facts by drawing deductions and inferences. Synthesis is (1) the creative structuring of the data, problems, and analysis into meaningful comprehensive problems and (2) the development of goals, strategies, and plans for the company which represent the solutions to the company's problems.

The average student has greatest difficulty in (a) knowing what questions to ask in order to begin analysis, (b) separating the "thinks" from the facts, and (c) thinking of more than one or two alternative courses of action from which the business can make the most effective decision. This book has been designed to assist the student in these three activities and should be reviewed while working out case solutions.

GENERAL TECHNIQUE FOR
DEVELOPING CASE SOLUTIONS

A student may, with experience, develop a preferred method of his or her own for attacking a case. Even so, it should be a *systematic* rather than an intuitive random procedure. In the long run, systems triumph over nonsystems. A step-by-step procedure for the development of a solution requires some recycling and is given below.

1. Read the case rapidly once to determine the general nature of the company and its setting.
2. Examine the case more carefully and jot down apparent objectives

of the company, policies, strategies, symptoms of problems, problems, and issues.

— 3. If appropriate, search outside sources for economic and industry information which will provide a setting for the company's situation.

— 4. Try to group related problems and issues into coherent, broad or even company-wide problems.

— 5. Create a framework for analysis which suits the particular case being studied. Some examples (explained further on in more detail) are:

    a. Organize the case around basic economic objectives, policies, strategies, plans, and implementation

    b. Organize the case around the process of administration such as:

       analysis of the situation
       basic objectives
       plans for action, schedules, and budgets
       implementation of plans
       control of operations

    c. Organize the case according to functional areas of the business and show functional interrelationships

    d. Organize the case around business systems: information flow and material flow systems

    e. Organize the case around key individuals in the case.

— 6. Within each subtopic of the chosen outline, state significant problems as *evidenced by data of the case,* whether direct or inferred. That is, state *why* you conclude such a problem exists; just don't dream up problems. This is particularly important when you identify problems which are due to *trends* of future events.

    Do not rehash case material; refer to case data or give data only to back up your arguments.

— 7. Identify *central* problems and the cluster of related problems for each central problem. These *problem clusters* may cut across your structure of subtopics.

— 8. Develop (synthesize) a reasonable number of feasible alternative actions or programs (generally, at least three) to solve each problem cluster. Seek basic objectives and broad strategies which will provide guides to the solutions of the problems. Specific plans implementing solutions should be developed. Alternatives for resolving key pressing issues should be staged.

— 9. Evaluate the alternative sets of goals, strategies, and problem solutions by analyzing the data and listing and weighing the advantages and disadvantages of each.

— 10. On the basis of your evaluations, prepare a set of specific *recommendations for action.* Assume action must be taken now, not after further lengthy research. Don't qualify, weasel, or hedge; action must be taken, the firm cannot be allowed to drift into further difficulty.

— 11. Organize your case solution and prepare your case report.

Case Structure Based on Plans and Implementation

We need to amplify on Step 5 above. First we examine the Step 5a alternative. In order to evaluate basic economic missions, we must answer such questions as:

1. Of what broad industries should the company be a part?
2. What do our competitive edge and resources capabilities suggest our product areas should be?
3. What are the trends of growth, the potentials, for these product areas?

With regard to policies, *we should structure major policies which will identify our firm and guide its operations.* For example, we may state that it is our policy not to take on defense contracts. Or we may state that it will be our policy to limit our business to the eastern U.S.A. and Europe. We may believe it important that all growth will come from our own product development rather than through acquisition of companies. (General Electric followed this policy to a great extent, historically.) Therefore, in analyzing the case, we may examine current policies and give alternatives and recommended policies.

What should be the competitive strategy of the company? The number and strengths of competitors need to be examined to answer this. What special opportunities in marketing, manufacturing, or design of products appear to be neglected by competitors? Which of these opportunities match our company's resources and talents? The development of alternative strategies is a highly creative process. A classic example is the introduction of the compact automobile, the Rambler, by American Motors Company in its effort to compete against the Big Three.

In a surprisingly large number of cases, the company will have no long-range, or even short-range, plans. The proposal of plans as a major topic for the case report is therefore often suitable.

Most case studies require the methods for implementing strategies and plans be given. Thus procedures for marketing programs, the specification of production systems, or implementation of shifts in the organization must be specified under the topic of implementation.

Case Structure Based on Administrative Process

The administrative process is not as broad-gauged an approach as the previous method. It is more an immediate examination of the firm's problems and how to dispose of them in terms of present objectives of the firm. In the previous structure, we examined the basic concepts of the firm and its position in future society. In this structure, we solve today's problems and plan for means of implementing the solutions. We must also specify how we can *control* implementation if it does not proceed according to plan.

With this approach, policies, problems, and issues are gathered together under subheadings used to describe the administrative process. One example of such headings is:

A. Objectives of the firm,
B. Organization,
C. Planning process and plans of the firm,
D. Implementation of plans of action.
E. Control systems and control as practiced in the firm.

While these topics are interrelated, nevertheless they do offer a procedure for classifying problems prior to clustering and tying the problems together. For each problem cluster or major problems, major alternative courses or *programs* of action should be given. For each program of action, analysis to demonstrate the pros and cons (advantages and disadvantages) of each should be given. When a major action or program is recommended as the best alternative, then other, more specific, procedures should be developed to carry out such a program within the firm. At this level, many of the secondary problems of the case must be handled. A number of *feasible alternative* procedures should be listed, and again pros and cons based on analysis should be supplied for each alternative. A single alternative should be recommended from each set of alternatives. Do not give conditional recommendations such as, "If this were the situation, we would recommend 'this' (specified), but if such-and-such a situation actually exists, we would recommend 'that' (specified)."

In order to integrate the analysis, a *summary* of several paragraphs of one or two pages will likely be needed to bind together the recommendations and the arguments in support of these.

The administrative process approach is essentially a systems approach. In a systems approach, objectives of the system are first formulated, current problems are identified and analyzed, the system is structured (organized) to seek objectives and deal with problems, plans are made and put into action, and control over the system is established.

The strategic plan, the operating plan, organizational structure, and control provide balance among demands of subsystems (suborganizations). Therefore, solutions to functional problems such as marketing, production, or accounting must be fitted into the plans and control systems of the company.

Case Structure Based on Functional Areas

The classification of problems by functional areas such as marketing, manufacturing, financial, and personnel is probably the most widely used structure for case analysis. This is because many textbook cases are themselves presented in a functional structure. The hazard of this method is that the analyst will fail to see problems which are caused by lack of *integration* of functional areas. Problems in the various functional areas must be tied together when they are related.

Since functions represent the subdivision of work by specialization, major and most secondary problems will fit obviously into a functional classification. Remember, that while this helps us with *analysis,* failure to observe or search out the functional *interrelationships* of problems will prevent *integration* of a solution to the case. To avoid this, when a problem is identified, it may be listed in its primary classification, say marketing, and underlined. It may then be listed under other functional areas it spills over into, but not underlined in the listing.

It is recommended in cases presenting financial statements that analysis start with the financial function. Symptoms of problems appear in the financial statements. These are usually symptoms of central problems which cut across functional areas. Functional subdivisions of operations may include some combination of the following, if they are relevant:

A. Financial planning and control
B. Marketing
C. Production
D. Engineering and research
E. Human resources (employee relations or personnel are narrower terms used)
E. International operations.

Other functional areas which are significant in some companies are Purchasing, Logistics, Systems and Procedures, Data Processing, or Land Development.

Company objectives and policies should be identified, appraised, and reformulated to guide the development of alternative solutions to functional problems.

Another suggestion for interrelating problems and policies is the preparation of a table such as in Table 14.1.

TABLE 14.1

Source of Problem
Manufacturing

Functional Areas Affected	Examples of Tradeoffs	Policy Recommendations
Marketing	Reduction in models vs. selling with promises of longer lead times	(as appropriate)
Human resources	Increased production planning and control vs. ceiling on employees on the payroll	(as appropriate)

Case Structure Based on Key Individuals

Sometimes the major problems of the company arise out of issues and strong protagonists on each side of the issues. The problems of the company may best be presented in terms of these issues and the character and viewpoints of the key individuals. Thus an analysis of each individual, his or her background, success record, and ideas relative to the opportunities and management of the company, offers a framework for the case study. This structure also has the advantage that it provides an easy starting point.

SUMMARY

The general approach to studying a case problem is really a general approach to problem solving. The framework for analysis of the case, however, may take on a number of forms. The particular form chosen should be one that is suitable to the available information—whether textbook case or actual business problem. It should also be a method that the analyst feels comfortable with. This permits improvisation and mixture of the structures given here. In brief, ill-structured problems call for creativity in approach to structuring analysis and solutions.

HOW TO WRITE A CASE REPORT

No matter how well the student has analyzed the case problem and synthesized strongly based recommendations, his or her work will be dissipated if the report is poor. The bases of a good report are:

1. Structure of the report as discussed above,
2. Organization of material within the structure as based on a good outline,
3. Format of presentation within the organization,
4. Style of writing, with simplicity, clarity, and conciseness as prime objectives.

HOW TO PREPARE THE OUTLINE

The purpose of the outline is to:

1. Organize the case material in a sequence which makes it easy for the reader to follow.
2. Highlight the major thoughts of the case and show the relationships among subsidiary ideas and major ideas,
3. Reinforce the student's memory of the case ideas and provide the framework for developing these ideas,
4. Serve to refresh the student's memory of the case, should he or she have to refer to it weeks later.

When the student has familiarized himself (herself) with the case, he or she will be able to select a structural pattern. Within this structure the student will proceed with the analysis. The analysis requires a *shifting of attention* from specific problems to a clustering or grouping of these specific problems according to their relationships. This latter is a synthesis which may involve trial and error. Out of this process will emerge a number of significant problem areas comprising subproblems. It is now possible to prepare the first draft of the outline.

The outline format should *avoid too fine a breakdown*. It is important to remember that there *must be no subdivision or at least two subdivisions for any heading*. That is, you cannot divide a heading into one subheading. The following format is traditional:

I.
  A.
    1.
    2.
  B.
    1.
    2.
    3.
II. Etc.

Parallel construction is important in an outline because it is logical, grammatically correct, and does not impose a burden on the reader to "shift gears" because of language structure. For example, all subheadings in a major section should be either (a) nouns or noun phrases, (b) similar verb forms, (c) questions, or (d) brief sentences. To illustrate each:

(a) Organizational System. Logistic System. Product Lines. Inventory Problems. Lack of Unified Objectives.
(b) Organizing. Analyzing the Logistics Problem. Planning for Action. Implementing the Recommendations.
    (Do not have one heading "Organizing" and another "Evaluation" or "Implementation." Either use "Organization" or change the other headings to "Evaluating" and "Implementing.")
(c) What are the major problem areas? What is the relationship of Acme Overseas Ltd. to the parent company? Why are sales down?
(d) The major problems are in marketing. The sales compensation plan is poor. Backup of salespeople is nonexistent. Manufacturing and sales organizations are not cooperating. Basic recommendations are to restructure sales and manufacturing procedures.

HOW TO SELECT A FORMAT

The student may be constrained by the desires of the instructor with respect to format, and he or she should question the instructor as to which formats are acceptable.

Listing and Outline Formats

There are two formats which have similarities. In one of these, each problem is identified in paragraph form. For each problem, possible alternative courses of action are *listed*. Following each alternative course of action, the pros and cons are *listed* and action recommended. As a variant, all recommendations may be tied together at the end of the analysis.

Another format is the *amplified outline*. After the original skeleton outline is prepared, either paragraphs or telegraphic-style sentences are added below each subheading to amplify on them. For example:
Competitive Patterns

A. National breweries in every area of the country
B. Large breweries in dominant position in each market
C. Number of breweries declining
D. Special premium brews of small companies successful in local areas
E. Light brews growing in popularity

The Business Report

Finally, the *business report* format may be used. Business reports may be classified as brief or long. A brief report is one that would be included in, say, a one- to three-page letter. If a report is longer than a few pages, the report is usually sent to the addressees with a cover letter which describes the problem and gives a summary of the recommendation. The report itself is written in paragraph style. The business report should *give the answer first* and then tie all ideas into the answer. Thus, in a case report, a resume of the problems and recommendations should appear first. The writer should then attempt to follow his or her outline to express the analysis and synthesis of the case by leading the reader smoothly through the report. The error that many students make in writing a case in this format is omitting alternatives and giving only single recommended courses of action, often without reasoning to back even these. The following ideas apply to letters of transmission and business reports in general.

Many firms have an already developed form that is required by management. If there is such a form, by all means, use it. Assuming, however, that this is not the case, we recommend that the following procedure be used at least on the first assignment.

While there is no one best form that fits every writer, it is only after experience with the company that an employee can judge the effect and effectiveness of creative changes in report structure, that might better fit the special talents of the writer and better illuminate the personality of the writer.

An outline of a typical letter which presents a business report is shown in Exhibit 14.1.

Name and Title of Addressee: Usually a request reaches the report writer from either an individual or a committee so that he or she has no choice as to the addressee. Occasionally this is not the case and the report writer can choose the individual or group of individuals to whom the report should be addressed. In this case the writer can make discreet inquiries as to which individual or group is most likely to act upon the report in the desired direction.

It is also important in addressing a memo to an individual to assess the impact on other people whose name or names may be omitted. Generally, it is better to include additional names rather than offend. Even the order in which the names appear may be important. A safe

EXHIBIT 14.1

Date _____

To: Mr. John Jones, President
Jones & Company

From: Robert Smith
Sales Correspondent

Subject: *Improving Sales Correspondence at a Lower Cost*

            Effectiveness of present sales correspondence

                 (Then follows a critique of present methods)

            Methods for improving sales correspondence
            1.
            2.
            3.

            Cost of suggested method vs. present system
            1. *Suggested cost*
            2. *Present cost*

            Dollar Savings Anticipated

                     Signed by hand

                 Robert Smith — Dept. 450

method, where a report is being addressed to several people, is to list them alphabetically without regard to rank. Recourse to the company organization chart is another possibility where the rank within the organization is clearly delineated.

Subject of the report: The subject of the report whenever possible should be:

1. Limited in length,
2. Descriptive of the report's contents,
3. Stated positively—i.e., improving, reducing costs, increasing sales, etc.,
4. A clear statement of the problem in the case of major reports, i.e., the problem that is most essential to be solved or the solution of which will clarify or lead to the solution of other problems,
5. Explicit—do not make vague general statements that are meaningless.

Content of the report: Approach—Thought should be given as to the best psychological approach.

Some addressees will be motivated by financial or cost or savings considerations. Others can best be "sold" by appeals to pride, company spirit, or even flattery, while still others can be forced into action with fear—fear of lost sales or what the competition is doing, etc.

During the early stages of a report writer's career, probably the best approach is to use a purely rational, hard-hitting, logical, factual attack.

Facts: Except for emphasis, students should *not* repeat facts. Your professor has read the same case material that you have and has enough wading through endless pages of repetition of facts repeated by each student in the class.

This is *not* true however, in business reports, where all the readers may *not* be familiar with the facts. In this type of report each section can contain facts or the facts can be placed near the beginning of the report so that all may be familiar with the foundation facts from which the conclusions are drawn.

Analysis and Conclusions: This section is the hardest to write. It requires logic, reasoning about the significance of factors and how they fit together, and a convincing explanation of the reasons underlying the conclusions. These types of errors are common:

1. Facts are needlessly recounted and bad situations decried but little analysis is included concerning the significance of the factors or why one is more important than another.
2. Problems are discussed independently without discussing their interrelationship.
3. Recommendations are mixed in with the analysis instead of being clearly and separately stated.
4. Constraints are often overlooked—for example, lack of capital precludes the use of expensive computers, yet the computers are recommended.
5. Definite recommendations for solving the main problems are not made, nor is a timetable realistically worked out.
6. The case analyst hedges or qualifies his recommendations and justifies this by citing a lack of facts. In case studies there are enough facts for the student to draw reasonable conclusions and inferences which will lead to decisions.

   In business there will be managers who jump to conclusions and others who research endlessly for facts because they are afraid to take the risk of making a firm decision. Only practice in decision making can point the way as to when to act and when to delay.

Mechanics: Enumeration, underlining of headings, indentation of subpoints as we have done above makes a paper far more useful and readable. Organization charts, systems diagrams, financial exhibits, and various types of charts and graphs greatly strengthen some reports.

Signature: In most companies a handwritten signature is a must even if there are twelve copies of a report. Always use it unless company policy precludes it.

HOW TO DEVELOP A GOOD BUSINESS STYLE

If there is one thing which every manager lacks, it is the *TIME* to do the work the way he or she would like to. The essence of good business communication is a style which is concise and easy to read. Both of these attributes will save the reader time. A strong thread of logic from "facts" to conclusions, adequate headings, good paragraphing, simple words for vague jargon, and avoidance of long, complex sentences such as this one make a report more readable.

We have seen case reports which extend to 12 typed pages without a single heading. We have seen paragraphs over one page long. We have seen sentences 10–12 lines in length. We have seen combinations of polysyllabic words strung out into one hot-air sentence after another. We have seen misspellings of common words which are incredible. The way to correct this type of writing is to set criteria in the form of a checklist and then check your case report against those criteria item by item.

Exhibit 14.2 suggests such a checklist. Each student should gather the instructor's criticisms of his or her style as a basis for preparing a personal checklist.

SUMMARY

Learning to write well is like learning carpentry or tennis. You must *want* to learn, you must *seek coaching,* and you must *practice and practice and practice.* You will be influenced by your coach instructor, and you must make continual efforts to learn his or her ideas about good writing. Eventually, you will develop a more refined skill of organizing and outlining, and you will develop a style which is easy both for you to write and your reader to read.

SELECTED BIBLIOGRAPHY ON HOW TO ANALYZE A CASE

Gilmore, Frank F., and Brandenburg, Richard G. Anatomy of Corporate Planning. *Harvard Business Review,* November–December, 1962.

Greenwood, William T. *Decision Theory and Information Systems.* Cincinnati, Oh.: South-Western Publishing Co., 1969.

Karger, D.W., and Murdick, R.G. Product Design, Marketing, and Manufacturing Innovation. *California Magagement Review,* Winter, 1966.

Lesikar, Raymond V. *Report Writing for Business,* 6th ed. Homewood, Illinois: Richard D. Irwin, 1981.

Mintzberg, Henry. The Science of Strategy-Making. *Industrial Management Review,* Spring, 1967.

Murdick, Robert G. *MIS: Concepts and Design.* Englewood Cliffs, N.J.: Prentice-Hall, 1980.

Paine, Frank T., and Naumes, William. *Organizational Strategy and Policy.* 2nd ed. Philadelphia: W.B. Saunders Co., 1978.

EXHIBIT 14.2

Written Performance Inventory

1. READABILITY

READER'S LEVEL

☐ Too specialized in approach

☐ Assumes too great a knowledge of subject

☐ So underestimates the reader that it belabors the obvious

SENTENCE CONSTRUCTION

☐ Unnecessarily long in difficult material

☐ Subject-verb-object word order too rarely used

☐ Choppy, overly simple style (in simple material)

PARAGRAPH CONSTRUCTION

☐ Lack of topic sentences

☐ Too many ideas in single paragraph

☐ Too long

FAMILIARITY OF WORDS

☐ Inappropriate jargon

☐ Pretentious language

☐ Unnecessarily abstract

READER DIRECTION

☐ Lack of "framing" (i.e., failure to tell the reader about purpose and direction of forthcoming discussion)

☐ Inadequate transitions between paragraphs

☐ Absence of subconclusions to summarize reader's progress at end of divisions in the discussion

FOCUS

☐ Unclear as to subject of communication

☐ Unclear as to purpose of message

2. CORRECTNESS

MECHANICS

☐ Shaky grammar

☐ Faulty punctuation

FORMAT

☐ Careless appearance of documents

☐ Failure to use accepted company form

COHERENCE

☐ Sentences seem awkward owing to illogical and ungrammatical yoking of unrelated ideas

☐ Failure to develop a logical progression of ideas through coherent, logically juxtaposed paragraphs

3. APPROPRIATENESS

A. UPWARD COMMUNICATIONS

TACT

☐ Failure to recognize differences in position between writer and receiver

☐ Impolitic tone—too brusque, argumentative, or insulting

SUPPORTING DETAIL

☐ Inadequate support for statements

☐ Too much undigested detail for busy superior

OPINION

☐ Adequate research but too great an intrusion of opinions

☐ Too few facts (and too little research) to entitle drawing of conclusions

☐ Presence of unasked for but clearly implied recommendations

ATTITUDE

☐ Too obvious a desire to please superior

☐ Too defensive in face of authority

☐ Too fearful of superior to be able to do best work

B. DOWNWARD COMMUNICATIONS

DIPLOMACY

☐ Overbearing attitude toward subordinates

☐ Insulting and/or personal references

☐ Unmindfulness that messages are representative of management group or even of company

CLARIFICATION OF DESIRES

☐ Confused, vague instructions

☐ Superior is not sure of what is wanted

☐ Withholding of information necessary to job at hand

MOTIVATIONAL ASPECTS

☐ Orders of superior seem arbitrary

☐ Superior's communications are manipulative and seemingly insincere

4. THOUGHT

PREPARATION

☐ Inadequate thought given to purpose of communication prior to its final completion

☐ Inadequate preparation or use of data known to be available

COMPETENCE

☐ Subject beyond intellectual capabilities of writer

☐ Subject beyond experience of writer

FIDELITY TO ASSIGNMENT

☐ Failure to stick to job assigned

☐ Too much made of routine assignment

☐ Too little made of assignment

ANALYSIS

☐ Superficial examination of data leading to unconscious overlooking of important pieces of evidence

☐ Failure to draw obvious conclusions from data presented

☐ Presentation of conclusions unjustified by evidence

☐ Failure to identify and justify assumptions used

☐ Failure to qualify tenuous assertions

☐ Bias, conscious or unconscious, which leads to distorted interpretation of data

PERSUASIVENESS

☐ Seems more convincing than facts warrant

☐ Seems less convincing than facts warrant

☐ Too obvious an attempt to sell ideas

☐ Lacks action-orientation and managerial viewpoint

☐ Too blunt an approach where subtlety and finesse called for

Source: John Fielden, "What Do You Mean I Can't Write?" *Harvard Business Review,* May–June 1964, p. 147.

Ronstadt, Robert. *The Art of Case Analysis: A Guide to the Diagnosis of Business Situations,* 2nd ed. Dover, MA: Lord Publishing, 1980.

Shay, Philip W. *How to Get the Best Results from Management Consultants.* New York: Association of Consulting Management Engineers, Inc., 1967.

Smalter, Donald J. Six Business Lessons from the Pentagon. *Harvard Business Review,* March–April, 1966.

Wingate, John W. *Management Audit for Small Retailers.* 2nd ed. Washington, D.C.: Small Business Administration, 1971.

limitations of personnel

15

CASE ANALYSIS ILLUSTRATED

THE SHAFT NURSERY AND LANDSCAPE COMPANY CASE

Shaft Nursery and Landscape Company in southeast Florida is a family-owned and -managed firm that was established in 1972. The company is currently divided into three main divisions: (1) Landscape Design and Installation, (2) Lawn and Garden Maintenance, and (3) Retail Nursery Operations. Total business is shared 55%, 30%, and 15%, *respectively*.

Thirty-seven-year-old president, Kent Gordon, says:

> "We want to be a 'landscape company' and not get too involved in the retail nursery business. Palm Beach and Broward Counties are among the fastest growing areas in the South. About 95% of our business comes from owners of private homes. We do very little business in industrial landscaping. While we are larger than average, a number of small firms keep entering and leaving the industry here."

Shaft's facilities are laid out on a six-acre site near the densely populated north-south strip of Florida coastline (see Exhibit 15.1). Financial statements for 19X1, 19X2, and 19X3 were the only ones in existence at the time of this case and are shown in Exhibits 15.2 and 15.3.

Method of Operation

The company designs the landscaping for a customer at no charge, and if the customer likes the design and contracts for the landscaping, he or she is billed upon completion.

EXHIBIT 15.1

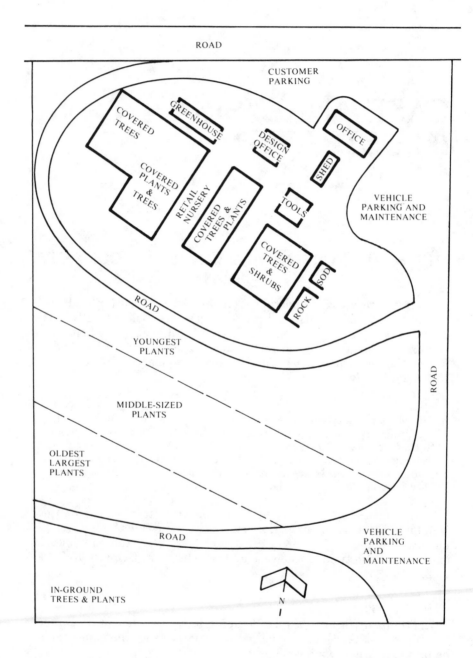

EXHIBIT 15.2

Income Statement

	19X1	19X2	19X3
Sales	562,000	620,000	640,000
Cost of Goods Sold			
Materials:			
purchased plants	30,000	42,000	40,000
peat, mulch, chemicals	9,200	8,400	10,800
Wages	236,000	276,000	292,000
Manufacturing Overhead	84,000	92,000	90,000
Total Cost of Goods Sold	359,200	418,400	432,800
Gross Profit	202,800	201,600	207,700
Selling Expense	62,000	70,000	70,000
General & Administrative Expense	86,000	89,800	92,000
Earnings before Taxes	54,800	41,800	45,200
Taxes	12,200	9,000	9,800
Earnings After Taxes	42,600	32,800	35,400

Lawn maintenance revenues come from customers under annual contract and random customers requesting a one-time service. The number of each class of customers varies erratically throughout the year.

Approximately 25,000 new plants are planted each year and there are approximately 83,000 plants on the site at any one time. There are approximately 200 varieties that may be growing at one time.

Presently, inventory is controlled by sight. The designer, Scott Gordon, age 29, can tell which types of plants are ready for installation. He then designs landscapes around the existing inventory. Since the same plants are being seeded each year, everyone in the company knows generally what is available. No records are kept.

Organization and Personnel

The Shaft Company is owned by two brothers, Kent and Scott Gordon, who started the firm after graduating from the local high school. The Shaft Company was initially founded as a partnership and incorporated in 1978. Kent is president and Scott handles miscellaneous activities as needed. The Shaft Company is organized as follows:

EXHIBIT 15.3

Balance Sheet

	19X1	19X2	19X3
Current Assets			
Cash	30,000	34,000	17,000
Accounts Receivable	1,600	7,400	14,400
Inventory	120,000	124,000	128,000
	151,600	165,400	169,400
Fixed Assets			
Trucks and Equipment	42,000	34,000	38,000
Buildings	74,000	64,000	54,000
Land	120,000	132,000*	140,000*
	236,000	230,000	232,000
Total Assets	387,600	395,400	401,400
Current Liabilities			
Accounts Payable	26,000	12,000	11,000
Fixed Liabilities			
Loan	40,000	40,000	40,000
	66,000	52,000	51,000
Capital	330,000	330,000	330,000
Retained Earnings	(8,400)	(13,400)	(20,400)
Total Equity	321,600	343,400	350,400

*Market value

A. Landscape Design and Installation Division—Kent Gordon, Manager
   1 landscape designer
   1 designer-estimator
   1 maintenance superintendent
   3 crane crew foremen with crews of 2 each
B. Retail Nursery Divsion—Kent Gordon, Manager
   2 salespeople
   1 grower-propagator
   5–6 nursery laborers
C. Lawn Maintenance and Spraying Divsion—Scott Gordon, Manager
   1 maintenance superintendent
   1 spraying superintendent
   18 people in 2- to 4-person crews

D. Service Group (reports to Kent Gordon)
    1 accountant
    1 secretary-receptionist
    1 mechanic

The company paid wages about 10% below the market for manual labor on the basis that it provided steady work. It offered no fringe benefits. The company claimed that workers would just drift in and out of manual labor anyway. The average number of workers with the company is 38, although the company sent out 217 W-2 tax forms.

Hiring, assignment, and miscellaneous personnel problems are handled on a casual basis by either Kent or Scott Gordon. The Gordons plan assignments and dispatch workers at the beginning of each day.

Financial

Barbara Pedolic, the "accountant" had been hired in 1978 shortly after graduating from high school with a major in commerce. As she gradually learned more about accounting systems from trying to solve daily problems and from outside reading, she attempted to develop records and systems. Most of the employees did not want to be bothered filling out even the few forms in use, the invoices and the purchase orders. Barbara spent much of her time just completing these forms and paying bills. The attempt to keep a cash account, accounts payable, and accounts receivable up-to-date was beginning to exhaust her. Other accounts such as capital assets were usually constructed at tax filing time.

The company owned, in addition to land, buildings, 3 crane trucks, 2 tractor-bulldozers, 5 pickup trucks, and 2 spraying trucks. No records of the smaller pieces of equipment such as mowers, edgers, trimmers, and diggers were kept.

Competition

Landscaping was a lucrative business which depended heavily on sales, design, and installation. A new nursery 10 miles away had opened in 1979 and was using personal selling and advertising very aggressively.

There were over a dozen firms which specialized in lawn spraying alone.

Lawn maintenance was an easy business to enter since it only required a pickup truck, a few mowers, edgers, rakes, and shovels, Many individuals and families were engaged in this business, despite the discomfort of laboring under the hot Florida sun.

ANALYSIS OF THE SHAFT COMPANY'S POLICIES AND PROBLEMS

Preliminary Reading

After a preliminary reading, the analyst will be able to identify some major policy issues and problems. He or she will then be able to structure his thoughts for a more detailed analysis and solution. Major policy and problem issues which are obvious are:

1. What strategy should the company adopt to give a *unified sense of direction?* What products, customers, and competitive edge should it specify as strategic objectives?

    We note that Kent Gordon wants to stay in the retail nursery business, but "not get too involved." However, the growing of trees and shrubs is more closely related to the main direction of landscaping than is lawn maintenance (which includes spraying).

2. What competitive edge should the company adopt for its strategy?

3. Does Shaft want to grow larger? If so, what plans may be made for acquiring land in an area where land is scarce and high priced?

4. No attempt is made to forecast sales and control inventory. This means that landscaping design is based upon whatever greenery is available or can be purchased from other nurseries. Further, without inventory control, the company cannot estimate its cost of production. The company is relying on "thinks" instead of facts about demand and supply.

5. The personnel policies are subject to question, in view of the high turnover and the attitude of management toward its labor force.

6. The physical layout of the nursery might be improved.

7. Just as basic direction, strategy, and plans are practically nonexistent, so are the financial planning and control of the company. The financial data must be put in order before an analysis can be made.

The preliminary reading suggests that the business is much like a manufacturing business. Relatively few data are given on the people involved. Let us therefore structure our case solution by just identifying strategy issues and solutions and then analyzing operating problems in a functional framework. We must first make a financial background analysis to determine the general health of the firm and unsuspected problems.

Background Financial Analysis

We note that the financial statements are summary in nature and do not permit an in-depth analysis. However, the balance sheet must first be adjusted. Land should be carried at cost, not market value. Current and long-term liabilities should be segregated. Trucks, equipment, and buildings should have been shown at cost with *Reserve for Depreciation* instead of net book value, but we can do nothing with the information as given. Exhibit 15.4 shows possible adjustments.

In Exhibit 15.5, we have converted items in the income statement to percentages of sales. We have also added *Earnings After Taxes* to this statement.

On the income statement we see sales are increasing rapidly. This indicates that Shaft is expanding with the rapidly growing population of south Florida.

From Exhibit 15.5 we note that the gross-profits percentages have

EXHIBIT 15.4

Adjusted Balance Sheet

| | End of Year | | |
	19X1	19X2	19X3
Current Assets			
Cash	30,000	34,000	27,000
Accounts Receivable	1,600	7,400	14,400
Inventory	120,000	124,000	128,000
	151,600	165,400	169,400
Fixed Assets			
Trucks	42,000	34,000	38,000
Buildings	74,000	54,000	54,000
Land	120,000	120,000	120,000
	236,000	218,000	212,000
Total Assets	387,600	383,400	381,400
Current Liabilities			
Accounts Payable	26,000	12,000	11,000
Noncurrent Liabilities			
Loan	40,000	40,000	40,000
Total Liabilities	66,000	52,000	51,000
Capital	330,000	330,000	330,000
Retained Earnings	(8,400)	1,400	400
Total Equity	321,600	331,400	330,400

declined. It is quite possible that in this highly inflationary time, the Gordons are not increasing their prices rapidly enough. A rapid increase in wages may also contribute to the decline. This increase in wages may be due to inflation, increased average number of workers, or both. It is a symptom of lack of control over personnel hiring, dispatching, or productivity of workers.

The company apparently paid excessive dividends in 19X1. The Current Assets to Current Liabilities ratios indicate that there is no lack of liquidity, however.

A critique of the format will be made in the functional analysis of the case. Other than this, trends appear reasonable except for earnings. The following ratios may be helpful in identifying major concerns of Shaft:

	19X1	19X2	19X3
Earnings/Sales	7.6	5.3	5.5
Earnings/Net Worth	13.2	9.6	10.1
Sales/Inventory	4.7	5.0	5.0

CASE SOLUTION: SHAFT NURSERY AND LANDSCAPE COMPANY

Strategy

Shaft has grown rapidly and successfully over the years primarily because of economic growth in Florida and *hard work* on the part of the owners. Evidence in the case indicates that more managerial skill will be needed for the firm to survive in a tough, competitive environment. As the Florida growth levels off, it is vital that the company have a clear strategy.

EXHIBIT 15.5

Earnings Statement Percent of Sales

	19X1	19X2	19X3
Sales	100%	100%	100%
Cost of Goods Sold			
Materials			
Purchased Plants	5.4	6.8	6.2
Peat, Mulch, Chemicals	1.6	1.3	1.7
Wages	42.0	44.5	45.6
Manufacturing Overhead	15.0	14.8	14.1
Total Cost of Goods	63.0	67.5	67.7
Gross Profit	36.0	31.2	32.4
Selling Expenses	11.0	11.6	11.0
G & A Expenses	15.3	14.5	14.4
Earnings before Taxes	9.8	6.7	7.1
Earnings after Taxes	7.6	5.1	5.5

The present scope of the company includes landscaping, lawn maintenance, and nursery operations. Landscaping and nursery operations are synergistic (mutually supportive). Lawn maintenance, on the other hand, other than sodding operations, is a distinctly different business. The only common characteristic with the other operations is some overlapping of customers. Shaft could continue with the current three businesses or choose to compete for a larger share of the lucrative landscaping business while also carrying the nursery business. The advantages of focusing on landscaping are (1) it will be easier to gain a larger share of the market now that the market is still growing, (2) landscaping service business is obtained through word-of-mouth so that building a strong reputation is important, and (3) the landscaping business requires the highest skills and is most lucrative.

The disadvantage of dropping the lawn maintenance business is that it represents 30% of sales. This may not be so significant, however, if it contributes little profit. We do know that most spraying of lawns is done by firms which specialize in spraying only. We also know that competition for mowing lawns is extremely intense with many firms in the field.

We *recommend* that Shaft phase out of the lawn maintenance business over the next five years and that it deploy its resources to build a strong market position in landscaping. In the marketing analysis further on, we propose the addition of a skilled landscape designer to further strengthen the company in this area. We recommend that Shaft consider opening a branch about 50 miles to the north to expand upon its more narrowly defined business.

Shaft, once its business has been defined, must identify its competitive edge. Rapid service, low prices, wide variety of plants to choose from, excellence in landscaping design, warranty on the survival of plants, and maintenance service of plants after installation are possible alternatives. Low prices do not appear appropriate to this type of business. Warranties on survival should be given based upon evidence of customer's care. A two-year service contract could add income and reduce warranty costs. We *recommend* that Shaft appeal to the well-to-do residential market, that it upgrade its design staff as much as possible, that it provide prompt estimates and rapid service, and that it price in terms of quality and uniqueness of service.

In order to obtain a larger market share, Shaft should purchase additional land as soon as possible. The rapidly rising land costs and the actual disappearance of available land are pressing factors. Shaft's very low debt/equity ratio would make borrowing easy. We *recommend* that Shaft pursue a policy of growth and purchase about four to five acres. Rapid appreciation of land in south Florida will outweigh high interest rate for a loan.

General Management

The Gordons' lack of formal management education is apparent. They have not tried to remedy this by utilizing consultants and specialists. We *recommend* that they retain a management consultant to work with them specifically on (1) development of planning procedures to implement the strategy we have recommended, (2) development of a very simple forecasting and control information systems, and (3) development of long-range development programs for Kent and Scott Gordon to improve their managerial skills.

Marketing

There are salespeople for the Retail Nursery Division, but only a designer-estimator for the Landscape Division where expansion is recommended. With a reduction in the Lawn Maintenance Division labor force, a salesperson-designer-estimator should be added to the Landscape Division. The company really needs to integrate and strengthen its total marketing activities. While an advertising agency could provide some specialized assistance including market research, a *marketing* consultant could help the Gordons establish a marketing plan.

We *recommend*, as consultants with the limited information available, that Shaft (1) identify areas of surrounding communities in which homeowners are able to afford landscaping, (2) determine landscaping installations which past customers have preferred, (3) begin an educational (promotional) program to convince marginal potential customers that landscaping adds both esthetic and dollar value to their homes, (4) develop a list of specific prospects including new home builders, and a plan, with schedule, for company salespeople to follow up promptly on prospects. Salespeople could be paid on a combination of salary, commission, and bonus or salary or commission alone. Because of the promotional work required, a base salary should be used. Commission and bonus represent incentives to increase sales. We *recommend* salespeople be paid a base salary of $12,000 plus a commission and bonus.

Once promotional effort and market potential have been established, a sales forecast should be prepared. Alternative appropriate methods are managerial judgment, time series analysis, or exponential smoothing. We *recommend* management judgment for one- to three-year forecasts and exponential smoothing for month-to-month forecasts. The latter is a simple arithmetical projection of historical sales which smooths out erratic data.

Production and Inventory Control

The site layout shown in Exhibit 15.1 could be improved (alternate layouts should be sketched and evaluated). Since vehicles are parked daily, the parking and maintenance areas should be combined close to the main road. There is considerable wasted space on the road side of the layout as well as between office buildings. We *recommend* that rock, sod, office buildings, and vehicles parking be brought to the roadside. A fence should be constructed around the nursery. A single road running from the south end of the nursery through the center, up to the buildings, and then dividing around the east and west sides of the buildings and covered areas is *recommended,* rather than the two looping east-west roads and north-south road.

Inventory control could be more exact than the present visual check. First, an investigation should be made to see if 200 varieties are required or whether this number could be cut in half. Perpetual inventory or monthly physical inventory to check on the physical condition of plants should be done at the same time. As a check of each plant is too time-consuming, we recommend calculating inventory by multiplying the estimated number of plants of a particular type per square and by the number of square yards of these plants. Value as a function of age and size can be estimated by experienced operators such as the Gordons.

Financial and Control Information Systems

The Shaft Company is not getting the kind of information it needs to make operating or strategic decisions. Under "marketing," we have discussed the lack of information required for growth. The company does not appear to have the information of sales and profit by division, or profit margins on varieties of plants needed to make operating decisions. Cost analysis for growth of each type of plant may be deduced as lacking on the basis of the simple error-prone financial statements.

On the balance sheet, it is apparent that only a guess at inventory has been made. With inflation and growth of sales, it is likely that inventory is growing more rapidly than indicated. In addition, land should be carried at cost or market value, whichever is lower. In Exhibit 15.4, we have shown land at cost.

Trucks, equipment, and buildings should be shown at cost and a reserve for depreciation subtracted to show net book value. There is insufficient data to make this correction. Liabilities should be separated into current and long-term to permit analysis.

Shaft has three apparent options to improve financial information. First, it may purchase consulting services to set up the books and further train Barbara Pedolic. Second, it may hire a CPA firm to maintain the books with Barbara assisting with record keeping. Third, Shaft may release Barbara and hire a fully qualified accountant. Our pros for the first are (1) that the accounting is basically simple and highly repetitive, so that Barbara could follow procedures once established, (2) a full-time accountant or accounting services would be more expensive, and (3) Barbara apparently has some desire to upgrade her skills. The argument against such a course of action is that the tax aspects of Shaft may be such that a fully qualified accountant would be profitable.

We *recommend* that Shaft follow the first option if Barbara is sufficiently capable.

Summary

Shaft has grown rapidly and profitably due to economic conditions and the hard work of the founders. In the years ahead, a professional approach to strategy and operations management will be required as the market potential levels out and new competitors enter the area. This type of business can be quite profitable provided a strong competitive edge of design and other services are maintained, total marketing is emphasized, and costs of operations are managed properly.

VOGUE CREATIONS, INCORPORATED, CASE

Eight years ago the International Apparel Company, one of the largest apparel companies in the world, bought 90% of the Robert Wood Company when the sole owner, Mr. Robert Wood, passed away. While International produced and sold all types of men's, women's, and children's apparel and shoes, the Robert Wood Company manufactured only lingerie and foundation garments (girdles and bras). The policy of International was one of decentralized management for all their subsidiaries. They felt that in the highly competitive apparel field with rapid style changes peculiar to each segment of the industry, the top management must be free to operate as they thought best.

Functional aspect

While International did change the name of the Robert Wood Company to Vogue Creations, Inc., no other changes were made except to place Mr. L. T. Johnson, former VP of Wood Company, in charge as president. Mr. Wood had run a "one man show" making all the major decisions himself. Mr. Johnson tried to follow in Mr. Wood's footsteps but even though he added many additional executives and departments, including electronic data processing (EDP) he had never been able to regain Wood's former profitability. In January of 1984, upon the retirement of Mr. Johnson, International sent Paul R. Putnam to Vogue as president, Mr. Putnam's conversation with the Chairman of the Board of International brought out the following:

1. International was dissatisfied with the operation of Vogue.
2. Mr. Putnam was to be president of Vogue for three years. He was to report back in two months to the Board of Directors what changes he was making to bring the return on equity up to International's 15% minimum.
4. If additional capital was required, Mr. Putnam would not be able to borrow from International but would need to raise the money on Vogue's assets.
4. Vogue could *not* call upon International for any help whatsoever, and Vogue was to stand upon its own two feet as a completely independent organization.

(Authors' Note: Mr. Putnam was given two sets of figures, short-range goals in Exhibit 15.6 and a five-year target plan. The "acceptable" figures are a one-year target plan and the "goal" figures, a five-year plan.)

Mr. Putnam embarked immediately upon arrival on three courses of action. First, he instructed the vice-president of Vogue to prepare immediately the 1983 statement which had not yet been completed. Second, he set up appointments with each person considered to be part of the management group. Third, he personally investigated each plant and functional area of the business.

During meetings with managers, Mr. Putnam decided to get answers on the following:

1. A brief history and background of each individual.
2. Exactly what the person did as he saw it, to whom he reported, and who reported to him.
3. An idea of the business philosophy of each person.
4. The problems of the business.
5. Ideas for solving the problems.

INTERVIEWS WITH KEY PERSONNEL

Walter White, 62, Executive Vice-President

"I have more friends in top management positions in retail stores than any other man in our industry—after all, I've been with this company and the original firm (Robert Wood Company) for over 25 years. Three of us, Mr. Wood, L. T. Johnson, and myself built this business from nothing to one of the most successful companies in our lines. That's why L. T. made me executive VP.

"We really made money before we went system crazy—nobody pays any attention to all those reports—all it does is cost us money, ruin deliveries, and make sales harder to get. What the hell, I'm a producer, not an expense. I'm glad I report directly to you—you're stuck with me (laughs) but, believe me, if you follow my ideas, we will both prosper.

"This is what we need: first, cut our expenses by getting rid of Sam Chapman and his department. I can merchandise the line if you put Toni (Head Designer) under me. Second, we don't need an advertising manager and his five people. Our advertising agency can do all that for nothing. Third, cut out about three quarters of the reports from our high and mighty systems V.P. Tom Evans. He doesn't know the first thing about the apparel business; he gives me quotas, industry potentials, all kinds of useless sales records that must cost the company hundreds of thousands. Fourth, with all the money we can save, let's cut prices 10% and give the customers a break. Fifth, increase our finished goods inventory so we can make faster deliveries to our customers. Sixth, concentrate on getting the merchandise out of our factories; we worry so much about quality control, industrial engineering, pay scales, and fringe benefits that we forget we are in business to sell first-class merchandise; not the 'seconds' that we have to give away.

"Do all those things, give us ten more salespeople, and I'll show how to get Vogue back on the track with much larger sales.

"One more thing, we need to broaden our line; our customers don't want only basics. We need more high fashion merchandise, more colors in each style and broader size ranges. Our sales would be far better if we went deeper into two additional product lines; hostess gowns and pajamas. What we have now leaves too many holes for competition to get into our accounts. Give us more to sell and the Sales Department will sell it."

Paul Trout, 54, Advertising Manager

"I greatly appreciate your frankness in telling me that you are unhappy with our sales and profits of the last few years and the possibility that International may decide to sell the company. This does not surprise me in any way, as prior to my being hired last year, I asked Mr. Johnson if I might look over the previous ten years' statements. I made an analysis and could see many problems—as a matter of fact, I came here only because Mr. Johnson assured me that he planned a reorganization and restructuring of the company. Actually, my first assignment was a report, which was finished last month. Unfortunately, Mr. Johnson never had an opportunity to look it over. I'll leave a copy with you.

"Answering your five questions in order:

1. My experience is fairly broad
   1946–50 University of Michigan-B.A.
   1950–52 University of Chicago-M.B.A.
   1952–56 Salesman for J & J Apparel
   1956–59 Military service, honorable discharge
   1959–67 Back at J & J where I was made assistant advertising manager in 1963, along with the accounts I continued to handle personally. In 1964, promoted to advertising manager, made assistant sales manager in 1967, as well as advertising manager. I was aiming at a marketing VP's job.
   1967–75 I was offered a real opportunity to return to the midwest, which both my wife and I wanted, to become sales manager for a good-sized apparel company, P. T. Brooks. In 1975, I was promoted to VP marketing and would still be with them except that both of our major principals died within three months of each other and the company was broken up and the parts sold. After assisting in the sale and liquidation, I was hired by Vogue. My job was advertising manager, with the understanding that I was to act, more or less, as a management consultant, and if my report was satisfactory, become vice-president of marketing.

"I reported to the president, and now to you, Mr. Putnam. Reporting to me are five people. It is not enough if we are ever going to get a real advertising program going again. Right now, and I realize the necessity for it, we do no national advertising—just 50/50 cooperative advertising, except for the trade magazines. Our competitors, the large ones, are strong national advertisers, and it sells goods for them and the retailers handling their lines.

"My business philosophy is simply that we should be run with a unified sense of direction and a complete devotion to the marketing concept, meaning: (1) we must be customer and consumer oriented; (b) the marketing effort should be an integrated, coordinated responsibility of every employee, each of whom should be devoted to serving the particular segment of the market top management agrees upon; and (c) we should focus on profitability as well as sales, using the proper budgeting, control, and other systems to achieve that profitability.

"In my opinion, we have a Pandora's box of problems, which I refer to in my report, so I won't repeat, except to say that we still have an excellent image in the trade and with the consumers. So I don't see any insurmountable obstacles; but we must have a unified sense of direction in our management team, which at present is sorely lacking."

Sam Chapman, 39, Merchandise Manager

"I am very unhappy here and I might as well tell you I am looking for another position—it is an intolerable situation. When Mr. Johnson hired me three years ago, he told me that I would have a free hand to merchandise the line, that our sales increases had slowed, that our profits were not what he wanted and he felt certain the problems were styling—lines that were too broad and not aimed at specific target markets—plus entirely too many price lines with too much emphasis on cheap merchandise rather than on quality consistent with the mass middle market in the 20 to 45 year old age groups.

"Instead of a free hand, I'm answering to Walter White (executive vice-president of sales), Toni DeMarco (head designer), Bill Winslow (vice-president of production), Vivian Morse (quality control), and even Dick Roberts (manager of industrial engineering), each of whom has a different idea of what we should have in the line, the target market, the sewing details, the quality and the intricacies of production. The people I've just named are all on the line selection committee, which is a sad joke. I keep my own records of sales by item, price, type, etc. with Tom Evans's (EDP) help and know what sells, what our customers want—but not one person on the committee pays any attention to the records.

"My ideas for improvement are simple. Give me the free hand I was promised—put Toni under me so I can guide her, put Vivian under me so we can have quality control consistent with the price of our merchandise. Yes, Ralph, the purchasing agent should come under me, too, so that I can see new materials as the piece goods salespeople present them and I should have the responsibility for finished goods inventory so that I am on equal footing with Putnam and Winslow. I've heard that in International, the marketing department of which I'm the key man, buys goods from manufacturing. Why don't we do that here?"

Toni DeMarco, 34, Head Designer

"I've been here for 13 years; started when I was just graduated from the School of Design. I like the business and appreciate the opportunities given me for regular advancement to my present position of head designer, reporting directly to the president.

"I think I'm justified in saying that we have the best-designed line in both of our major product categories.

"My only problem is that production constantly wants to take manufacturing shortcuts which spoil the detailing in our products—they don't understand the inspiration and art that goes into our merchandise that makes the garments sell by setting them apart from other designer's styles. Of course, our new sales force doesn't sell them as well as they should because I don't have any opportunity to train them."

Tom Evans, 48, VP Systems

"I'm simply delighted to have this chat with you. I've been pretty frustrated with the lack of acceptance of the systems approach I've tried to introduce this last year and a half. Mr. Johnson realized when he hired me that it would be rough, as most of our people are 'seat of the pants' operators and don't know a system when they see one. For example, I tried to show Walt White how to use quotas and sales potentials for every city over 20,000 population, etc., which I copied from the previous firm I was with in hard goods, but he just lets them accumulate. I was going to install an inventory system both for sales and production control but decided it was no use, although Sam Chapman was really enthusiastic about the idea. He thought sales forecasting could be tied in at the same time.

"Actually, we really don't make very good use of our electronic data processing equipment and perhaps it is my fault for not selling my ideas better; but try talking to people that won't hear. I would like to do a complete job that would help every management person in our company; sales, merchandising, production, purchasing, production control, quality control, and even personnel. Right now, you don't need me to do only accounts receivable and accounts payable, which is all I'm doing that's effective.

"I really don't know what to do to sell our people, but one look at our profit and loss statement convinces me that we certainly need a systems approach."

Bill Winslow, 61, Vice-President of Production

"I started here 25 years ago. As a matter of fact, I'm entitled to my gold watch on February 23rd. I don't have a college degree, but I can still teach the younger men quite a few tricks. I learned the hard way, and I'm proud of it.

"We need a strong leader. L. T., unfortunately, was not himself these last few years before he died and, as a result, we are all running off in 17 different directions. I'll admit that I'm not about to take orders from guys like Walter White who hasn't the foggiest idea of how run factories. Since he was made executive vice-president, there is no living with him. He wants every style rushed; never works with John Fogarty (production control manager). That was a mistake, too, having John report to Bob Kelly. Guess it was because they are both Irish, but who ever heard of the production control manager not reporting to the vice-president of production—me. We don't have sales forecasts and if we do, they don't mean anything; so our 'runs' are so small, half the time we have to put our people on time work. Ask Dick Roberts. He agrees with me; makeup pay is killing us. Walter White and both his assistants make life miserable for all of us, with their constant yammering for price, price, price! One day he says to me, 'To hell with quality, your job is to get the goods manufactured and at a competitive price which we don't have.' I try to do a good job, but how can you with people like him?

"Old L. T. used to tell me that I should run our factories and, if anyone gave me any trouble, to come and see him; but now he's not here.

"I don't rightly know what to tell you to do. You're the boss so I guess you'll figure out what to do."

Robert Kelly, 59, Vice-President of Operations

"My background is in accounting and finance. I'm a C.P.A., having been with two of the leading public accounting firms for 25 years, then VP of the First National Bank in charge of loans.

"My job here has grown and grown. I handle real estate, credit, accounting, purchasing, production control and now, secretary-treasurer, since Mr. Johnson died. I didn't really want purchasing and production control, but Mr. Johnson thought I could handle them better than anyone else, and asked me as a favor to him to take them on a few years ago, when we started having trouble. As far as I am concerned, I would like to give them up, as I don't have many capabilities along the merchandise line. It is my opinion, if you are asking for it, that we have two capable men who could handle both departments (purchasing and production control). They are Sam Chapman and Dick Roberts.

"From a financial point of view, I can give you many ideas. Would you like me to give you them in writing? I have already prepared a detailed memo broken down by functions as well as a full financial report. I would like you to study them at your leisure and then let's talk about them."

Harry Thomas, 43, Personnel Manager

Mr. Thomas reported that his department was not having any particular problems. None of the plants were unionized, and employee relations were excellent because of the firm's enlightened policies and fringe benefits. His job, he said, was stimulating, and he particularly liked reporting to the president.

Vivian Morse, 56, Quality Control

Vivian was away on a long vacation, paid for by the company, in recognition of 40 years of service. Apparently, she and Bill Winslow (VP Production) saw eye to eye on quality control and she had no problems with Ralph Nolan, the purchasing agent for the raw materials which Vivian inspected.

Richard Roberts, 32, Chief Engineer

Dick Roberts immediately impressed Mr. Putnam as a young, aggressive, well-trained articulate engineer with an excellent education in mechanical engineering. In addition, he had been taking additional courses at night in a wide range of subjects for seven years at a good university near his home. He said that he was not aiming for a Ph.D. in engineering but rather a broad general background that would help him rise further in the company. He was currently taking a course in human resources management, having finished courses in production, production control, management information systems, etc., including two marketing courses.

He was very confident that a new method for cutting was going to bring large savings to the company in labor, but more importantly, in material usage. He pointed out that this was extremely important, as materials were in excess of 35% of the sales dollar.

Dick said that he had excellent men under him and proudly said that Pete, one of his men, had recently developed two machine attachments they had built in the shop which, he predicted, would lower labor costs.

When asked about other people in the organization, he merely said that he got along with nearly everybody and was too busy concentrating on his own job to become involved in company politics.

When Mr. Putnam pushed him on the size of his research budget, he said he thought it was about right, although if the machine attachments resulted in real savings, then he felt he might ask for additional funds to explore other areas his men had in mind.

FUNCTIONAL AREAS

During Mr. Putnam's plant visits, analysis of company records, including correspondence and conversations with both major suppliers and customers, coupled with his intimate knowledge of the business, added the following insight.

Marketing

Vogue sold lingerie and foundation garmets to 10,011 department and specialty stores. While distribution was nationwide, strength was predominant in the smaller towns and outlying areas of larger cities with evident weakness in the largest department stores, particularly on both coasts. Medium-sized cities in the Midwest were Vogue's stronghold.

Approximately 65% of volume came from sales of foundation garments, with 35% from lingerie. This was exactly the opposite of national sales reported by the U.S. Department of Commerce, which showed lingerie out-selling foundations two to one. Total industry sales were approximately $6 billion.

Salespeople were paid a per diem expense allowance, a monthly salary, and ¼ of 1% commission on all sales shipped into their territories (divided by geographical areas). All salespeople handled both lines. No commission was paid on sales of marked-down merchandise which was closed out at the end of each season at a reduction of 40% from regular wholesale price.

Customers held the company in high repute. Complaints centered around late delivery with occasional mention of mismatching of finishings (shoulder straps, ribbon trim, etc.).

Exclusive distribution rights were given to customers if purchases were sufficiently large in the sales manager's view, although quite often it was obvious that salespeople merely did not call on other accounts in the town or section of a large city, if they did not agree with the sales manager. Salespeople supposedly were to send in call reports but rarely did so. Most of the salesperson's correspondence was regarding late delivery or a notation that a shipment was about to be returned for any number of reasons such as "buyer overbought." Contests were held frequently; the most recent of which was a cash bonus offered to salespeople for each new account opened with a $100 minimum order. See Exhibits 15.7 and 15.8 for additional data.

Personnel and Labor Relations

Turnover of employees was low, as generous fringe benefits for the industry were paid. Plants were located in small towns surrounding the main office and cutting facilities, which were in a large mid-western city. Unions presented no problems, as the company was not organized. Many of the employees had been with the company over five years. Most of the salespeople had been employed for over ten years. Training was practically nonexistent in every part of the company except for designers, where every senior designer (four of them) had two assistants who attended classes held twice a week, by Ms. DeMarco. Included in the classes were pattern makers, who took paper patterns and transferred them to hard board. Seniority and promotion from within was strictly enforced for all but managers earning in excess of $40,000 per year.

Organization

No formal organization existed. Exhibit 15.13 was worked out from statements made by each individual.

Manufacturing

The factories were clean, air-conditioned, well-lighted, and good housekeeping was evident.

Cutting for foundations was mainly done by clickers (large press cutters using steel dies) with some electric knife cutting and a minimum of hand cutting for small lots. Lingerie was done with both electric cutters and by hand. Quality cutting to close tolerances with the least amount of fall-offs was a matter of pride for the head cutter. Cutting was done centrally at the headquarters plant, with all materials shipped by truck to the outlying sewing factories.

Due to the increasing number of items in each line, production scheduling had decreased lot sizes for cutting, which prevented efficient utilization of the clickers and increased the number of steel dies required (including in cutting costs at an average cost of $1200 per set for a range of sizes in one style).

The plant managers all complained about shortages of one or two minor findings (parts) which held up finishing, pressing, and packaging. Each manager was therefore asking for more than he needed, so as to build up a little extra inventory locally.

Most of the sewing operators were paid by piecework but when small lots were run requiring a change in machine threading or attachments, they were switched to time work, which was shown on the

EXHIBIT 15.6

Vogue Creations, Incorporated
Income Statement (In thousands)
For Year Ending December 31

	1973	1974	1975	1976	1977	1978	1979	1980	1981	1982	1983
Sales	$32,040	$35,980	$40,016	$45,996	$47,980	$49,500	$50,960	$52,920	$52,480	$50,980	$53,006
Sales Returns and Allowances	820	1,030	1,146	1,076	1,150	1,330	1,730	2,360	2,710	2,900	3,056
Net Sales	31,220	34,950	38,870	44,920	46,830	48,170	49,230	50,560	49,770	48,080	49,950
Cash Discounts	2,420	2,690	2,970	3,470	3,606	3,710	3,830	3,834	3,748	3,496	3,414
Cost of Goods Sold											
Net Sales After Discounts	28,800	32,260	35,900	41,450	43,224	44,460	45,400	46,826	46,022	44,584	46,536
Materials	12,480	14,000	15,540	17,950	18,732	19,060	19,600	20,320	20,118	20,098	21,014
Packaging, Labels, Etc.	370	420	480	530	562	610	630	660	630	620	610
Freight-In	94	104	116	134	140	194	242	252	244	238	280
Direct Labor:											
Cutting	460	528	584	668	702	788	914	944	1,164	1,228	1,324
Sewing	3,902	4,392	4,922	5,644	5,814	5,960	6,166	6,512	6,284	6,184	6,482
Makeup Pay	312	350	384	454	468	710	908	948	1,332	1,414	1,514
Fringe Benefits	62	134	264	384	422	472	478	502	488	490	508
Manufacturing Expenses:											
Supervision	1,862	2,004	2,266	2,556	2,648	2,588	2,714	2,656	2,896	2,910	2,998
Nonproductive Labor	240	256	296	312	328	508	666	868	782	750	778
Fringe Benefits	124	138	154	178	186	188	194	202	194	188	186
Occupancy	334	340	368	536	512	520	530	580	522	514	504
Machinery and Equipment	200	218	234	386	438	470	520	588	584	618	510
Other	62	70	78	90	94	92	98	112	104	94	94
Gross Profit on Sales	8,298	9,306	10,214	11,628	12,178	12,300	11,740	11,682	10,680	9,238	9,734
Operating Expenses:											
Selling	2,580	2,830	3,020	3,486	3,646	3,870	4,420	4,384	4,162	4,006	4,202
Advertising	728	766	1,016	1,094	1,136	1,230	1,732	2,306	1,346	850	744
Shipping and Warehousing	676	734	802	908	984	1,030	1,070	1,150	1,072	1,036	1,030
Administrative	1,400	1,570	1,742	2,020	2,088	2,118	2,192	2,670	2,522	2,474	2,458
Inventory Markdowns	472	484	498	562	608	772	1,116	1,290	1,710	2,210	3,002
Bad Debts	30	28	32	24	22	36	54	84	106	132	152
Net Operating Income (Loss)	2,412	2,894	3,104	3,534	3,694	3,244	1,156	(202)	(238)	(1,470)	(1,854)
Interest Expense	10	-	-	38	36	34	56	72	28	26	110
Net Profit (Loss) Before Taxes	2,402	2,894	3,104	3,496	3,658	3,210	1,100	(274)	(266)	(1,496)	(1,964)
Income Tax (Refund)	1,140	1,374	1,474	1,660	1,738	1,520	520	(244)	(266)	(74)	-0-
Net Profit (Loss)	$ 1,262	$ 1,520	$ 1,630	$ 1,836	$ 1,920	$ 1,690	$ 580	$ (30)	$ -0-	$(1,422)	$(1,964)

EXHIBIT 15.7

Vogue Creations, Incorporated
Income Statement (%)
For Year Ending December 31

	1973	1974	1975	1976	1977	1978	1979	1980	1981	1982	1983
Sales	102.62	102.94	102.94	102.39	102.45	102.76	104.97	104.66	105.44	106.03	106.11
Sales Returns and Allowances	2.62	2.94	2.95	2.39	2.45	2.76	4.97	4.66	5.44	6.03	6.11
Net Sales	100.00	100.00	100.00	100.00	100.00	100.00	100.00	100.00	100.00	100.00	100.00
Cash Discounts	7.75	7.69	7.65	7.72	7.70	7.70	7.77	7.38	7.53	7.27	6.83
Net Sales After Discounts	92.25	92.31	92.35	92.28	92.30	92.30	92.23	92.62	92.47	92.72	93.17
Cost of Goods Sold:											
Materials	39.97	40.05	39.97	39.95	40.00	39.56	39.81	40.18	40.42	41.80	42.07
Packaging, Labels, Etc.	1.18	1.20	1.23	1.17	1.20	1.26	1.27	1.30	1.26	1.28	1.22
Freight-In	.30	.29	.29	.29	.29	.40	.49	.49	.49	.49	.56
Direct Labor:											
Cutting	1.47	1.51	1.50	1.48	1.49	1.63	1.85	1.86	2.33	2.55	2.65
Sewing	12.49	12.56	12.66	12.56	12.41	12.37	12.52	12.87	12.62	12.86	12.97
Makeup Pay	.99	1.00	.98	1.01	.99	1.47	1.84	1.87	2.67	2.94	3.03
Fringe Benefits	.19	.38	.67	.85	.90	.97	.97	.99	.98	1.01	1.01
Manufacturing Expenses:											
Supervision	5.96	5.73	5.82	5.69	5.65	5.37	5.51	5.25	5.81	6.05	6.00
Nonproductive Labor	.76	.73	.76	.69	.70	1.05	1.35	1.71	1.57	1.55	1.55
Fringe Benefits	.39	.39	.39	.39	.39	.39	.39	.39	.38	.39	.37
Occupancy	1.06	.97	.94	1.19	1.09	1.07	1.07	1.14	1.04	1.00	1.00
Machinery and Equipment	.64	.62	.60	.85	.93	.97	1.05	1.16	1.17	1.28	1.02
Other	.19	.20	.20	.20	.20	.19	.19	.22	.20	.19	.18
Gross Profit on Sales	26.57	26.62	26.27	25.88	26.00	25.53	23.84	20.73	21.45	19.21	19.48
Operating Expenses:											
Selling	8.26	8.09	7.76	7.76	7.78	8.03	8.97	8.67	8.36	8.33	8.41
Advertising	2.33	2.19	2.61	2.43	2.42	2.55	3.51	4.56	2.70	1.76	1.48
Shipping and Warehousing	2.16	2.10	2.06	2.02	2.10	2.13	2.17	2.27	2.15	2.15	2.06
Administrative	4.48	4.49	4.48	4.49	4.45	4.39	4.45	5.28	5.06	5.14	4.92
Inventory Markdowns	1.51	1.38	1.28	1.25	1.29	1.60	2.26	2.55	3.43	4.59	6.01
Bad Debts	.09	.08	.08	.05	.04	.07	.10	.16	.21	.27	.30
Net Operating Income (Loss)	7.72	8.28	7.98	7.86	7.88	6.73	2.34	(.39)	(.47)	(3.05)	(3.71)
Interest Expense	.03	-		.08	.07	.07	.11	.14	.05	.05	.22
Net Profit (Loss) Before Taxes	7.69	8.28	7.98	7.78	7.81	6.66	2.23	(.54)	(.53)	(3.11)	(3.93)
Income Tax (Refund)	3.65	3.93	3.79	3.69	3.71	3.15	1.05	(.48)	(.53)	(.15)	-0-
Net profit	4.04	4.34	4.19	4.08	4.10	3.51	1.17	(.05)	-0-	(2.96)	(3.93)

EXHIBIT 15.8

Vogue Creations, Incorporated
Balance Sheet (in thousands)

	1973	1974	1975	1976	1977	1978	1979	1980	1981	1982	1983
Current Assets:											
Cash and Marketable Securities	$ 960	$1,106	$1,356	$1,118	$ 816	$ 928	$ 506	$ 664	$ 792	$ 218	$ 140
Accounts Receivable	3,520	4,000	4,400	5,140	5,600	6,600	6,060	6,160	5,740	4,980	4,340
Inventories											
Raw Material	1,920	2,160	2,400	2,300	2,800	2,960	2,860	2,640	2,340	2,980	3,190
Work in Process	1,440	1,620	1,800	1,840	2,040	2,380	2,520	3,060	2,880	3,140	3,360
Finished Goods	3,840	4,320	4,800	5,060	5,960	6,660	6,920	5,500	6,180	6,580	6,800
Income Tax Refund Due	-	-	-	-	-	-	-	244	266	74	-
Prepaid Expenses	160	200	280	300	360	290	194	170	140	188	134
Total Current Assets	$11,840	$13,406	$15,036	$15,758	$17,576	$18,818	$19,060	$18,438	$18,338	$18,160	$18,014
Fixed Assets:											
Land and Building (Net)	2,240	2,180	2,120	3,040	2,760	2,880	2,800	2,720	2,640	2,560	2,480
Machinery and Equipment (Net)	1,920	1,880	1,840	2,760	2,660	2,560	2,460	2,360	2,540	2,386	2,232
Total Fixed Assets	$ 4,160	$ 4,060	$ 3,960	$ 5,800	$ 5,620	$ 5,440	$ 5,250	$ 5,080	$ 5,180	$ 4,946	$ 4,712
Total Assets	$16,000	$17,466	$18,996	$21,558	$23,196	$24,258	$24,320	$23,518	$23,518	$23,106	$22,726
LIABILITIES											
Current Liabilities											
Account Payable	$ 1,920	$ 2,160	$ 2,400	$ 2,760	$ 2,860	$ 3,040	$ 3,440	$ 3,500	$ 3,660	$ 5,220	$ 5,954
Accrued Expenses	328	500	560	640	700	640	840	950	840	830	310
Notes Payable (Bank)	200	-	-	-	-	-	400	600	-	-	1,400
Income Taxes Payable	1,140	1,374	1,474	1,660	1,738	1,520	532	-	-	-	-
Dividends Payable	500	500	500	500	500	500	500	500	-	500	500
Total Current Liabilities	4,088	4,534	4,934	5,560	5,798	5,700	5,712	5,470	4,500	6,550	8,164
Long Term Debt	-	-	-	-	-	-	-	-	-	-	-
Mortgage Payable	-	-	-	600	580	550	520	490	460	420	390
Total Liabilities	$ 4,088	$ 4,534	$ 4,934	$ 6,160	$ 6,378	$ 6,250	$ 6,232	$ 5,960	$ 4,960	$ 6,970	$ 8,554
STOCKHOLDERS EQUITY											
Common Stock	$10,000	$10,000	$10,000	$10,000	$10,000	$10,000	$10,000	$10,000	$10,000	$10,000	$10,000
Retained Earnings (Deficit)	1,912	2,932	4,062	5,398	6,818	8,008	8,088	7,558	7,558	6,136	4,172
Total Stockholder's Equity	11,912	12,932	14,062	15,398	16,818	18,008	18,088	17,558	17,558	16,136	14,172
Total Liabilities and Stockholder's Equity	$16,000	$17,466	$18,996	$21,558	$23,196	$24,258	$24,320	$23,518	$23,518	$23,106	$22,726

EXHIBIT 15.9

Sales Index of Combined Lingerie and
Foundation Garment Sales
(From Industry Sources)

Year	1983	1982	1981	1980	1979	1978	1977	1976	1975	1974	1973
Index	160	150	141	138	133	127	120	118	114	108	100

EXHIBIT 15.10

Target Figures
(Based on a product mix of 65% Foundation Garment Sales and
35% Lingerie.)

Item	Goal	Acceptable
Annual Growth in Sales	10.00%	5.00%
Net Profit on Net Sales	6.00%	4.00%
Sales Returns and Allowances	2.50%	3.00%
Material to Net Sales	37.00%	40.00%
Cutting to Net Sales	1.50%	1.85%
Sewing to Net Sales	12.15%	12.60%
Makeup Pay to Net Sales	1.00%	1.30%
Supervision to Net Sales	5.00%	5.40%
Nonproductive Labor to Net Sales	.65%	.95%
Gross Profit on Net Sales	33.00%	26.00%
Selling Expense to Net Sales	7.50%	8.30%
Administrative Expenses to Net Sales	4.00%	4.60%
Markdowns to Net Sales	1.25%	1.65%
Operating Expenses to Net Sales	18.00%	21.80%
Profitability		
Growth in Net Profit on Net Sales	10.00%	5.00%
Net Profit to Net Worth	25.00%	15.00%
Liquidity		
Current Ratio	3.50:1	2.50:1
Acid Test Ratio	1.25:1	1.00:1
Fixed Assets to Net Worth	28.00%	33.00%
Funded Debt to Net Working Capital	10.00%	20.00%
Leverage		
Current Debt to Net Worth	22.00%	27.00%
Total Debt to Net Worth	35.00%	40.00%
Funded Debt to Net Worth (D/E)	20.00%	15.00%
Turnover		
Raw Materials	13.0 times	11.0 times
Work-in-Process	16.5 times	14.5 times
Finished Goods	6.5 times	5.5 times
Accounts Receivable	36 days	42 days

EXHIBIT 15.11

Distribution of Customer Accounts

Annual Purchases	Number of Accounts
Under $1,000	3,927
$ 1,001 to $ 2,000	1,985
$ 2,001 to $ 6,000	1,506
$ 6,001 to $10,000	1,227
$10,001 to $20,000	797
$20,001 to $40,000	463
Over $40,000	110
Total Sales $53,006,000	Total Accounts 10,015

EXHIBIT 15.12

Competitive Analysis

	Vogue		Competition*	
Item	Price Lines ($)	Number of Styles Offered	Price Lines ($)	Number of Styles Offered
Short Bras	2.22 to 9.00	113	4.50 to 6.50	18
Long Bras	3.95 to 15.00	44	7.00 to 10.00	6
Padded Bras	3.68 to 10.00	31	4.50 to 6.50	9
Regular Girdles	2.47 to 21.00	76	8.95 to 13.00	21
Panty Girdles	3.22 to 19.50	69	5.00 to 13.95	34

*The competitor's product line was taken from his printed catalogue. This particular competitor was the most successful company in the industry.

books as makeup pay. New operators' (learners') earnings were charged to the makeup pay account, as were all operators who were not on a piecework basis. Mr. Putnam was aware that this was not the usual practice in the industry.

Quality control was tightly controlled in each plant, with the individual operator rectifying any error caught by the inspectors.

A new cutting system introduced by Dick Roberts for increasing material usage had been begun for lingerie as had other sewing machine innovations on which patents were pending. The operators liked the new systems and machine attachments, as they could increase their output and earnings. Mr. Roberts felt that $150,000 per year

EXHIBIT 15.13

Vogue Creations, Incorporated

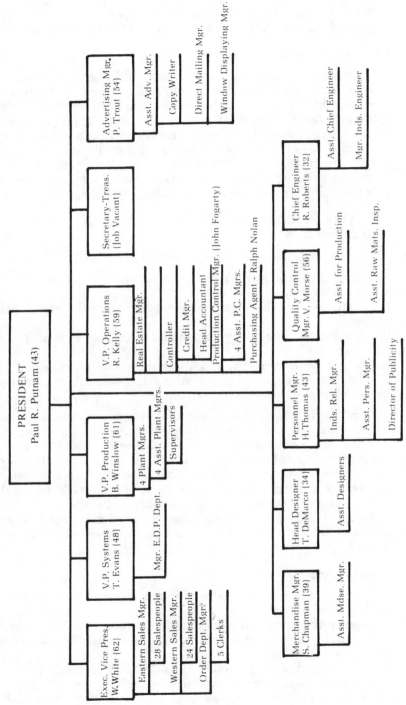

PRESIDENT Paul R. Putnam (43)

Exec. Vice Pres. W. White (62)
- Eastern Sales Mgr.
  - 28 Salespeople
- Western Sales Mgr.
  - 24 Salespeople
- Order Dept. Mgr.
  - 5 Clerks

V.P. Systems T. Evans (48)
- Mgr. E.D.P. Dept.

V.P. Production B. Winslow (61)
- 4 Plant Mgrs.
- 4 Asst. Plant Mgrs.
- Supervisors

V.P. Operations R. Kelly (59)
- Real Estate Mgr.
- Controller
- Credit Mgr.
- Head Accountant
- Production Control Mgr. (John Fogarty)
- 4 Asst. P.C. Mgrs.
- Purchasing Agent - Ralph Nolan

Secretary-Treas. (Job Vacant)

Advertising Mgr. P. Trout (54)
- Asst. Adv. Mgr.
- Copy Writer
- Direct Mailing Mgr.
- Window Displaying Mgr.

Merchandise Mgr. S. Chapman (39)
- Asst. Mdse. Mgr.

Head Designer T. DeMarco (34)
- Asst. Designers

Personnel Mgr. H. Thomas (43)
- Inds. Rel. Mgr.
- Asst. Pers. Mgr.
- Director of Publicity

Quality Control Mgr. V. Morse (56)
- Asst. for Production
- Asst. Raw Mats. Insp.

Chief Engineer R. Roberts (32)
- Asst. Chief Engineer
- Mgr. Inds. Engineer

added to his research budget would lower costs in cutting material usage and labor within two years by over $600,000 per year.

Finance and Accounting

Profit-center accounting was not used although it was in use at International. Cost accounts for internal purposes were exactly as shown in the exhibits. Work in process and finished goods inventory valuation was "eyeballed" in conjunction with Mr. Ralph Nolan and Walter White. Ralph Nolan had complete charge of purchasing, which primarily, was placing repeat orders for materials and supplies, such as boxes from long-established sources. When additional cash was required, either Vogue withheld payment on accounts payable or increased their borrowing from their bank.

ANALYSIS OF VOGUE'S POLICIES AND PROBLEMS

Read through the case to get an overall perspective. We note that:

A. Mr. Putnam must make recommendations for changes in operations as appear necessary.
B. A number of issues (points of disagreement) exist among personnel.
C. Interrelated marketing, production, and cost control problems exist.
D. Sales have leveled out, which signals potential problems.
E. The company has been sustaining increasing losses each year, which signals very serious problems.

From the first scanning of the case it appears reasonable to use what is basically a functional approach to the case. We start with a financial analysis because symptoms of operating and management problems may be observed easily from such an analysis. The purpose of the analysis is to identify possible problems and solutions. The analysis is prepared in the form of "working papers." The results of the analysis will be used to evaluate courses of action which will improve the operations of the firm. Therefore, the analysis we show here first is preliminary to the development of the presentation of the case soltuion.

Financial Analysis

Question 1: How do the sales of Vogue compare with industry figures in Exhibit 15.9?

Question 2: From the comparative figures and your cursory reading of the rest of the case, what general conclusions may be drawn regarding management?

Vogue lagged the industry in 1978, 1979, 1980, 1981, 1982, 1983. Vogue beat the industry record in 1974, 1975, 1976, 1977, and then never matched industry gains thereafter. If 1978 is used as a base year, the record appears even more dismal.

Comparison of Vogue's Sales With Industry Sales

Year	Industry Index	% Change	Vogue Index	% Change
1973	100	....	100	....
1974	108	+8	111	+11
1975	114	+5	124	+11
1976	118	+3	143	+15
1977	120	+1	150	+4
1978	127	+5	154	+2
1979	133	+4	157	+1
1980	138	+3	161	+2
1981	141	+2	159	1
1982	150	+6	154	3
1983	160	+7	159	+3

Conclusion: After a strong start in the first four years, something happened in the management of Vogue. Since top management remained the same, either key people left the company, management grew less effective at internal control, or management failed to adapt to changing external conditions.

Question 3: What symptoms of what problems are indicated by the trends of sales and manufacturing expenses? (Supplementary data may be brought in for comparison).

Symptoms

1. Sales have increased very slowly and remained almost level in the most recent four years. See Exhibit 15.10 for acceptable growth.

2. Steep upward trend in sales returns as indicated by Exhibit 15.7 by 2.62 for 1973 and 6.11 in 1983.

3. Somewhat low inventory turnover. (Cost of Goods Sold/Inventory)
   Raw materials   10.6 ('73)
   15.1 ('81)
   12.7 ('83)

Possible Problems

1. (a) Inept marketing
   (b) Poor product styling
   (c) Production problems which affect delivery or quality
   (d) Lack of unified sense of direction of activities aimed at marketing

2. (a) Return-goods policy
   (b) Product or price inferiority resulting in lower sales
   (c) High pressure selling
   (d) Late delivery
   (e) Product-line proliferation causing items to compete with each other.

3. (a) Size of inventory or safety stock may be too large.
   (b) Product proliferation.

Work in Process	14.2 ('73)	*Possible Problems* (Continued)
	16.2 ('76)	
	10.9 ('83)	
Finished Goods	6.6 ('80)	
	5.7 ('81)	
	5.4 ('83)	

4. Upward trend of cost-of-goods-sold as a percent of sales.

Material, labor, or manufacturing expense problems as determined by analyzing detailed breakdown of costs and expenses.

5. Creeping increase in materials cost.

(a) Purchasing practices and control deteriorating due to new personnel or inattention of long-service personnel
(b) Poor pattern layout
(c) Cutting errors
(d) Pilferage
(e) Inflation in the economy

6. "Cutting" labor cost rapidly increasing in recent years. Exhibit 15.10 shows 1.49 ('79), 1.86 ('80), 2.65 ('83).

(a) Production control
(b) Proliferation of products and too short runs so that learning time and setup time increase
(c) External factors such as union or inflation.

7. Increased makeup pay .99 ('77), 1.84 ('79), 2.67 ('81), 3.03 ('83).

Too many switchovers from piecework to hourly pay as indicated by "poor forecasts, short runs, too many rushes, and too many styles"

8. Increasing manufacturing expense as a percent of sales. Supervision expense, while stable, is high compared with acceptable goal (Exhibit 15.7 vs. Exhibit 15.10). Nonproductive labor shows a steep upward trend (Exhibit 15.7). Machinery and equipment expense follows a steeply rising trend.

(a) With control by Mr. Wood gone due to his death, no control system or procedures may have been instituted.
(b) Need for better training of indirect labor employees.
(c) Lack of equipment replacement and maintenance program.

Question 4: The increase in operating expenses is due to huge increases in inventory markdowns. We should start with the biggest problem, as this appears to be, in rectifying a company's situation. What could such a change be caused by?

Symptoms	Possible Problems
Huge increase in inventory markdown, likely related closely with the increase in sales returns and allowances.	(a) Product or price inferiority
	(b) Poor sales forecasting with overproduction
	(c) Poor inventory policy and control
	(d) Aggregate forecast is OK, but forecast of individual styles is way off.
	(e) Ineffective marketing
	(f) Production delays resulting in poor delivery and consequent buildup of inventory after fashions change
	(g) Defective goods getting into inventory
	(h) Too many styles in the line competing with each other

Question 5: What leads may be obtained from ratio analysis and further financial analysis as described in Chapter 7?

Net Profits/Net Sales were never very good. The ratio was below an "acceptable" 5%: 4.04 ('73), 4.34 ('74), 4.19 ('75) ('76), 4.10 ('77). It went even lower: 3.51 ('78), 1.17 ('79), loss .05 ('80), 0 ('81), loss 2.96 ('82), loss 3.93 ('83).

Net Profit/Net Worth

10.6 ('73)	11.4 ('77)	0 ('81)
11.7 ('74)	9.4 ('78)	-8.8 ('82)
11.6 ('75)	3.2 ('79)	-13.8 ('83)
11.9 ('76)	.17('80)	

From 1973 to 1977 this ratio was somewhat below the acceptable level when compared with Exhibit 15.10 value of 15%. Thereafter the bottom fell out and the indication is that Johnson was not up to the job, perhaps because of his illness.

Liquidity
Current Ratio is no problem but will be if losses continue

High	3.83 ('79)	Goal	3.50
Low	2.44 ('83)	Acceptable	2.50

Acid Test Ratio indicates that Vogue will have trouble paying its bills if the loss trend continues.

High	1.45 ('81)	Goal	1.25
Low	0.54 ('83)	Acceptable	1.00

Fixed Assets/Net Worth

High	0.37 ('76)	Goal	0.28
Low	0.28 ('75)	Acceptable	0.33
	0.33 ('83)		

This ratio is low enough so that if Putnam wants to, he could refinance the mortgage to borrow more on the building, machinery, and equipment. He could thus increase liquidity by increasing long-term debt.

Funded Debt/Net Working Capital

High	0.06 ('76)	Goal	0.10
Low	0.03 ('81)	Acceptable	0.20
	0.04 ('83)		

This ratio is low in comparison with most companies, in which 0.60 often is reached. This low ratio reinforces the advisability of increasing long-term debt, reducing short-term debt, and increasing cash.

Leverage
  Current Debt/Net Worth

High	0.57 ('83)	Goal	0.22
Low	0.26 ('81)	Acceptable	0.27

The high leverage indicates low net worth in relation to current debt. A leverage of 80% is considered extremely dangerous.

Total Debt/Net Worth

High	0.60 ('83)	Goal	0.35
Low	0.30 ('81)	Acceptable	0.40

This leverage ratio, like the previous, has gone from low to high in the last ten-year period. If total debt exceeds net worth, the equity of the creditors in the assets of the business exceeds that of the owners.

Funded Debt/Net Worth

0.039 ('76)	0.028 ('80)
0.034 ('77)	0.026 ('81)
0.031 ('78)	0.026 ('82)
0.029 ('79)	0.027 ('83)

If the profitability trend can be reversed so that Vogue can earn, say, 10% on sales, then by borrowing and employing more money, Vogue may increase dollar earnings greatly. If the investment in the company is constant, then these increased earnings will increase the return on investment. In other words, Vogue would be earning more on the funds borrowed than it costs to borrow the funds.

Turnover
  Raw Materials

High	15.1 ('81)	Goal	13
Low	10.7 ('83)	Acceptable	11
	12.7 ('83)		

Apparently no problem exists, but it would be desirable to know the composition of the inventory, how it is priced, and what it is really worth. If it is priced too high, profit will be overstated.

Work-in-Process

High	16.2 ('76)	Goal	16.5
Low	10.9 ('83)	Acceptable	14.5

Too much work-in-process is evident. This may be a symptom of (a) poor production control, (b) bottlenecks in the production process, (c) shop workers' hoarding work so as to always have a backlog to work, and (d) increase in pricing methods from comparison figures.

Finished Goods

High	6.1 ('81)	Goal	6.5
Low	5.3 ('75)	Acceptable	5.5
	5.4 ('83)		

No urgent problem is indicated.

Accounts Receivable Turnover Rate

High	32 days ('83)	Goal	36 days
Low	44.1 days ('80)	Acceptable	42 days

No apparent problem.

Symptoms and Problems

Comment: Each individual analyst will find a method which he or she prefers for identifying major problem clusters. The more skilled the analyst, the more likely he or she is to identify the big problems from rereading the case with its many facts and "thinks" and relating problems to the evidence of the financial analysis. For the student who has not had experience of practice in case analysis, a more non-creative approach is suggested. This consists first of making a "laundry list" of small problems, large problems, and issues under functional headings. The "small" problems may be independent small problems, or they may be symptoms of larger problems. After all problems have been listed, we must somehow seek major problems which, when cured, will solve related minor problems or prepare the way for their solution.

The major problems may be identified by (a) examining company policies; (b) finding a cluster of many small related problems; or (c) noting a symptom of impending disaster from the financial analysis.

We will attempt to place ourselves in the shoes of the average inexperienced student to show a kind of elementary thinking process. The problem list by function follows. We show a "Systems" function because of its emphasis in the organization and the case.

Marketing

1. Merchandising and advertising expenses are too high and should be reduced by drastic reduction of personnel and reorganization. (A think by White)
2. Prices could and should be cut 10%. (A think by White)

3. Customers want, and could obtain faster delivery. Finished goods inventories are too small. (A think by White)
4. Broaden the merchandise lines to give customers more colors in each style and more size ranges. More high fashion merchandise is needed. (A think by White)
5. Vogue should do national advertising. (A think by Trout)
6. A larger advertising staff is needed.
7. Marketing responsibility is confused, and the organization is impossible to work in effectively. (A think by Chapman)
8. Vogue is weak competitively in the largest department stores which are the potentially big accounts.
9. In terms of available market, Vogue is either doing very well in foundation garment sales or very poorly in lingerie sales.
10. Commission rate above salary to salespeople is so small as to be negligible. Payment of a $100 bonus for opening new accounts apparently provides more incentive to salespeople as indicated by Exhibit 15.11. This means big accounts are not being cultivated.
11. Customer complaints centered on late deliveries.
12. Exhibit 15.12 indicates that Vogue maintained a much wider range of prices and styles than a competitor did.

Production

1. Manufacturing is now made too complicated by adding quality control, industrial engineering, and personnel policies. Vogue should concentrate on producing goods quickly and getting them out of the factory, i.e., reduce work-in-process. (A think by White)
2. Manufacturing is taking shortcuts which are spoiling the detailing in the design. (A think by DeMarco)
3. White has no idea of how to run a factory, keeps interfering with production, and doesn't work with the production control manager. (A think by Winslow)
4. Lack of sales forecasts and consequent short runs are requiring makeup pay which is driving production costs sky high. (A think by Winslow)
5. Chapman and Roberts are capable men who could and should handle purchasing and production. (A think by Kelly)
6. An increasing number of items in each line reduced lot sizes, prevented efficient utilization of clickers, increased the number of steel dies required, and prevented "learning curve" gains by workers. For example of cost, 113 styles of short bras at $1200 per die represents an investment of $135,600.
7. Hoarding of parts by plant manager resulted in increased work-in-process inventory.

Personnel

1. Chapman, an apparently capable merchandise manager is looking outside for another job.
2. Personnel, except for Chapman, are seat-of-the-pants operators and

have not been indoctrinated or trained to use analytical data and reports. (A think by Evans)
3. Bitter conflict between Exec. VP White and VP of production Winslow.
4. Thomas is either oblivious to organizational conflicts and dissatisfactions or is trying to conceal these from Putnam.
5. Training was limited to designers only.
6. No formal organizational charts and policy guides apparently existed.
7. The use of makeup pay was contrary to industry practice. Combined with the production of small lots due to poor forecasting, production control, and many styles, this practice was extremely costly.

Systems and Control

1. Too many reports nobody reads cost too much. (A think by White)
2. Forecasting and control systems are not accepted by management, except Chapman, and the EDP equipment is poorly utilized. (A think by Evans)

Basic Business Philosophy Issues

1. Cut expenses to the bone outside of personal selling. (A think by White)
2. A unified sense of direction with clearly stated company objectives is needed. (A think by Trout)
3. Vogue should be dedicated to the marketing concept. (A think by Trout)
4. Strong leadership of the company is needed. (A think by Winslow)
5. White believes that low cost and low price should override quality considerations. (A think by Winslow)
6. What product mix, price and style range, and new products should Vogue establish?
7. What short- and long-range goals and plans should Vogue establish if Putnam decides to continue operation?

Presentation of Case Solution

Comment: The order in which topics are shown in the presentation of the case is not usually the order in which the topics are developed. For example, the first work which is done, the financial analysis, if it is long and detailed, may be given in appended working papers at the end of the case. On the other hand, a summary of problems and recommendations is often placed at the beginning of the case to give the reader a perspective, yet this summary cannot be written until the case has been analyzed completely.

Although the solution presented here is a guide to the analyst, it does not mean that other forms of presentation, other solutions, or other recommendations are not equally worthy. A case solution should be evaluated on the analysis, logic, and practical creativity. Prior to putting the recommendations into effect, nobody can foretell how well reasonable policies or courses of action will turn out. It does happen that we have "Mr. Putnam" in our midst to provide a little authenticity and validity of hindsight for the case solution.

SUMMARY OF PROBLEMS AND RECOMMENDATIONS

The leveling off of sales and the rapidly declining trends in profit and ROI are symptoms of a sick company. The lack of a unified sense of direction and resultant functional problems are apparent. We recommend that Mr. Putnam, in consultation with key executives (a) establish a competitive niche and basic long-range business objectives for Vogue, (b) establish specific long- and short-range plans for moving toward these objectives, and (c) restructure the organization and make personnel changes to achieve better functional responsibility and a unified sense of direction.

We recommend that a product strategy and appropriate product policies be formulated to achieve the long-range business objectives and to guide the functional operations.

We recommend that, in the marketing function, (a) appropriate sales forecasts be prepared, (b) sales analyses and distribution cost analyses by prepared *to the extent that they are needed and used* by managers and other employees, (c) advertising expenditures be greatly increased to include a national campaign, (d) the salesperson's compensation be revised to provide incentives to carry out company strategies, and (e) additional salespeople be hired and all salespeople be given training.

Our detailed analysis in a later section shows that if the above recommendations are put into effect, most production problems will vanish. As a result, previously mentioned production problems as well as late deliveries and excessive returns, will be greatly alleviated or cured.

For the systems function, we recommend a short management seminar on management information systems so that managers may learn the role of information in their decision making and the role of the systems function in serving them. At the same time, Evans should be coached to search for information needs of managers rather than trying to sell them on the use of computer output.

ANALYSIS

Lack of unified sense of direction is a problem as indicated by the lack of basic objectives, lack of agreement on product and advertising objectives, and organizational conflicts between White and others.

Alternative 1: Since Putnam has full responsibility for the success of Vogue in the next three years, he could call upon his experience and judgment to lay down objectives and policies for Vogue utilizing the present organization.

Pro 1: Time is of the essence if Vogue is to be saved. With clearcut objectives the present management would fall in line behind a new strong leader.

Pro 2: It takes time to build a new management team so that restructuring the organization or replacing executives would hamper efforts to keep Vogue afloat in the short run. New executives hired from outside would have to learn Vogue's operation.

Con 1: If Putnam does not consult with key people to work out a sense of direction *with* them, they may not accept objectives and policies. Openly in agreement, they may thwart implementation covertly.

Con 2: Putnam needs to reorganize the company immediately and get new key people in place so that he will be consulting with the proper people, those whose support he will need, rather than someone he will soon fire.

Alternative 2: As shown below, under the organization problem, there is a need for restructuring the organization and retiring White. Therefore, Putnam could immediately *restructure the organization* in a way so that no outside executives need be hired. The goals and policies could then be *worked out with the key people* involved in their implementation.

Pro 1: Although in emergencies an authoritarian leadership approach is preferred, this particular emergency could certainly allow one or two months to set the direction for a solution. This is adequate time to reorganize and bring a consultative method of leadership into play.

Pro 2: There are a number of competent people in the organization such as DeMarco, Kelly, Evans, Winslow, Chapman, Roberts, and Morse. Not only will they have valuable ideas, but by participating in the formulation of objectives they will obtain a broader understanding of company direction.

Pro 3: Failure to retire White and to clarify functional relationships by defining the new organization will make development of company objectives a time-consuming and even bitter process. The objectives may be distorted by White's influence.

Pro 4: The entire competitive edge of Vogue appears to be the designer, DeMarco. If DeMarco is not given strong immediate reassurance about Vogue's direction and her part in it she may leave. Good designers are very hard to find and are often paid equivalent to the vice-presidents of the firm.

Con 1: Putnam could impose his own ideas for the direction of the firm if the present *dis*organization were maintained. In fact, subordinates might welcome *any* ideas which gave a sense of direction to a disorganized conflicting group.

Con 2: It would be easier for Putnam to consult his employees to develop objectives so that he would not be subject to the pressures from his immediate staff which may arise in well-designed homogeneous functional organizations.

Recommendation: We recommend that Putnam immediately reorganize Vogue and eliminate executives whom he does not want on his management team. He should proceed immediately, in consultation with key personnel, to formulate basic objectives and general plans. Necessary policies should be disseminated promptly to all managers, supervisors, forepersons, and key personnel in Vogue.

What unified sense of direction should be set for Vogue? This is a problem which must be answered for all levels of activity from basic business direction to functional goals. The problem is evidenced by the lack of direction and the need for direction. It involves formulating the kind of business in which the company wants to be engaged in the long run and the competitive niche it wishes to carve out.

Alternative 1: Continue as a manufacturer of women's foundation garments and lingerie, competing with the present wide variety of price lines and styles. In brief, compete across the board with all kinds of competitors and attempt to obtain X percent of the *total industry* market.

Pro 1: Vogue's image has been established over the years by its line and designs.

Pro 2: Vogue was once successful, probably with its broad price-line, and the solution of other problems should pave the way back to profits.

Pro 3: A change to fewer items or fewer styles, even if a change were desirable, might end up with the wrong items or styles. At such a critical time, such an error would be disastrous.

Pro 4: A small, but slightly larger than the present, percentage of total industry business could represent a large sales volume.

Con 1: Many of the marketing and production problems are derived from short production runs and late deliveries attributable to the large number of styles offered.

Con 2: It is difficult, if not impossible from a practical standpoint, to produce both a very cheap and a high quality item in the same manufacturing plant. Worker and management psychology, substitution of parts during inventory shortages, and quality control differences argue against this practice.

Con 3: Vogue far exceeds the product/price styles of its successful competitors.

Con 4: It is difficult to compete effectively for many market segments against competitors who specialize in one market alone. To do so would require considerably more resources than Vogue now possesses.

Alternative 2: Retain the present items of foundation garments and lingerie but reduce the number of styles to about 20% of the present. Seek a competitive niche at the medium to good quality (middle to higher price) styles.

Pro 1: This reduction would give Vogue slightly more styles than one of its successful competitors, Exhibit 15.12, to cover a broader market segment.

Pro 2: The U.S. is growing rapidly more affluent so that the large, fairly homogeneous, middle-class market segment will continue to buy more good quality goods and move up to high fashion merchandise. For such personal items as foundation garments and lingerie, women will prefer to move away from "cheap" lines.

Pro 3: The reduction in number of styles will greatly alleviate manufacturing, late delivery, and returns problems.

Pro 4: Manufacturing costs will be reduced because of longer runs, fewer setups, and reduced makeup time.

Pro 5: Selling costs will be reduced since fewer styles will need to be shown to customers and billing may be simplified with fewer items/invoice.

Pro 6: Vogue's competitive edge is its designer, DeMarco. Greater gains over competition can be achieved in the design of higher quality lines.

Con 1: Either more than 20%, say 50%, or less, say 10%, of the current styles might be more profitable. In fact, a sudden drop to 20% might be traumatic to customers who will know Vogue is in trouble. It might be preferable to lower the items by 10% each year to see how profit is affected.

Con 2: Producing low- to medium-price items only, instead of quality goods, would lower inventory costs greatly and reduce quality control costs. Vogue needs every cost reduction possible to keep afloat. The low-price market segment is still a good sized one and the poor will always be with us.

Con 3: Good scheduling based on good forecasting should be able to eliminate production problems.

Alternative 3: Ask the basic question, "What business does Vogue want to be in ten years from now?" to develop the firm's direction.

Comment: The development of additional alternatives beyond the obvious should be encouraged. We simply list Alternative 3 and do not analyze it in the interest of space. However, the creative problem solver will raise questions (problems, alternatives) about whether Vogue should cut back to lingerie and expand to sportswear, produce male and female medical body support items, seek only special private brand markets such as Sears, Roebuck, etc.

Recommendation: We recommend that Vogue reduce the number of styles by dropping its low-price styles and many other more expensive styles as soon as current orders have been filled. DeMarco should design a related line of styles for the medium to upper price range leading to about 20% of the present number of styles over a period of three years.

How Should Vogue Be Organized and Staffed? This is a problem as evidenced by White's interference in manufacturing, Chapman's desire to have DeMarco and the purchasing function under him, and production control and secretary-treasurer functions assigned to VP of operations. The question of timing has already been discussed and the recommendation made for immediate change.

Alternative 1: See Proposed Vogue Organization Chart, Exhibit 15.14. Retire White immediately. Putnam should be acting VP of operations so as to work closely with Evans to make him more effective. Thomas should be released and replaced. A controller would be hired immediately under this alternative. Kelly would be made secretary-treasurer.

Pro 1: Marketing must be unified to integrate business goals, product styles and markets, and total selling effort.

Pro 2: A unified marketing function will permit emphasis on the marketing concept throughout Vogue.

Pro 3: Evans is competent in his field but needs coaching to get him to work more effectively with top management. Putnam can coach him to see his function as a service which must be marketed to the line VP's.

Pro 4: Design is one aspect, and a major aspect of merchandising. Although DeMarco may be paid far more than the merchandise manager, she should nevertheless report to him so that all merchandising activities may be integrated.

Pro 5: Kelly has apparently performed well as secretary-treasurer by keeping Vogue's financial position as good as possible in view of the operational losses. As controller, he appears to have done little and failed competely to recognize that he should be working closely with Evans. His performance in each area may be evaluated against the functions given by the Financial Executive's Institute:

Controllership.	*Treasurership*
1. Planning for control (P)	1. Provision of capital (G)
2. Reporting and interpreting (P)	2. Investor relations
3. Evaluating and consulting (P)	3. Short-term financing (G)
4. Tax administration	4. Banking and custody (G)
5. Government reporting	5. Credits and collections (G)
6. Protection of assets (G)	6. Investments
7. Economic appraisal (P)	7. Insurance

From the information given in the case, we indicated P for Poor and G for Good as we deduced Kelly's performance. We would have to evaluate as Unknown or Satisfactory the remaining activities.

Pro 6: Purchasing should be in manufacturing so that raw materials inventories may be economically maintained and production uninterrupted. Chapman's view that purchasing should be under him so he will see the new patterns has little merit. His designer De Marco sets specifications for materials, and salespeople coming to Vogue will be aware that they must sell Chapman first and purchasing second.

— *Pro 7:* White likes to play in sand piles. Modern business requires planning, forecasting, clear lines of communications and responsibility, and a team approach. He has been erratic, interfering, and oblivious to marketing and systems changes. He is close to retirement.

— *Pro 8:* Thomas, the personnel manager, failed conspicuously to contribute any kind of estimate of Vogue's problems. The lack of a formal organization and policy guide and the obvious organizational problems indicate that he is unfit for his job.

Cons: The cons must be arguments that alternative organizations are better or that the transfers and releasing of personnel are ill-advised. As alternatives to the organization shown, we could argue that the real estate manager should report to the secretary-treasurer or that the accounting manager should report to the controller.

A plant manager who has only one individual, assistant plant manager, reporting to him is frowned upon by some organization theorists as too limited a span of responsibility (one-over-one). The idea is that if the plant manager is out because of illness or business, he should rotate the job of acting plant manager among his supervisors to train them and identify leaders.

Another alternative is to place the systems manager under the controller, the real estate manager under the secretary-treasurer, and eliminate the VP-operations position entirely. This is further recognition of the importance of the controllership functions.

Another variant would be to add a new position, director of long-range planning, reporting to the president, to assist him by getting together the detailed plans once the president and VP's have set general objectives.

Recommendation: We recommend the removal of White and Thomas from Vogue. We recommend the adoption of the organization structure proposed subject to elimination of the position of VP-operations, the assignment of the systems function to the controller, and the assignment of the real estate function to the secretary-treasurer. A strong competent controller should be hired immediately.

Lack of Product Strategy is a problem that must be resolved after the firm's direction has been selected. Strategy is the means by which objectives are achieved in a competitive situation. It is a set of rules which guide action in response to competitors' action and to environmental changes. The case gives little information concerning competition and the industry. Because of time limitations, we will simply list basic categories of strategic action with some alternatives.

1. Single product line, i.e., lingerie only.
2. Related product lines, i.e., lingerie, foundation garments, housecoats, blouses.
3. Unrelated products, but user-related, such as women's apparel in general.

Product Breadth and Overlap Alternatives:

1. Number of styles total and the selection of number of styles for particular items.
2. Development of competing lines.
3. Identifying Vogue with quality items and developing a new brand name for medium price lines.
4. Producing for private brands.
5. Giving emphasis (or not) to customized items, styles, or sizes.

Product Pricing and Service Alternatives:
Pricing alternatives have been listed in the marketing section. These alternatives depend heavily on the originality of design, product qual-

EXHIBIT 15.14

Proposed Vogue Organization Chart

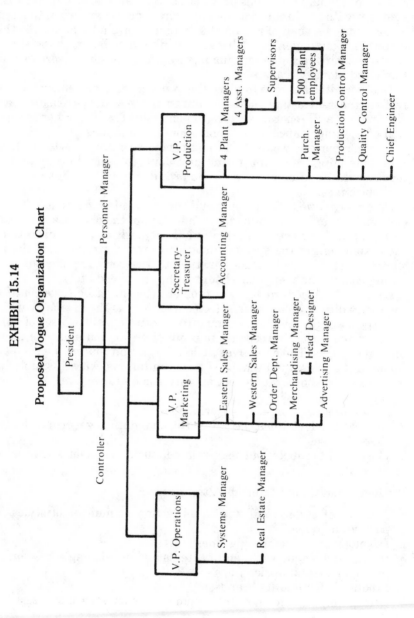

ity, competitive strategies, and consumer vagaries, that "tactics" may be more important than strategy for this type of business.

Exhibit 15.15 indicates that Vogue's high costs, and hence relative high pricing, are matched with only average product differentiation. Therefore, its competitive position is poor.

Market Segmentation Alternatives:

1. Women only.
2. Women and teenagers.
3. Women, teenagers, and female children.
4. Standard Metropolitan Statistical Areas only.
5. Expand items to direct Vogue towards men's as well as women's underwear.
6. Segment the market and reach only the "average" women or only the "heavy" women, or produce separate lines for tall women or other special body shapes.
7. Segment by quality/price and select one or more segments to aim at, with, perhaps, different brands.

Competitive Strategy Alternatives:

1. Compete head-on against principal competitor.
2. Find niches around principal competitors.
3. Compete head-on against one small competitor after another.

Marketing Problems are evidenced by flattening of the sales trend, the large amount of returns, Evans' complaint about the line selection committee, Trout's statement about the need for the marketing concept and his complaint about the advertising program, and finally an analysis of Exhibits 15.11 and 15.12 showing product line and selling problems. The development of a unified sense of direction will contribute to the solution of many of these problems, but more specific action must be stipulated.

Sales forecasting and sales analysis is required in any modern business. The questions for Vogue are: Who uses such information for decision making? How often do users require it up-dated? How accurately must it be performed? What detail is needed? and Who at Vogue shall be responsible?

Alternative 1: An annual sales forecast of total dollar sales only and a revised forecast could be made each quarter for units of each item. Analysis of sales by item, salesperson, and profit contribution could be made at the end of each year.

Pro 1: This is inexpensive yet more than is now being done.

Con 1: Such aggregate forecasting and analysis is far too crude to really assist the decision making for production, merchandising, and selling. Information is needed on at least a monthly basis and most preferably on a weekly basis.

Con 2: The computer has the capability of easily supplying better data than these.

EXHIBIT 15.15

Vogue's Product Differentiation and Costs Relative to Competition

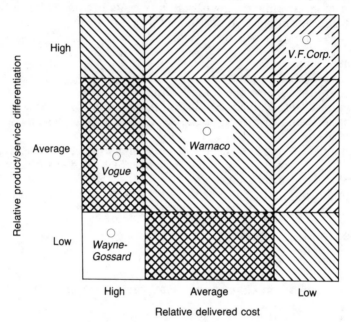

	Financial Performance	**Differentiation Product/Service**	**Relative- Delivered Cost**
V.F. Corporation	*(A) leader	** leader	***low
Warnaco. Inc.	*(B) average		***average
Vogue	marginal	marginal	high
Wayne-Gossard (did discontinue lingerie lines)	*(C++) marginal	** marginal	***high

Leadership position in market and financial performance

Average position in market and financial performance

Marginal position in market and financial performance

Disastrous position in market and financial performance

* Value Line rating ** Value Line annual reports, Standard & Poor's *Industry Surveys* *** Value Line ratios, Standard & Poor's *Industry Surveys*

(Matrix developed by William K. Hall in "Survival Strategies in a Hostile Environment." *Harvard Business Review,* Sept.–Oct., 1980.)

Alternative 2: Let Evans put out all forecasts and analyses of which the computer is capable, and let managers use these as needed.

Pro 2: Too many data are better than too few.

Con 1: Any report which is issued and not used represents a waste of time and money.

Alternative 3: Have Evans prepare weekly sales forecasts and analyses by item, style, size, salesperson, and profit contribution as specified by Chapman. Analysis of sales to accounts should be prepared monthly. Annual sales forecasts by the same classification should be prepared by Chapman, the merchandising manager with the assistance of Evans. Approval by the VP-marketing and Putnam would make the forecast official and a part of the annual business plan.

It would be up to Evans to convert computer data into charts, as Chapman requests, so that the data become meaningful to managers and capable of being more rapidly interpreted.

Pro 1: Weekly forecasts at this level are necessary for good production control and merchandising.

Pro 2: Centralization of forecasting permits use of the computer, application of statistical forecast models, consolidation of the latest field information, and prompt reporting.

Pro 3: The sales force composite method and executive judgment method of forecasting are too crude, too slow, and too inaccurate compared with the method proposed.

Pro 4: Chapman has the responsibility for selection of items, lines, styles, and pricing. He must therefore have responsibility for obtaining information for decision making and evaluation.

Cons: Alternative methods, such as committees for annual forecasting, assigning forecasting responsibility to Evans instead of Chapman, etc., all have obvious drawbacks. We have not detailed these because of time limitations.

Line selection committee conflicts will have vanished with establishment of a sense of direction and the placing of responsibility for all merchandising with Chapman, the newly hired VP-marketing, and Putnam, in that order of accountability.

Advertising as a problem will be resolved to some extent by the new organization. Whatever Trout recommends will be reviewed by the VP-marketing in relation to sales objectives, direct selling, and competitive pressures.

Alternative 1: Keep costs down by continuing low-budget cooperative advertising.

Alternative 2: Eliminate cooperative advertising but maintain a low-budget national campaign.

Alternative 3: Contribute less to a low-budget cooperative campaign and institute a low-budget national campaign. The total budget will be a fixed 2% of sales.

Alternative 4: Institute for one year a national campaign with a lower contribution to cooperative advertising. Set the advertising

COOPERATIVE ADVERTISING: INVOLVES
MIDDLEMEN + PRODUCERS SHARING IN
COST OF ADS.

budget at $1,500,000. The advertising should be synchronized with the reduced number of styles, some special designs, and good quality control maintenance. Further, it should be synchronized with the availability of additional salespeople and subsequent to a sales training program.

➤ *Pro 1:* National advertising is a must to secure volume sales of most consumer items. Since Vogue has not been using national advertising, it must try to make a big initial impact; it doesn't have time to wait ten years to build its image. The $1,500,000 is only suggested. Putnam would need to make the final decision as to how much Vogue could afford and how much it *must afford.* Bold risks are needed in desperate times.

Pro 2: Vogue is losing market position rapidly as evidenced by Exhibit 15.9. It may eventually have zero percent of a larger market at this rate.

Con: Gross sales are not the cause of Vogue's losses, but rather *net* sales. The solution is not to increase costs, but institute a cost reduction program and reduce returns on sales to about $1,000,000 where it used to be when the business was profitable. The reduction of styles and the new organization will eliminate late deliveries and consequently cut back returns.

Recommendation: We recommend Alternative 4.

Sales management problems are evidenced by analysis of Exhibit 15.11. We are assuming that the midpoint of the Annual Purchase class represents the class and have calculated the table below.

Average Annual Purchase	Number of Accounts	Sales (1,000s)
$ 500	3,927	1,964
1,500	1,985	2,978
4,000	1,506	6,024
8,000	1,227	9,816
15,000	797	11,954
30,000	463	13,890

Total sales except for highest class		46,626
Total sales, Exhibit 15.6.		53,006

$$58,000 = \frac{6,380,000}{110}$$
110   6,380 Balance in highest class

It is apparent that the present compensation of $100 for new accounts is causing salespeople to spend their time looking for new accounts. Of the approximately 4,000 accounts serviced at the low end of the sales classes, $4,942,000 resulted. This combined amount for two classes is out of all proportion to sales in the other individual classes.

Alternative 1: Drop the $100 bonus for *any* new account, but give an additional 5% commission on new account sales which provide billings of $2,000 or more in the first year. A new account with a large department store which yielded less than $2,000 the first year but had large potential would be reviewed by the VP-marketing for possible bonus payment to the salesperson. Old small accounts would be solicited by mail.

Pro 1: This incentive system would redirect the salesperson to larger accounts.

Pro 2: Salespeople would have more time to increase business from present large accounts.

Con 1: Potentially large accounts might not be approached if the salesperson figured that the first year's orders would be under $2,000 and chances of a bonus would be slim.

Con 2: It might be more profitable to the salesperson to work up old accounts than to open any new ones.

Alternative 2: Give a bonus of $100 for each new account, but don't accept any orders for less than $2,000.

Pro: This would stimulate salespeople to open both small and large new accounts yet ensure Vogue of good-sized sales with minimum account servicing.

Recommendation: We recommend Alternative 1.

Another closely related sales management problem may be observed from the fact that there are 52 salespeople calling on approximately 10,000 accounts. This implies that a salesperson must call on almost 200 accounts in 250 working days. If 50 days are required for reports, sales meetings, illness, and personal business, a salesperson would be able to contact a single account only about four times a year. This is not adequate for so many items and for new designs constantly coming out.

Alternative 1: Hire more salespeople.

Alternative 2: Reduce the number of accounts as recommended above.

Alternative 3: Hire more salespeople, reduce the number of accounts, and train salespeople to adjust the number of sales per year per account in accordance with the billings from the account.

Recommendation: We recommend Alternative 3.

Manufacturing Problems: The production problems of makeup time, short runs, late deliveries, shortages of findings, and inefficient use of clickers will tend to be eliminated by the previous courses of action recommended. We recommend that the effectiveness of production control be carefully monitored for the first six months in which sales and production forecasts are instituted and the number of styles are drastically reduced. We recommend that the cost of checking shipment of parts to the plants be compared with cost of the plant manager's building extra inventory at their plants.

We recommend also that the compensation plan for operators be reviewed.

Also we recommend that, on the basis of past successes, Mr. Roberts' budget for research be increased. The amount should depend on an evaluation of his detailed proposals.

Systems Problems exist to a great extent because of present organizational obstacles. However, even with the new organization, both Evans and top management should be treated to a two-day seminar on Management Information Systems. Evans must be coached to develop systems which support management's needs for information for decisionmaking and control. At the same time, Vogue's management must be taught the value of information, information systems, and the power of the computer. The new controller should play a continuing role in keeping management aware of information planning and control systems.

Human Resource Problems abound in Vogue. The new organization and staff only provide a clear pattern of communication and responsibility. Under one-man domination for many years, and beset by internal bickering, there has been no opportunity for managers to develop their leadership, and particularly their decision-making skills.

We recommend that Putnam give considerable attention to developing his managers so that they will take on responsibility and risks. This should be done primarily by coaching and counseling. We recommend, however, that each VP and manager, as well as key personnel such as DeMarco, be sent to at least one seminar, conference, or educational program each year to gain breadth in his or her field or in business in general.

We further recommend a continuing program of training for all salespeople.

All compensation plans should be reviewed and revised as the new personnel manager may recommend, subject to top management approval.

A monthly newsletter to all employees should be instituted to show company goals, operational results, and reinforce the sense of direction concept and marketing concept. Noteworthy news about employees, events of interest to them, and gripes and how they are handled could be included to increase group cohesion.

APPENDICES

APPENDIX A
SOURCES OF FINANCIAL ANALYSIS
COMPUTER SOFTWARE

IBM, P.O. Box 1385, Atlanta, GA 30055

Management Science America, Inc., 3445 Peachtree Road, N.E., Atlanta, GA 30326

MicroPro International Corporation, 33 San Pablo Avenue, San Rafael, CA 94903

Software International, Elm Square, Andover, MA 01810

APPENDIX B
SYMBOLS USED IN EVALUATION OF REPORTS

P   You have overlooked many problems or missed the central problem completely

GS   Glittering generality; be specific

A   Too few, or no alternatives; you are solving the problems by assertion

I   Inconsistent with other statements you have made

Q	Quantify or put a dollar value on it
NS	Nonsupport of statement or conclusion by data or analysis
SW	Too few pros and cons. So What? What are you trying to show?
N	Nonsense. No basis in fact or theory
R	Rehash of case
O	Lack of any organization structure for the case or poorly organized
C	Conclusions or recommendations not supported by your analysis
?	I doubt this. You may be right, who knows?
T	Irrelevant or trivial
✔	Good
SA	Relate this to all affected areas of the business system or amplify on it to develop its significance

INDEX